Fodor's

LAS VEGAS

WELCOME TO *Fabulous* LAS VEGAS NEVADA

Welcome to Las Vegas

Las Vegas knows what everyone wants and delivers it in spades. Megaresorts fund their 45-foot bronze lions, half-size Eiffel Towers, and towering glass pyramids with the collective desires and dollars of more than 30 million annual visitors. From a Wolfgang Puck dinner to a Wolfpack-like adventure on the Strip, you're sure to find your perfect indulgence. Swim up to a blackjack table, chow down at a buffet, or chill out in an ultralounge. As you plan your upcoming travels to Las Vegas, please confirm that places are still open and let us know when we need to make updates by writing to us at this address: editors@fodors.com.

TOP REASONS TO GO

★ **Resorts:** Colossal hotels present exotic themes and over-the-top amenities.

★ **Dining:** Few cities in the world can claim a higher concentration of top restaurants.

★ **Gambling:** Novices and pros alike come to Vegas for legendary casino action.

★ **Shopping:** Lavish malls and bargain outlets provide retail options for every budget.

★ **Nightlife:** Master mixologists serve creative cocktails and famous DJs spin nightly.

★ **Shows:** Cirque du Soleil, international singers, and local stars perform day and night.

Contents

Fodor's Features

EXPERIENCE LAS VEGAS

29 ULTIMATE EXPERIENCES

Las Vegas offers terrific experiences that should be on every traveler's list. Here are Fodor's top picks for a memorable trip.

1 Fountains at Bellagio

The most recognizable sight in all of Las Vegas, the "dancing fountains" in front of Bellagio, go off every 30 or 15 minutes, depending on the time and day of the week. *(Ch. 4)*

2 High Roller

At 550 feet high, the High Roller—right on the Strip—is the tallest observation wheel in the world. It's also the best way to see the Las Vegas Valley at night. *(Ch. 3)*

3 Music Residencies

Las Vegas is once again the hottest place on the planet to see live music as mega-stars have signed contracts to perform in the Strip's relatively intimate settings. *(Ch. 12)*

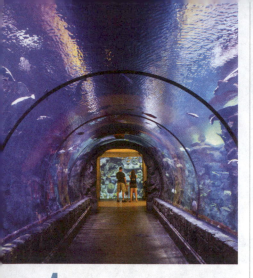

4 Shark Reef Aquarium

Mandalay Bay's aquarium lets you get up close and personal with more than 100 different species of sea creatures (more than 2,000 animals in all), not all of them sharks. *(Ch. 3)*

5 The Big Apple Coaster

What makes the coaster at New York–New York Hotel & Casino thrilling is that it hugs both indoor and outdoor track, giving riders a varied experience the entire time. *(Ch. 3)*

6 Eataly Las Vegas

The very best Italian-made food and products are yours for sampling at this marketplace and restaurant, one of the newest eateries at Park MGM on the South Strip. *(Ch. 3)*

7 Thunder from Down Under

More than 10 million visitors to Vegas have flocked to see nearly naked, chiseled Aussies bumping, grinding, and engaging in cheeky humor on stage since 1991. *(Ch. 3)*

8 Mirage Volcano

Marvel at modern-day pyrotechnics of Volcano Las Vegas, the not-so natural disaster outside of The Mirage that erupts in flame and fireworks three times daily. *(Ch. 4)*

9 Fremont Street Experience

Think of the Fremont Street Experience as one six-block party along pedestrian-only Fremont Street, all covered by a canopy lined with programmed LED lights. *(Ch. 6)*

10 Venetian Gondoliers

Even if the canals are fake, sitting in an authentic gondola and being serenaded by your gondolier remains one of the most romantic outings in all of Las Vegas. (*Ch. 5*)

11 Golden Knights Game

A Golden Knights home hockey game is unlike anything else in Las Vegas. The beloved Knights were the first pro sports team to come to Sin City, and local fans love them. (*Ch. 3*)

12 Area 15

The star of this new attraction is Omega Mart, an interactive grocery store theater from Meow Wolf that is sure to bend your mind. (*Ch. 9*)

13 Peking Duck at Mott 32

The first Hong Kong–style Chinese restaurant on the Las Vegas Strip offers its impeccable (and delicious) signature dish in addition to myriad dumplings and street food. (*Ch. 5*)

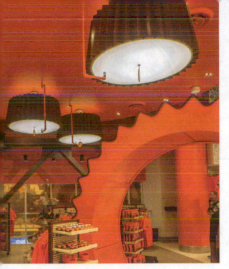

14 Hershey's World Las Vegas

Chocolate and more chocolate is on the menu at this attraction and monument to the great American chocolate bar. This is not a place to go when you're on a diet. *(Ch. 3)*

15 Gold & Silver Pawn Shop

The television show *Pawn Stars* has made this pawn shop on the outskirts of Downtown into a famous set—and a destination for reality TV fans from every walk of life. *(Ch. 6)*

16 Downtown Container Park

This open-air shopping pavilion—composed of dozens of repurposed shipping containers surrounding a three-story treehouse—proves that malls can be cool. *(Ch. 6)*

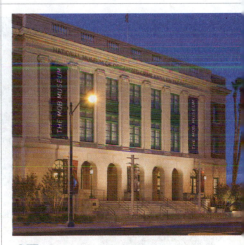

17 Mob Museum

Housed in a former federal courthouse, this museum pays homage to mafiosos throughout U.S. history. Downstairs is a speakeasy bar and brewery that brews its own beer. *(Ch. 6)*

18 SlotZilla

The city's most famous zip line starts at the east end of the Fremont Street and shoots thrill-seekers up to 30 mph from about halfway up the world's largest slot machine. *(Ch. 6)*

19 Arts District

The city's hottest neighborhood is the most eclectic; galleries and working studios sit side-by-side with hipster coffee shops, classic dive bars, and great restaurants. *(Ch. 6)*

20 Neon Museum

The Boneyard is a big lot where the neon signs of Old Vegas get second lives and become the small handful that museum docents light up at night. *(Ch. 6)*

21 Spiegelworld

Combining potty humor, physical comedy, and eccentric characters, Spiegelworld's three shows are unlike any others in Vegas: raunchy, hilarious, and absolutely nuts. *(Ch. 12)*

22 The Strat

The tallest freestanding tower in the United States—at 1,149 feet—keeps visitors busy with a fancy restaurant, a trio of insane thrill rides, and an observation deck. *(Ch. 5)*

23 Tea at Waldorf Astoria Las Vegas

Afternoon tea at the Waldorf Astoria inside CityCenter is an elevated experience—in more ways than one, offering exquisite service to accompany the breathtaking views. *(Ch. 4)*

24 Cirque Du Soleil

Cirque has been in Sin City since Mystère opened in 1993; today there are five different productions that have helped to reinvent the Strip entertainment scene. *(Ch. 12)*

25 The Chandelier

Cocktails take on new meaning at the casino bar in The Cosmopolitan of Las Vegas offering innovative spins on an ever-changing menu of reinvented classics. *(Ch. 4)*

26 Hoover Dam

A total of 3.25 million cubic yards of concrete was used to build the Hoover Dam, which stopped up the Colorado River to create Lake Mead outside of Las Vegas. *(Ch. 13)*

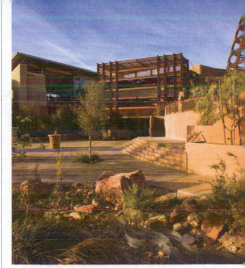

27 Las Vegas Springs Preserve

This all-ages attraction in North Las Vegas is five or six museums wrapped up into one, teaching visitors about the history and climate of the Las Vegas valley. *(Ch. 6)*

28 Grand Garden Arena

The MGM Grand has hosted some of the city's most legendary boxing matches. It remains a spectacular place to see a fight, with great sight lines all around. *(Ch. 3)*

29 Red Rock National Conservation Area

Near Summerlin, the expansive park—dubbed Red Rock after the ochre-red hillsides all around—is a great destination for day-trippers and campers alike. *(Ch. 10)*

WHAT'S WHERE

1 South Strip. Most hotels along the Strip between Mandalay Bay and Park MGM are within 15 minutes of the airport. Farther south are some large resorts, budget motels, the Town Square shopping mall, and chain restaurants.

2 Center Strip. A 15- to 20-minute cab ride from the airport, the heart of the Strip goes from CityCenter north to The Mirage.

3 North Strip. About a 30-minute ride from the airport, it extends north from The Venetian to the Strat and includes the new Resorts World Las Vegas.

4 Downtown. The center of old Las Vegas has made a comeback with the opening of Circa Las Vegas, The Smith Center for the Performing Arts, and the Downtown Project, powered by the late Tony Hsieh. The Arts District, between the Strat and Downtown, is also a hot neighborhood. North of Downtown is the neighborhood known on maps as North Las Vegas. It's home to the Las Vegas Motor Speedway and some locals' casino hotels.

5 Paradise Road and the East Side. Parallel to the Strip, a short drive or 15-minute walk east, is the mellower Paradise Road area, which includes the original Convention Center. There's monorail service along one stretch. Beyond are the University District and Boulder Strip.

6 Henderson and Lake Las Vegas. Southeast of the Strip but west of Lake Las Vegas, this area's perhaps the most stereotypically "suburban" in the Valley. Still, its outlet malls and the Green Valley Ranch Resort & Spa Casino draw locals (and visitors).

7 West Side. West of the Strip, on the other side of I–15, are several large resort hotels, including the Palms. It's too far from the Strip to walk.

8 Summerlin and Red Rock Canyon. On the far west side of the Las Vegas Valley, this tony neighborhood sits in the shadow of Red Rock National Conservation Area. It's home to a couple of resorts, the city's new minor league baseball park, and a burgeoning downtown of its own.

Great Under-the-Radar Experiences in Las Vegas

THE UNDERGROUND

It should come as no surprise that the Mob Museum has a speakeasy of its own. The bar and working brewery are in the basement level and has a separate door. A password—available on the bar's social media channels—is required for entry. The cocktail list tends toward midcentury classics.

BRILLIANT!

Since it opened in 1996, the Neon Museum has become a popular spot to relive the neon glory of Old Vegas. This show, which is ticketed separately, takes this homage to new heights. The action unfolds in a small lot of old signs to the north of the main Boneyard; over the course of about 30 minutes, an elaborate laser light show projected onto the signs has the effect of bringing them back to life. Think of the experience like a musical history of Vegas told by signs. It's worth the extra $20.

GOLDEN KNIGHTS GAME PARTIES

Can't get a ticket to see the Las Vegas Golden Knights play live at T-Mobile Arena? Just head to City National Arena in Summerlin, where game-days are all-out parties at the on-site Mackenzie River Pizza Pub & Grill. The bar airs all Knights games on its big screens and offers a variety of food and drink specials to keep the masses happy. Because City National doubles as the team's practice facility, most of the time you feel as if you're right behind the glass at center ice.

JAZZ BRUNCH AT NOMAD BAR

Get your groove on every Sunday at the NoMad Bar inside Park MGM. From 11 to 2, the bar pairs its special brunch menu with live jazz and delicious cocktails. Menu items include lemon poppyseed pancakes with whipped ricotta and blueberries, and a breakfast burrito with suckling pig, eggs, spinach, and *chile de arbol*. There's also a delicious spin on a margarita, served in a giant copper chicken. Be sure to make a reservation, as waits can be long.

LATE-NIGHT AT THE PEPPERMILL

All-nighters in Vegas aren't the same without a stop at the Peppermill. Yes, the North Strip fixture has classic diner dishes such as club sandwiches and mozzarella cheese sticks. But the real reasons to go are the scorpion bowls, the 1980s music videos that play on a loop, and the sunken fire pits—some of which have bubbling fountains. The vibe at the Peppermill isn't necessarily Old Vegas, but it's throwback enough to make you feel like you've entered another dimension for an hour, which is always fun.

NATIONAL ATOMIC TESTING MUSEUM

One of the best ways to bone up on the history of the Las Vegas Valley as a testing site for atomic bombs is to visit the National Atomic Testing Museum on the East Side. The main collection

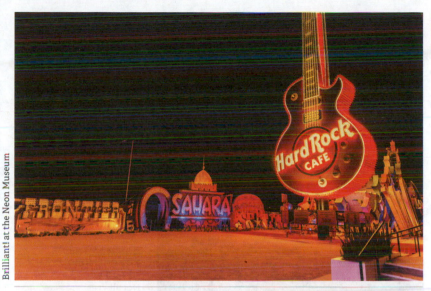

Brilliant! at the Neon Museum

comprises more than 3,500 artifacts, and the museum houses more than 16,000 official government and unofficial personal photos. Perhaps the best (and most disturbing) exhibit is a simulated atom bomb blast, which unfolds in a space that museum officials call "Ground Zero Theater."

OPIUM

Sword-swallowers! Hula-hooping experts! Raunchy humor! Sci-fi drama! *Opium*, one of three zany shows from Spiegelworld, has all of it and more. The show unfolds in the Opium Theater in the Chelsea Tower at The Cosmopolitan of Las Vegas. It's a schlep from the casino floor, but the feats of derring-do are totally worth the hike. Bartenders also have created a menu of eccentric drinks for the theater bars, including one that comes in a bag and another that comes with pop rocks.

SEVEN MAGIC MOUNTAINS

The seven towers that comprise Ugo Rondinone's "Seven Magic Mountains" stand alone in the desert 10 miles south of Mandalay Bay, commanding attention from just about every angle. Each tower is composed of giant boulders painted different colors; each tops out at about 30 feet tall. Since it opened in May 2016 the art installation has become a favorite spot for selfies. If you're single, it's also a popular pick-up spot.

SIN CITY SMASH

Everybody needs to let off some steam now and again, and the rage rooms at Sin City Smash are great (and safe!) places to get it done. The place is built on the concept of "Destruction Therapy." You pay for a set amount of time to lock yourself in a room, take a hammer, and break as much as you possibly can.

This particular facility even lets customers bring their own stuff to smash. It's a surprisingly fun and cathartic way to spend an afternoon.

THE VIEW FROM RIVEA

Rivea, the Alain Ducasse–helmed restaurant at the top of Delano Las Vegas, has one of the most incredible views of the Las Vegas Strip and the entire Vegas Valley. Naturally, then, if you book a table near one of the windows facing north, it's a spectacular place to spend an important meal. Ducasse is famous for his French cuisine, and the menu has a notably Mediterranean flair. Surprisingly, the wine list has a treasure-trove of great California wines, too.

Extravagant (But Affordable) Las Vegas Experiences

MYRON'S CABARET JAZZ

Held almost nightly in the 240-seat Boman Pavilion next door to The Smith Center, Myron's Cabaret Jazz is unique in Las Vegas. Seats come with tables, and you can get drinks and light snacks. Close your eyes and you feel like you've time-traveled to the 1920s. It's always a night to remember.

DINNER ON THE PATIO AT LAGO

The patio at Lago by Julian Serrano isn't very large but it commands one of the best spots in all of Vegas. The eight-table terrace looks out on the Fountains of Bellagio, putting those who choose to sit there front-and-center for the waterworks throughout their meals. Understandably, reservations are required for these popular seats, and the patio often books up months in advance.

GHOST DONKEY AT THE COSMOPOLITAN OF LAS VEGAS

Amid the hubbub of Block 16 at The Cosmopolitan hides Ghost Donkey, a speakeasy that specializes in tequila, mezcal, and drinks made with both (or either). Patrons can either order set drinks off a modest menu or spend five minutes telling bartenders what sort of agave liquor they like and letting the experts drive. The bar offers an all-nachos menu for those who get the munchies. Wondering how to access this paradise? Simply look for the black door with the donkey picture.

GOLF AT LAKE LAS VEGAS

The man-made Lake Las Vegas sits like an oasis in the middle of the desert, and one of the best ways to experience it is by playing golf. There are two courses operating currently—Reflection Bay and South Shore. Both are open to members only, but guests of area hotels usually can get a tee time with help from the concierge. After a day on the links, return to either clubhouse for a stiff drink and a soak in the spa.

HAMMAM INSIDE THE COSMOPOLITAN OF LAS VEGAS

Not all Vegas spas are created equal. Case in point: The Sahra Spa at The Cosmopolitan, which is one of the only spas in town to boast a Turkish-style hammam. The hammam room features what massage therapists refer to as the "motherstone slab," a giant circular rock that's heated and is used as a relaxation platform before massage treatments. Hammam time can be added to any massage; the spa also offers exclusive treatment packages that include hammam time and other special features.

HAPPY HALF HOUR ON THE HIGH ROLLER

It's one thing to take a ride on the High Roller, the tallest observation wheel in the world. It's entirely something else to sign up for the Happy Half Hour—one complete 30-minute rotation in a pod with an all-you-can-drink open bar.

The Cosmopolitan Spa

This option is available whenever the wheel is working, and it makes the standard experience feel ultraexclusive. What's more, there's something magical about throwing back gin-and-tonics while you're circling the Vegas Valley 550 feet above the desert floor.

HUGO'S CELLAR

Old-school elegance is on tilt at Hugo's Cellar, a basement restaurant at the Four Queens Resort & Casino downtown. Servers—they're all men—wear tuxedos, female patrons receive a long-stemmed rose, and everyone is greeted formally. Dishes are throwbacks, too—Caesar salad and Bananas Foster are prepared tableside, and the menu includes dishes such as Queen's Lobster, Beef Wellington, and tournedos Rossini. Everybody gets complimentary chocolate-dipped strawberries with dessert.

MOËT VENDING MACHINE AT WALDORF ASTORIA LAS VEGAS

The Waldorf brand is synonymous with luxury, which explains why the only vending machine you'll find on the property serves up splits and full-size bottles of Moët & Chandon Champagne. The machine sits in the lobby near the elevators, providing everyone with an opportunity to buy and pop their favorite bubbly at any time of day. If you're feeling particularly hifalutin, you can hand your bottle to a server or bellhop who will open it for free.

OYSTER BAR AT PALACE STATION

There are only 18 seats at the iconic oyster bar inside Palace Station Hotel & Casino, but that doesn't stop locals and visitors alike from lining up by the dozens. Regulars swear by the oyster special, which can feature raw mollusks from just about anywhere in the world, depending on when you go. The limited menu also features gumbos, oyster pan roasts, and chowders. Oh, and because the bar is open 24 hours, you can squeeze it into your Vegas schedule at any time.

SHOPPING AT EATALY LAS VEGAS

Fans of imported Italian goods cheered when the international chain, Eataly, came to Las Vegas in December 2018. Today, the marketplace inside Park MGM offers prosciutto, pasta, sundried tomatoes, cookware, and literally hundreds of other items on any given day. If you're looking for a particular item, you can request a personal shopper to help you to find it. Of course, you'll have to hit the gelato stand before you head back to your hotel.

Best Pools in Las Vegas

MANDALAY BAY
Mandalay Bay's wave pool, which sends four-foot waves toward swimmers every 60 seconds or so, is the only one of its kind on the Las Vegas Strip. Also worth checking out: The Lazy River, around which visitors can float for hours on inflatable life rafts, and a beach with real sand.

ARIA
Everything here is over-the-top, from attentive service to food and drink specials. Cabanas come with music docking stations upon request. In addition to three main pools, a separate and private pool serves guests of the ARIA SkySuites, while tops at the adults-only Liquid Pool Lounge are optional.

CAESARS PALACE
Seven pools comprise the "Garden of the Gods Pool Oasis." The largest, the Temple Pool, has a small temple in the center. The Neptune Pool is loaded with giant floaties that your friends will love seeing on Instagram. The Jupiter Pool is kid-friendly, while the Fortuna Pool has swim-up blackjack.

THE COSMOPOLITAN OF LAS VEGAS
The pool deck at The Cosmopolitan is known for fun. In summer, the resort shows movies at night; in winter, the pools are turned into ice-skating rinks. There's ping-pong and foosball year-round. From April through October, a portion of the pool deck becomes part of Marquee Dayclub. Be on the lookout for alcoholic popsicles and boozy milk shakes.

CIRCA LAS VEGAS
Without question, Stadium Swim is the hottest pool scene in Downtown Vegas. Think of it like a sports book where you can swim. There are six pools in all, and all of them face a 143-foot, sports book–style screen. An added bonus: the pool is open year-round.

M RESORT
Think of the M Pool at the M Resort in Henderson as one giant trapezoid of water, split in half by a walkway straight down the middle. The walkway makes navigating the area easy; it also provides a great vantage point for people-watching. There are a handful of cabanas on either side, as well as a variety of events geared toward locals.

VIRGIN HOTELS LAS VEGAS
Though the former Hard Rock rebranded as Virgin Hotels Las Vegas, Curio Collection by Hilton in March 2021, the party pool scene didn't change all that much. The highlight: the Elia Beach Club, which has a live-music stage and

Encore

a penchant for booking big-name acts.

RED ROCK CASINO RESORT & SPA
For a locals' casino, this place has the pool deck dialed in. The main pool here is a circular number called the Sandbar Pool with an "island" in the center where you can hoist yourself out of the water and sunbathe. To the south, the pool is flanked by shallower wading areas, a spot for poolside gambling, and a full-service café.

THE VENETIAN RESORT LAS VEGAS
Considering how large The Venetian really is, a pool deck with four large pools isn't too far-fetched. The main pools are on the Venetian side, and they are flanked by lounge chairs and cabanas alike. Over on the Palazzo side, everything is on a slightly smaller scale. All pools are decked out with tiny mosaic tile art on the bottoms. And celebrity chef Wolfgang Puck concocts the poolside menus.

RESORTS WORLD LAS VEGAS
At 5.5 acres (and with 7 individual pools), this is the largest pool deck in Las Vegas, and it's on the 5th floor of the Resorts World hotel complex. The reservation-only VIP area has an infinity pool that will overlook the still-developing surfing pool below. And the Ayu Dayclub is yet another pool area devoted to hedonistic enjoyment.

WYNN LAS VEGAS
The pools at Wynn include a multitude of private cabanas as well as a "European" pool for topless sunbathing. There's also gambling under a tent. The real action is at Encore Beach Club. The only downside is the maze you must navigate to find the pool from the rooms upstairs.

Best Celebrity Chef Restaurants on the Strip

JALEO
Chef (and human rights activist) José Andres offers myriad tapas at his restaurant in The Cosmopolitan of Las Vegas, many starring the spectacular Jamón Ibérico Fermin. But paellas prepared over burning wood are the best.

BARDOT BRASSERIE
Michael Mina's signature parfait is on the menu here with foie gras instead of caviar, along with throwbacks like lobster Thermidor and the oh-so-Gallic scallops Veronique. The Belle Époque atmosphere of this restaurant on ARIA's mezzanine seems particularly well-suited to brunch, which is served on weekends.

GIADA
This Cromwell spot with an expansive corner view of Las Vegas's most bustling intersection was Giada de Laurentiis' first restaurant anywhere. Her fresh, seasonal take on traditional Italian cuisine is shown here in signatures such as spaghetti with shrimp, mascarpone, lemon, and basil. The desserts are second to none. Brunch was added to accommodate the masses.

MOMOFUKU LAS VEGAS
David Chang brings his conventional unconventional game to The Cosmopolitan of Las Vegas, freely borrowing from a variety of Asian and non-Asian cuisines. Bring a group for one of the large-format options like the Bo Ssam (slow-roasted pork shoulder).

JEAN-GEORGES STEAKHOUSE

Jean-Georges Vongerichten set the standard for Las Vegas steak houses, including Prime at Bellagio and this one at ARIA. Genuine Kobe A5 (the best of the best) is showcased here, along with tableside-carving presentations of smoked wagyu brisket, a 42-ounce wagyu tomahawk, and 32-ounce bone-in Chateaubriand.

JOËL ROBUCHON

The late French culinary lion's American flagship has long been considered the pinnacle of fine dining in Las Vegas, even earning three Michelin stars. Although Robuchon himself passed in 2018, a flock of disciples maintains his standards of excellence.

GORDON RAMSAY STEAK

Ramsay's Las Vegas flagship is at Paris Las Vegas. His signatures like beef Wellington and sticky toffee pudding are on the menu here, but the menu focuses on steaks. There's a tasting menu and a preshow menu, too. (Ramsay has four other Las Vegas restaurants in addition to this one.)

Morimoto Las Vegas

RESTAURANT GUY SAVOY

Guy Savoy established a beachhead at Caesars Palace for lovers of all things opulent, especially those things that happen to have French accents. So here you'll find the master's signatures such as artichoke and black truffle soup, but you can also indulge in a caviar tasting menu accompanied by Krug Grand Cuvée.

MORIMOTO LAS VEGAS

The Iron Chef himself drops in from time to time at this expansive spot at MGM Grand. Morimoto's talent for deploying the unexpected and sometimes whimsical shows in dishes such as his pork chashu salad and Duck Duck Goose entrée, but there's more conventional sushi and sashimi, too.

AMALFI

Bobby Flay is always innovating, so when he closed fan-favorite Mesa Grill in 2020, he immediately announced a plan to open Amalfi in its place. The menu has a fish-centric theme, complete with a "market" of catches flown in straight from the Mediterranean.

What to Read and Watch Before You Go

OCEANS 11

If you're wondering where the Rat Pack started, it was here. The 1960 original, starring Frank Sinatra, Dean Martin, Sammy Davis Jr., Joey Bishop, and Peter Lawford band together to rob five casinos on New Year's Eve. The much-better 2001 remake, starring George Clooney and Brad Pitt (and directed by Stephen Soderbergh) recycles much of the plot and also has a more positive resolution for the gang and their robbery.

LEAVING LAS VEGAS

Nicolas Cage won both a Golden Globe and Oscar for Best Actor for this black-as-night story of an alcoholic who loses everything before heading to Las Vegas to drink himself to death; while there he meets Sera (Elizabeth Shue), a hooker with a heart of gold, who loves him enough to let him die. The movie was based on the book of the same name by writer John O'Brien, who killed himself after selling the film rights to the book. The movie is well-regarded, but no one anyone ever needs to see twice.

CASINO

Directed by Martin Scorcese, the film stars Robert DeNiro, Joe Pesci, and Sharon Stone. DeNiro plays Sam Rothstein, who is based on real-life casino boss Frank Rosenthal, who helped build the giant mob-controlled Las Vegas casinos of the 1970s and '80s. Ultimately, the FBI shuts down much of the mob business, and the casinos are bought by the same giant corporations that have transformed Las Vegas to the mega-tourist destination it is today. Based on the nonfiction book *Casino: Love and Honor in Las Vegas* by Nicholas Pileggi, it's both successful as a film and conveys a sense of how Las Vegas has evolved. Watch it if you have nostalgia for Las Vegas of yore.

THE GODFATHER II

At the end of *The Godfather,* Michael Corleone decides to move the family's business to Las Vegas (and Moe Greene gets it in the eye). The sequel, perhaps the most successful in cinematic history, continues the Corleone story in two different ways: with Robert DeNiro playing a young Vito Corleone establishing himself in New York City, and Al Pacino continuing his role as Michael, now sheltered in a beautiful midcentury mansion on the shores of Lake Tahoe. Michael survives an assassination attempt and a Senate-organized crime hearing, and seeks more revenge on his enemies, this time including his brother Fredo.

SHOWGIRLS

One of the worst movies of modern cinema, *Showgirls* has achieved something of a cult status. It's the rags-to-riches story of Nomi Malone, who goes from runaway to stripper (at Cheetah's, which is still very much in business), to showgirl at the Stardust (which is now long gone), and finally to Hollywood. The debate about whether this film is a schlock fest or misunderstood masterpiece (or perhaps both) continues.

VERY BAD THINGS

Murder, death, and unhappiness are the results for a group of friends who come to Las Vegas for a bachelor party and accidentally kill a prostitute (and not-so-accidentally kill a security guard) then don't deal well with the aftermath. Some call it an exceptionally dark comedy, others simply tasteless and mean-spirited.

THE HANGOVER

Another hapless bachelor party is played for laughs in this film starring Bradley Cooper, Ed Helms, and Zach Galifianakis. The trio awakens to find a chicken, a tiger, and a baby in their trashed hotel suite at Caesars Palace as well as a missing groom-to-be. As they travel around Las Vegas and try to piece together what happened, hilarity ensues, this time without actual murder and death, which puts *The Hangover* far ahead of *Very Bad Things* on the comedy scale.

ELECTRICK CHILDREN

In this low-budget indie film, a girl from a fundamentalist Mormon community in Utah discovers that she is pregnant. Believing she has immaculately conceived after listening to a cassette tape for the first time, she flees an arranged marriage (with her brother accidentally in tow) for Las Vegas, where she falls in with a group of skaters and falls in love with one of them. She eventually meets her biological father, returns to her community, but decides not to stay and instead starts a life with her skater boyfriend. The well-received film, a first-time directorial effort by Rebecca Thomas from 2012, was a festival hit.

THE GOLDFINCH

Donna Tartt's 2013 novel won the 2014 Pulitzer Prize for Fiction. Although commercially popular, it was not loved by all critics, despite winning such a major literary award. It's a coming-of-age novel about a boy named Theo whose mother is killed during a bombing at the Metropolitan Museum, while he is viewing *The Goldfinch,* a 17th-century Dutch painting that Theo takes after the bombing. A section of the novel finds Theo in Las Vegas, where he's been taken by his father, an addicted gambler and drunk.

FEAR AND LOATHING IN LAS VEGAS

Hunter S. Thompson's most famous novel is a fictionalized autobiographical story of a journalist and his friend who go to Las Vegas to cover a motorcycle race in 1971 but instead have a series of destructive, drug-fueled, hallucinatory experiences. For Thompson, Las Vegas represented the height of mainstream, consumerist American culture for which he had nothing but disdain, but he felt his novel was not entirely successful (most critics disagreed). Over time, the book's reputation grew, and it was adapted into an unsuccessful 1998 film starring Johnny Depp and Benicio del Toro.

MARS ATTACKS!

Sin City serves as one of the main settings for this 1996 satire about an alien invasion full of kitschy gore and strange characters. Surviving the apocalyptic destruction of the city are Tom Jones, Annette Bening, and a waitress named Cindy, who take refuge in a cave overlooking Lake Tahoe.

THE LAST HONEST PLACE IN AMERICA: PARADISE AND PERDITION IN THE NEW LAS VEGAS

Marc Cooper writes about the nascent years of contemporary Las Vegas in the early 2000s by writing about his own love of the city (and gambling) and talking to the dealers and others who have seen Las Vegas develop into a more corpratized resort destination after its more free-wheeling Mob days. Many consider it the best history of modern Las Vegas.

21/BRINGING DOWN THE HOUSE

A purported nonfiction account of the MIT Blackjack Team in the early 1990s was written by Ben Mezrich. It follows the exploits of several MIT students who find success in Las Vegas playing blackjack (and counting cards); when the casinos discover their tactics, most of the players are banned. Later examinations of the real events led the *Boston Globe* to conclude that the book was highly fictionalized, but the book was wildly popular and adapted into a film called *21* in 2008 starring Kevin Spacey and Jim Sturgess.

Free Things To Do

Yes, Vegas brims with cash, glitz, and glamour, but that doesn't mean you can't find freebies (or cheapies).

Experience Fremont Street. The Downtown casinos' answer to the spectacle of the Strip is the Fremont Street Experience, played out on a 90-foot-high arched canopy that covers the entire street. Every hour between sunset and midnight it comes alive with an integrated video, graphics, and music show. Several different programs run each night and contribute to a festive outside-in communal atmosphere that contrasts with the Strip's every-man-for-himself ethic.

Watch a Free Show. You can easily spend $100 or more on seats at a typical Vegas concert or big-name production, but several casinos offer fabulous, eye-catching extravaganzas that won't cost you a penny. There's the erupting volcano at The Mirage, the graceful Fountains of Bellagio, and the Wildlife Habitat (with a flamboyance of flamingos!) at the Flamingo Las Vegas. People-watching is a free show of a different kind, too.

See the New Old Downtown. The Downtown casinos don't attempt to compete with the opulence of the Strip, but area streets have their own charm. The Downtown Container Park is a collection of shipping containers that have been converted into an outdoor mall of shops, bars, and restaurants. Also, stroll through history as you marvel at Vegas Vic and other vintage neon signs (curated by the Neon Museum).

Preview a TV Show. Vegas is home to several preview studios, where you're asked to watch and offer feedback on TV shows. Some studios offer a small cash stipend for your time; for others you'll have to be satisfied with free refreshments, coupons, and the thanks of a grateful nation. We like **CBS Television City** (✉ *3799 Las Vegas Blvd. S, South Strip* ☎ *702/891–5753* ⊕ *tvcityresearch. com* ⊙ *Daily 10–10*) at the MGM Grand. ■ **TIP→ No kids under 10.**

Cruise the Strip. You haven't done Vegas until you've been caught—either intentionally or unwittingly—in the slow-mo weekend-night crawl of traffic down the Strip. You can handle the experience like a been-there local, or you can play the delighted tourist: relaxed, windows down, ready to engage in silly banter with the carload of players in the convertible one lane over. We suggest the latter, at least once. Just be mindful of all the pedestrians, who can crowd the crosswalks and are just as dazed as you are by the cacophony.

Appreciate Architecture. Las Vegas as a hot spot for architectural design? In recent years, yes. Check out the art deco–inspired **Smith Center for the Performing Arts,** which was designed to match the sweeping grandeur of the Hoover Dam. Elsewhere around Downtown, check out the **Antonio Morelli House,** a classic example of midcentury residential architecture, and the modern Frank Gehry–designed **Lou Ruvo Center for Brain Health.** Of course, you always can wander through the older hotels on the Strip and Downtown that will, eventually and inevitably, be torn down to make way for new construction.

Continued on page 36

HISTORY, VEGAS-STYLE

by Matt Vilano

Over the last few years, we've all heard the brilliant marketing slogan "What happens in Vegas stays in Vegas." But a whole lot has happened in Vegas in the last few hundred years, and most of the stories have made it into the history books.

Archaeologists believe civilization in the area now known as Sin City stretches back almost 2,000 years. This once lush area was home to numerous Native American tribes, including the Kawaiisu, Kitenamuk, and Serrano. In the 1820s, Spaniards traveling from Mexico to northern California on the Old Spanish Trail named the area "Las Vegas" (meaning "The Meadows"). When the area became part of the U.S. in 1855, the name stuck.

The railroad arrived in 1905, and, over the next decades, Las Vegas grew from a rail hub to a leisure destination. The Hoover Dam, built in the 1930s, played a large part in development, but gambling put the city on the map. Since 1940, Las Vegas has seen casinos rise, fall, and rise again—bigger than before. These casinos have launched some of the greatest names in show business, including Frank Sinatra, Dean Martin, and Wayne Newton.

Today, Las Vegas and its environs (population: more than 2 million) shelter those who make the casinos whir. And nothing here sits for long; the town becomes hipper, bolder, and more sophisticated every year. The city is now home to 11 of the 21 largest hotels in the world. From a place nicknamed Sin City, you'd expect nothing less.

1829: water-rich Las Vegas valley (the Meadow) gets its name.

1855: Mormons build fort.

1864: Nevada becomes 36th state.

1885: State La Act attracts farmers.

Precolonial Era   1800   1850   1900

COL. FREMONT

(left) Detail from poster for John C. Fremont 1856; (above) Las Vegas circa 1895; (right) construction workers working Hoover Dam spillway between 1936 and 1946.

Native Occupation

1500s–1800s

Cultural artifacts indicate that human settlers including the Kawaiisu, Kitanemuk, Serrano, Koso, and Chemehuevi occupied the area as far back as the 100 or 200 A.D. Archaeologists have said the land would have been hospitable—the region's artesian wells would have provided enough water to support small communities, and skeletal remains indicate wildlife was prevalent. It also stands to reason that many of the earliest inhabitants took advantage of the lush meadows after which the region ultimately was named; excavated pieces of detailed weavings and basketry support these theories.

Early Settlers

1820s–90s

Spaniards settled the area in the 1820s, but John Fremont, of the U.S. Army Corps of Engineers, quickly followed on a scouting mission in 1844. After annexation, in 1855, Brigham Young sent a group of missionaries to the Las Vegas Valley to convert a number of modern Native-American groups, including the Anasazi. The missionaries built a fort that served as a stopover for travelers along the "Mormon Corridor" between Salt Lake City and a thriving colony in San Bernardino, California. Dissension among leaders prompted the Mormons to abandon Las Vegas by the 1860s, leaving only a handful of settlers behind.

Industrialization Arrives

1890s–1920s

Everything in Las Vegas changed in the 1900s. Just after the turn of the century, local leaders diverted the spring and resulting creek into the town's water system. The spring dried up and the once-vibrant meadows turned into desert. Then, in 1905, the transcontinental railroad came through on its inexorable push toward the Pacific. The city also began to serve as a staging point for all the area mines; mining companies would shuttle their goods from the mountains into Las Vegas, then onto the trains and out to the rest of the country. With the proliferation of railroads, however, this boom was short-lived.

1905. Las Vegas is founded as a city.	1911: Divorce laws are liberalized in Nevada	1931: construction begins at Hoover Dam sight. Population booms. Gambling is legalized.	1941: El Rancho Vegas, first hotel and casino on the Strip.	1951: First Atomic Bomb is detonated north of Las Vegas.

1920   **1940**   **1960**

(above) The Flamingo Hotel; (below) Bugsy Siegel; (top right) The Rat Pack.

1930s

Early Casinos

Las Vegans knew they needed something to distinguish their town from the other towns along the rails that crisscrossed the United States. They found it in gambling. The Nevada State Legislature repealed the ban in 1931, opening the proverbial floodgates for a new era and a new economy. Just weeks after the ban was lifted, the now-defunct Pair-O-Dice opened on Highway 91, the stretch of road that would later become known as the Las Vegas Strip. The city celebrated another newcomer—dedicating the Boulder (now Hoover) Dam on the Colorado River in 1935.

1940s–50s

Bugsy Takes Charge

No person had more of an impact on Las Vegas's gambling industry than gangster Ben "Bugsy" Siegel. The Brooklyn, New York native aimed to build and run the classiest resort-casino in the world, recruiting mob investors to back him. The result was the Flamingo Hotel, which opened (millions of dollars over budget) in 1946. Though the hotel was met with historic fanfare, it initially flopped, making Siegel's partners unhappy and suspicious of embezzlement. Within six months, Siegel was "rubbed out," but the Flamingo lived on—a monument to the man who changed Vegas forever.

1950s–60s

Rat Pack Era

Frank Sinatra, Dean Martin, Sammy Davis, Jr., Peter Lawford, and Joey Bishop were a reckless bunch; upon seeing them together, actress Lauren Bacall said, "You look like a goddamn rat pack." The name stuck. The quintet appeared in a number of movies—who can forget the original *Ocean's Eleven?*—and performed live in Las Vegas. Their popularity helped Sin City grow into an entertainment destination. They also played an important role in desegregation—the gang refused to play in establishments that wouldn't give full service to African-American entertainers, forcing many hotels to abandon their racist policies.

(left) Howard Hughes; (center top) Frank Rosenthal interviewing Frank Sinatra; (center bottom) Elvis Presley; (top) Liberace; (right top) Steve Wynn; (right bottom) Siegfried and Roy; (right) Bellagio's dancing fountains.

1960s
A Maverick Swoops in

Multimillionaire Howard Hughes arrived in Vegas in 1966 and began buying up hotels: Desert Inn, Castaways, New Frontier, Landmark Hotel and Casino, Sands, and Silver Slipper, to name a few. He also invested in land—then mostly desert—that today comprises most of the planned-residential and commercial community of Summerlin. Hughes also wielded enormous political and economic influence in Nevada and nearly single-handedly derailed the U.S. Army's plan to test nuclear weapons nearby. His failure in this matter led to a self-imposed exile in Nicaragua until his death in 1976.

1960s–80s
Mob Era

Elvis Presley made his comeback in 1969 at The International (now the Las Vegas Hotel) and played there regularly until the middle of the next decade. In the same era, East Coast mobsters tightened their grip on casinos, prompting a federal crackdown and forcing some to return to the east when gambling was legalized in Atlantic City, New Jersey, in 1976. Frank "Lefty" Rosenthal, largely seen as the inventor of the modern sports book, narrowly survived a car bomb in 1982. Others, such as Tony "The Ant" Spilotro, were not as lucky—Spilotro and his brother, another casino gangster, were beaten and strangled to death in 1986 and buried in a cornfield in Indiana.

Late 1980s–90s
Era of Reinvention

The years immediately following the mob crackdown weren't pretty. The nation was in a recession, and tourism was down. Large fires at major resorts such as MGM Grand, Aladdin, and Monte Carlo devastated the city's economy and image. Gradually, Las Vegas recovered. Big corporations purchased hotels off the scrap heap, and several properties underwent major renovations. With the help of clever marketing campaigns, properties began attracting tourists back to experience the "new" Vegas. In 1989, Steve Wynn opened the city's first new casino in 16 years—the Mirage—and triggered a building boom that persists today.

1993: Work begins in Fremont Street Experience.	1996: Las Vegas Motor Speedway opens.	2001: Green Valley Ranch Resort and Spa opens.	2005: The Wynn opens; Las Vegas celebrates its centennial.	2010: The new Las Vegas CityCenter is completed.	2016: The T-Mobile (home to the Las Vegas Golden Knights NHL franchise) Arena and Park Theater open.

2000   **2010**   **BEYOND**

In Focus | HISTORY, VEGAS-STYLE

1990s

Age of the Mega-Hotel

In all, more than a dozen new mega-resorts opened in the 1990s. The Mirage, which opened in 1989, started the domino effect of new hotels up and down the Strip. It was followed by the Rio and Excalibur in 1990; Luxor and Treasure Island (now TI) in 1993; the Hard Rock Hotel in 1995; the Stratosphere and the Monte Carlo in 1996; Bellagio in 1998; and Mandalay Bay, the Venetian and Paris Hotel & Casino in 1999. These, coupled with the $72-million, 1,100-acre Las Vegas Motor Speedway, which took the city from exclusively gambling destination to a NASCAR destination, made the city incredibly visitor-friendly. Tourists obliged, arriving in record numbers.

2000s

Variations on a Theme

Never fans of complacency, Vegas hoteliers have continued to innovate. Steve Wynn, of Mirage and Bellagio fame, opened arguably the city's most exquisite resort, Wynn Las Vegas, in 2005. Sheldon Adelson, CEO of Sands Corporation, countered by opening The Palazzo next door to the Venetian, giving the two properties 7,000 rooms combined. Off the strip, multimillion dollar mega-resorts such as the Palms and Red Rock offered more exclusive, intimate experiences. Then, toward the end of this decade, Vegas experienced a new trend: hotels without casinos of any kind, outfitted for nothing but complete relaxation.

2010s

Mixing It Up

By 2010 non-gaming revenue had exceeded gaming revenue on the Strip for more than 10 years, and every major resort had fully adapted to this new normal with ever-greater investments in clubs, restaurants, shows, and shops. The mega resorts mega-merged, with MGM Mirage becoming MGM Resorts International and Harrah's Entertainment becoming Caesars Entertainment in 2010, dominating the Strip with more than 20 properties between them. Mixed-use spaces such as the mammoth CityCenter and major attractions such as the High Roller and the Park ushered in a new age of visitor amenities that emphasized entertainment inside and outside the resorts.

Tie the Knot

Vegas wedding chapels: they're flowers and neon and love ever after (or at least until tomorrow's hangover). They're also mighty quick, once you get that marriage license.

A Little White Wedding Chapel. The list of ALWWC alums is impressive: Demi Moore and Bruce Willis, Paul Newman and Joanne Woodward, Michael Jordan, Britney Spears, and Frank Sinatra. Patty Duke liked it so much, she got married here twice. Try the Hawaiian theme, where the minister plays a ukulele and blows into a conch shell to close out the ceremony. Or, get hitched in a pink Cadillac while an Elvis impersonator croons. One of the five chapels is a drive-through, for the ultimate in shotgun weddings. ⊠ *1301 Las Vegas Blvd. S, North Strip* ☎ *800/545–8111, 702/382–5943* ⊕ *www.alittlewhitechapel.com.*

Chapel of the Flowers. Enjoy a brief facsimile of a traditional ceremony at this venue, designed to be a turnkey wedding operation, with two chapels and an outdoor garden, as well as on-site flower shop, photography studio, and wedding coordinators. It's still Las Vegas, so an Elvis impersonator is available for all ceremonies. ⊠ *1717 Las Vegas Blvd. S, North Strip* ☎ *800/843–2410, 702/735–4331* ⊕ *www.littlechapel.com.*

Clark County Marriage License Bureau. A no-wait marriage certificate can be yours if you bring $77 cash (there's an additional fee for credit cards), identification, and your beloved to the Clark County Marriage License Bureau. Unless the office is unusually busy, the process normally takes less than an hour. ⊠ *201 E. Clark Ave., Downtown* ☎ *702/671–0600* ⊕ *mlic.vegas.*

Little Church of the West. This cedar-and-redwood chapel on the South Strip is one of the city's most famous. The kitsch is kept under control, and the setting borders on picturesque (it's even listed on the National Register of Historic Places—ah, Vegas). Since it opened in 1942, the church has been the site of more celebrity marriages than any other chapel in the world. ⊠ *4617 Las Vegas Blvd. S, South Strip* ☎ *702/739–7971, 800/821–2452* ⊕ *www.littlechurchofthewest.com.*

Office of Civil Marriages. If you don't want to be married by Elvis or a Klingon, head for the Office of Civil Marriages downtown, where a commissioner will do the deed for $77.75 on a credit card. The catch: you must call ahead to make an appointment. At least one witness is required. ⊠ *330 S. 3rd St., 6th fl., Suite 660, Downtown* ☎ *702/671–0577* ⊕ *www.clarkcountynv.gov/government/ elected_officials/county_clerk/other_services/civil_marriage.php.*

Viva Las Vegas Wedding Chapels. An endless variety of wedding themes and add-on shtick is available, ranging from elegant to casual to camp. You can say your vows in the presence of Elvis, the Blues Brothers, or Liberace. Live webcams stream nuptials on the chapel's website in real time. Of the four chapels, one has a Doo-Wop Diner theme. ⊠ *1205 Las Vegas Blvd. S, North Strip* ☎ *702/384–0771, 800/574–4450* ⊕ *www.vivalasvegasweddings.com.*

Chapter 2

TRAVEL SMART

Updated by
Matt Villano

★ **STATE CAPITAL:**
Carson City

POPULATION:
634,773 (2.2 million in metropolitan area)

LANGUAGE:
English

$ **CURRENCY:**
U.S. dollar

☎ **AREA CODES:**
702, 725

⚠ **EMERGENCIES:**
911

🚗 **DRIVING:**
On the right

⚡ **ELECTRICITY:**
120–220 v/60 cycles; plugs have two or three rectangular prongs

🕐 **TIME:**
PST; same as Los Angeles

⊕ **WEBSITES:**
visitlasvegas.com, review-journal.com, lasvegas.com

✈ **AIRPORT:**
LAS, McCarran International Airport

Know Before You Go

KNOW THE SLOWEST VS. MOST CROWDED TIMES

Big events (the Super Bowl in February and all large conventions) rather than traditional tourist seasons affect business more in Las Vegas. Summers tend to be slower because of the heat. And Sunday through Thursday hotel rates are always significantly cheaper than weekends.

FIND THE BEST WEATHER

Winter in Las Vegas can be extremely unpredictable. Ultramild weather in 2017/2018 was followed by a winter with a number of snowfalls (exceedingly rare in the Valley) in 2018/2019 and again in 2021. Spring and autumn tend to be particularly pleasant, with moderate temperatures coupled with the famous low humidity. But watch out for summer; highs in July and August can easily reach 116°F, and while it may be a dry heat, it can be deadly if you're taken unawares. Hydrate, hydrate, hydrate, and make sure you can get to a space that's air-conditioned or at least shady.

KNOW WHAT TO EXPECT AFTER COVID-19

The COVID-19 global pandemic of 2020 and 2021 threw Las Vegas for a loop, but by mid-2021, things had already begun to return to normal. You might still spot some vestiges of pandemic-related public health protocols, and open hours may continue to be erratic through fall 2021.

KNOW HOW TO GET DISCOUNTED SHOW TICKETS

The biggest local dealer probably is ⊕ *Tix4Tonight.com*, which sells tickets online and at 10 booths around the valley. They advise showing up early in the morning; for booth locations and more advice, visit tix4tonight.com. Other popular (legitimate) websites are ⊕ *lasvegas.showtickets.com* and ⊕ *vegas.com*. Check out the regular ticket prices before you shop so you know if you're getting a good deal. If you're staying in a hotel with a concierge, check with them, and if you're a premium player, talk to your casino host.

AIRPORT TRANSPORT: FAST VS. CHEAP

The most economical way to get from the airport to your hotel is via the Regional Transportation Commission's Centennial Express, which stops at Sands Avenue/Spring Mountain Road and the Strip, downtown, and at the UNLV transit center. This will likely not be the fastest, and will not take you door to door. For a quick trip and luxurious ride, opt for a stretch limousine, but a ride share or taxi will be just as speedy in terms of both speed and will cost less; ride shares tend to be noticeably cheaper than regular taxis. Shuttles are also quite popular in Las Vegas, but they make multiple stops; still, the price is right if you're on a budget or traveling alone.

HOW TO TRAVEL THE STRIP

The Strip is about 4 miles from one end to the other, although most visitors seem to stick mostly to their clusters at the south, center, and north ends. Even though two resorts may be right next to each other, the walk can be very long because of the sheer size of the properties. Free trams can make things easier: a popular one links Bellagio, Vdara, ARIA, The Shoppes at Crystals, and Park MGM; another goes from Mandalay Bay to Excalibur; yet another connects Mirage and Treasure Island (all of these on the west side of the Strip). But your best foot-saving option may be the Regional Transportation Commission's The Deuce, Strip, and Downtown Express (SDX), which is $8 for 24 hours, or $20 for three days.

WHAT ABOUT THE MONORAIL?

Las Vegas also has a monorail that connects several of the major resorts on the east side of the Strip to the Convention Center. When does it pay to use the monorail? Should you get a pass? The Las Vegas Monorail doesn't go to and from McCarran International Airport, but if you'll be attending a convention or other event at the Las Vegas Convention Center, it's extremely convenient—especially during CES, when taxis, buses, and ride-sharing vehicles choke the areas near the center. There are stations at MGM Grand, Bally's/Paris, the Flamingo, Harrah's/The LINQ, the Westgate, and the SLS Las Vegas. If you're staying at a hotel on the west side of the Strip (including Bellagio and Caesars Palace), just walk across the street, though be aware that it can also be a very long walk to the monorail stations, which are typically on the back sides of the resorts. One-ride tickets are $5, and one-day passes $13 ($23 and $29 for two- and three-day passes, respectively), so plan according to your travel needs.

PARKING: IT'S NO LONGER FREE

The free resort parking that Las Vegans and visitors once considered practically a right is no longer—not even for hotel guests. The only exceptions on or near the Strip are The Venetian and The Palazzo, Tropicana, Westgate, the Rio, and Orleans resorts, which still have free parking, as do the resorts in the outlying areas. Wynn and Encore have free parking only for resort guests. Most other resorts charge nothing for the first hour, but rates vary thereafter, and there's generally a fee for valet parking in addition to the tip. At MGM

Resorts properties, their M life Rewards Mastercard entitles you to free parking; so do some of the players' clubs, provided you reach a high enough level. Some resorts, including the Westgate, may charge for parking during large conventions because of their proximity to the action.

RESORT FEES ARE NOW UBIQUITOUS

Resort fees (which hotels say cover things like pools and Internet access, but which are mandatory for every guest) have become common on the Strip and can add up to $45 a day to the room rate—and they don't include parking. Hotels that don't charge them tend to be off the Strip and often are noncasino properties (and they usually trumpet their lack of a resort fee), so cruise around the Internet to find one without the charge.

YOU CAN GET A GOOD AND CHEAP BREAKFAST NEAR THE STRIP

The Omelet House, west of the Strip at Charleston Boulevard and Rancho Drive, just celebrated its 40th anniversary, and social media is guiding crowds of visitors to it. Breakfast places have grown exponentially in Las Vegas during the past few years; somewhat farther afield (but easily reachable by ride-share, taxi, or rental car) are the various outlets of Blueberry Hill, the Cracked Egg, the Egg Works, Rise and Shine, Hash House a Go Go, Babystacks, Metro Diner, Black Bear Diner, and Squeeze Inn.

THERE'S PLENTY TO KEEP YOU BUSY OFF THE STRIP

Visitors who confine their trips to the Strip are missing out on some of the best things Las Vegas has to offer. Downtown Las Vegas has seen a resurgence in recent years, particularly the Arts District and the Fremont East area, including the Downtown Container Park. And what a lot of visitors don't know is that the Las Vegas Valley is filled with natural wonders. Three popular spots are Red Rock Canyon National Conservation Area, Valley of Fire State Park, and Mt. Charleston; the latter tends to be at least 20 degrees cooler than the Valley and also offers skiing and snowboarding in the winter. There are a number of fun museums, including the Mob Museum, Neon Museum, and Discovery Children's Museum Downtown; the Las Vegas Natural History Museum is just north of Downtown; the National Atomic Testing Museum east of Downtown, and the Clark County Museum in Henderson. And the Springs Preserve on the west side is a way to get out in nature and learn about the history of the area.

Getting Here and Around

The sprawling city of Las Vegas is fairly easy to get around by car, as it's laid out largely in a grid, bisected by two Interstates, and mostly surrounded by a beltway. Traffic along the Strip, especially at its major intersections, as well as on parallel Interstates 15 and 515 (the latter of which is U.S. Highway 93/95 at most points), can be horrendous. It's particularly bad on weekend evenings and whenever there are conventions in town. Give yourself plenty of time when you're traveling to or from the Strip.

Outside the Strip, the city sprawls in all directions, and renting a car is the best way to get around, especially if you're staying in Lake Las Vegas, Summerlin, or similar areas more than a few miles away from the Strip. Las Vegas is also served by public buses; the one that travels up and down the Strip (it's called The Deuce) is particularly popular with visitors.

✈ Air

Approximate flying times to Las Vegas: from New York, 5 hours; from Dallas, 2 hours; from Chicago, 4 hours; from Los Angeles, 1 hour; from San Francisco, 1½ hours.

If you're leaving Las Vegas on a Sunday, be sure to arrive at the airport at least two hours before your scheduled departure time. Though the TSA has improved its operations at McCarran International, security lines on busy days still seemingly stretch forever, and inevitably, travelers miss flights.

AIRPORTS

The gateway to Las Vegas is McCarran International Airport (LAS), 5 miles south of the business district and immediately east of the southern end of the Strip. The airport, just a few minutes' drive from the Strip, is well served by nonstop and connecting flights from all around the country and a handful of international destinations. The airport is consistently rated among the most passenger-friendly airports in the United States.

Also, McCarran is close enough to the Strip that, if you ever find yourself there with a few hours to kill, you can easily catch a 15-minute cab ride to one of the South Strip casinos (Mandalay Bay and Luxor are closest) to while away some time. Additionally, as you might expect, McCarran has scads of slot machines to keep you busy.

AIRPORT TRANSFERS

Bus: If you're heading Downtown or to the south end of the Strip, the Regional Transportation Commission's public bus is the cheapest, and often quickest, way from the airport. RTC's Centennial Express (CX) travels from McCarran Airport all the way to Centennial Hills Transit Center in North Las Vegas and includes a stop along the Strip at Tropicana Avenue and Las Vegas Boulevard (between New York–New York and Excalibur), Las Vegas Premium Outlets (near Downtown), and at Casino Center Boulevard and Fremont Street Downtown. The service operates seven days a week from approximately 5 am to midnight. The bus runs approximately every hour. Just know that while the bus is clean and comfortable, it contains no racks for luggage. ■ TIP→ **When boarding the bus, tell the driver where you're going before paying. When on board, alert them to your approaching stop by ringing the buzzer.**

The Terminal 1 transit stop for CX is on Level Zero, below baggage claim, at the south end of the bus plaza. Follow signs for Ground Transportation. Once outside, proceed across the pedestrian crosswalk, turn right toward the parking garage, and follow signs for the public bus stop. Exact change of $2 ($1 with a Medicare card, student ID [ages 6–17] or reduced-fare card from another system) is the fare for a single ride. The ticket vending machine accepts credit or debit cards to purchase a 2- or 24-hour pass, $6 and $8, respectively; passes also can be purchased aboard Deuce buses and SDX vehicles. The ride from the airport to the Strip will take 10 to 20 minutes, depending on ridership and traffic; to Downtown about 30 to 55 minutes. The transit stop for CX in Terminal 3 is on the Departures Level. Follow signs for Ground Transportation and then for Public Transportation. ■TIP➜ **Download a free Park & Ride Airport Guide at ⊕ tcsnv.com.**

Ride share: Both Uber and Lyft are allowed to both drop off and pick up at McCarran International Airport. Use the app on your phone to book them. The pickup spots at the airport are on Level 2M of the Terminal 1 parking garage and the Valet Level of the Terminal 3 parking garage. They are not allowed to pick up at the arrivals or departures area of either terminal.

Shuttle van: This is one of the cheapest ways to get from McCarran to your hotel if you don't take the public bus. Shuttle service operated by SuperShuttle, BellTrans, and ODS is shared with other riders, and costs $15 to $18 per person, depending on the location of the hotel (excluding tips). If you have a large party, group rates are available. The vans wait for passengers outside the terminal in marked areas. Because the vans often make numerous stops at different hotels, it's not the best means of transportation if you're in a hurry. For round-trip service, save time and money by booking online and printing out your vouchers beforehand. ■TIP➜ **Before you jump on a shuttle,**

check with your hotel, because several of them, such as Green Valley Ranch in Henderson and Red Rock Resort in Summerlin, offer customers free round-trip shuttle rides.

Taxi: There are still taxis in Las Vegas, and metered cabs operated by more than 10 companies and awaiting your arrival at McCarran remain one of the quickest ways to get to your destination (see Taxi Travel below for more information).

Town car: These rides by companies, including AWG Ambassador, Bell Limousine, and ODS, are a bit more expensive than the average taxi and must be reserved ahead of time, but they are cleaner and more convenient. A chauffeur from Bell Limousines, for example, will meet and greet you at baggage claim, assist with luggage, and whisk you away in a luxury sedan, with seating for up to five, for $55 an hour.

FLIGHTS

The major airlines operate frequent service from their hub cities and, as a whole, offer one-stop connecting flights from virtually every city in the country. In addition to nonstop service from the usual hub cities (e.g., Atlanta, Chicago, Cincinnati, Dallas, Denver, Houston, Minneapolis, Newark, New York City, Phoenix, Salt Lake City, San Francisco), nonstop service is offered to many other destinations, sometimes by smaller airlines. Southwest remains a dominant airline, offering frequent flights to many cities in the south and west, including San Diego, Los Angeles, San Francisco, Oakland, Seattle, Salt Lake, Denver, Albuquerque, and Phoenix. Be sure to check the rates of the airlines that serve Las Vegas frequently from multiple cities, such as Delta, JetBlue, Frontier Airlines, United, American, and Alaska Airlines.

Getting Here and Around

Bus

THE DEUCE

The Deuce is a special double-decker RTC bus that rides the Strip for $6 for two hours. All Deuce fares include transfers on residential routes as well. The Deuce certainly is a unique way to explore new and old Vegas alike. Buses stop on the street in front of all the major hotels about every 15 minutes (in a perfect world) between 7 am and 2 am and every 20 minutes between 2 am and 7 am. Because traffic is quite heavy along the Strip, delays are frequent. Also, because the bus route has become popular among tourists, 24-hour passes ($8), and 3-day passes ($20) are available.

INTERCITY BUSES

Greyhound, Megabus, Flixbus, and CoachRun (and a few others) provide regular Las Vegas service; the Greyhound bus terminal is Downtown, but other lines serve other stations (Megabus, for example, stops at the RTC South Strip Transfer Station). Visit the bus line's website for fare, schedule, and baggage-allowance information. Cash and credit cards are accepted. Seating is on a first-come, first-served basis. The most frequent route out of Las Vegas is the one to Los Angeles, with departures several times a day; the trip takes five to eight hours, depending on stops. Fares begin at around $19 one-way, if you take advantage of the substantial discounts offered on the website. On Sunday evening and Monday morning, arriving an hour or more before departure is recommended.

RTC

Nonlocals typically ride RTC buses only up and down the Strip, between Mandalay Bay and the Strat. Some continue on to the Bonneville Transit Center. If you're heading to outlying areas, you may need to change buses Downtown. Mornings and afternoons the buses are frequently crowded, with standing room only. The fare for residential RTC buses is $2.

Car

Though you can get around central Las Vegas adequately without a car, the easiest way to experience the city can be to drive it. A car gives you easy access to all the casinos and attractions; lets you make excursions to Lake Mead, Hoover Dam, and elsewhere at your leisure; and gives you the chance to cruise the Strip and bask in its neon glow. If you plan to spend most of your time on the Strip, a car may not be worth the trouble, but otherwise, especially given the relatively high costs of taxis, renting or bringing a car is a good idea.

Valet parking is available at most major hotels but can take a while at busy times, and in most cases there is a fee in addition to your tip for the valets ($2 to $3 is expected). Self-parking on and around the Strip is, for the most part, no longer free. Still, it's usually less expensive to rent a car and drive around Vegas, or to use the monorail (or even—gasp!—to walk), than to cab it everywhere.

CAR RENTALS

The airport's rental-car companies are off-site at McCarran Rent-a-Car Center, about 3 miles from the main airport complex, and visitors must take the Rental Car Shuttle buses from the center median, located just outside the baggage claim Ground Transportation exits from Level 1 (Terminal 1) and Level Zero (Terminal 3) to get there. The facility reduces congestion in and around the airport, and offers visitors the opportunity to check bags for flights on some airlines without setting foot in the main terminal. But getting there can add 15 to 25 minutes to your travel time to or from the airport. If you rent a car, be sure to leave yourself plenty of time to return the vehicle and catch your flight.

Rental Car Rates: For 2021, the Las Vegas average was running anywhere from $25 to $80 a day for intermediate to full-size cars. Usually you can find a car for less than $40 a day (and at very slow times for less than $30), but during very busy times (and in the aftermath of COVID-19), expect sky-high rates, especially at the last minute. Las Vegas also has among the country's highest car-rental taxes and surcharges: 8.1% Nevada sales tax for car rentals, a 2% Clark County rental tax, 10% concession recovery fee, and a 4% vehicle licensing fee. If you rent your car at the airport, an additional $3 per-day "customer facility charge" applies as well. During special events and conventions, rates frequently go up as supply dwindles, but at other times you can find bargains. For the best deals, check with the various online services or your airline, or contact a representative of the hotel where you'll be staying, as many hotels have business relationships with car-rental companies.

Although there are several local car-rental companies along the Strip itself, they tend to be more expensive than those at the airport or elsewhere in the city.

Rental Car Requirements: In Nevada you must be 21 to rent a car, and some major car-rental agencies have a minimum age of 25. Those agencies that do rent to people under 25 often assess surcharges to those drivers. There's no upper age limit for renting a car. Non–U.S. residents will need a reservation voucher, a passport, a driver's license, and a travel policy that covers each driver when picking up a car.

DRIVING

The principal north–south artery is Las Vegas Boulevard (Interstate 15 runs roughly parallel to it, less than a mile to the west). A 4-mile stretch of Las Vegas Boulevard South is known as the Strip, where a majority of the city's hotels and casinos are clustered. Many major streets running east–west (Tropicana Avenue, Flamingo Road, Desert Inn Road, Sahara Avenue) are named for the casinos—past and present—built at their intersections with the Strip. Highway 215 circumnavigates the city, and the Interstate 515 freeway connects Henderson to Las Vegas; the Summerlin Parkway connects the city and that suburb. Because the capacity of the streets of Las Vegas hasn't kept pace with the city's incredible growth, traffic can be slow at virtually any time, especially on the Strip, and particularly in the late afternoon, in the evening, and on weekends. At those times drive the streets parallel to Las Vegas Boulevard: Koval Lane and Paradise Road to the east; Frank Sinatra Drive and Industrial Road/Dean Martin Drive/Sammy Davis Jr. Drive to the west. That last shortcut (from Tropicana Avenue almost all the way to Downtown) can save you an enormous amount of time. You can enter the parking lots at Fashion Show mall, Trump Las Vegas, and Circus Circus from Sammy Davis Jr. Drive. Exit Frank Sinatra Drive off Interstate 15 North, and you can access most of the hotels from Mandalay Bay to Caesars Palace (including CityCenter).

■ **TIP→ Visitors from Southern California should at all costs try to avoid traveling to Las Vegas on a Friday afternoon and returning home on a Sunday afternoon. During these traditional weekend-visit hours, driving times (along Interstate 15) can be more than twice as long as during other, nonpeak periods.**

Getting Here and Around

GASOLINE

It's easy to find gas stations, most of which are open 24 hours, all over town, within a mile of the Strip in either direction, along the main east–west cross streets. Gas is relatively expensive in Las Vegas, generally 30¢ to 40¢ per gallon above the national average, and the stations nearest the airport tend to charge a few cents more per gallon—it's prudent to fill up your rental car a few miles away from the airport before returning it.

PARKING

You can't park anywhere on the Strip itself, and Fremont Street in the casino district Downtown is a pedestrian mall closed to traffic. Street parking regulations are strictly enforced in Las Vegas, and meters are continuously monitored, so whenever possible it's a good idea to leave your car in a parking lot or garage. Self-parking is available at most of the massive garages and lots of virtually every hotel, although you may have to hunt for a space and possibly wind up in the far reaches of immense facilities. It's also no longer free. You can avoid this challenge by opting for valet parking, but most hotels now charge for that as well. Parking in the high-rise structures Downtown is generally free or inexpensive, as long as you validate your parking ticket with the casino cashier or restaurant host.

The long tradition of free parking at all Strip resorts ended in mid-2016, when MGM Resorts International starting charging for both self-parking and valet at all of its resorts. Caesars Entertainment Corporation followed suit, as did The Cosmopolitan of Las Vegas. Self-parking is still free at Wynn/Encore (although there's a fee for valet), The Venetian/ The Palazzo, the Westgate Las Vegas (although there may be a fee there during conventions), the new Virgin hotel, and nongaming hotels in the tourism corridor. Also note that some players' card holders and holders of company-branded bank cards get free parking. (Most Downtown hotel-casinos charge, but you generally get a few hours of free parking if you gamble, dine, or otherwise patronize the property). Parking rates can vary, even within the same company, so check with the property you'll be visiting.

ROAD CONDITIONS

It might seem as if every road in Las Vegas is in a continuous state of expansion or repair. Orange highway cones, road-building equipment, and detours are ubiquitous. But once the roads are widened and repaved, they're efficient and comfortable. The city's traffic-light system is state of the art, and you can often drive for miles on major thoroughfares, hitting green lights all the way. Signage is excellent. The local driving style is fast and can be less than courteous. Watch out for unsignaled lane changes and turns.

There are rarely weather problems in Las Vegas, but flash flooding can wreak havoc. For information about weather conditions, highway construction, traffic incidents, and road closures, visit the website of the Nevada Department of Transportation, or call its Travel Info system by dialing ☎ 511 in Nevada or ☎ 877/687–6237 if calling outside Nevada.

ROADSIDE EMERGENCIES

Call ☎ 911 to reach police, fire, or ambulance assistance. Dial ☎ *647 to reach the Nevada Highway Patrol.

RULES OF THE ROAD

Right turns are permitted on red lights after coming to a full stop. Nevada requires seat-belt use in the front and back seats of vehicles. Chains are required on Mt. Charleston and in other mountainous regions when snow is fresh and heavy; signs indicate conditions.

Children: Always strap children under age six or less than 60 pounds into approved child-safety seats. In Nevada children must wear seat belts regardless of where they're seated.

DWI: The Las Vegas police are extremely aggressive about catching drunk drivers—you're considered legally impaired if your blood-alcohol level is 0.08% or higher (this is also the law in most neighboring states, but Utah's limit at 0.05% is even lower).

Speed Limits: The speed limit on residential streets is 25 mph. On major thoroughfares it's 45 mph. On the interstate and other divided highways within the city the speed limit is 65 mph; outside the city the speed limit is 70 or 75 mph. Police officers are highly vigilant about speeding laws within Las Vegas, especially in school zones, but enforcement in rural areas is rare.

Ⓜ Public Transport

The Las Vegas Monorail stretches from MGM Grand, in the south, to Sahara Avenue Station, to the north, with five stops in between, including the Las Vegas Convention Center. All told, the trains make the 4-mile trip in about 14 minutes, arriving every 4 to 8 minutes. The monorail runs Monday 7 am–midnight; Tuesday–Thursday 7 am–2 am; and Friday–Sunday 7 am–3 am. Fares are $5 for a single-ride ticket, $13 for a one-day pass, $23 for a two-day pass, $29 for a three-day pass, and so forth. Unlimited Ride passes are also available. You can purchase tickets at the vending machines at the entrance to each station or in advance online, where special deals on passes are sometimes offered. Children age five or under ride free.

In 2021, the Las Vegas Convention & Visitor Authority unveiled underground tunnels connecting the old Convention Center to a new West Hall. The tunnels were built by Elon Musk's Boring Company, and Tesla vehicles shuttle visitors from one convention facility to the next. At this writing, the tunnels and their chariots were only available to convention attendees.

A number of properties on the west side of the Strip are connected by free trams that run roughly every 10 minutes. There's one that runs between Excalibur and Mandalay Bay, from 9 am to 12:30 am (2:30 on weekends) one that runs between The Mirage and Treasure Island, from 9 am to 1 am, extending until 3 am on Friday and Saturday; and one that stretches from Monte Carlo through CityCenter to Bellagio, from 8 am to 4 am.

🚗 Ride-Sharing

All the major Strip resorts are served by both Uber and Lyft, but there's a designated ride-sharing pickup/drop-off area, and it's generally not near the taxi stand. Just ask a hotel employee if you can't spot it. There also are designated pickup/drop-off locations at large events, such as the Electric Daisy Carnival and Life Is Beautiful festival, and event spaces such as T-Mobile Arena. Be aware that rates can fluctuate rapidly, especially in the cases of holidays and special events, when surge pricing may be in effect. And surge pricing can happen almost anytime on the weekends or during large conventions. Anecdotal evidence suggests that pick-up time estimates aren't always reliable in Las Vegas because of traffic and lights.

After some rough spots in the early days of serving Las Vegas, the process of using both Uber and Lyft has become

Getting Here and Around

much smoother. Uber Pool, X, XL and Select are available, along with Lyft Line, Lyft, Plus and Premier. Both services also are allowed to pick up and drop off passengers at McCarran Airport. Sometimes customers may even receive autonomous vehicles (with human monitors).

Taxi

Taxis aren't allowed to pick up passengers on the street, so you can't hail a cab New York–style. You have to wait in a hotel or other taxi line or call a cab company. If you dine at a restaurant off the Strip, the restaurant will call a cab to take you home.

FARES

The fare is $3.50 on the meter when you get in and 23¢ for every 1/12th mile, or $2.76 per mile (there's also a $32.40 per-hour charge for waiting). Taxis are limited by law to carrying a maximum of four passengers, and there's no additional charge per person. No fees are assessed for luggage, but taxis leaving the airport are allowed to add an airport surcharge of $2. There's also a 3% excise tax on all rates and fees.

Flat-rate, zone-based taxi fares from McCarran Airport were unveiled at the end of 2019; hotels closest to the airport cost $19, the heart of the Strip is $23, and anything from the Strat or beyond is $27. Before these flat rates, the trip from the airport to most hotels on the south end of the Strip cost about $16 to $20, to the north end of the Strip about $22 to $29, and to Downtown about $24 to $27.

Ride-sharing applications can provide either cheaper or dramatically more expensive service depending on surge pricing.

SUGGESTED ROUTES

Drivers who take passengers through the airport tunnel without asking are committing an illegal practice known as "long-hauling." You have every right to ask your driver about the routes they are using; don't be afraid to speak up. If you have trouble with your cabdriver, be sure to get their name and license number and call the Taxicab Authority to report the incident. ■TIP➜ **Be sure to specify to your driver that you don't want to take Interstate 15 or the airport tunnel on your way to or from the airport. This is always the longer route distance-wise, which means it's the most expensive, but it can sometimes save you 5 to 10 minutes on the trip if traffic is heavy on the Strip.**

TIPPING

Drivers should be tipped around 15% to 18% for good service (see Tipping in Essentials). Some drivers can't accept credit cards (and those who do usually add a surcharge); all drivers carry only nominal change with them.

Essentials

🏃 Activities

AUTO RACING

The Las Vegas Motor Speedway in North Las Vegas hosts both NASCAR and NHRA events throughout the year. It's a very popular destination, though far from both Downtown and the Strip. If you intend to take in a race, you'll need a car.

BASEBALL

The Las Vegas Aviators is a minor-league team in the Pacific Coast League that plays between April and early Labor Day in the brand-new Las Vegas Ballpark in downtown Summerlin.

BASKETBALL

Las Vegas has no professional NBA team, but the Las Vegas Aces of the WNBA play their season in the Mandalay Bay Events Center on the South Strip.

BIKING

One of the best ways to explore the Las Vegas Valley is by bike. Outside of the urban area, roads are flat with spacious shoulders, providing great opportunities for serious road biking (early in the day, of course, before the desert sun has a chance to set the region to broil). Local conservation land offers epic options for mountain biking, too; in addition to hundreds of miles of mixed-use trails in the Red Rock National Conservation Area, the bike-specific trails of Bootleg Canyon, near Boulder City, are internationally renowned as challenging and fun. Perhaps the crown jewel of the local bicycling scene is the River Mountains Trail, a 36-mile trail that winds past Lake Mead National Recreation Area, Lake Las Vegas, Henderson, and Boulder City.

BOWLING

Bowling in Vegas incorporates elements of casinos, bars, and nightclubs, with lively crowds to match. Locals take their leagues seriously, so "spare" yourself

some heartache and call ahead to make a lane reservation.

FOOTBALL

The Oakland Raiders relocated to Las Vegas in fall 2020 and were renamed the Las Vegas Raiders. They will play in a new domed facility named Allegiant Stadium west of the Strip and south of Mandalay Bay. The stadium did not welcome fans for NFL games during the 2020 season due to COVID-19 but was expected to operate at close to full capacity for the 2021 season.

GOLF

With an average of 315 days of sunshine a year and year-round access, Las Vegas's top sport is golf. The peak season on the greens is any nonsummer month; only mad dogs and Englishmen are out on the courses in the noonday summer sun. However, most of the courses in Las Vegas offer reduced greens fees during the summer months, sometimes as much as 50%–70% lower than peak-season fees. If you want to golf a course on a weekend, call before you get into town, as the 8–11 am time slots fill up quickly. Starting times for same-day play are possible (especially during the week), but if you're picky about when and where you play, plan ahead. Some of the big Strip resorts have a dedicated golf concierge who can advise you on a course that fits your tastes. In some cases, these people can get you access to private courses.

HIKING

Sweeping vistas. Ocher-color rocks. Desert flora and fauna. These are just some of the reasons to love hiking in and around Las Vegas. Most pedestrian trails in the area are mixed-use, meaning they double as bicycle and equestrian trails. All of the trails offer respite from the bustle of the resorts. The very best trails in the region are in Red Rock National Conservation Area. Here, the Ice Box

Essentials

Canyon trail heads 2.6 difficult miles from the exposed desert up into a shady box canyon, where waterfalls appear after rainstorms, and La Madre Springs trail stretches 3.3 miles up an old fire road to a spectacular vista point. What's more, the Willow Springs Loop, which is only 1.5 miles, takes hikers past some pictographs that have adorned the rocks for hundreds of years.

Trails on the other side of the Spring Mountains, in the Spring Mountain National Recreation Area, are breathtaking in a different way; in winter, there's snow all over the place, and the shade of the canyon keeps temperatures about 15 degrees cooler than they are on the Valley floor. Popular hikes there include the 3-mile round-trip to Mary Jane Falls (a waterfall at the back of a pristine mountain bowl) and Bristlecone Trail, a strenuous 6-mile loop at the end of Lee Canyon that hugs the ridgeline and offers some of the most incredible vistas in the entire Las Vegas Valley. For more information about hikes in the Spring Mountains, check out the Spring Mountains Visitor Gateway on Kyle Canyon Road, about an hour outside of Downtown Las Vegas.

Before you lace up those hiking shoes, remember that trails at all the region's top spots dot the landscape across a variety of sites, and you'll need a car to get from one trailhead to the next. And, of course, this is the desert, so you'll need to bring plenty of water, especially if you plan to spend at least part of your hike in the heat of the day.

HOCKEY
Wildly popular, the Las Vegas Golden Knights play at T-Mobile Arena on the South Strip. During their inaugural season in 2017/2018, the Golden Knights swept their playoff series, becoming the first expansion team in the history of the NHL to do so in their first season. They later played for the Stanley Cup in 2018, losing to the Washington Capitals. They didn't do quite as well in their second and third seasons, but were considered favorites for the Cup in 2021.

Dining
It's no secret that Las Vegas has become one of the most exciting dining destinations in the world. Less well known is that a few years ago it surpassed New York as the most expensive dining city in the country. But there are comparative bargains to be had if you know where to look, generally casual and off-Strip locations.

BUFFETS
For years buffets have been a mainstay of the Las Vegas dining scene. COVID-19 threatened that. Most buffets have come back after COVID, but none of them allows guests to serve their own food as they did in days of yore. The experience is different, but it's also safer, which is a good thing.

RESERVATIONS
As the Vegas dining landscape has become rife with showstopping, one-of-a-kind restaurants, reservations at dinner (and occasionally even at lunch) have become a necessity in many cases. Generally, if you have your heart set on dinner at any of the celeb-helmed joints at the bigger Strip casinos, you should book several days, or even a couple of weeks, ahead. On weekends and during other busy times, even at restaurants where reservations aren't absolutely essential, it's still prudent to phone ahead for a table.

WHAT TO WEAR
Although virtually no Vegas restaurants (with the exception of Joël Robuchon at the Mansion inside MGM Grand) require

formal attire, men will likely feel a bit out of place at some of the top eateries on the Strip if not wearing a jacket—at the very least, avoid jeans in these spots. Dressing according to the mood of the restaurant (smart, stylish threads at the better ones) will generally help you out in terms of how you're treated and where you're seated. Casual attire is the norm at lunch, at less fancy venues, and virtually anywhere off the Strip or outside upmarket resorts.

HOURS

The majority of the top restaurants on the Strip are dinner only, although there are plenty of exceptions to this rule. Unless otherwise noted, the restaurants listed in this guide are open daily for lunch and dinner. Hours vary greatly from place to place, with 5 to 10 pm typical for dinner hours, but many of the more nightlife-driven venues serve until after midnight or even around the clock. Las Vegas is definitely a city where it's best to phone ahead and confirm hours.

TIPPING AND TAXES

In most restaurants, tip the waiter 16%–20%. (To figure the amount quickly, just double the tax noted on the check and add a bit more.) Bills for parties of eight or more sometimes include the tip already. Tip at least $1 per drink at the bar.

CHILDREN

Although it's unusual to see children in the dining rooms of Las Vegas's most elite restaurants, dining with youngsters doesn't have to mean culinary exile. Some of the restaurants reviewed in this chapter are excellent choices for families, and are marked with "Family."

PRICES

Las Vegas's status as a bargain-food town has evaporated steadily, even rapidly, as the restaurant scene has evolved and the city has been thrust into the gastronomic spotlight; it's now ranked as the most expensive restaurant city in the country. At top restaurants in town it's unusual to experience a three-course meal (including a bottle of wine, tips, and tax) for less than $100 per person, and prices can be two to three times that at many establishments. You can save money by trying lunch at some of the top eateries, and by checking out the increasingly noteworthy crop of restaurants that have developed off the Strip. Credit cards are widely accepted, but some restaurants (particularly smaller ones off the Strip) accept only cash. If you plan to use a credit card, it's a good idea to double-check its acceptability when making reservations or before sitting down to eat.

What It Costs in U.S. Dollars			
$	$$	$$$	$$$$
RESTAURANTS			
under $12	$12–$20	$21–$30	over $30

🇺🇸 Embassy/Consulate

All foreign governments have embassies in Washington, D.C., and most offer consular services in the embassy building. Several countries have consulates in Los Angeles. In Las Vegas, you'll find the Consulate Republic of Austria (✉ 8215 S. Eastern Ave. ☎ 702/706–5180 ⊕ austrian-consulatelasvegas.org/aclv); the Honorary Consul General of France (✉ 8337 W. Sunset Rd. ☎ 702/582–5476); the Honorary Consul of Ireland for Nevada (✉ 516 S. 6th St. ☎ 415/823–7150); the Honorary Consul General of Mexico (✉ 330 S. 4th St. ☎ 702/383–0623); and the Honorary Consul General of Romania (✉ 711 Rancho Circle ☎ 702/878–5534).

Essentials

➕ Health and Safety

You can't sugarcoat it: the COVID-19 pandemic hit Las Vegas hard. When the pandemic was first declared in March 2020, most of Sin City's casinos literally shuttered their doors for the first time ever. The city stayed shut down until June 2020, when it opened at reduced capacity. Gradually the place came back to life. By May 2021, Las Vegas was back, though, of course, it was different.

Today Las Vegas has some vestiges of the pandemic. Visitors are still required to wear face coverings while indoors. They are required to stand six feet from each other. Many public-oriented events and happenings are struggling to be themselves with reduced capacity. Some casinos also are still requiring people to stand or sit behind plexiglass barriers when they are playing table games. Enforcement of these rules is not uniform, so you may just have to go with the flow. Ultimately, the fact that some visitors to Las Vegas are taking seriously COVID-19 precautions is a step toward greater public health safety for all of us.

The dry desert air in Las Vegas means that your body will need extra fluids, especially during the punishing summer months. Always drink lots of water even if you're not outside very much. When you're outdoors, wear sunscreen and always carry water with you if you plan a long walk. In the aftermath of COVID-19, always carry a face covering in case you need to wear it when you go indoors.

The well-known areas of Las Vegas are quite safe for visitors. With so many people carrying so much cash, security is tight inside and out. The casinos have visitors under constant surveillance, and hotel security guards are never more than a few seconds away. Outside, police are highly visible, on foot and bicycles and in cruisers. However, you should take the same precautions you would in any city—be aware of what's going on around you, stick to well-lighted areas, and quickly move away from any situation or people that might be threatening—especially if you're carrying some gambling cash. When Downtown, it's wise not to stray too far off the three main streets: Fremont, Ogden, and Carson between Main and Las Vegas Boulevard.

Be especially careful with your purse around slot machines. Grab-and-run thieves are always looking for easy pickings, especially Downtown.

Apart from their everyday vulnerability to aggressive men, women should have few problems with unwanted attention in Las Vegas. If something does happen inside a casino, simply go to any pit and ask a boss to call security. The problem will disappear in seconds. Outside, crowds are almost always thick on the Strip and Downtown, and there's safety in numbers. Still, be aware of pickpockets.

Men in Las Vegas also need to be on guard against predatory women. "Trick roller" is the name of a particularly nasty breed of female con artist. These women are experts at meeting single men by "chance." After getting friendly in the casino, the woman joins the man in his hotel room, where she slips powerful knockout drugs into his drink and robs him blind. Some men don't wake up. Prostitution is illegal in Clark County, although it is legal in the rural counties of Nevada.

■ TIP➜ **Distribute your cash, credit cards, IDs, and other valuables between a deep front pocket, an inside jacket or vest pocket, and a hidden money pouch. Don't reach for the money pouch once you're in public.**

IMMUNIZATIONS

There are no immunization requirements for visitors traveling to the United States for tourism, though some facilities and businesses may require proof of COVID-19 vaccination.

🛏 Lodging

Las Vegas is blessed with a wide variety of lodging choices, from the classic (Caesars Palace, MGM Grand) to the hip and trendy (The Cosmopolitan of Las Vegas, ARIA, Virgin Las Vegas) and elegant (Bellagio, The Venetian, Wynn, Resorts World Las Vegas). Boutique hotels-within-hotels such as Nobu and NoMad add another dimension. Family-friendly, nongaming chain hotels are right off the Strip.

TIMING YOUR TRIP

Especially on weekends, accommodations in Las Vegas fill up fast. When it's time for a big convention—or a big sporting event—it's not unusual for all of the Las Vegas area's roughly 150,000 hotel rooms to sell out completely. Combine those with three-day holidays, and you can see why it's wise to make lodging arrangements for busy weekends as far ahead as possible.

The age of the last-minute deal seems to be coming to an end. There was a time when many hotels, eager to fill rooms, offered rock-bottom prices and tempting packages for as low as $79 per night. These types of deals still exist, but with Vegas enjoying high-occupancy rates year-round now, they're increasingly more difficult to find. However, if you're not traveling during a busy weekend and have the luxury of waiting until the last minute, you can still find some discounted rates.

GETTING THE BEST ROOM

There's no surefire way to ensure that you'll get the room you want, when you want it, and for the lowest price possible. But here are a few tips for increasing your chances:

Book early. This town's almost always busy, so book as early as possible. Generally, if you book a room for $125 and later find out that the hotel is offering the same category of room for $99, the hotel will match the lower price, so keep checking back to see if the rates have dropped. Of course, this won't work if you prepay for a room on a hotel-booking website. It also won't work if you buy in for a prepaid package deal. Once you go this route, you either can't get out of the reservation or you may have to pay a hefty cancellation fee.

Getting the room you want. Actual room assignments aren't determined at most Vegas hotels until the day before, or the day of, arrival. If you're hoping for a particular room (for example, a room with a view of the Strip), phone the hotel a day before you arrive and speak with somebody at the front desk. This applies whether you booked originally through the hotel or some other website. Don't be pushy or presumptuous. Just explain that although you realize the hotel can't guarantee a specific room, you'd appreciate it if they'd honor your preference.

Your second-best bet. Simply check in as early as possible on the day of arrival—even if no rooms are yet available (and you have to wait in the casino), you're likely to get first preference on the type of room you're seeking when it opens up.

What about upgrades? It's virtually never inappropriate to request a nicer room than the one you've booked. At the same time, it's virtually always inappropriate to expect that you'll receive the

Essentials

upgrade. The front-desk clerk has all the power and discretion when it comes to upgrades, and is unlikely to help you out if you act pushy or haughty. Gracious humility, smiles, and warmth go a long way.

Do I tip for an upgrade? It's not customary to tip hotel clerks for upgrades, especially at nicer properties. If you wave some cash around discreetly, it might not hurt, but it won't necessarily help either.

THE LOWDOWN ON RATES
In general, at an average of about $129 per night (per the Las Vegas Convention and Visitors' Authority), rates for Las Vegas accommodations are lower than those in most other American resort and vacation cities. Still, the situation is changing; though rack rates for fancy properties are higher than ever, many hotels still offer fantastic deals. There are about a hundred variables that impact price, depending on who's selling the rooms (reservations, marketing, casino, conventions, wholesalers, packagers), what rooms you're talking about (standard, deluxe, minisuites, standard suites, deluxe suites, high-roller suites, penthouses, bungalows), and demand (weekday, weekend, holiday, conventions or sporting events in town).

When business is slow, many hotels reduce rates on rooms in their least desirable sections, sometimes with a buffet breakfast or even a show included. Most "sales" occur from early December to mid-February and in July and August, the coldest and hottest times of the year, and you can often find rooms for 50% to 75% less midweek than on weekends. Members of casino players' clubs often get offers of discounted or even free rooms, and they can almost always reserve a room even when the rest of the hotel is "sold out."

Over the last few years, most Strip hotels have clustered "amenities" such as Wi-Fi, fitness center access, and morning newspapers into mandatory resort fees. These fees vary from property to property, and generally range from $30 to $45. In addition to the resort fees, starting in 2016, most Las Vegas resorts began to charge for parking. ■TIP➜ **If you book a room through a casino host, request that they eliminate resort and parking fees from your folio.**

What It Costs in U.S. Dollars			
$	$$	$$$	$$$$
HOTELS			
under $150	$150–$230	$231–$330	over $330

✚ Marijuana

So long as you're over 21, recreational cannabis (up to 1 ounce) is legal in Las Vegas, and in recent years the city has seen a proliferation of dispensaries. Some of these dispensaries are tiny storefronts in suburbia; others are giant, tourist-friendly destinations right off the Strip (especially the North Strip). Still others boast 24-hour drive-thru windows. All dispensaries require identification before you buy, and all transactions must be in cash. Also, be forewarned: no casino allows marijuana smoking on the gaming floor, and you cannot legally smoke in a hotel room.

Where Should I Stay?

	VIBE	PROS	CONS
South Strip	Fun! Resorts here are glamorous, but not as serious as Center and North Strip properties. With roller coasters, arcades, shows, and beaches, properties are also the most kid-friendly.	Close to airport; plenty of diversions for the whole family; bargains at top Strip properties can be found here.	Need to take a taxi or monorail to hit Center Strip. Fewer shopping options than Center and North Strip.
Center Strip	Happening, hip section of Strip has the newest resorts with all of the latest and greatest amenities. Shopping in this part of town also is second to none.	Many rooms are new or recently renovated; spas are among the largest and most popular in town.	Traffic congestion, both on sidewalks and off; rooms generally pricier than they are elsewhere in town.
North Strip	Glitz and glamour rule. Rooms are among the largest and most ornate, and on-property amenities are all top-of-the-line.	Most (but not all) rooms are suites; incredible restaurant options.	Highest prices on-site; long (and pricey) cab ride from the airport.
Downtown	Vegas as it used to be—back when rooms were an afterthought and everything was about the casino downstairs.	Affordable lodging; classic casinos; proximity to other diversions in the area.	Rooms are bare-bones; streets aren't entirely safe after dark; expensive taxi ride to big resorts on the Strip.
West Side and Summerlin	Smaller, more amenity-heavy resorts sit west of the Strip, with the most lavish of the bunch offering glamorous pools and golf courses nearby. Many resorts appeal to locals.	Quieter and away from the hustle of the Strip; lower room rates; incredible views of the Spring Mountains and the Strip.	Summerlin is a half hour from the Strip.
East Side and Henderson	Resorts here (and along Paradise Road) are functional. Instead of offering the latest and greatest in amenities, rooms are on the small side.	Lower prices than the Strip; on-site diversions such as bowling; proximity to local services.	Long taxi ride to the Strip (half hour from Henderson); doesn't have the excitement of the Strip.

Essentials

$ Money

Prices in Las Vegas can be gratis or outrageous. For example, you can get a sandwich wrap or hot dog at one of the rock-bottom casino snack bars (Circus Circus, Four Queens) or from a food cart for $3–$4, or you can spend upward of $100 for a 17-inch-long sandwich at the Ike's Love & Sandwiches in the Fashion Show Mall. A cup of coffee in a casino coffee shop or Starbucks will set you back $2 to $5, whereas that same cup is free if you happen to be sitting at a nickel slot machine when the cocktail waitress comes by. Taxis from the airport are now priced on flat-rate zones that range from $19 to $27, depending on how far you're headed. The more you know about Las Vegas, the less it'll cost you.

ATMs are widely available in Las Vegas; they're at every bank and at virtually all casinos, hotels, convenience stores, and gas stations. Casino ATMs generally tack on a fee of up to $6 per transaction (this, of course, is on top of any fees your bank might charge). In addition, all casinos have cash-advance machines, which take credit cards. You just indicate how large a cash advance you want, and when the transaction is approved, you pick up the cash at the casino cashier. But beware: you pay a service charge up for this "convenience"—up to 18% or more— in addition to the usual cash-advance charges and interest rate; in most cases, the credit-card company begins charging interest the moment the advance is taken, so you won't have the usual grace period to pay your balance in full before interest begins to accrue. To put it another way, don't obtain cash this way.

♈ Nightlife

Inspired by the "What happens in Vegas, stays in Vegas" attitude, and that it usually happens after dark, nightlife impresarios keep dipping into their vast pockets to create over-the-top experiences where party-mad Visigoths—plus, well, you and me—can live out some wild fantasies. The number of high-profile nightclubs, trendy lounges, and sizzling strip bars continues to grow, each attempting to trump the other to attract not just high rollers, but A-list celebrities and the publicity that surrounds them.

Many of the newest clubs even have gambling. Though, we ask: Why bother when you can lounge beside the pool by day and bellow at the moon by night while dancing half clad at a club until noon the following day (when it's back into the pool you go)?

In the late 1990s, once the Vegas mandarins decided that the "family experience" just wasn't happening, Sin City nightlife got truly sinful again, drawing raves from clubbers worldwide. A wave of large dance clubs, such as the Luxor's (now-defunct) Ra, opened their doors, followed by a trendy batch of cozier ultralounges—lounges with dance floors and high-tech amenities.

The game of one-upmanship has continued—recent additions that have kept the city hopping include the massive Omnia at Caesars Palace and more intimate On the Record at Park MGM. What's more, bawdy 1950s-era burlesque lounges are continuing their comeback with a gaggle of clubs now dedicated to the art of striptease.

Few cities on Earth match Vegas in its dedication to upping the nightlife ante. So with all these choices, no one—not even the Visigoths—has an excuse for not having fun, however you define the "f" word.

FIND OUT WHAT'S GOING ON

With the number of nightlife options in Las Vegas, it's easy to get overwhelmed. Several local publications can steer you in the right direction and help you plan your ultimate Vegas night out. Remember that party schedules—as well as the popularity of any one spot—can change overnight, so the best way to keep current is to consult these publications.

Eater Vegas (⊕ *www.eater.com*) provides information on dining and nightlife, many times long before the newspapers.

Anthony Curtis's **Las Vegas Advisor** (⊕ *www.lasvegasadvisor.com* ☎ *702/252–0655*) is a monthly newsletter that's invaluable for its information on Las Vegas dining, entertainment, gambling promotions, comps, and news.

If you're here for a short visit, pick up free copies of **Las Vegas Magazine** (⊕ *lasvegasmagazine.com*) at hotels and gift shops.

The **Las Vegas Review-Journal,** the city's daily newspaper, publishes a tabloid pull-out section each Friday. It provides entertainment features and reviews, and showroom and lounge listings with complete time and price information. The **Review-Journal** maintains a website (⊕ *www.reviewjournal.com*) where show listings are updated each week. The **Las Vegas Sun,** once a competing daily, is now a section inside the **Review-Journal** but maintains its own editorial staff and website (⊕ *www.lasvegassun.com*).

Las Vegas Weekly is an excellent alternative weekly newspaper distributed at retail stores and coffee shops around town and maintains a comprehensive website (⊕ *www.lasvegasweekly.com*).

HOW TO GET IN

Nobody comes to Las Vegas to wait in line. So how exactly do you get past those velvet ropes? Short of personally knowing the no-nonsense bouncers and serious-looking women holding clipboards who guard the doors, here are a few pointers.

First, know that even though this is a 24-hour town, lines start forming around 10 pm (or earlier). If you're not on a list, get there after dinner and dress the part—which is to say, don't expect to go straight from the pool to the club. Vegas bars and clubs have pretty strict dress codes, so leave those T-shirts, baseball caps, and ripped jeans in your hotel room (unless you're headed to the Griffin Lounge or some other hipster haven). Arguing that your sneakers were made by Alexander McQueen probably won't help, either. At most of the trendier spots, at least for women, skin is in—this *is* Sin City, after all. And needless to say, the universal rule of big-city nightlife also applies in Vegas: groups of guys almost always have a harder time getting in without a few women in the mix. If your group is gender-impaired, consider politely asking some unaccompanied women to temporarily join you, perhaps in exchange for some drinks once you're all inside. Too shy, you say? If there was ever a place to check your shyness at the airport, it's this town.

Most spots have two lines: a VIP line (for those on the guest list or who have a table with bottle service reserved) and a regular line. You can either ask your hotel concierge for help contacting a club to get on a guest list, or contact the club directly. Some websites such as ⊕ *www.vegas.com* sell passes they guarantee will get you past the crush, but save your money for the door—better to slip the bouncer $20 per person than hope they'll

Essentials

acknowledge the Internet ticket you've bought for the same amount. If you have a few people in your group, it might be worth it to splurge on a table reservation: without one, a group of five could easily spend $20 each getting in good with the bouncers, plus $20 each for the cover charge, and then there's always the expensive drinks.

A further note on going deluxe: if you're getting a table with bottle service, note that your VIP host will expect something from you, as will the busboy who actually lugs over your booze. On holiday weekends and New Year's Eve, expect to multiply what you plan to give them by at least two.

🧳 Packing

Although Las Vegas casinos were filled with people dressed to the nines during the Rat Pack era, things have gotten much more casual over the past couple of decades. The warm weather and informal character of Las Vegas render casual clothing appropriate day and night. However, there are some exceptions. A very small number of restaurants require jackets for men, and some of the city's increasingly exclusive and overhyped "ultralounges" and high-profile dance clubs have specific requirements, such as no sneakers or jeans, or that you must wear dark shoes or collared shirts. At a minimum, even if there's no set dress code, you're going to fit in with the scene if you make some effort to dress stylishly when heading out either to the hipper nightclubs or even trendier restaurants (i.e., those helmed by celeb chefs or with trendy followings and cool decor). Just as an example, where jeans and T-shirts might be technically allowed at some establishments, try to wear plain, fitted T-shirts versus those with logos

and designs, and choose jeans that are appropriate for a venue (crisp and clean for a nice restaurant, designer labels for a top club). It's always good to pack a few stylish outfits for the evening, and when you're making dinner reservations at an upscale spot or considering a visit to a nightclub, ask for the dress-code specifics. Also, flip-flops are best kept to pool areas.

Although the desert sun keeps temperatures scorching outside in warmer months, the casinos are ice-cold. Your best insurance is to dress in layers. The blasting air-conditioning may feel good at first, but if you plan to spend some time inside, bring a light sweater or jacket in case you feel chilly.

Always wear comfortable shoes; no matter what your intentions, you cover a lot of ground on foot.

🌐 Passport

All visitors to the United States require a valid passport that is valid for six months beyond your expected period of stay.

🛍 Shopping

Vegas is an international shopping destination. The square footage in The Forum Shops at Caesars alone makes it some of the most valuable retail real estate in the country; bankrolls are dropped there as readily as on the gaming tables. It's the variety that has pushed Las Vegas near the ranks of New York City, London, and Milan: you could send home a vintage slot machine or tote back a classic Hermès handbag.

Most Strip hotels offer designer dresses, swimsuits, jewelry, and menswear; almost all have shops offering logo merchandise for the hotel or its latest show. Inside the casinos the gifts are often elegant and exquisite. Outside, all the Elvis clocks and gambling-chip toilet seats you never wanted to see are available in the tacky gift shops. Beyond the Strip, shopping in Vegas can encompass such extremes as finding a couture ball gown in a vintage store and, in a Western store, a fine pair of Tony Lama boots left over from the town's cowboy days. Shoppers looking for more practical items can head for neighborhood malls, supermarkets, shopping centers, and specialty stores. Bargain-hunters seeking to avoid the stratospheric prices on the Strip, and not averse to traveling a bit, can usually find the same high-ticket items at discounted prices in the local or nearby factory outlet malls.

GETTING AROUND

Shopping in Las Vegas—so demanding, yet so rewarding. With malls encompassing millions of square feet of retail space, you won't have any trouble finding ways to part with your cash. But to make the most of your time and money, you should map out your shopping safaris. Distances are deceiving because of the scale of the resort casinos. What looks like a quick walk might take a half hour, or more. Because of crowd-control measures, you'll find yourself squeezing around barriers and leaping over bridges instead of just crossing a street. Grab a cab or ride the monorail ($5 a trip) and save the time for shopping. Buses, which are $8 for 24 hours along the Strip, are a cheaper option, but crowded at all hours.

Got a car? Unfortunately, very few resorts still offer free parking and/or free valet service. Mandalay Bay, Luxor, Excalibur, MGM Grand, New York–New York, Park MGM, ARIA, Bellagio, The Cosmopolitan, Caesars Palace, and The LINQ now charge for self-parking and valet. Rates vary depending on the amount of time parked.

SEND THEM PACKING

Who wants to lug packages from store to store? Most stores are happy to send your purchases back to your hotel or even ship them back home for you.

HOURS OF OPERATION

Although Las Vegas may be up all night, the people who work in the retail establishments need a little rest. Many places are open from 10 am to 11 pm during the week, and stay open an hour later on weekends. And the shopping, like the gambling, goes on every day.

💲 Taxes

The Las Vegas and Reno-Tahoe international airports assess a $4.50 departure tax (which is usually included in the ticket price), or passenger facility charge. The hotel room tax is 13.35% in Las Vegas. Moreover, virtually all hotels on the Strip—and many Downtown—will charge an additional (and outrageous) resort fee of up to $45 per room per night. These fees are sometimes waived, however, for high-tier players-club members or deluxe-room bookings, so be sure to check.

The sales tax rates for the areas covered in this guide are Las Vegas, 8.38% (4.6% for the State of Nevada and 3.78% for Clark County); Arizona, 5.6%; and California, 7.25% (though in the latter two cases, individual counties can and do add their own).

💵 Tipping

Just as in other U.S. destinations, workers in Las Vegas are paid a minimal wage and rely on tips to make up the primary part of their income. A $1 tip per drink is appropriate for cocktail waitresses, even when they bring you a free drink at a slot machine or casino table. On package

Essentials

Tipping Guidelines for Las Vegas	
Bartender	$1 to $5 per round of drinks, depending on the number of drinks
Bellhop	$1 to $5 per bag, depending on the level of the hotel
Coat Check Personnel	$1 to $2 per item checked; if there's a fee, nothing
Hotel Concierge	$5 or more, if they perform a service for you
Hotel Doorman	$1 to $2, if he helps you get a cab
Hotel Housekeeping	$2 to $5 a day (daily preferably, or at the end of your stay, in cash)
Hotel Room-Service Waiter	$2 to $3 per delivery, even if a service charge has been added
Porter at Airport or Train Station	$1 per bag
Restroom Attendants	$1 or small change
Skycap at Airport	$1 to $3 per bag checked
Taxi Driver or Chauffeur	15% to 20%, but round up the fare to the next dollar
Valet Parking Attendant	$2 to $3, but only when you get your car
Waiter	16% to 20%, with 20% being the norm at high-end restaurants; nothing additional if a service charge is added to the bill

tours, conductors and drivers usually get $10 per day from the group as a whole; check whether this has already been figured into your cost. For local sightseeing tours, you may individually tip the driver-guide $5 if they have been helpful or informative. Tip dealers with the equivalent of your average bet once or twice an hour if you're winning; slot-machine change personnel and keno runners are accustomed to a buck or two. Ushers in showrooms may be able to get you better seats for performances for a gratuity of $5 or more. Tip the concierge 10%–20% of the cost of a ticket to a hot show. Tip $5–$10 for making dinner reservations or arrangements for other attractions.

◉ Visitor Information

Before you go, contact the city and state tourism offices for general information. When you get there, you might want to visit the Las Vegas Convention and Visitors Authority for brochures and general information. Hotels and gift shops on the Strip have maps, brochures, pamphlets, and free-events magazines—such as *Las Vegas Magazine*—that list shows and buffets and offer discounts to area attractions.

Anthony Curtis's *Las Vegas Advisor,* a monthly print newsletter and website, keeps track of the constantly changing Las Vegas landscapes of gambling, accommodations, dining, entertainment, Top Ten Values (a monthly listing of the city's best deals), complimentary offerings, coupons, and more, and is an indispensable resource for any Las Vegas visitor. Visit the website (⊕ *www. lasvegasadvisor.com*) for a free sample issue; annual online memberships begin at $37 per year.

As ⊕ *VEGAS.com* advertises, to do Vegas right, it's who you know. The website offers information and instant-booking capabilities for everything from air and hotel packages to shows and tours. ⊕ *TripSavvy.com* has an excellent online Las Vegas travel guide, which includes dozens of original articles and reviews as well as links to many other Vegas resources, as does the website of the **Las Vegas Review-Journal**. The **Review-Journal**'s weekly **Neon** magazine lists information on shows and events, and its annual Best of Las Vegas lists reader favorites in various categories. Visit ⊕ *www.reviewjournal.com* or ⊕ *bestoflasvegas.com*.

One of the oldest sites is the **Las Vegas Leisure Guide**, which is full of hotel, restaurant, and nightlife info. Las Vegas Online Entertainment Guide has listings for hotels and an online reservations system, plus local history, restaurants, a business directory, and even some gambling instruction. ⊕ *VisitLasVegas. com*, the official Las Vegas tourism website, has a little bit of everything going on in Sin City. Find out about events, book hotels, get special deals, and find out other vital travel info; the Las Vegas Convention and Visitors Authority, which runs the site, also broadcasts great deals and updates on Twitter (⊕ *www.twitter. com/vegas*). The City of Las Vegas has its own website (⊕ *www.lasvegasnevada. gov*), which is a great resource for service-related information, including how to pay a ticket or citation. Remember, what happens in Vegas, stays in Vegas.

📅 When to Go

LOW SEASON

There are no defined high, low, and shoulder seasons in Las Vegas; crowds—and, correspondingly, hotel and ride-sharing rates—can fluctuate from week to week, depending on factors such as whether there's a big convention in town. While the first 10 days to two weeks of December tend to be busy because of the National Finals Rodeo, and the days right before and after New Year's Eve are some of the craziest of the year, the late-December period between them tends to be one of the quietest times in Las Vegas, and with the holiday decorations and generally mild weather, one of the most pleasant.

SHOULDER SEASON

Summer is kind of a mixed bag in Las Vegas. Families and casual travelers like to visit at this time of year, but the extreme heat (highs of 116 in July are not uncommon) keeps others away. It therefore falls between the busiest and slowest times.

HIGH SEASON

You'll want to avoid early January, when the CES convention brings more than 180,000 people to town for exhibits at 10 or more local venues including the sprawling Las Vegas Convention Center. Check the Las Vegas Convention and Visitor Authority website for convention dates and avoid those with the most attendees.

Contacts

✈ Air

AIRLINES Alaska Air.
☎ *800/426–0333* ⊕ *www.
alaskaair.com.* **American
Airlines.** ☎ *800/433–7300*
⊕ *www.aa.com.* **Delta
Airlines.** ☎ *800/221–1212*
⊕ *www.delta.com.* **Frontier
Airlines.** ☎ *800/432–1359*
⊕ *www.flyfrontier.com.*
jetBlue. ☎ *800/538–2583*
⊕ *www.jetblue.com.*
Southwest Airlines.
☎ *800/435–9792* ⊕ *www.
southwest.com.* **United
Airlines.** ☎ *800/864–8331*
⊕ *www.united.com.*

**AIRPORTS McCarran
International Airport (LAS).**
⊠ *Paradise Rd., Airport*
☎ *702/261–5211* ⊕ *www.
mccarran.com.*

**AIRPORT TRANSFERS Bell
Trans.** ☎ *800/274–7433*
⊕ *www.airportshut-
tlelasvegas.com.* **ODS
Chauffered Transportation.**
☎ *702/688–7353.* **Super-
Shuttle.** ☎ *800/258–3826*
⊕ *supershuttle.com.*

🚌 Bus

CONTACTS CoachRun.
⊕ *www.coachrun.
com.* **Flixbus.** ⊕ *www.
flixbus.com.* **Greyhound.**
☎ *702/384–9561* ⊕ *www.
greyhound.com.* **Megabus.**
⊕ *www.megabus.com.*
**Regional Transportation
Commission of Southern
Nevada.** ☎ *702/228–7433*
⊕ *www.rtcsnv.com.*

🚗 Car

**CAR RENTAL CENTER
McCarran Rent-A-Car
Center.** ☎ *702/261–6001*
⊕ *www.mccarran.com.*

**NEVADA DEPT. OF
TRANSPORTATION Nevada
Department of Transpor-
tation.** ☎ *775/888–7000
or call 511 locally for
travel information*
⊕ *www.nevadadot.
com.* **Nevada Highway
Patrol.** ☎ *702/486–4100,
775/687–5300* ⊕ *nhp.
nv.gov.*

Ⓜ Public Transport

**LAS VEGAS MONORAIL
Las Vegas Monorail Com-
pany.** ☎ *702/699–8200*
⊕ *www.lvmonorail.com.*

🚕 Taxi

CONTACTS Desert Cab.
☎ *702/555–5151* ⊕ *www.
desertcabinc.com.* **Taxicab
Authority.** ☎ *702/668–4005*
⊕ *taxi.nv.gov.* **Whittlesea
Blue Cab.** ☎ *702/555–5151*
⊕ *whittleseabluecab.
com.* **Yellow Checker Star.**
☎ *702/873–2000* ⊕ *www.
ycstrans.com.*

📍 Visitor Information

**CONTACTS City of Las
Vegas.** ☎ *702/229–6011*
⊕ *www.lasvegasne-
vada.gov.* **LasVegas.
com.** ⊕ *www.lasvegas.
com* . **Las Vegas Advi-
sor.** ☎ *800/244–2224,
702/252–0655* ⊕ *www.
lasvegasadvisor.com.*
**Las Vegas Convention and
Visitors Authority.** ⊠ *3150
Paradise Rd., Paradise
Road* ☎ *877/847–4858,
702/892–0711* ⊕ *www.vis-
itlasvegas.com.* **Las Vegas
Leisure Guide.** ⊕ *www.
lasvegas-nv.com.* **Las
Vegas Online Entertainment
Guide.** ⊕ *www.lvol.com.*
Las Vegas Review-Journal.
⊕ *www.reviewjournal.
com.* **Nevada Commission
on Tourism.** ☎ *800/638–
2328* ⊕ *travelnevada.com.*
TripSavvy.com. ⊕ *www.
tripsavvy.com.* **VEGAS.com.**
⊕ *www.vegas.com.*

Chapter 3

SOUTH STRIP

Updated by
Steven Bornfeld

👁 Sights	🍴 Restaurants	🛏 Hotels	💼 Shopping	🍸 Nightlife
★★★★☆	★★★★☆	★★★★★	★★★☆☆	★★★☆☆

NEIGHBORHOOD SNAPSHOT

TOP EXPERIENCES

■ **Big Apple Coaster:** Turn your visit upside-down at New York–New York.

■ **Las Vegas Golden Knights:** "Knight up" in black and gold and head to T-Mobile Arena to cheer on Las Vegas's first pro sports team.

■ **Topgolf Las Vegas:** Practice your tee shots in style at this fancy driving range (with a bar).

■ **Visting Eataly:** Shop the market of Italian imports at inside Park MGM.

■ **"Welcome to Fabulous Las Vegas":** Welcome yourself to Sin City with a visit to the famous sign at the southern end of the Strip.

GETTING HERE

Everything on the South Strip is relatively close. Most resorts are within a 10- or 15-minute taxi or rideshare from the airport, and all are accessible by public transportation. A monorail connects Mandalay Bay with Luxor and Excalibur; another connects Park MGM with City Center and Bellagio on the Center Strip. Pedestrian bridges across Las Vegas Boulevard and Tropicana Avenue link other casino resorts. If it's not July or August, a walking tour of this area is a fun activity. From ground level, the heft of casinos never gets old.

The Las Vegas Monorail begins (or ends) on this part of the Strip at the MGM Grand station. The RTC (Regional Transportation Commission of Southern Nevada) services this part of the Strip with public buses and double-deckers.

PLANNING YOUR TIME

The best way to explore the theme casino resorts of the South Strip is on foot. Start at Mandalay Bay and wind your way from the tropics through medieval times (Excalibur) to NYC (New York–New York) and the great outdoors (Park MGM). Allow at least four hours to see it all.

QUICK BITES

■ **Beerhaus.** This restaurant in The Park offers a fresh take on the classic beer hall, with dozens of craft brews and a menu of savory bites. On warm days, grab a picnic table outside and play giant Jenga or cornhole while you relax. ✉ *3784 Las Vegas Blvd. S* ⊕ *www.theparkvegas.com*

■ **LaLa Noodle.** While this eatery inside Park MGM serves pan-Asian cuisine, it is known best for its noodles, which range from lo mein and Singapore-style to pork belly and delicious Dan Dan. ✉ *Park MGM, 3770 Las Vegas Blvd. S* ⊕ *park-mgm.mgmresorts.com*

■ **Table 34.** This understated eatery in a strip mall south of Town Square mall is known for its duck confit quesadillas and cajun-seasoned fries. It also has a legendary happy hour with half-price drinks and snacks. ✉ *600 E. Warm Springs Rd.* ⊕ *table34lasvegas.com*

Fun and fantasy collide on the South Strip. Close to the airport, the resorts and attractions at this end of Las Vegas Boulevard go from Mandalay Bay (and the Delano Las Vegas) all the way to Park MGM, and include the sprawling MGM Grand Resort. Whether it's a man-made beach lagoon, a glass pyramid, a medieval castle, or an Oz-like complex, imagination in these parts most certainly runs wild.

A first-time tour should start at the iconic "Welcome to Las Vegas" sign, just west of the runways at McCarran International Airport. From there, swing through the shark habitat at Mandalay Bay, check out the "Sphinx" in front of Luxor, and view the circa-1950 stained-glass skylights inside the renovated Tropicana.

The kitschy jousting in the *Tournament of Kings at Excalibur* is topped only by the gravity-defying loops of the roller coaster at New York–New York. Park MGM, the South Strip's newest resort, has an Eataly Italian market and restaurants galore. Then, of course, there's the MGM Grand—one of the largest hotels in the world—that now has Topgolf, one of the swankiest driving ranges from which you'll ever swing.

Dig deeper and you start to appreciate the details of the South Strip resorts. The palm-frond fans inside Mandalay Bay. The apartment-style rooms at NoMad Las Vegas. Even New Yorkers say the West Village–inspired food court at New York–New York feels like home. And the giant bronze lion in front of MGM Grand is a

throwback to the hotel's affiliation with the movie company, but it's also a veiled reference to the *Wizard of Oz,* which inspired the building's green hue.

Noncasino destinations are worth visiting, too. The multicolor rock towers of Seven Magic Mountains inspire rumination. Hershey's Chocolate World satisfies chocolate desires of every age. Town Square, an open-air mall, is a great place to spend the day to escape the casino vibe and spend a day shopping. Then there's The Park, with an arena that's home to Sin City's first professional sports franchise, the NHL's Golden Knights. Compared with the rest of the Strip, which is more modern and, at times, stuffy, the South Strip is whimsical and just plain neat.

The area that loosely stretches from the McCarran Rental Car facility south of 215 to Southern Highlands is a mix of stand-alone hotels (such as the Silverton and the South Pointe), big-box stores, time-share resorts, and residential neighborhoods. It's also the first stretch of metropolitan Las Vegas that road-trippers from Los Angeles encounter on their approach. Without traffic, travel time from these parts to the South Strip is about 15 to 20 minutes. During rush hour, however, you might be better off dealing with traffic lights on Las Vegas Boulevard.

👁 Sights

★ Big Apple Coaster and Arcade
AMUSEMENT PARK/WATER PARK | FAMILY
There are two reasons to ride the Coney Island–style New York–New York roller coaster (aka Manhattan Express): first, with a 144-foot dive and a 360-degree somersault, it's a real scream; and second, it whisks you around the amazing replica of the New York City skyline, giving you fabulous views of the Statue of Liberty, Chrysler Building, and, at night, the Las Vegas lights—you climb to peak heights around 200 feet above the Strip. Get ready to go 67 mph over a dizzying succession of high-banked turns and camelback hills, twirl through a "heartline twist" (like a jet doing a barrel roll), and finally rocket along a 540-degree spiral before pulling back into the station. ✉ *New York–New York, 3790 Las Vegas Blvd. S, South Strip* ☎ *866/815–4365, 702/740–6969* ⊕ *newyorknewyork.mgm-resorts.com* 🎟 *From $19.*

★ Dig This Las Vegas
LOCAL INTEREST | This attraction is perfect for adults who like to play in a life-size sandbox—and use big toys to do it. In this case, the toys are heavy construction machinery: bulldozers, excavators, mini-excavators, and skid-steer track loaders. Guests don hard hats and spend about 90 minutes driving the equipment on a big dirt lot, moving around giant tires, digging holes, and more. You can even crush a car. Dig This also partners with a number of other local businesses to get people off the Strip. ✉ *800 W. Roban Ave., South Strip* ☎ *702/222–4344* ⊕ *digthisvegas.com* 🎟 *From $269.*

Hershey's Chocolate World Las Vegas
STORE/MALL | FAMILY | Chocoholics rejoiced in 2014 when the two-story, West Coast flagship of Hershey's Chocolate opened as part of the streetscape fronting New York–New York. The attraction includes an 800-pound Statue of Liberty made of chocolate, a retail store, a café, and a tester area where visitors can sample some of Hershey's newest confections. Visitors also can personalize Hershey's chocolate bar wrappers, star in a Reese's Peanut Butter Cup ad, or put together a bag of different-flavored Hershey's Kisses (almond, mint, and so on) chocolates wrapped in a variety of different colors. ✉ *New York–New York, 3790 Las Vegas Blvd. S, South Strip* ☎ *702/437–7439* ⊕ *www.hersheyschocolateworldlasvegas.com.*

Level Up
AMUSEMENT PARK/WATER PARK | Tucked just inside the main Strip entrance to the MGM Grand resort, this expansive space (which opened in the former Rainforest Cafe space at the end of 2016) is essentially an arcade for hipsters, along with a great bar. Games include everything from Pop-A-Shot and foosball to table hockey and more; most cost about $1 apiece. Beer pong tables are available and they're free, so long as you keep drinking beer (balls are 50 cents apiece). There's also a game that bills itself as the World's Largest Pac-Man. Golf fans love GolfStream Laser Golf, which essentially is virtual reality golf. Because it's Vegas, there's gambling here, too, in the form of electronic craps, roulette, blackjack, and baccarat. ✉ *MGM Grand, 3799 Las Vegas Blvd. S, South Strip* ☎ *702/891–7871* ⊕ *leveluplv.com* 🎟 *Free; games from $1* 🕑 *Closed Mon.–Thurs.*

Luxor Las Vegas
RESORT—SIGHT | Welcome to the land of the Egyptians—Vegas-style. This modern-world wonder is topped with a xenon light beam that burns brighter than any other in the world and can be seen from

anywhere in the Valley at night; for that matter, it's supposedly visible even from space. The exterior is made with 13 acres of black glass. Forget elevators; climbing the slanted walls of the Luxor pyramid requires four "inclinators" to reach guest rooms. Above the casino is the world's largest atrium—you get the full impact of the space from the second floor, where "BODIES…The Exhibition" gives guests an eerie view of the human body. This atrium also is home to *Fantasy*, a seductive adult revue that's fun to share with your significant other, and Carrot Top, who—believe it or not—is still performing live shows in Vegas after nearly 20 years. For something entirely unique, head outside the casino, walk past the porte cochere, and follow the sidewalk inside a replica of the Great Sphinx of Giza. Only in Vegas. ⊠ *3900 Las Vegas Blvd. S, South Strip* ☎ *877/386–4658* ⊕ *www. luxor.com.*

Mandalay Bay Resort & Casino, Las Vegas

RESORT—SIGHT | Mandalay Bay is famous for a few things: the House of Blues, which brings in some epic concerts throughout the year; the Shark Reef aquarium, which boasts a 1.6-million-gallon saltwater tank with more than 2,000 different animals; and an A-list of restaurants from celebrity chefs such as Charlie Palmer, Hubert Keller, and Wolfgang Puck. Additionally, international flavors are tasty attractions here, among them the authentic Emerald Isle experience at Rí Rá Irish Bar and the exquisite Japanese food, framed in delicate Asian ambience, at Morimoto. Technically the complex is three separate brands: Mandalay, the Delano Las Vegas, and the Four Seasons Hotel Las Vegas. If you're into design, the lobby for the Delano incorporates natural features from around the Vegas Valley and is one of the sharpest lobbies you'll find in Nevada. Also worth noting: Minus5 Ice Bar, which is located in the Mandalay Place shopping corridor that connects Mandalay Bay with the Luxor; for the price of admission you get to borrow a parka,

waltz into a subzero drinking establishment, and throw back vodka from a glass made of ice. ⊠ *3950 Las Vegas Blvd. S, South Strip* ☎ *877/632–7800* ⊕ *www. mandalaybay.com.*

MGM Grand Las Vegas

RESORT—SIGHT | A regal, bronze rendering of the roaring MGM lion mascot fronts the four emerald-green, fortresslike towers of the MGM Grand, one of the largest hotels in the world. Over the years, the property has become synonymous with big fights, most of which take place in the hotel's Grand Garden Arena. In recent years, the property also has added Hakkasan, an upscale restaurant and nightclub; Level Up, a hipster arcade with booze; Topgolf Las Vegas, a state-of-the-art driving range; and Brad Garrett's Comedy Club, where the beloved comic from *Everybody Loves Raymond* performs regularly. The hotel also has its share of restaurants from celebrity chefs, including Morimoto's first foray into Las Vegas. ⊠ *3799 Las Vegas Blvd. S, South Strip* ☎ *877/880–0880* ⊕ *www. mgmgrand.com.*

New York–New York Las Vegas Hotel & Casino

RESORT—SIGHT | The mini-Manhattan skyline that forms the facade of this hotel is one of our favorite parts of the Strip—there are third-size to half-size re-creations of the Empire State Building, the Statue of Liberty, and the Chrysler Building, as well as the New York Public Library, Grand Central Terminal, and the Brooklyn Bridge. Inside, portions of the casino floor have been made to look like neighborhoods of the real New York City. The Little Italy/Greenwich Village area is such an accurate replica many New Yorkers momentarily get confused. Without question, the big attraction is the Big Apple Coaster. A close second: Hershey's Chocolate World. Then, of course, there's The Park, which sits just north of the back side of the hotel and stretches from the Strip all the way to

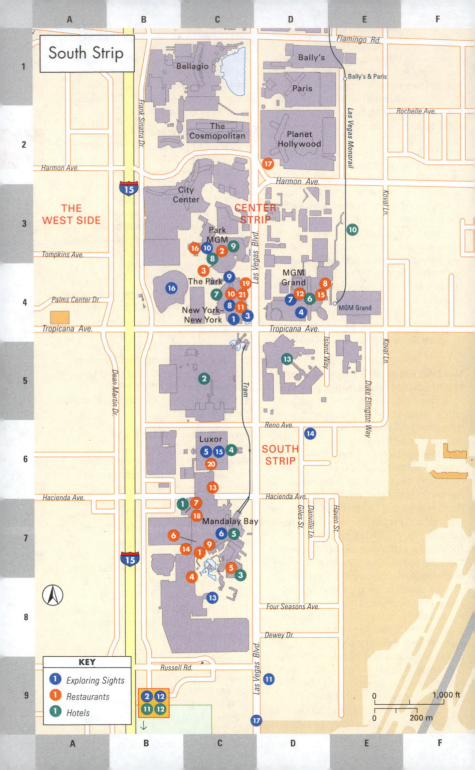

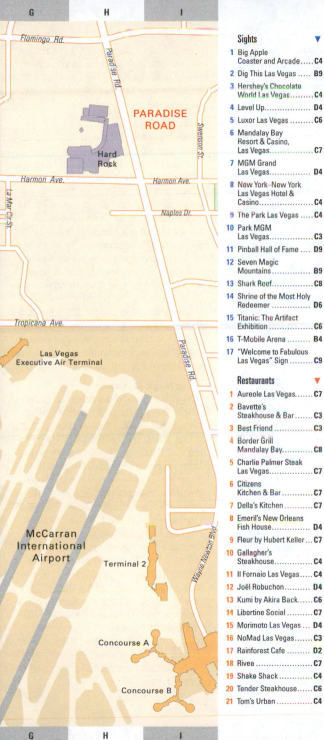

Flamingo Rd.

Paradise Rd

PARADISE ROAD

Swenson St.

Hard Rock

Harmon Ave.

Harmon Ave.

La Mar Cir St.

Naples Dr.

Tropicana Ave.

Paradise Rd.

Las Vegas Executive Air Terminal

McCarran International Airport

Terminal 2

Wayne Newton Blvd.

Concourse A

Concourse B

G H I

T-Mobile Arena. ✉ *3790 Las Vegas Blvd. S, South Strip* ☎ *866/815–4365* ⊕ *www. newyorknewyork.com.*

★ The Park Las Vegas

CITY PARK | Ever since the razing of The Boardwalk casino in the early 2000s, the space between New York–New York and the Monte Carlo (now the Park MGM) sat vacant, a veritable eyesore on the south end of the Strip. Finally, in 2015, landowner MGM Resorts decided to do something about it. The result, inventively dubbed The Park, is a small public park that runs from the Strip itself back west to the T-Mobile Arena, home to the city's first professional sports franchise, the Las Vegas Golden Knights hockey team. Along the way, The Park offers natural touches such as desert vegetation and rock from local quarries. It also has features such as a water wall, shade structures made to look like trees, and a 60-foot-tall statue of a dancing naked woman named "Bliss Dance." Restaurants on the New York–New York side offer outdoor seating and games for patrons to play while they relax. On the Park MGM side, The Park Theater provides a venue for intimate musical concerts. ✉ *3784 Las Vegas Blvd. S, South Strip* ☎ *702/740–6969* ⊕ *www. theparkvegas.com.*

Park MGM Las Vegas

RESORT—SIGHT | The resort formerly known as Monte Carlo was reborn at the end of 2018 as Park MGM, an homage to The Park, just outside its door. The property features dozens of nods to nature, including a lobby sculpture designed to replicate the roots of a tree from below. The resort also features a hotel within a hotel: the NoMad's foray into Las Vegas. On-site food and beverage options such as Eataly and Roy Choi's Best Friend make the property stand out further. The Park Theater, an intimate performing arts venue, was home to Lady Gaga's Vegas residency in 2020. The hotel still connects to City Center and Bellagio via a tram; on hot days, this is a great way to minimize outside time as you travel the Strip on foot. ✉ *3770 Las Vegas Blvd. S, South Strip* ☎ *888/529–4828* ⊕ *www. parkmgm.com.*

Pinball Hall of Fame

MUSEUM | **FAMILY** | This fun facility has more than 25,000 square feet (twice the size of its original location) filled with games that were created between the 1950s and the 1990s, including the old wood-rail models. Though it may sound more like an arcade than a museum, the local club is a nonprofit organization whose goal is to preserve these pieces of Americana and share the joy of the silver ball with as many folks as possible. All excess revenues go to nondenominational charities. The museum relocated to the South Strip in April 2021. ✉ *4925 Las Vegas Blvd. S, South Strip* ✛ *Across from Welcome to Fabulous Las Vegas sign* ⊕ *www.pinballmuseum.org* ✉ *Free entry, from 25¢ per game.*

Seven Magic Mountains

PUBLIC ART | The "mountains" of Seven Magic Mountains aren't actually mountains at all; instead they're towers of multicolor stacked boulders standing more than 30 feet high. The art installation from renowned Swiss artist Ugo Rondinone is a commentary about human presence in the desert, and it stands tall about 10 miles south of town near Jean Dry Lake. Visitors to the site can walk right up to the towers and pose with the towers in the background. As such, the spot has become a popular place for selfies. The exhibit opened in 2016 and was only scheduled to run until 2018, but due to public demand the Bureau of Land Management extended it through 2021. Proponents hope that the extension will be made permanent. ✉ *South Strip* ✛ *About 10 miles south of Mandalay Bay on I–15* ⊕ *www.sevenmagicmountains. com* ✉ *Free.*

Great Walks: South Strip 👁

Mummies to Big Apple: Inside Luxor's pyramid, follow the enclosed walkways to Excalibur. From there, it's an easy walk across a pedestrian bridge to New York–New York's gaming floor. Total time: 15 minutes.

All about M's: Inside the MGM Grand, resort guests can explore the grounds—both the MGM Grand and the area surrounding the Signature towers. Then you can join the masses and hit the Strip heading north toward M&M's World, one of the town's biggest candy stores. Total time: 30–40 minutes.

See an Icon: Head south on Las Vegas Boulevard from Mandalay Bay and you'll spot the famous "Welcome to Fabulous Las Vegas" sign. If you want to take a picture directly under the sign, be careful crossing the street; the sign sits in the center median and there's no crosswalk. Total time from Mandalay and back: about 40 minutes.

Shark Reef

ZOO | FAMILY | Your journey through Mandalay Bay's long-running Shark Reef attraction begins in the mysterious realm of deep water at the ruins of an old Aztec temple. It's tropical and humid for us bipeds, but quite comfy for the golden crocodiles, endangered green sea turtles, and water monitors. Descend through two glass tunnels, which lead you deeper and deeper under the sea (or about 1.6 million gallons of water), where exotic tropical fish and other sea creatures swim all around you. The tour saves the best for last—from the recesses of a sunken galleon, sharks swim below, above, and around the skeleton ship. Elsewhere you'll find a petting zoo for marine life, a Komodo dragon exhibit, and a special jellyfish habitat. If you plan to visit other MGM Resorts attractions you can save with their three-for-$57 promotion. ⊠ *Mandalay Bay, 3950 Las Vegas Blvd. S, South Strip* ☎ *702/632–4555* ⊕ *www.sharkreef.com* 🎫 *From $24.*

Shrine of the Most Holy Redeemer

RELIGIOUS SITE | Churchgoers staying in the South Strip area stagger into this iconic Roman Catholic church for mass seven days a week. Among the more popular offerings: the two Saturday and five Sunday masses. ⊠ *55 E. Reno Ave., South Strip* ☎ *702/891–8600* ⊕ *the-shrinelv.org.*

Titanic: The Artifact Exhibition

MUSEUM | FAMILY | Travel down to the bottom of the North Atlantic where the "ship of dreams" rests after grazing an iceberg in 1912. The 25,000-square-foot exhibit inside Luxor Las Vegas includes a replica of guest compartments, the grand staircase, and a promenade deck that movie fans will recognize from a little film by James Cameron. Among the 250 emotionally arresting artifacts: luggage, clothing, a bottle of unopened champagne, and pieces of the ship, including a massive section of the iron hull, complete with bulging rivets and portholes. ⊠ *Luxor Las Vegas, 3900 Las Vegas Blvd. S, South Strip* ☎ *702/262–4000, 800/557–7428* ⊕ *www.luxor.com/entertainment* 🎫 *From $37* 🕐 *Closed Mon.–Wed.*

T-Mobile Arena

SPORTS VENUE | FAMILY | T-Mobile Arena has probably become most widely known beyond Las Vegas as the home of the National Hockey League's Vegas Golden Knights, an expansion team that reached the Stanley Cup finals during its inaugural season. It's also a popular concert venue, attracting acts from George Strait to Ariana Grande to Kiss. And it's rich in amenities, with a variety of restaurants, bars and guest services. When there's downtime, you can even tour the arena's backstage areas, but these tours are offered only sporadically. ⊠ *3780 Las Vegas Blvd. S, Center Strip* ☎ *702/692–1600* ⊕ *www.t-mobilearena. com* 🎫 *Arena tours from $25.*

"Welcome to Fabulous Las Vegas" Sign
HISTORIC SITE | This neon-and-incandescent sign, in a median of Las Vegas Boulevard south of Mandalay Bay, is one of Sin City's most enduring icons. The landmark dates back to 1959, and was approved for listing on the National Register of Historic Places in 2009. Young Electric Sign Company leases the sign to Clark County but the design itself was never copyrighted, and currently exists in the public domain. (This, of course, explains why you see so many likenesses all over town.) The parking lot in the median just south of the sign was expanded in 2015. If you prefer to go on foot, expect a 10-minute walk from Mandalay Bay. ⊠ *5100 Las Vegas Blvd. S, South Strip* 🎫 *Free.*

🍴 Restaurants

Aureole Las Vegas
$$$$ | **AMERICAN** | Celebrity-chef Charlie Palmer re-created his famed New York restaurant for Mandalay Bay. It was extensively renovated in late 2016 but retains designer Adam Tihany's four-story wine tower, which holds more than 60,000 bottles that are reached by "flying wine angels," who are hoisted up and down via a system of electronically activated pulleys. **Known for:** Charlie Palmer's innovative cuisine; wine tower with "angels" on cables; windows that look out on picturesque fountain. ⑤ *Average main: $50* ⊠ *Mandalay Bay Resort & Casino, 3950 Las Vegas Blvd. S, South Strip* ☎ *702/632–7401* ⊕ *www.*

Taxi! 👁

You're never far from a taxi in Las Vegas, but it's downright impossible to hail a cab on the Strip. Hotels welcome you to their taxi stand lines in the hope that you'll come back and play in their casinos. Ride-sharing services such as Uber and Lyft also are also available; drivers for these services usually pick up in separate locations. See casino signage for details.

charliepalmer.com/location/aureole-las-vegas 🕐 *Closed Sun. No lunch.*

Bavette's Steakhouse & Bar
$$$$ | **STEAKHOUSE** | With tufted leather banquettes and dark lighting, Bavette's, inside Park MGM, offers a much stronger dose of Gallic flair than the typical Las Vegas steak house. The restaurant offers a full complement of popular steak cuts ranging from bone-in rib eye to fillet, as well as baked crab cakes, raw-bar items, including a decent vegetarian menu. **Known for:** French flair; stiff cocktails and lively bar scene; classic steak-and-seafood preparations. ⑤ *Average main: $60* ⊠ *Park MGM, 3770 Las Vegas Blvd. S, South Strip* ☎ *702/730–6700* ⊕ *bavettessteakhouse. com/las-vegas* 🕐 *Closed Mon.–Wed.*

Best Friend
$$$$ | **KOREAN** | Famous Los Angeles chef Roy Choi debuted in Las Vegas with this lively concept inside Park MGM serving Korean BBQ as well as a panoply of favorites from Choi's Koreatown experience. While a live DJ spins tunes at a turntable in the corner, the meal starts with a sampling of *banchan*: tiny dishes that include kimchi, broccoli, cucumbers, spinach, and more. **Known for:** working convenience store out front; all-you-can eat option; family-style dishes made for sharing. ⑤ *Average main: $40* ⊠ *Park MGM, 3770 Las Vegas Blvd. S, South*

Strip ☎ 702/730–7777 ⊕ www.parkmgm.
com/en/restaurants/best-friend.html
⊙ No lunch. Closed Wed. and Thurs.

Border Grill Mandalay Bay

$$$ | SOUTHWESTERN | FAMILY | Mary Sue
Milliken and Susan Feniger are the pop-
ular, green-minded chefs who created
this cheery, sophisticated outpost of their
now-closed Santa Monica restaurant. Ser-
vice is snappy, and you'd be hard-pressed
to find a tastier margarita in town—par-
ticularly the mango-cilantro and raspber-
ry-chipotle versions. **Known for:** urban
Mexican cuisine; fun, flavored margaritas;
patio overlooking Mandalay Bay Beach.
⑤ Average main: $30 ⊠ Mandalay Bay
Resort & Casino, 3950 Las Vegas Blvd.
S, South Strip ☎ 702/632–7403 ⊕ www.
bordergrill.com.

Charlie Palmer Steak Las Vegas

$$$$ | STEAKHOUSE | Charlie Palmer
understood that the Four Seasons, a
quiet enclave within a busy hotel-casino
complex, needed a similar restaurant.
Although his Aureole at Mandalay Bay
can be something of a scene, this nearby
steak house is easygoing and understat-
ed. **Known for:** top-quality steaks; great
"cut of the week" deal; quiet refuge
from the hubbub. ⑤ Average main: $45
⊠ Four Seasons Hotel, 3960 Las Vegas
Blvd. S, South Strip ☎ 702/632–5120
⊕ www.charliepalmersteak.com/loca-
tions/las-vegas ⊙ Closed Sun. No lunch.

Citizens Kitchen & Bar

$$$ | AMERICAN | This pub serves up
some of the best comfort food Vegas
has to offer. Dishes include beer-braised
bratwurst; bacon, egg, and cheese sandwiches; a prime rib dinner; and ultimate
nachos with corn chips, black beans,
jalapeños, and your choice of meat.
Known for: tasty comfort food; convenient
location right off the casino; fun sides
such as loaded nachos. ⑤ Average main:
$25 ⊠ Mandalay Bay, 3950 Las Vegas
Blvd. S, South Strip ☎ 702/632–9200
⊕ mandalaybay.mgmresorts.com ⊙ No
dinner Mon.–Wed.

Della's Kitchen

$$$ | AMERICAN | Della's is of the new
school of updated, farm-to-table resort
coffee shops. Both breakfast and lunch
are available all day. **Known for:** best
casual breakfast and lunch spot at the
Delano; regional specialties like Portu-
guese sausage; quiet atmosphere for a
coffee shop. ⑤ Average main: $25 ⊠ The
Delano Las Vegas, 3940 Las Vegas Blvd.
S, South Strip ☎ 702/632–9250 ⊕ www.
delanolasvegas.com/en/restaurants/del-
las-kitchen.html ⊙ No dinner.

Emeril's New Orleans Fish House

$$$$ | SOUTHERN | Chef Emeril Lagasse's
first restaurant in Las Vegas dates back
to the opening of the MGM Grand, but
it's still a popular choice and has been
periodically updated. The menu still
puts the spotlight on the chef's Cre-
ole-inspired cuisine, such as barbecued
shrimp, Louisiana-style jambalaya, and
oysters on the half shell with watermel-
on mignonette. **Known for:** Creole and
Cajun specialties; lively, family-friendly
atmosphere; killer banana cream pie.
⑤ Average main: $40 ⊠ MGM Grand
Hotel & Casino, 3799 Las Vegas Blvd. S,
South Strip ☎ 702/891–7374 ⊕ emerilsre-
staurants.com/emerils-new-orleans-fish-
house ⊙ No lunch.

Fleur by Hubert Keller

$$$$ | INTERNATIONAL | Chef Hubert Keller's
Fleur has two dining spaces, one fairly
intimate and one open to Mandalay Bay's
restaurant row, so you can watch the
world (or at least Las Vegas) go by. Small
plates themed to various cuisines around
the world can be enjoyed à la carte or
as a tasting menu for two or four. **Known
for:** upscale yet fun menu of small plates;
indulgent Wagyu "Burger 5000" with foie
gras, truffles, and Chateau Petrus; great
people-watching on the indoor patio.
⑤ Average main: $37 ⊠ Mandalay Bay
Resort & Casino, 3950 Las Vegas Blvd.
S, South Strip ☎ 702/632–7200 ⊕ www.
mandalaybay.com/en/restaurants/fleur-by-
hubert-keller.html.

Dining with Kids

Las Vegas is not really a family destination, but you'll still find plenty of spots around town—both on and off the Strip—that happily welcome kids. Here's a look at several restaurants worth a trip if you have kids in tow.

Grimaldi's. Exceptionally tasty pizza and a casual dining room draw crowds to this cheery restaurant at The Palazzo (where there's a little outdoor patio that's good fun on a nice day) and Henderson.

Hard Rock Cafe. The last-remaining Vegas outpost of this national chain (located near M&M's World) still delivers family-friendly dishes and hearty portion sizes for the whole brood.

Honey Salt. The menu at this Summerlin restaurant was created by kids for kids (age 10 and under), with both delicious (mac and cheese, margherita pizza) and nutritious (steamed broccoli and cheddar) offerings. There are cookies and milk for dessert and a "sushi" option that comprises rice crispy treats with gummies.

The Patisserie. With locations in both ARIA and Bellagio, the draws here are beautifully displayed cakes, cookies, gelato, and dessert crepes, and a fanciful Wonka-esque ambience, with a chocolate fountain at the Bellagio location.

Rainforest Cafe. If you want to be sure the kids won't fuss during dinner, take them to this popular spot in the Harmon Corner so they can dine among animatronic animals and listen to (faux) weather reports.

322 Pizza Bar. Nothing goes better together than kids and pizza, and they fit hand in glove at this upbeat joint smack in the middle of the Fremont Street action, serving up huge slices of tasty 'za. A happy, lip-smackin' experience.

Gallagher's Steakhouse

$$$$ | STEAKHOUSE | This credible remake of the famed 1927 Manhattan original offers an old-school carnivore experience inside the cleverly decorated New York–New York casino. The convivial tavern's walls are lined with black-and-white photos of sports stars, actors, and politicos, and the hardwood floors and tray ceilings transport guests directly to Gotham. **Known for:** aged meat display near entrance; old New York atmosphere; sublime sauces. $ *Average main: $55* ✉ *New York–New York Hotel & Casino, 3790 Las Vegas Blvd. S, South Strip* ☎ *702/740–6450* ⊕ *newyorknewyork. mgmresorts.com/en/restaurants/gallaghers-steakhouse.html* ☾ *No lunch.*

Il Fornaio Las Vegas

$$$$ | ITALIAN | FAMILY | This soothingly neutral Italian restaurant will satisfy carb cravings as well as yearnings for dishes that Grandma used to make. Crusty loaves of freshly baked bread, pasta, and dough for its excellent thin-crust, wood-oven pizzas are all made in-house. **Known for:** hearty and reliable breakfast; wood-oven-baked pizzas; people-watching from indoor terrace. $ *Average main: $35* ✉ *New York–New York Resort & Casino, 3790 Las Vegas Blvd. S, South Strip* ☎ *702/650–6500* ⊕ *newyorknewyork.mgmresorts.com/en/restaurants/il-fornaio.html.*

★ Joël Robuchon

$$$$ | FRENCH | The late chef Joël Robuchon left his mark on Vegas with haute cuisine at two gorgeous, side-by-side restaurants. The more glamorous manse that bears his name offers the ultimate gastronomical rush, with elaborate dishes and luxurious ingredients in several multicourse menus. **Known for:** elegant, formal atmosphere; elaborate tasting menus; small plates in the Atelier. ⑤ *Average main: $400* ✉ *MGM Grand Hotel & Casino, 3799 Las Vegas Blvd. S, South Strip* ☎ *702/891–7925* ⊕ *www.mgmgrand.com/en/restaurants/joel-robuchon-french-restaurant.html* ◷ *No lunch* ⛨ *Jacket required.*

Kumi by Akira Back

$$$$ | JAPANESE FUSION | Chef (and former professional snowboarder) Akira Back presents a Japanese menu with a slight Korean twist in a sleek space with natural woods and hammered steel. Menu items include dishes such as Jidori chicken with kimchi Brussels sprouts and *hirame* carpaccio with dried shallots, as well as more conventional tataki, tempuras, and a wide variety of rolls and sushi. **Known for:** Japanese food with a Korean twist; sleek, contemporary decor; artisanal cocktails. ⑤ *Average main: $45* ✉ *Mandalay Bay, 3590 Las Vegas Blvd. S, South Strip* ☎ *702/632–7200* ⊕ *mandalaybay.mgmresorts.com* ◷ *No lunch. Closed Mon.–Wed.*

Libertine Social

$$$$ | AMERICAN | This casual spot from James Beard Award–winning chef Shawn McClain and modern mixologist Tony Abou-Ganim puts the emphasis on "social." The food's fun but seriously good, such as the Modern Fried Egg, in which an empty egg shell is filled with corn pudding, a fluffy egg and caviar, or the social toasts and dips, flatbreads, and charcuterie and cheese boards. **Known for:** serious but fun menu; updated versions of historic cocktails; emphasis on the "social". ⑤ *Average main: $35* ✉ *Mandalay Bay, 3950 Las Vegas Blvd. S, South Strip* ☎ *702/632–7558* ⊕ *www.mandalaybay.com/en/restaurants/libertine-social.html* ◷ *No lunch. Closed Sun.–Thurs.*

Morimoto Las Vegas

$$$$ | JAPANESE FUSION | "Iron Chef" Masaharu Morimoto has opened his restaurant in what he proudly called "the most famous city in the world," and it marked his first foray into teppanyaki, sure to be popular with conventioneers. There's also sushi, of course, and some of his standbys: braised black cod with a ginger-soy reduction, and tuna pizza with anchovy oil, olives, and jalapeño. **Known for:** food by the original Iron Chef; sushi, teppanyaki, and conventional dining; dramatic black-and-white interior. ⑤ *Average main: $40* ✉ *MGM Grand, 3799 Las Vegas Blvd. S, South Strip* ☎ *702/891–3001* ⊕ *www.mgmgrand.com/en/restaurants/morimoto.html* ◷ *No lunch. Closed Tues. and Wed.*

★ NoMad Las Vegas

$$$$ | ECLECTIC | Grandiose, spectacular, and heart-stopping are three words to describe the restaurant at NoMad Las Vegas. The restaurant has 40-foot ceilings and is ringed with shelves of real books—a backdrop that creates an intimate and sophisticated vibe. **Known for:** breathtaking atmosphere; delicious communal dishes; jazz brunch in the bar on weekends. ⑤ *Average main: $43* ✉ *Park MGM, 3772 Las Vegas Blvd. S, South Strip* ☎ *702/730–6785* ⊕ *www.thenomadhotel.com/las-vegas.*

Rainforest Cafe

$$$ | AMERICAN | FAMILY | The Rainforest Cafe moved out of its longtime berth in the MGM Grand in 2015, but its current location just up the Strip on Harmon Avenue still has plenty of animatronic animals. The menu offers an eclectic mix of classic American food like fried chicken and pot roast with a mix of pastas, burgers, and Caribbean and South American influences. **Known for:** animatronic wildlife; periodically changing (indoor)

Las Vegas Hamburger Roundup

A number of casino resorts have opened eateries dedicated to that most quintessentially American of cuisines—the compact and delicious hamburger. All of these restaurants are casual affairs; most don't even accept reservations.

Black Tap Las Vegas. How American is this? You can actually nosh a burger and quaff an icy milk shake while overlooking the outdoor canals at The Venetian—or take in the indoor action in the resort's poker room. ⊠ *The Venetian, 3355 Las Vegas Blvd. S, North Strip* ☎ *702/414–1000*

Bobby's Burger Palace. Bobby Flay is the original grillmaster, and he proves it at this colorful spot that serves not only burgers but also salads and drinks and shakes, many of them spiked. ⊠ *Residences at the Mandarin Oriental, 3750 Las Vegas Blvd. S, Center Strip* ☎ *702/598–0191*

Fatburger. With 11 locations throughout the city, this is an ever-present ol' reliable, Whether it actually lives up to its tagline, "The Last Great Hamburger Stand," can be debated, but they are true to their name: they make burgers—and make them to order per your preference—and they make them fat. Also medium-size or even smaller, for more modest appetites. ⊠ *Multiple locations.* ⊕ *fatburger.com.*

Gordon Ramsay Burger. The volcanic Scottish chef now has four restaurants in Las Vegas and his burger spot, where the main attraction is cooked over an open flame, is among the most popular. ⊠ *Planet Hollywood, 3667 Las Vegas Blvd. S, Center Strip* ☎ *702/785–5462*

LVB Burgers and Bar. Burger choices in this restaurant near The Mirage sports book include duck, salmon, lamb, and turkey. Spiked milk shakes—including "rum in the coconut," with Myers's rum, coconut, pineapple, and vanilla ice cream—make great accompaniments. ⊠ *Mirage Las Vegas, 3400 Las Vegas Blvd. S, Center Strip* ☎ *702/792–7888*

Shake Shack. These branches of the New York original offer the famous burgers made with a proprietary blend of meat. There's a second location in downtown Summerlin. ⊠ *New York–New York, 3970 Las Vegas Blvd. S, South Strip* ☎ *725/222–6730*

weather; family-friendly food. $ *Average main: $25* ⊠ *Harmon Corner, 3717 Las Vegas Blvd. S, South Strip* ☎ *702/891–8580* ⊕ *www.rainforestcafe.com.*

Rivea

$$$$ | **FRENCH FUSION** | Culinary lion Alain Ducasse replaced his iconic Mix with the equally stunning Rivea, offering unparalleled views of the Strip and Riviera-style interpretations of his cuisine from the 64th floor of the Delano Las Vegas. It's suitably more casual fare, with such shared plates as paccheri pasta with braised short rib, and sautéed calamari and prawns with artichokes and crushed red chilies. **Known for:** Riviera spin on Alain Ducasse's cuisine; 64th-floor location; unparalleled views up the Strip. $ *Average main: $50* ⊠ *Delano Las Vegas, 3940 Las Vegas Blvd. S, South Strip* ☎ *877/632–5400* ⊕ *www. delanolasvegas.com/en/restaurants/ rivea.html* ☾ *No lunch.*

Shake Shack

$ | **AMERICAN** | **FAMILY** | This fast-casual favorite born in New York City finally arrived in Las Vegas in 2014, and the only thing different about it is that the lines aren't so long. It's a great place to stop for a ShackBurger and fries, and don't forget the concretes (frozen custard), especially the flavor of the day. **Known for:** burgers made from a proprietary meat mix; crinkle-cut fries; shakes and concretes made from frozen custard. $ *Average main: $12* ✉ *New York–New York, 3790 Las Vegas Blvd. S, South Strip* ☎ *702/222–6730* ⊕ *www.shakeshack.com.*

Tender Steakhouse

$$$$ | **STEAKHOUSE** | Tender is the steak house that it seems every Las Vegas hotel-casino is required to have, but it offers a menu that veers off the beaten path. In addition to the typical steak offerings, you'll find a wide selection of fish and seafood. **Known for:** dry- and wet-aged steaks; selection of seafood; classic steak-house styling. $ *Average main: $55* ✉ *Luxor Las Vegas, 3900 Las Vegas Blvd. S, South Strip* ☎ *702/262–4778* ⊕ *www.luxor.com/en/restaurants/tender-steakhouse.html* ☾ *No lunch. Closed Mon.–Wed.*

Tom's Urban

$$$ | **AMERICAN** | **FAMILY** | From restaurant-industry veteran and Smashburger founder Tom Ryan, this gastropub bridges a space at New York–New York between the casino and the Brooklyn Bridge that runs along the Strip, delivering great views of the action. The large menu of drinks and beers is matched by an extensive food menu, including burgers, pizzas, and other entrées. **Known for:** varied menu of gastropub favorites; huge selection of drinks; great Happy Hour deals. $ *Average main: $25* ✉ *New York–New York, 3790 Las Vegas Blvd. S, South Strip* ☎ *702/740–6766* ⊕ *www.tomsurban.com/las-vegas.*

🛏 Hotels

With an Oz-like structure that stretches forever, a pyramid with a light you can see from space, and a replica of the New York City skyline, the southern third of the Strip between CityCenter and the iconic "Welcome to Fabulous Las Vegas" sign could be considered the entertainment hub of Vegas.

Major resorts in this area include the Tropicana, Mandalay Bay, Luxor, Excalibur, MGM Grand, New York–New York, and Park MGM. Rooms here are generally within 10 to 15 minutes of the airport and are slightly more affordable than their Center and North Strip counterparts. After the addition of The Park and T-Mobile Arena, the South Strip has reestablished itself as the most popular section of Sin City's most famous street.

This part of town has a small claim on Strip history as well; the Tropicana dates back 50 years, and the MGM, Mandalay Bay, and the Luxor were early entrants in the megaresort race of the 1990s. In November 2017, when the puck dropped for the first time at T-Mobile Arena, the city welcomed its first-ever major professional sports franchise in the National Hockey League's Las Vegas Golden Knights. Las Vegans are equally excited for Raiders football to start with the 2020 season.

Another trend here: ultraluxurious hotels within the ordinary hotels. Mandalay has Delano Las Vegas and the Four Seasons; MGM has Skylofts; Park MGM has NoMad Las Vegas. You don't have to splurge to have a great time on the South Strip, but enjoying sumptuous linens, exclusive amenities, and unparalleled service every once in a while sure is special.

★ Delano Las Vegas

$$$ | **RESORT** | South Beach meets desert Zen at this all-suites tower inside Mandalay Bay. Elaborate wet bars, giant 42-inch plasma TVs, plush carpeting, and floor-to-ceiling windows make the all-white guest

rooms oases in the Nevada desert. **Pros:** lavish suites; great views; separate and swanky entrance. **Cons:** long walk to main casino; hard-to-find entrance; white can get monotonous. ⑤ *Rooms from: $279* ✉ *3950 Las Vegas Blvd. S, South Strip* ☎ *877/632–7800, 702/632–7777* ⊕ *www.delanolasvegas.com* ↘ *1117 suites* ⦿ *No meals.*

Excalibur Hotel and Casino

$ | **RESORT** | **FAMILY** | The giant castle is popular with families—child-oriented attractions include the basement arcade (dubbed the Fun Dungeon) and the medieval-theme *Tournament of Kings* dinner show—but recent makeovers in all of the property's rooms make much of it look more grown-up (though still nondescript). **Pros:** low table minimums make for more accessible gambling; easy access to Luxor and Mandalay Bay; lively casino atmosphere. **Cons:** low table minimums also attract huge crowds; most on-site dining options are mediocre; few legitimately cool attractions. ⑤ *Rooms from: $149* ✉ *3850 Las Vegas Blvd. S, South Strip* ☎ *702/597–7777, 800/937–7777* ⊕ *www.excalibur.com* ↘ *3981 rooms* ⦿ *No meals.*

★ Four Seasons Hotel Las Vegas

$$$$ | **RESORT** | **FAMILY** | If peace and quiet are what you're after, this is your spot; with its own ground-level lobby and separate floors, the Four Seasons is cushioned from the general casino ruckus. **Pros:** kid-friendly; ultraposh; access to the elaborate resort facilities at Mandalay Bay. **Cons:** pricey; far from rest of Vegas action; stuffy at times. ⑤ *Rooms from: $429* ✉ *Mandalay Bay Resort, 3960 Las Vegas Blvd. S, South Strip* ☎ *702/632–5000* ⊕ *www.fourseasons.com/lasvegas* ↘ *424 rooms* ⦿ *No meals.*

Luxor Las Vegas Hotel & Casino

$$ | **RESORT** | Unlike other hotels on the Strip, this one has no elevators—at least in the main pyramid; instead, in order to reach rooms, guests must climb the slanted walls in one of four "inclinators." On each floor, open-air hallways overlook

the world's largest atrium. **Pros:** decent value; hip casino; expansive pool. **Cons:** slanted room walls; removed from main Strip action; cheesy decor. ⑤ *Rooms from: $219* ✉ *3900 Las Vegas Blvd. S, South Strip* ☎ *702/262–4000, 877/386–4658* ⊕ *www.luxor.com* ↘ *4400 rooms* ⦿ *No meals.*

★ Mandalay Bay Resort & Casino, Las Vegas

$$$ | **RESORT** | **FAMILY** | Mandalay Bay remains as swanky as ever, decked out like a South Seas beach resort, complete with cavernous rooms and one of the best pool areas on the Strip. **Pros:** large rooms; ample options for everything; the beach. **Cons:** concerts can be loud; so large it's easy to get lost; nothing comes cheap here, including the resort fee. ⑤ *Rooms from: $239* ✉ *3950 Las Vegas Blvd. S, South Strip* ☎ *702/632–7777, 877/632–7800* ⊕ *www.mandalaybay.com* ↘ *3209 rooms* ⦿ *No meals.*

MGM Grand Las Vegas

$$$ | **RESORT** | The MGM Grand is one of the largest hotels in the world, with five 30-story towers with rooms in nine different categories. **Pros:** something for everyone; StayWell rooms; fantastic restaurants. **Cons:** easy to get lost; schlep to parking lot; check-in can have very long lines. ⑤ *Rooms from: $239* ✉ *3799 Las Vegas Blvd. S, South Strip* ☎ *702/891–1111, 877/880–0880* ⊕ *www.mgmgrand.com* ↘ *5044 rooms* ⦿ *No meals.*

New York–New York Las Vegas Resort & Casino

$$ | **RESORT** | The mini-Manhattan skyline is one of our favorite parts of the Strip—there are third-size to half-size re-creations of the Empire State Building, the Statue of Liberty, and the Chrysler Building, as well as the New York Public Library, Grand Central Terminal, and the Brooklyn Bridge. **Pros:** authentic New York experience; art deco lobby; casino floor center bar. **Cons:** layout is somewhat confusing; cramped sports book; mediocre pool. ⑤ *Rooms from: $179*

✉ *3790 Las Vegas Blvd. S, South Strip* ☎ *702/740–6969, 800/689–1797* ⊕ *www.newyorknewyork.com* ⤳ *2024 rooms* ⫶◉⫶ *No meals.*

★ NoMad Las Vegas

$$ | RESORT | The swanky NoMad hotel chain made its Las Vegas debut in late 2018 with a hotel that comprises the top four floors of the Park MGM but with its own check-in area, a separate high-limit casino, and the NoMad Restaurant & Bar down below. **Pros:** impeccable service; one-of-a-kind rooms with wood floors and standalone tubs; unreal food at NoMad Restaurant & Bar. **Cons:** private pool small and hard to find; access to separate lobby from casino is not intuitive; restaurant reservations hard to come by. ⑤ *Rooms from: $219* ✉ *Park MGM, 3772 Las Vegas Blvd. S, South Strip* ☎ *702/730–7000* ⊕ *www.thenomadhotel.com/las-vegas* ⤳ *293 rooms* ⫶◉⫶ *No meals.*

Park MGM Las Vegas

$$ | RESORT | FAMILY | Park MGM, formerly the Monte Carlo Resort, opened in late 2018, and the transformation has been remarkable. **Pros:** new design emphasises the outdoors; small but nice and relaxing rooms; proximity to T-Mobile Arena. **Cons:** taxi entrance not close to main entrance; small pool area; busy on game days at arena next door. ⑤ *Rooms from: $189* ✉ *3770 Las Vegas Blvd. S, South Strip* ☎ *702/730–7777, 888/529–4828* ⊕ *www.parkmgm.com* ⤳ *2700 rooms* ⫶◉⫶ *No meals.*

★ The Signature at MGM Grand

$$ | RESORT | FAMILY | The three towers that comprise this spacious and well-appointed luxury resort adjacent to the MGM Grand are perhaps most notable for what they lack: a casino. **Pros:** relatively inexpensive room rates; spacious suites; en suite kitchens to save money on food. **Cons:** inconvenient off-Strip entrance; a trek to nearest casino (at MGM Grand); views of Topgolf. ⑤ *Rooms from: $199* ✉ *145 E. Harmon Ave., South Strip* ☎ *702/797–6000, 877/612–2121* ⊕ *www.signaturemgmgrand.com* ⤳ *1728 suites* ⫶◉⫶ *No meals.*

Silverton Casino Hotel

$ | HOTEL | FAMILY | Don't overlook this Rocky Mountain lodge–theme hotel with popular attractions such as a huge Bass Pro Shop, a 117,000-gallon saltwater aquarium (complete with mermaid shows), and the Shady Grove Bar and Lounge, which has plasma-screen televisions and a mini–bowling alley. **Pros:** Bass Pro Shop is a fisherman's heaven; mermaid shows are one-of-a-kind; great value not too far from Strip. **Cons:** casino underwhelms; mediocre dining options; rooms are small and have very few frills. ⑤ *Rooms from: $109* ✉ *3333 Blue Diamond Rd., South Las Vegas* ☎ *702/263–7777, 866/722–4608* ⊕ *www.silvertoncasino.com* ⤳ *300 rooms* ⫶◉⫶ *No meals.*

South Point Hotel Casino & Spa

$ | HOTEL | FAMILY | Perk or quirk—the South Point houses an equestrian center, a venue that frequently hosts rodeos and other horse-oriented shows. **Pros:** pool area; equestrian center; lively sports book. **Cons:** proximity to airport; distance from Strip hotels; rooms could use a refresh. ⑤ *Rooms from: $109* ✉ *9777 Las Vegas Blvd. S, South Las Vegas* ☎ *702/796–7111, 866/796–7111* ⊕ *www.southpointcasino.com* ⤳ *2163 rooms* ⫶◉⫶ *No meals.*

Tropicana Las Vegas—A DoubleTree by Hilton Hotel

$$ | RESORT | Today's "Trop" (as it's been known for more than 50 years) features some of the most spacious rooms in town with a pleasant (and whitewashed) South Beach/Miami style. **Pros:** views from the new Sky Villa Suites; breezy style; pool still has pizzazz. **Cons:** small casino; interior layout can be confusing; restaurants better at other casino resorts. ⑤ *Rooms from: $179* ✉ *3801 Las Vegas Blvd. S, South Strip* ☎ *702/739–2222, 800/462–8767* ⊕ *www.troplv.com* ⤳ *1454 rooms* ⫶◉⫶ *No meals.*

☿ Nightlife

BARS AND LOUNGES

The lounges of the Las Vegas casino-hotels were once places where such headliners as Frank, Dean, and the gang would go after their shows, taking a seat in the audience to laugh at the comedy antics of Shecky Greene or Don Rickles. For a while lounges were mostly reduced to small bars within the casino where bands played Top 40 hits in front of people pie-eyed from the slots. The turn of the 21st century, however, brought an explosion of hybrid nightspots—the so-called ultralounges—that aimed for the middle ground between dance club and conventional lounge. Some of the best of them are worth a separate trip, given how much of a pleasure-jolt they offer.

Coyote Ugly

PIANO BARS/LOUNGES | Barmaids in tight clothes break into choreographed bar-top dances intended to make Hooters look like a church picnic at this noisy tourist trap, a reincarnation of the 2000 movie's title nightspot (which is, fittingly, in New York). If you want to gaze at galvanized aluminum siding, old license plates, and an impressive bra collection, who are we to stop you? ⊠ *New York–New York, 3790 Las Vegas Blvd. S, South Strip* ☎ *702/740–6969* ⊕ *www.coyoteuglysaloon.com/vegas.*

Eyecandy Sound Lounge

PIANO BARS/LOUNGES | High technology hits the Strip at this vast "interactive" ultralounge in the center of Mandalay Bay's casino floor. For "future shock" freaks, there are tented "touch tables" on which you can draw messages, words, and images projected onto video screens above the dance floor, and "sound stations" that let you send music of your choice to the DJ. More important than the technology here, though, is the cocktail menu; crafted by a master mixologist, drinks are so scrumptious they could call the place "mouthcandy,"

too. Best of all, there's no cover charge. ⊠ *Mandalay Bay, 3950 Las Vegas Blvd. S, South Strip* ☎ *702/632–4760* ⊕ *www.mandalaybay.com/en/nightlife/eyecandy-sound-lounge.html.*

Foundation Room

PIANO BARS/LOUNGES | Ancient statues, tapestry-covered walls, pirated Mississippi road signs—the Foundation Room gets high marks for aesthetic appeal. Though the joint is members-only at certain times, this secluded subsidiary of the House of Blues is open to everyone seven nights a week—provided you're willing to wait in line. The venue itself is a series of different rooms, each with its own set of design themes and type of music that could range from Top 40 hits to house, depending on the night. ■**TIP→** **A main attraction is the view of the Strip; because the club is on the 43rd floor, it provides some of the best panoramic vistas of the entire town, but the views come with a hefty cover charge.** ⊠ *Mandalay Bay, 3950 Las Vegas Blvd. S, South Strip* ☎ *702/632–7631* ⊕ *www.mandalaybay.com/en/nightlife/foundation-room.html.*

Franklin

PIANO BARS/LOUNGES | The Delano gives its classy lobby lounge a moniker that goes with its theme: the 32nd president. Bourbons, whiskeys, and barrel-aged drinks are specialties here, so belly up, let the DJs help you relax, and ask the bartender to prep you a little something. Woodford Reserve barrel service was a nice addition in 2018. What's more, since it's a lobby lounge, there's no cover. ✉ *Delano Las Vegas, 3940 Las Vegas Blvd. S, South Strip* ☎ *702/632–7888* ⊕ *www.delanolasvegas.com/en/restaurants/franklin.html.*

Juniper Cocktail Lounge

BARS/PUBS | Gin is the specialty of the house at Juniper, which is named after one of the berries used to flavor the spirit, but thirsty patrons can get just about any craft cocktail they wish at this Park MGM lounge. The menu features a curated cocktail program using house-made juices and syrups alongside an expertly selected spirits menu. There's also a live DJ on many nights. ✉ *Park MGM, 3770 Las Vegas Blvd. S, South Strip* ☎ *702/730–7777* ⊕ *www.parkmgm.com/en/nightlife/juniper-cocktail-lounge.html.*

Mermaid Restaurant & Lounge

PIANO BARS/LOUNGES | Head to the Silverton's frontier-theme, salt-of-the-earth casino (or its sensational, museumlike hunting-fishing Bass Pro Shop), where it's well worth stopping by for a drink and taking a long look at the gigantic, sharks 'n' all aquarium. The tanks hold 117,000 gallons of water and are home to more than 4,000 fish and a handful of mermaids (yes, really). ✉ *Silverton Hotel & Casino, 3333 Blue Diamond Rd., South Las Vegas* ☎ *702/263–7777* ⊕ *silvertoncasino.com.*

Minus5 Ice Bar

PIANO BARS/LOUNGES | Did you ever think you'd be wearing a winter parka in the Las Vegas desert? If not, then you've underestimated just how gimmicky these 21st-century bars can be. Don the parka provided by Minus5, pay attention to your orientation speech, buy those drink tickets, and step into the Ice Bar, where the temperature is always 5 below zero Celsius (23 Fahrenheit). This frosty clime ensures that you'll have a "cool" time here, but it also keeps the walls, bar, cocktail glasses, chairs, couches, and decorative sculpture in their frozen-solid state. Expensive fun for the sheer weirdness of it? Definitely! The drinks are tasty, too. Additional locations are at *The Venetian (3355 Las Vegas Blvd. S) and LINQ Promenade (3545 Las Vegas Blvd. S).* ✉ *The Shoppes at Mandalay Place, 3930 Las Vegas Blvd. S, South Strip* ☎ *702/632–7714* ⊕ *www.minus5experience.com.*

Press

PIANO BARS/LOUNGES | The very swanky but very inviting Press features fire pits with seating overlooking the private pool at the Four Seasons, cooled off by misters in the hotter months. Like everything at the upscale resort, the libations and accompanying bites (mmm, flatbreads) are near perfection. Free high-speed Internet, 12 charging docks, and access to 2,000 digital newspapers and magazines from 100 countries in 56 languages highlight the complimentary services at this lobby bar that doubles as a coffee shop by day. ✉ *Four Seasons Hotel Las Vegas, 3960 Las Vegas Blvd. S, South Strip* ☎ *702/632–5000* ⊕ *www.fourseasons.com/lasvegas/dining/lounges/press.*

Skyfall Lounge

PIANO BARS/LOUNGES | Head up to the 64th floor of the Delano for the 180-degree views of the city inside Skyfall Lounge. Everything up here is higher, including the prices for craft cocktails. Around sunset the crowds can become unbearable but later in the evening, when live DJs play tunes, the vibe is chill. Be sure to step into the bathrooms for a different view of the city while you relieve yourself. ✉ *Delano Las Vegas, 3940 Las Vegas Blvd. S, South Strip* ☎ *877/632–5400* ⊕ *www.delanolasvegas.com/en/nightlife/skyfall-lounge.html.*

You can have a particularly cold drink in the middle of the desert at Minus5 Ice Bar at The Shoppes at Mandalay Place.

COMEDY CLUBS

Brad Garrett's Comedy Club

COMEDY CLUBS | Brad Garrett, he of *Everybody Loves Raymond* and *Single Parents* fame, has returned to his stand-up roots in a classic comedy-club setting—a bar with plenty of photos of … Brad Garrett on the walls. He handpicks the comedians and headlines almost monthly himself: "It was either this or *Jews on Ice* at the Stratosphere," he likes to tell audiences. There's usually a hefty cover charge of at least $75. ✉ *MGM Grand, 3799 Las Vegas Blvd. S, South Strip* ☎ *866/740–7711* ⊕ *www.bradgarrettcomedy.com.*

DANCE CLUBS AND NIGHTCLUBS

Vegas dance clubs come in three basic flavors—up-to-the-moment trendy (such as Marquee and Omnia), established classic (Tao and XS), and fun for the great unwashed masses (*ahem*, Chateau). The usual Catch-22 of nightlife applies: the more "in" the place, the harder it is to get in and the more oppressively crowded and noisy it'll be once you do. Cover charges have crept into the $20 to $40 range—and don't be surprised to find that, even in these enlightened times, men pay higher cover charges than women. Although the level of capital investment gives these clubs a longevity their New York counterparts don't enjoy, dance clubs are still by nature a fickle, fleeting enterprise, so check with more frequently updated sources (such as the Fodor's website as well as local periodicals) to ensure they're still hot.

★ Hakkasan

DANCE CLUBS | The 80,000-square-foot Vegas haunt is one of the latest iterations of the nightclub brand that started in London. The space is one part nightclub, one part modern Cantonese restaurant—five floors in all with three dedicated to nightlife. To fill this space, the venue has booked some of the biggest DJs in the world, including Lil' Jon, Calvin Harris, Steve Aoki, and Tiësto. For a more casual experience, head to the third-level Ling Ling Club. ✉ *MGM Grand Hotel & Casino, 3799 Las Vegas Blvd. S, South Strip*

☎ *702/891–3838* ⊕ *hakkasannightclub. com* ☻ *Closed Mon.–Wed.*

Light Nightclub

DANCE CLUBS | Combining the acrobatics of co-creators Cirque du Soleil with a nightclub environment gives this hot spot an element of theatrics. State-of-the-art lighting, sound, and special effects give this DJ-driven nightclub the upper hand. The aerialists floating over the masses tip it over the edge. Even if you're not ordering bottle service, the video screens behind the DJ booth will wow. ⊠ *Mandalay Bay, 3950 Las Vegas Blvd. S, South Strip* ☎ *702/693–8300* ⊕ *thelightvegas.com.*

★ On the Record

DANCE CLUBS | As the name suggests, the nightclub at Park MGM is all about sound. Sure, the brainchild of L.A.'s Houston brothers brings in live DJs every night. But it also offers three hidden karaoke rooms, as well as a hidden vinyl bar in the middle of the club. Perhaps the coolest detail is the hallway lined with cassette tapes. Don't miss the double-decker bus in the open-air courtyard either; it's like nothing at any other club in town. On the Record is open Wednesday, Friday, and Saturday nights. ⊠ *Park MGM, 3770 S. Las Vegas Blvd., South Strip* ☎ *702/730–6773* ⊕ *www.parkmgm. com/en/nightlife/on-the-record.html.*

Stoney's Rockin' Country

DANCE CLUBS | What do you get when you fill a country-theme Texas saloon with slick dance-music-crazed nightclubbers? Madness—10-gallon-hat madness. Behind the Texas-shape neon sign, Stoney's Rockin' Country has all the glam hot-spot fixings: one of the largest dance floors in Nevada, private tables, a VIP lounge, bottle service, and music that can segue from Merle Haggard to Jay-Z. You can't beat the prices either. The location in Town Square makes the club convenient to visit from casinos on the Strip. ⊠ *Town Square, 6611 Las Vegas Blvd. S, South Las Vegas* ☎ *702/435–2855* ⊕ *stoneysrockincountry. com* ☻ *Closed Sun.–Wed.*

IRISH PUBS

Nine Fine Irishmen

BARS/PUBS | Don't be surprised to see patrons break into impromptu bouts of step-dancing at this authentic Irish pub inside New York–New York. It's so authentic that the place was built in Ireland, shipped over, and reassembled in Vegas. Today, barkeeps pour Guinness, Harp Lager, Killian's Red, and all sorts of Irish whiskeys, while cooks crank out Irish food and traditional Irish breakfast all day long. Live Irish music rounds out the toe-tapping sing-along entertainment here. UFC closed-circuit live-viewing events are scheduled regularly. A happy hour runs from 2 to 5 pm weekdays, and live entertainment begins nightly at 9. Go before then if you want a table for dinner. ⊠ *New York–New York, 3790 Las Vegas Blvd. S, South Strip* ☎ *866/815–4365* ⊕ *www. mgmresorts.com/en/restaurants/new-york-new-york/nine-fine-irishmen.html.*

Rí Rá Irish Pub

BARS/PUBS | Like the Statue of Liberty, this pub was constructed in Europe, then shipped over piecemeal and reassembled in The Shoppes at Mandalay Place (yes, Lady Liberty is in New York; you know what we mean). Highlights include the music—which regularly comprises Irish sessions—and the menu, which boasts enough sausage rolls and fish-and-chips to make you feel like you've flown to Dublin. Another authentic touch: Most of the wait staff are from Ireland. ⊠ *The Shoppes at Mandalay Place, 3930 Las Vegas Blvd. S, South Strip* ☎ *702/632–7771* ⊕ *www.rira.com.*

LIVE MUSIC

Small, medium, or large? From bohemian indie-band showcases and kooky kitschy lounges to big concert halls—and *then* on to truly *gargantuan* venues like the new T-Mobile Arena, The Smith Center for the Performing Arts, the Park Theater, and the MGM Grand Garden Arena— Vegas is a world capital of live music. The trick, as always with local nightlife, is to check current news listings for performers, showtimes, and locations. (Why locations? Because even certain hot spots not ordinarily given over to live music—Drai's Nightclub, for example—will host concerts when you least expect it.) And, of course, the Vegas lounge act has come a long way. Nearly every big Strip resort features a high-energy dance band that expertly performs hits from the '60s to today's hottest tunes.

★ House of Blues

MUSIC CLUBS | This nightclub–concert hall hybrid at Mandalay Bay was the seventh entry in this chain of successful, intimate music clubs. As if the electric roster of performers taking the stage almost nightly wasn't enough (past acts include Carlos Santana, Billy Idol, Social Distortion, Joe Walsh, Slash, the Dropkick Murphys, and Seal), the decor is lusciously imaginative. (Our favorite decoration isn't inside, though—it's the Voodoo Mama statue greeting you outside.) The Gospel Brunch on Sunday has great live music and is worth a visit. Also, buy music, books, hot sauce, and T-shirts at the souvenir shop, where an expansive, remarkable collection of colorful folk art decorates the walls. ⊠ *Mandalay Bay, 3950 Las Vegas Blvd. S, South Strip* ☎ *702/632–7600* ⊕ *www.houseofblues.com.*

LOCALS HANGOUTS

Blue Martini Lounge

PIANO BARS/LOUNGES | It's in a shopping mall eight minutes from the Strip (by taxi), but we won't hold that against the Blue Martini, because it's still pretty cool. The cream of local bands plays here nightly, an attractive blue interior curves from room to room, and the cocktail menu is impressive (the signature martinis are served in the shaker). Also, there's a legendary happy hour. Best of all, hordes of the kind of people you'll want to meet (that is, sexy nontourists of all genders) keep pouring in. ⊠ *Town Square, 6593 Las Vegas Blvd. S, South Las Vegas* ☎ *702/949–2583* ⊕ *lasvegas.bluemartinilounge.com.*

🛍 Shopping

FOOD AND DRINK

★ Eataly Las Vegas at Park MGM

FOOD/CANDY | Take some time to "eat, shop and learn" (their tagline/motto) at this vast Italian marketplace, an Italian grocery and food hall that occupies the main entrance to Park MGM. What are you eating, shopping, and learning about? High-quality Italian food in an immersive simulation of a trip to that famous boot on the map. A 12-seat Chef's Table allows guests to pay for a dining and learning experience from some of the Eataly great Italian chefs. Perhaps the highlight of the experience is a modest gift shop and extensive market that sells a variety of goods imported straight from the motherland. But visitors may be more interested in the Cucina del Mercato, numerous food stalls that serve everything from wine and cheese to meats, pizza, pasta, gelato, and Italian pastries. Other highlights, mi amore? Eyeball a replica of the famous bull mosaic in Milan (said to bestow good luck); drink wine poured "on tap"; sample the goodies at the Nutella counter (serving crepes, cookies, and croissants); and even purchase souvenir poker chips (sporting symbols of espresso, gelato, pizza, and Parmigiano Reggiano). ⊠ *Park MGM, 3770 Las Vegas Blvd. S, South Strip* ☎ *702/730–7617* ⊕ *www.eataly. com/us_en/stores/las-vegas.*

M&M's World

FOOD/CANDY | FAMILY | Every day till midnight, all manner of M&M's merchandise is sold here—a slot machine that dispenses M&M's jackpots is a best seller—and the popular candy may be purchased by the pound. Four air-conditioned levels of colorful, milk-chocolate goodies attract crowds of families with children (and strollers). Those who use the personalized printing machine can create and print custom messages on M&M's, or select from unique Las Vegas images (the "Welcome to Las

Las Vegas has its first Eataly Italian marketplace filled with both Italian products and restaurants, including Manzo, which is devoted to roasted meats.

Vegas" sign or a deck of cards). NASCAR champion Kyle Busch hails from Las Vegas, and a full-size reproduction of his M&M's-sponsored #18 racing Toyota Camry is on display (floor 4) along with racing merchandise. About every half hour, the short 3-D movie *I Lost My M in Vegas* (G-rated, free), starring spokescandies Red and Yellow, is screened on floor 3 until 6 pm. ⊠ *Showcase Mall, 3785 Las Vegas Blvd. S, next to MGM Grand, South Strip* ☎ *702/740–2504* ⊕ *www.mymms.com/category/store-locations/las-vegas.do.*

GIFTS AND SOUVENIRS
Guinness Store
GIFTS/SOUVENIRS | The only Guinness Store in the United States features all things that go with the dark Irish beer. Have etched Guinness glasses personalized while you restock your bar with coasters, bar mats, and an essential authentic pouring spoon for making a perfect black and tan. The store was renovated in 2017 and now offers a tasting bar where visitors can sample brews or pay $20 to learn the six steps to pouring the perfect pint. ⊠ *The Shoppes at Mandalay Place, 3930 Las Vegas Blvd. S, South Strip* ☎ *702/632–7773* ⊕ *www.guinness.com/en-us/home.html.*

MALLS
The Shoppes at Mandalay Place
SHOPPING CENTERS/MALLS | Request the savings booklet at the north end of this sky-bridge mall, which spans the gap between Mandalay Bay and the Luxor, to receive immediate discounts at 40 shops and eateries. As you stroll from store to store, you can look at the most extensive collection of Guinness merchandise outside Ireland at the Guinness Store, or pick up clothing and accessories made from bamboo at Cariloha. Beauty fans will love the all-natural Lush with its "cosmetic deli." You can also buy new sandals at Flip Flop Shops or surf gear at Ron Jon Surf Shop. ⊠ *Mandalay Bay, 3930 Las Vegas Blvd. S, South Strip* ☎ *702/632–4760* ⊕ *www.mandalaybay.com/en/amenities/the-shoppes-at-mandalay-bay-place.html.*

Where to Refuel

If you're on a shopping mission on the Strip, keep your strength up at one of these delicious pit stops.

Malls on the Strip

Bellagio: Spago

Caesars Palace: Mesa Grill

Fashion Show: Stripburger

The Forum Shops at Caesars: Sushi Roku, The Palm

Paris Las Vegas: Mon Ami Gabi

Planet Hollywood Resort & Casino: Gordon Ramsay BURGR

The Venetian: Sushisamba

Outlet Malls

Fashion Outlets of Las Vegas: Alex's Mexican Food Factory

Las Vegas North Premium Outlets: The Cheesecake Factory

Town Square: California Pizza Kitchen or Capriotti's Sandwich Shop

Showcase Mall

SHOPPING CENTERS/MALLS | FAMILY | "Mall" is a bit of a misnomer here, where stores are more like highly evolved interactive marketing concepts. First off, there's M&M's World, the four-story homage to the popular candy, where huge dispensers with every color and type line one wall. More sugar awaits you at the Coca-Cola Store, where $8 buys either the Around the World sampler of 16 colorful, international soda flavors or eight flavors of floats. Be sure to get a photo of the 100-foot bottle of Coca-Cola outside. Branded apparel, accessories, and interesting collectibles are also for sale. Post–sugar buzz, you can head to the Hard Rock Cafe to browse the interactive video Rock Wall or buy T-shirts, Las Vegas–branded clothing, and souvenirs. The Showcase Mall's parking structure is right next to MGM Grand; the best access is from the fifth floor, where a pedestrian bridge crosses into the mall. A less hectic option is to park at any of the surrounding hotels (MGM Grand, NY–NY, Park MGM) and walk here. ⊠ 3785 Las Vegas Blvd. S, near corner of Tropicana Ave., South Strip ☎ 702/597–3117.

Town Square

SHOPPING CENTERS/MALLS | FAMILY | Constructed to resemble Main Street America with open-air shopping and dining, this 100-acre complex contains more than 150 shops, including MAC and Sephora cosmetics, H&M, Apple, Saks Off Fifth, and Banana Republic. When you tire of shopping (or the kids do, anyway), there's also a children's play area, multiplex cinema, and rides on the Town Square train. Lazy Dog lets you bring Fido on the patio, while Yard House brings pub fare. There's also a Capriotti's, Tommy Bahama's, and several other on-site eateries, including a Whole Foods Market. Stoney's Rockin' Country dance and live-music venue fires up the country tunes Thursday through Saturday. ■TIP→ Need to make a quick stop? Town Square offers curbside parking so you don't have to schlep all the way from one of three parking garages to your shopping destination. ⊠ 6605 Las Vegas Blvd. S, at junction of I–15 and I–215 Beltway, Airport ☎ 702/269–5000 ⊕ www. mytownsquarelasvegas.com.

🏃 Activities

GOLF

★ Bali Hai Golf Club

GOLF | This island-theme course is dotted with palm trees, volcanic outcroppings, and small lagoons. The entrance is a mere 10-minute walk from Mandalay Bay, and the course touts that it's less than 1,000 steps from the Strip itself. The clubhouse includes a pro shop and restaurant. Online specials can cut rates in half. ✉ *5160 Las Vegas Blvd. S, South Strip* ☏ *888/427–6678, 702/450–8191* ⊕ *www.balihaigolfclub.com* 🖃 *From $199 for nonresidents* 🏌 *18 holes, 7002 yards, par 71.*

★ Topgolf Las Vegas

GOLF | Sin City's newest driving range takes golf to another level. Situated on the back side of the MGM Grand, this three-story outpost of the national chain has 108 climate-controlled bays, all of which offer food and beverage service and TVs, just like a sports bar. State-of-the-art technology tracks each ball and gives an immediate distance reading on monitors so you can compare with your friends. Five bars make the vibe lively even when nobody's golfing. There are also two pools, in case you decide you want to take a dip. ✉ *MGM Grand, 4627 Koval La., South Strip* ☏ *702/933–8458* ⊕ *www.topgolf.com* 🖃 *From $30 per hr (up to 6 players).*

HOCKEY

Las Vegas Golden Knights

HOCKEY | Las Vegas's first professional sports team became a cult sensation overnight when the Golden Knights made it to the Stanley Cup Finals in their inaugural year. The team, owned by wine magnate Bill Foley, plays at T-Mobile Arena, a state-of-the-art facility at the west end of The Park between New York–New York and Park MGM. Tickets are hard to come by but standing-room spots are usually available on the day of game.

✉ *T-Mobile Arena, 3780 Las Vegas Blvd. S, South Strip* ☏ *702/692–1600* ⊕ *www.nhl.com/goldenknights.*

SPAS

Bathhouse Spa

FITNESS/HEALTH CLUBS | Dark slate and suede-covered walls wrap this modern and sexy boutique spa at the Delano. The 16,000-square-foot spa features 12 treatment rooms and a nightclub-like scene, but with the thump, thump, thumping music replaced with the serene melody of water trickling. Baths are a specialty, with treatments such as the Moor mud bath that beautifies and soothes arthritis, respiratory issues, and more; and the signature fizz bath, which bubbles with fragrances that turn into essential oils. ✉ *Delano, 3940 Las Vegas Blvd. S, South Strip* ☏ *877/632–9636* ⊕ *www.delanolasvegas.com/en/amenities/bathhouse-spa.html.*

Grand Spa & Fitness Center

FITNESS/HEALTH CLUBS | Though this well-managed spa lacks the stunning architecture of other Strip spas, it makes up for it with accommodating attendants and a serene, feng shui–designed atmosphere. The World Therapies menu features creative treatments, including the Dreaming Ritual inspired by Aboriginal culture in Australia, and the Moroccan Hydration Ritual that combines exfoliation with a moisture treatment applied with hot stones. Too adventurous? Detox your hangover with the Morning Latte, an exfoliating scrub with coffee, or the Citrus Splash with salt grains. A salon also offers blow-out services. ■ **TIP→ Spa services are available to nonguests Monday through Thursday only.** ✉ *MGM Grand, 3799 Las Vegas Blvd. S, South Strip* ☏ *702/891–3077* ⊕ *www.mgmgrand.com/en/amenities/grand-spa-fitness-center.html.*

Nurture Spa

FITNESS/HEALTH CLUBS | Perhaps one of the most accessible spas on the Strip, Nurture Spa features a bright and airy setting giving it an inviting, earthy feel. Try one of the signature treatments such as the peppermint foot and leg therapy to recuperate from a long day of walking the Strip or the sugar scrub, a 20- or 50-minute treatment that nourishes skin all over your body. Massage therapists also offer a special treatment for pregnant moms. Open 24/7. ⊠ *Luxor Las Vegas, 3900 Las Vegas Blvd. S, South Strip* ☎ *800/258–9308* ⊕ *www.luxor.com/ en/amenities/nurture-spa.html.*

Spa Mandalay

FITNESS/HEALTH CLUBS | Modeled after Turkish-style baths, the hot, warm, and cold plunges at this spa are surrounded by marble, fountains, and plenty of places to lounge. Try the Aromatherapy Massage, which uses essential oils and Swedish massage techniques, or the Foot Focus that uses reflexology on legs and tired feet. The spa offers what may be the only hot-stone pedicure in town. If you're spending multiple nights at the resort, consider the three-, or five-day spa pass, which are much cheaper than buying individual passes each day. ⊠ *Mandalay Bay, 3950 Las Vegas Blvd. S, South Strip* ☎ *877/632–7300* ⊕ *www.mandalaybay. com/en/amenities/spas.html.*

CENTER STRIP

4

Updated by
Steven Bornfeld

👁 **Sights**
★★★★★

🍴 **Restaurants**
★★★★★

🛏 **Hotels**
★★★★★

🛍 **Shopping**
★★★★★

🍸 **Nightlife**
★★★★★

NEIGHBORHOOD SNAPSHOT

TOP EXPERIENCES

■ **Bellagio Conservatory & Botanical Garden:**
Visited by 6 million people a year, the garden
celebrates the partnership of man and nature.

■ **Caesars Palace:** The landmark continues to deliver
cutting-edge dining, shopping, and gaming
experiences.

■ **The Cosmopolitan of Las Vegas:** This trendy Strip
hotel makes an art form of balancing naughty and
nice.

■ **Fountains at Bellagio:** The fountains are world-
famous for their mesmerizing dancing aquatics
synchronized to music.

■ **High Roller:** For a true eagle's-eye view of the Strip
take a gentle and scenic 30-minute ride.

GETTING HERE

Expect heavy traffic, both vehicle and pedestrian.
There's a major bottleneck at the Fountains of Bellagio, especially on weekend evenings. One way to
avoid these backups is to take the free Aria Express
Tram connecting the Park MGM (in the South Strip)
with ARIA, Vdara, The Shops at Crystals, and Bellagio
(all in the Center Strip). Taxis take anywhere from 20
to 25 minutes to the airport, and 10 to 15 minutes to
get to other parts of town.

Las Vegas Monorail stations here include the Bally's/
Paris station, Flamingo/Caesars Palace station, and
farthest north, the Harrah's/LINQ station. RTC
services this part of the Strip with public buses and
double-deckers.

PLANNING YOUR TIME

The Center Strip really is in the middle of the action,
with Las Vegas icons like Caesars Palace and Bellagio sharing the crowds with the newer Cosmopolitan
of Las Vegas and the various attractions at CityCenter. Give yourself at minimum a half-day to explore it
on foot, the most effective way.

QUICK BITES

■ **Block 16 Urban Food
Hall.** Offering a variety of
eclectic tastes, you can have
Hattie B's Hot Chicken from
Nashville, or Lardo and Pok
Pok Wing from Portland.
⊠ *The Cosmopolitan of Las
Vegas, 3708 Las Vegas Blvd.
S* ⊕ *www.cosmopolitanlas-
vegas.com.*

■ **La Creperie.** For a
delectable taste of Parisian
street food, stop by this
window, where you can
get breakfast, lunch, and
dinner crepes, either sweet
or savory (with ice cream,
if you like). ⊠ *Paris Las
Vegas, 3655 Las Vegas Blvd.
S* ⊕ *www.caesars.com/
paris-las-vegas.*

■ **Sprinkles Cupcake.**
Here's a great place to get
yourself a sweet treat,
sandwiched around ice
cream, if you like. And the
cupcake ATM is available
24/7. ⊠ *The LINQ Prom-
enade, 3535 Las Vegas Blvd.
S* ⊕ *sprinkles.com.*

It's fitting that this part of the Strip comprises the heart of today's Las Vegas. It is, quite literally, where modern Vegas was born.

It began with the Flamingo more than 70 years ago. The Mirage ushered in the age of the modern megaresort in the late 1980s. That renaissance gained momentum with Bellagio and snowballed from there. Today the stretch includes other classics such as Caesars Palace and Bally's, as well as thematic wonders such as Paris and Planet Hollywood. The centerpiece is, fittingly, CityCenter, a city-within-the-city that includes everything from public art to apartment-style living and more. Then, of course, there's the relative new kid on the block: the uber-hip Cosmopolitan of Las Vegas.

There's no shortage of spectacles in this part of town. From the fountains in front of ARIA and Bellagio to the Eiffel Tower at Paris and the volcano in front of The Mirage, the Center Strip truly is a feast for the eyes. Art is on display here as well; CityCenter has a $42-million public art collection for visitors to enjoy, and Bellagio has one of the most highly regarded galleries in town. Another popular pastime: shopping. A day of exploration here should include strolls through vast retail destinations such as Crystals, Miracle Mile, and The Forum Shops—all of which offer some of the finest boutiques and shops in the United States.

No visit to the Center Strip would be complete without a little pool time. For an intimate vibe, check out The Cosmopolitan's eighth-floor pool deck that looks down on the Strip, which turns into a skating rink and winter wonderland during the chilly months. To live like royalty, check out the seven-pool Garden of the Gods Pool Oasis at Caesars Palace. Reclining on a lounger, soaking up the sun, you'll be experiencing Vegas the way countless others have over the years. The more things change, apparently, the more they stay the same.

◉ Sights

ARIA Resort & Casino

RESORT—SIGHT | Glistening like a futuristic oasis in the heart of the Strip, ARIA is a modern spin on the Las Vegas casino of old. Its soaring, three-story atrium is bathed in natural light (a novel concept in this town). The casino has windows, too. Many onlookers come to marvel at the artwork in the atrium, including Maya Lin's *Silver River*, an 84-foot sculpture of reclaimed silver that mirrors the route of the Colorado River and hangs in the lobby behind the check-in desk. Much like the gardens at properties such as Bellagio and Wynn, the floral arrangements here change with the seasons. Other remarkable attractions include restaurant offerings on the mezzanine, as well as the design of the high-limit rooms, which are masked from the rest of the casino by opaque stained glass. ARIA remains one of the largest buildings in the world to achieve LEED Gold certification from the U.S. Green Building Council. ✉ *3730 Las Vegas Blvd. S, City Center* ☎ *866/359-7757* ⊕ *www.aria.com.*

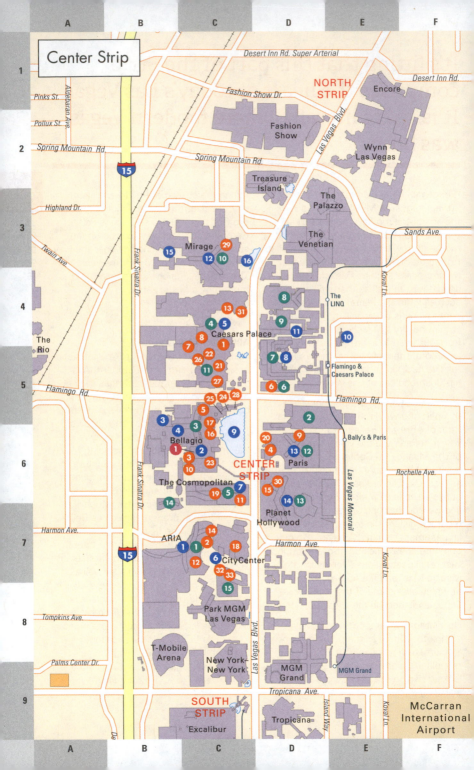

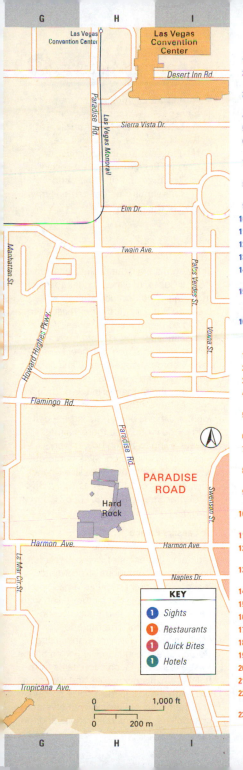

Sights ▼

1 ARIA Resort & Casino... **C7**
2 Bellagio Conservatory and Botanical Gardens....... **C6**
3 Bellagio Gallery of Fine Art.................. **B5**
4 Bellagio Las Vegas **B6**
5 Caesars Palace **C4**
6 CityCenter Fine Art Collection............. **C7**
7 The Cosmopolitan of Las Vegas................. **C6**
8 Flamingo Wildlife Habitat **D5**
9 Fountains of Bellagio.... **C6**
10 High Roller................ **E4**
11 LINQ Promenade **D4**
12 Mirage Las Vegas **C3**
13 Paris Las Vegas **D6**
14 Planet Hollywood Resort & Casino......... **D6**
15 Siegfried & Roy's Secret Garden & Dolphin Habitat **B3**
16 Volcano at Mirage...... **C3**

Restaurants ▼

1 Amalfi by Bobby Flay.... **C5**
2 Bardot Brasserie **C7**
3 Bellagio Patisserie **C6**
4 Eiffel Tower Restaurant.............. **D6**
5 FIX Restaurant & Bar..................... **C5**
6 Giada.................... **D5**
7 Gordon Ramsay Hell's Kitchen............. **C5**
8 Gordon Ramsay Pub & Grill **C4**
9 Gordon Ramsay Steak **D6**
10 Harvest by Roy Ellamar............... **C6**
11 Jaleo **C6**
12 Jean-Georges Steakhouse at ARIA..... **C7**
13 Joe's Seafood, Prime Steak & Stone Crab **C4**
14 Julian Serrano Tapas.... **C7**
15 Koi Las Vegas **D6**
16 Lago **C6**
17 Le Cirque................. **C5**
18 Mastro's Ocean Club.... **C7**
19 Momofuku Las Vegas **C6**
20 Mon Ami Gabi.......... **D6**
21 Mr Chow................. **C5**
22 Nobu Restaurant Las Vegas................ **C5**
23 Petrossian Bar **C6**
24 Picasso **C5**
25 Prime Steakhouse **C5**
26 Rao's **C5**
27 Restaurant Guy Savoy .. **C5**
28 Spago by Wolfgang Puck.......... **C5**
29 Stack Restaurant and Bar **C3**
30 Strip House **D6**
31 Sushi Roku............... **C4**
32 Tea Lounge at the Waldorf Astoria **C7**
33 Twist by Pierre Gagnaire................. **C7**

Quick Bites ▼

1 Bellagio Patisserie **C6**

Hotels ▼

1 ARIA Resort & Casino... **C7**
2 Bally's Las Vegas Hotel & Casino **D5**
3 Bellagio Las Vegas **C6**
4 Caesars Palace **C4**
5 The Cosmopolitan of Las Vegas.............. **C6**
6 The Cromwell Hotel & Casino **D5**
7 Flamingo Las Vegas **D5**
8 Harrah's Las Vegas Hotel & Casino **D4**
9 The LINQ Hotel & Casino **D4**
10 Mirage Las Vegas **C3**
11 Nobu Hotel at Caesars Palace **C5**
12 Paris Las Vegas......... **D6**
13 Planet Hollywood Las Vegas Resort & Casino......... **D6**
14 Vdara Hotel & Spa at ARIA Las Vegas................ **B7**
15 Waldorf Astoria Las Vegas **C8**

★ Bellagio Conservatory and Botanical Gardens

GARDEN | FAMILY | The flowers, trees, and other plants in Bellagio's soaring atrium are fresh and alive, many of them grown in a 5-acre greenhouse. The artistic floral arrangements and ornamental landscaping here is breathtaking and in some cases monumental in scale. Displays change each season, and the holiday displays in December (for Christmas) and January (for Chinese New Year) are particularly dramatic. ⊠ *Bellagio Las Vegas, 3600 Las Vegas Blvd. S, Center Strip* ☎ *702/693–7111, 888/987–6667* ⊕ *www. bellagio.com/attractions* ⊠ *Free.*

★ Bellagio Gallery of Fine Art

MUSEUM | This gallery—one of the last of its kind inside Strip hotels—originally was curated from Bellagio founder Steve Wynn's private collection. Today, with Wynn long gone, the gallery operates independently, bringing in an average of two traveling exhibits each year from some of the most famous art museums in the world. Shows have featured works by Picasso, Fabergé, and Warhol. A new feature is the adjacent Artist Studio, where guests can interact with the artist in residence to discuss their art and observe the creation of it. ⊠ *Bellagio Las Vegas, 3600 Las Vegas Blvd. S, Center Strip* ☎ *702/693–7871, 888/488–7111* ⊕ *www.bellagio.com/attractions* ⊠ *$15.*

★ Bellagio Las Vegas

RESORT—SIGHT | Sightseers come to Bellagio for three main reasons: the fountains out front, the Dale Chihuly installation of glass flowers in the lobby, and the conservatory gardens. Any one of these attractions is worth the trip. All three make the casino resort a must-see. The fountains are a spectacle in and of themselves: 1,200 jets in all, streaming and bursting in a choreographed water ballet across the man-made Bellagio lake. The conservatory gardens are particularly stunning during Christmas and Chinese New Year. The glass flowers are pretty

Cooling Misters 👁

Numerous casinos and restaurants have public water misters. Our favorites: outside Mon Ami Gabi at Paris Las Vegas, at Spanish Steps, the frozen-margarita bar outside Caesars Palace (northwest corner of Flamingo and the Strip); and various shops outside Fashion Show mall in the North Strip.

amazing, as well; the sculpture is named Fiori di Como, and it continues to inspire more than two decades after it was created. But there are other reasons to spend some time at Las Vegas's first real destination resort. For starters, with restaurants from Michael Mina, Jean-Georges Vongerichten, and Julian Serrano, Bellagio still has one of the best restaurant rosters in town. Then, of course, there's the patisserie's chocolate fountain; this is one of the largest of its kind in the world, and there's almost always a line to watch how it works. Finally, the Bellagio contains numerous luxe boutiques with names like Chanel, Dior, and Gucci. ⊠ *3600 Las Vegas Blvd. S, Center Strip* ☎ *888/987–6667* ⊕ *www. bellagio.com.*

★ Caesars Palace

RESORT—SIGHT | The opulent entrance, fountains, Roman statuary, bas-reliefs, and roaming centurions all add up to the iconic, over-the-top Las Vegas hotel. Here you can get your picture taken with Caesar, Cleopatra, and the centurion guard; find the full-size reproduction of Michelangelo's *David*; or amble along Roman streetscapes in The Forum Shops to see replicas of iconic fountains from Italy. Vegas history is alive and well here, too, with the iconic main porte cochere and the old-school casino with crystal chandeliers. Several renovations and the

Did You Know?

The Center Strip is still the heart of Las Vegas, where you'll find classics like Caesars Palace and The Mirage, as well as newer developments like CityCenter and The LINQ (and its popular LINQ Promenade).

THE MIRAGE

CASINO & RESORT

Learn more at mlife.com/MasterCard

THE VOICE ENTERTAINMENT
TERRY FATOR

THE FORUM SHOPS

THE LINQ

Bigger than the London Eye, the High Roller offers visitors some of the best views of the city.

addition of Nobu Hotel have ensured the resort remains current. Shopping here at The Forum Shops is among the best in the city. The hotel's pool complex, dubbed Garden of the Gods Pool Oasis, is arguably the nicest set-up on the Strip. ✉ *3570 Las Vegas Blvd. S, Center Strip* ☎ *866/227–5938* ⊕ *www.caesars.com.*

CityCenter Fine Art Collection

MUSEUM | CityCenter includes $42 million in public art. Pieces range from sculptures to paintings and elaborate fountains. Our favorite: *Big Edge,* an amalgam of kayaks and canoes by Nancy Rubins. ✉ *CityCenter, Las Vegas Blvd. S, Center Strip* ⊕ *www.aria.com.*

The Cosmopolitan of Las Vegas

RESORT—SIGHT | The Cosmopolitan is a truly different Las Vegas resort experience—a blend of arty sophistication and comfortable elegance. This is evidenced by the digital artwork on the columns near the registration desk, as well as the vending machines with wood-block paintings from local artists. Don't miss The Chandelier, a three-story bar that, as the name suggests, sits inside a giant crystal concoction. The property mixologist is an expert in crafted cocktails and comes out with a brand-new menu for the bar seasonally. Elsewhere on the property, hipsters love Marquee nightclub and dayclub. A slate of restaurants includes offerings from José Andrés (Jaleo, China Poblano) and Bruce and Eric Bromberg (Blue Ribbon). There's also a Momofuku and a Milk Bar, both of which have cult followings from across the country. Plus, there's Chef David Chang helming Bang Bar, a quick spot to grab freshly griddled flatbread sandwiches and rice bowls. Shopping at The Cosmopolitan also is second to none. One-of-a-kind boutiques include Stitched (men's clothes), Retrospecs & Co. (eyewear), and CRSVR (sneakers). ✉ *3708 Las Vegas Blvd. S, Center Strip* ☎ *702/698–7000* ⊕ *www.cosmopolitanlasvegas.com.*

Flamingo Wildlife Habitat

ZOO | **FAMILY** | Just next to the pool area at Flamingo Las Vegas, a flamboyance of live Chilean flamingos lives on islands and in streams surrounded by sparkling waterfalls and lush foliage. Other animals on-site include swans, ducks, koi, goldfish, pelicans, hummingbirds, and turtles. The small habitat makes for a fun, brief stroll. Be sure not to miss the daily pelican feedings at 11:30 and 2. ⊠ *3555 Las Vegas Blvd. S, Center Strip* ☎ *702/733–3349* ⊕ *www.flamingolasvegas.com* ⊠ *Free.*

★ Fountains of Bellagio

FOUNTAIN | At least once on your visit you should stop in front of Bellagio to view its spectacular water ballet from start to finish. The dazzling fountains stream from more than 1,000 nozzles, accompanied by 4,500 lights, in 27 million gallons of water. Fountain jets shoot 250 feet in the air, tracing undulations you wouldn't have thought possible, in near-perfect time with music ranging from Bocelli and the Beatles to "Billie Jean" and tunes from Tiësto. Some of the best views are from the Eiffel Tower's observation deck, directly across the street (unless you've got a north-facing balcony room at The Cosmopolitan). Paris and Planet Hollywood have restaurants with patios on the Strip that also offer good views. ⊠ *Bellagio, 3600 Las Vegas Blvd. S, Center Strip* ☎ *888/987–6667, 702/693–7111* ⊕ *www.bellagio.com/attractions.*

High Roller

LOCAL INTEREST | Standing more than 100 feet taller than the London Eye, the High Roller opened in 2014 as the largest observation wheel in the world. The giant Ferris wheel at the east end of the LINQ features 28 glass-enclosed cabins, each of which is equipped to hold up to 40 passengers. One full rotation takes about 30 minutes; along the way, riders are treated to a dynamic video and music show on TV monitors in the pod, as well as one-of-a-kind views of Sin City and the surrounding Las Vegas Valley. The experience begins and ends in a state-of-the-art wheelhouse, where visitors can read about the engineering behind the project as they wait in line, buy drinks to take with them on the ride,

or pick up souvenirs commemorating the spin. The best time to ride the wheel is nighttime, when 2,000 LED lights on the wheel itself create an otherworldly vibe. ⊠ *3545 Las Vegas Blvd. S, Center Strip* ☎ *855/234–7469* ⊕ *www.caesars.com/linq/high-roller.html* ⊠ *From $21, depending on time of day and options.*

LINQ Promenade

STORE/MALL | **FAMILY** | Yes, the name is confusing, but the LINQ Promenade, the shopping, dining, and entertainment complex between the Flamingo and the LINQ Hotel, is worth the trip. Some of the notable attractions include the two-story I Love Sugar, complete with "candy martini bar"; Purple Zebra, a bar devoted solely to frozen daiquiris; a namesake comedy club for late-night host Jimmy Kimmel (who grew up in Las Vegas); and Brooklyn Bowl, which is one-part bowling alley, one-part live music venue. Of course, there's also a new iteration of O'Shea's, the Irish-theme casino that was razed to create the new streetcape. The big draw, however, is the **High Roller**, a 550-foot-tall observation wheel with spectacular views of the city. ⊠ *3545 Las Vegas Blvd. S, Center Strip* ☎ *800/223–7277* ⊕ *www.caesars.com/linq.*

Mirage Las Vegas

RESORT—SIGHT | **FAMILY** | When Steve Wynn opened The Mirage in 1989, the $630-million property was the most expensive resort-casino in history; the hotel's distinctive gold windows got their color from actual gold used in the tinting process. Today the main attractions are *The Beatles: LOVE from Cirque du Soleil,* the dolphins at Siegfried & Roy's Secret Garden & Dolphin Habitat, and the volcano with breathtaking fire effects and music composed by Grateful Dead drummer Mickey Hart. Inside the casino, the sports book remains one of Vegas's finest. ⊠ *3400 Las Vegas Blvd. S, Center Strip* ☎ *702/791–1111, 800/374–9000* ⊕ *www.mirage.com.*

Great Walks: Center Strip

See the Fountains: Catch the dancing fountains outside Bellagio. Showtimes (basically) are every half hour. It's best to go at night, when the fountains are illuminated with spotlights. Total time: 20–30 minutes.

Retail Therapy: Start by circling the stores in Crystals at CityCenter, then hit the Miracle Mile Shops at Planet Hollywood. Stroll through the Grand Bazaar Shops in front of Bally's. Then, to wrap things up, cross the street and explore The Forum Shops at Caesars Palace. Total time: three hours, depending on stops and dressing-room time.

Molten Fun: The Mirage's volcano is worth a gander, but the best views are from the opposite side of the Strip. From the LINQ, head north and stop in front of the Casino Royale. It's best to go at night, when the "lava" glows like the real stuff. Total time: 25 minutes.

Paris Las Vegas

RESORT—SIGHT | FAMILY | At this homage to the City of Light, replicas of the Arc de Triomphe, Paris Opera House, Hôtel de Ville, and Louvre, along with an *Around the World in Eighty Days* balloon marquee, are *magnifique*, but the crowning achievement is the 50-story, half-scale replica of the Eiffel Tower where guests are whisked 460 feet to the top for spectacular views of the Valley. Need more near-authenticity? Look up at the ceiling painted like a sky with clouds and pretend you're actually in France. ⊠ *3655 Las Vegas Blvd. S, Center Strip* ☎ *702/946–7000, 877/796–2096* ⊕ *www.parislasvegas.com.*

Planet Hollywood Resort & Casino

RESORT—SIGHT | Everything at Planet Hollywood is designed to make ordinary people feel like stars. Perhaps the main attraction in recent years is *Criss Angel's Mindfreak*, which relocated from the Luxor in 2019. Because the property is obsessed with celebrities, it often hosts residencies like the recent one by Gwen Stefani, and world-premiere events that attract stars from all over the world. There's something for everybody in the on-site Miracle Mile Shops, including clothing stores, restaurants, and more.

Just be sure you bring a map, as the corridors of the mall wind around in circles and it's easy to get lost. ⊠ *3667 Las Vegas Blvd. S, Center Strip* ☎ *702/785–5555, 866/919–7472* ⊕ *www.planethollywoodresort.com.*

Siegfried & Roy's Secret Garden & Dolphin Habitat

ZOO | FAMILY | The palm-shaded sanctuary has a collection of the planet's rarest and most exotic creatures. Animals are rotated regularly, but at any time you're likely to see white tigers, as well as lions, a snow leopard, and more. Atlantic bottlenose dolphins swim around in a 2.5-million-gallon saltwater tank at the Dolphin Habitat. Pass through the underwater observation station to the video room, where you can watch tapes of two dolphin births at the habitat. In addition to the regular admission, there are VIP edu-tours as well as a paint-with-the-dolphins experience, and a deluxe trainer-for-a-day program. ⊠ *Mirage Las Vegas, 3400 Las Vegas Blvd. S, Center Strip* ☎ *702/791–7111* ⊕ *www.mirage.com/attractions* ⛵ *$22.*

Volcano at Mirage

LOCAL INTEREST | This erupting volcano, a 54-foot mountain-fountain surrounded by a lake of miniature fire spouts, is a

The Mirage Volcano still erupts three times every night, as it has since the hotel opened in 1989.

must-see free attraction on the Strip. Two or three times a night the whole area erupts in flames, smoke, and eerily backlit water that looks like lava. The thundering island percussion sound track was created by Grateful Dead drummer Mickey Hart. The best vantage point is near the main drive entrance, or on the east side of Las Vegas Boulevard in front of Casino Royale. ⊠ *Mirage Las Vegas, 3400 Las Vegas Blvd. S, Center Strip* ☎ *702/791–7111* ⊕ *www.mirage.com/ attractions* ✉ *Free.*

🍴 Restaurants

Amalfi by Bobby Flay

$$$$ | ITALIAN | Chef Bobby Flay scores a new, hoped-for hotspot at Caesars Palace with his replacement for the popular Mesa Grill. With a menu emphasizing seafood (thanks to Flay's visits to Italy's Amalfi Coast), the new restaurant encourages diners to visit a "market" section near the back, where they can choose a whole fish and one of three ways to prepare it. **Known for:** fish sold by weight (which can get expensive quickly); some meat options for nonseafood lovers; Italian-inspired cocktails. $ *Average main: $50* ⊠ *Caesars Palace, 3570 Las Vegas Blvd. S, Center Strip* ☎ *702/650– 5965* ⊕ *www.caesars.com* ⊙ *No lunch.*

Bardot Brasserie

$$$$ | FRENCH | Michael Mina's stunning Belle Époque dark-wood-and-glass wonder on the mezzanine level of ARIA has, as you might expect, a decidedly French accent, and old-world glory shines in dishes such as *duck presse a l'orange* (pressed duck with orange sauce) and *loup de mer Provençal* (branzino cooked with Pastis, artichokes, and fennel). At brunch in the main restaurant, which runs into weekend afternoons, you can indulge in the complexity of pastrami-cured salmon with marble rye profiteroles, or enjoy the simple purity of the "world's best butter" on some fresh crusty bread. **Known for:** foie gras parfait; Parisian gnocchi; dayboat scallops. $ *Average main:* ⊠ *ARIA Resort & Casino, 3730 Las Vegas Blvd. S, Center Strip*

☎ 702/590–8544 ⊕ www.aria.com ⊗ No lunch. Closed Mon.–Wed.

Eiffel Tower Restaurant

$$$$ | FRENCH | This Paris Las Vegas Resort restaurant is a room with a view, all right—it's about a third of the way up the hotel's half-scale Eiffel Tower replica, with vistas from all four glassed-in sides (request a Strip view when booking for the biggest wow factor—it overlooks the fountains at Bellagio, across the street). But patrons are often pleasantly surprised that the food here measures up to the setting. **Known for:** view overlooking Bellagio fountains; fine French cuisine; caviar by the ounce. ⑤ *Average main: $60* ✉ *Paris Las Vegas, 3655 Las Vegas Blvd. S, Center Strip* ☎ *702/948–6937* ⊕ *www. eiffeltowerrestaurant.com.*

FIX Restaurant & Bar

$$$$ | AMERICAN | The ceiling, constructed almost entirely of Costa Rican padouk wood, curves like a breaking wave at this upscale comfort-food restaurant, where childhood favorites get updated twists. You'll find modern takes on grilled cheese, mac and cheese, and eggs Benedict. **Known for:** menu of fun hipster favorites; undulating wooden ceiling; late-night menu. ⑤ *Average main: $55* ✉ *Bellagio Las Vegas, 3600 Las Vegas Blvd. S, Center Strip* ☎ *702/693–8865* ⊕ *www.bellagio.com/restaurants* ⊗ *No lunch. Closed Sun.–Thurs.*

Giada

$$$$ | ITALIAN | The first restaurant from TV personality and classically trained chef Giada de Laurentiis sits on a prime piece of real estate at the intersection of the Strip and Flamingo Road. The wide expanse of floor-to-ceiling windows provide commanding views, and the food's pretty impressive, too. **Known for:** Giada's first restaurant; expansive view of Strip; huge dessert cart. ⑤ *Average main: $50* ✉ *The Cromwell, 3595 Las Vegas Blvd. S, Center Strip* ☎ *855/442–3271* ⊕ *www. caesars.com/cromwell.*

Gordon Ramsay Hell's Kitchen

$$$$ | BRITISH | Gordon Ramsay's fifth Las Vegas restaurant is a reflection of his popular Fox TV show, right down to the red and blue teams in the kitchen and TV monitors dotted around. The sprawling restaurant is a lively, noisy place where fire is a frequent motif. **Known for:** beef Wellington; lively, fiery atmosphere that evokes Ramsay himself; innovative bar menu. ⑤ *Average main: $70* ✉ *Caesars Palace, 3570 Las Vegas Blvd. S, Center Strip* ☎ *702/731–7373* ⊕ *www.caesars.com.*

Gordon Ramsay Pub & Grill

$$$$ | BRITISH | FAMILY | Three things stand out at this comfortable, casual restaurant, conceptualized by tyrannical celeb chef Gordon Ramsey: the libations, the cheery across-the-pond ambience, and the elevated British pub grub—in that order. The cocktails are strong and diverse, but it's the beer here that's to die for. **Known for:** Ramsay's pub favorites; fun, lively atmosphere; across from Coliseum. ⑤ *Average main: $40* ✉ *Caesars Palace, 3570 Las Vegas Blvd. S, Center Strip* ☎ *702/731–7410* ⊕ *www.caesarspalace.com.*

Gordon Ramsay Steak

$$$$ | STEAKHOUSE | Gordon Ramsay's heavily British-theme Las Vegas flagship bridges the geographic gap with a Chunnel-like entrance connecting it to Paris Las Vegas. It bridges the culinary gap with a wide variety of cuts of beef, showcased before dinner on a rolling cart. **Known for:** classic steak-house favorites with Ramsay flourish; meat displayed on carts; entryway that bridges Paris to London. ⑤ *Average main: $60* ✉ *Paris Las Vegas, 3655 Las Vegas Blvd. S, Center Strip* ☎ *877/346–4642* ⊕ *www. parislasvegas.com* ⊗ *No lunch.*

Harvest by Roy Ellamar

$$$$ | ECLECTIC | It's no easy feat coming up with a truly original restaurant in Las Vegas that offers more than just a gimmicky theme or celebrity-chef pedigree. Harvest, a casual but cosmopolitan spot that's secluded from Bellagio's noisy

gaming areas, succeeds on all counts by presenting a locally sourced, sustainable menu. **Known for:** farm-to-table menus; snack and dessert carts; interior evokes the outdoors. $ *Average main: $50 ✉ Bellagio Las Vegas, 3600 Las Vegas Blvd. S, Center Strip ☎ 702/693–8865 ⊕ www.bellagio.com/restaurants ⊙ Closed Sun.–Thurs.*

Jaleo

$$$$ | SPANISH | Chef José Andrés was one of the first to capitalize on the tapas concept in the United States (at his original Washington, D.C. location), and small plates are the highlights of the menu here, too. You haven't thoroughly explored the menu until there are stacks of plates on your table. **Known for:** tapas and paellas; fine Spanish ham; fun atmosphere. $ *Average main: $35 ✉ The Cosmopolitan of Las Vegas, 3708 Las Vegas Blvd. S, Center Strip ☎ 702/698–7000 ⊕ www.cosmopolitanlasvegas.com ⊙ Closed Sun. and Mon.*

Jean-Georges Steakhouse at ARIA

$$$$ | STEAKHOUSE | This steak house, named for famed chef Jean-Georges Vongerichten, serves up a modern spin on the traditional meat and potatoes. To wit: dishes such as the soy-glazed short rib with apple and rosemary and cheeseburger with truffle mayo and brie, plus the full component of beef including tomahawk rib eyes, Chateaubriand, and porterhouse steaks. **Known for:** the famous chef's latter-day spins; fine dry-aged steaks; tableside carving. $ *Average main: $65 ✉ ARIA Resort & Casino, 3730 Las Vegas Blvd. S, Center Strip ☎ 877/230–2742 ⊕ www.arialasvegas.com/dining ⊙ No lunch. Closed Wed. and Thurs.*

Joe's Seafood, Prime Steak & Stone Crab

$$$$ | SEAFOOD | Drop by this bustling branch of the famed South Miami Beach restaurant for, at the very least, a pile of fresh stone crabs and a beer. But Joe's is worth a try whether for a light lunch or snack (or a full meal) to remember. **Known for:** stone crab year-round; lots

of steaks and chops; table-side service. $ *Average main: $55 ✉ The Forum Shops at Caesars Palace, 3500 Las Vegas Blvd. S, Center Strip ☎ 702/792–9222 ⊕ www.joes.net/las-vegas.*

Julian Serrano Tapas

$$$$ | SPANISH | Chef Julian Serrano—renowned for Picasso at Bellagio—chose to honor his homeland's tapas and paella traditions at his eponymous restaurant in ARIA. Tapas include classics as well as those with Serrano's special touch. **Known for:** authentic tapas; creative Julian Serrano twists; people-watching in ARIA lobby. $ *Average main: $50 ✉ ARIA Resort & Casino, 3730 Las Vegas Blvd. S, Center Strip ☎ 877/230–2742 ⊕ www.arialasvegas.com/dining.*

Koi Las Vegas

$$$$ | ASIAN | Koi has garnered a reputation as a see-and-be-seen restaurant in New York, Bangkok, Los Angeles, and Las Vegas. The cavernous 220-seat Las Vegas outlet offers sublime Asian-fusion fare. **Known for:** inventive sushi rolls; loud dining room; drinks in the lounge. $ *Average main: $45 ✉ Planet Hollywood Resort & Casino, 3667 Las Vegas Blvd. S, Center Strip ☎ 702/454–4555 ⊕ www.planethollywoodresort.com ⊙ No lunch. Closed Mon. and Tues.*

Lago

$$$$ | ITALIAN | Renowned chef Julian Serrano, who long has had the award-winning Picasso at Bellagio (and an eponymous tapas spot at ARIA), has added more frontage on the resort's lake with his first Italian restaurant, which specializes in small plates. There's a three-course tasting menu as well as à la carte choices at lunch, an intermezzo menu for late afternoon, and the à la carte dinner, with such standards as Caesar and caprese salads and more esoteric choices like risotto with tripe and tomato, and shrimp-stuffed squid with lemoncello dressing. **Known for:** Italian-style small plates; tasting menus; view of Bellagio fountains. $ *Average* main: $45 ⊠ Bellagio, 3600 Las Vegas Blvd. S, Center Strip ☎ 702/693–8865 ⊕ www.bellagio.com.

Le Cirque

$$$$ | **FRENCH** | This sumptuous restaurant, a branch of the now-closed New York City landmark, remains one of the city's true temples of haute cuisine, despite increased heavy-hitting competition. The mahogany-lined room is all the more opulent for its size: in a city of mega-everything, Le Cirque seats only 80 under its draped silk-tent ceiling. **Known for:** tiny, jewel-box room; food not often found elsewhere; fine, attentive service. $ Average main: $65 ⊠ Bellagio Las Vegas, 3600 Las Vegas Blvd. S, Center Strip ☎ 702/693–8865 ⊕ www.bellagio. com/restaurants ☾ Closed Mon. No lunch.

Mastro's Ocean Club

$$$$ | **SEAFOOD** | In addition to food that is upscale and delicious, this impressive restaurant has two other attractions. The first is a piano lounge that serves stellar martinis; the second is the "Tree House," a two-story wooden sculpture that rises from the ground level and houses the main dining room 30 feet above the ground. **Known for:** warm, welcoming service; "tree house" structure; warm butter cake. $ Average main: $50 ⊠ The Shops at Crystals, 3270 Las Vegas Blvd. S, Center Strip ☎ 702/798–7115 ⊕ www. mastrosrestaurants.com ☾ No lunch.

Momofuku Las Vegas

$$$$ | **ASIAN FUSION** | David Chang's budding New York–based restaurant empire went way west for the first time with this spot at The Cosmopolitan, which offers a mix of Momofuku favorites and only-in-Vegas choices. You can also set up fried chicken and caviar for parties of four to six; other group options are salt-and-pepper lobster and shrimp, or five-spice roasted chicken for three or four. **Known for:** classics honed at New York original; some only-in-Vegas choices; fried chicken and caviar for large parties. $ Average

main: $50 ⊠ Cosmopolitan of Las Vegas, 3708 Las Vegas Blvd. S, Center Strip ☎ 877/893–2001 ⊕ www.cosmopolitan-lasvegas.com.

Mon Ami Gabi

$$$$ | **FRENCH** | This French bistro and steak house that first earned acclaim in Chicago has become much beloved here in Las Vegas, in large part because it was the first restaurant to have a terrace overlooking the Strip. For those who prefer a quieter environment, a glassed-in conservatory conveys an outdoor feel, and still-quieter dining rooms are inside, adorned with chandeliers dramatically suspended three stories above. **Known for:** view of Strip from outdoor patio; lots of steak frites variations; great for breakfast or brunch. $ Average main: $35 ⊠ Paris Las Vegas, 3655 Las Vegas Blvd. S, Center Strip ☎ 702/944–4224 ⊕ www. monamigabi.com.

Mr Chow

$$$$ | **CHINESE** | It was a long time coming, but the venerable celebrity magnet Mr Chow opened its Las Vegas branch in Caesars Palace in 2015. On the second floor overlooking the Garden of the Gods pool complex, the predominantly white restaurant is centered on a circular suspended "kinetic sculpture" that periodically descends and opens itself to the room. **Known for:** kinetic sculpture centerpiece; lots of Mr Chow classics; superb, friendly service. $ Average main: $45 ⊠ Caesars Palace, 3570 Las Vegas Blvd. S, Center Strip ☎ 702/731–7888 ⊕ www.caesars.com ☾ No lunch. Closed Mon.–Wed.

Nobu Restaurant Las Vegas

$$$$ | **SUSHI** | Celebrity chef Nobu Matsuhisa established a foothold in the Vegas market with a namesake restaurant at the Hard Rock Hotel, but later added this modern location at the base of his hotel tower at Caesars Palace. The result: one of the hottest tables in town. **Known for:** Nobu classics like black cod miso; extensive sushi and sashimi list;

imported Japanese Wagyu. $ *Average main: $45* ✉ *Nobu Hotel Caesars Palace, 3570 Las Vegas Blvd. S, Center Strip* ☎ *702/785-6628* ⊕ *www.nobuhotels.com* ⊙ *No lunch.*

Petrossian Bar

$$$$ | ECLECTIC | This elegant bar with dark-wood paneling and a baby grand piano sits just off Bellagio's lobby, near the famous Dale Chihuly glass ceiling. The best time to visit for cocktails is during the lavish afternoon tea, held daily from 1 to 4 pm. **Known for:** numerous caviar choices; afternoon tea; soothing piano music. $ *Average main: $35* ✉ *Bellagio Las Vegas, 3600 Las Vegas Blvd. S, Center Strip* ☎ *702/693-7111* ⊕ *www.bellagio.com.*

★ Picasso

$$$$ | EUROPEAN | Adorned with some original works by Picasso, this restaurant raised the city's dining scene a notch when it opened in Bellagio in 1998. Although some say Executive Chef Julian Serrano doesn't change his menu often enough, the artful, innovative cuisine—based on French classics with strong Spanish influences—is consistently outstanding. **Known for:** artworks by the master; Julian Serrano's award-winning food; overlooking Lake Bellagio. $ *Average main: $135* ✉ *Bellagio Las Vegas, 3600 Las Vegas Blvd. S, Center Strip* ☎ *702/693-8865* ⊕ *www.bellagio.com/restaurants* ⊙ *No lunch. Closed Mon.–Thurs.*

Prime Steakhouse

$$$$ | STEAKHOUSE | Even among celebrity chefs, Jean-Georges Vongerichten has established a "can't touch this" reputation. Prime—with its gorgeous view of the fountains—is a place to see and be seen at Bellagio. **Known for:** excellent prime steaks; sophisticated decor; view of Bellagio fountains. $ *Average main: $65* ✉ *Bellagio Las Vegas, 3600 Las Vegas Blvd. S, Center Strip* ☎ *702/693-8865* ⊕ *www.bellagio.com/restaurants* ⊙ *No lunch.*

Rao's

$$$$ | ITALIAN | FAMILY | Whereas its 10-table New York counterpart is notorious for a never-changing reservation list, this 200-seat outpost at Caesars Palace lets someone besides the regulars eat, too. Hearty portions of family-style, rustic, southern Italian cuisine are featured on the menu. **Known for:** accessibility, unlike NY original; traditional red-sauce dishes; bocce court. $ *Average main: $45* ✉ *Caesars Palace, 3570 Las Vegas Blvd. S, Center Strip* ☎ *702/731-7267* ⊕ *www.caesarspalace.com* ⊙ *No lunch. Closed Mon.–Wed.*

★ Restaurant Guy Savoy

$$$$ | FRENCH | In an ultraswank dining room on the second floor of the Augustus Tower, Michelin three-star chef Guy Savoy introduces diners to his masterful creations, such as roasted turbot with bean sprouts and green curry. The 14-course, jumbo-priced Prestige Menu is the restaurant's crown jewel, featuring signature dishes such as artichoke-and-black-truffle soup, and hazelnut-crusted sweetbread. **Known for:** one of Las Vegas's best; caviar room; Krug chef's table. $ *Average main: $125* ✉ *Caesars Palace, 3570 Las Vegas Blvd. S, Center Strip* ☎ *877/346-4642* ⊕ *www.caesarspalace.com* ⊙ *Closed Mon. and Tues. No lunch.*

Spago by Wolfgang Puck

$$$$ | AMERICAN | After more than 25 years at The Forum Shops at Caesars Palace—where it launched Las Vegas's enduring romance with celebrity chefs—Spago moved to Bellagio in 2018, in a spot overlooking the famous Fountains of Bellagio. The menu's still vintage Wolfgang Puck, of course, which means his signature pizzas, house-made pastas, and entrées with produce fresh from the market. **Known for:** Wolfgang Puck's signature cuisine; farm-to-table produce; pretheater menu. $ *Average main: $50* ✉ *Bellagio, 3600 Las Vegas Blvd. S, Center Strip* ☎ *702/693-8181* ⊕ *www.bellagio.com* ⊙ *No lunch. Closed Wed.–Thurs.*

Stack Restaurant and Bar

$$$$ | **AMERICAN** | Curvy strips of exotic wood form the "stacked" walls of this beautiful restaurant, owned by nightclub impresarios the Hakkasan Group. Inventively prepared comfort classics dominate the menu. **Known for:** grown-up comfort foods; undulating wooden walls; sirloin on hot rock. $ *Average main: $40* ✉ *Mirage Las Vegas, 3400 Las Vegas Blvd. S, Center Strip* ☎ *866/339–4566* ⊕ *www.mirage. com/restaurants* ⏱ *No lunch.*

Strip House

$$$$ | **STEAKHOUSE** | This lavish but cheeky steak joint with sisters in New York wears its bordello-chic atmosphere with a healthy touch of irony. The red-flocked wallpaper and other decor may suggest you're inside an early-20th-century house of ill repute, but the menu of artfully presented chops and classic American foods reflects a highly skilled, contemporary kitchen. **Known for:** bordello-chic interior; indulgent steaks and chops; 24-layer chocolate cake. $ *Average main: $60* ✉ *Planet Hollywood Resort & Casino, 3667 Las Vegas Blvd. S, Center Strip* ☎ *702/737–5200* ⊕ *www.planethollywoodresort.com* ⏱ *No lunch.*

Sushi Roku

$$$$ | **JAPANESE** | On the top floor of the towering atrium at the Strip entrance to The Forum Shops, Roku occupies an airy dining room lined with bamboo stalks and tall windows facing the Strip. Sushi is the main draw, but there's much more. **Known for:** huge selection of sushi; many seasonal dishes; view of the Strip. $ *Average main: $45* ✉ *The Forum Shops at Caesars Palace, 3500 Las Vegas Blvd. S, Center Strip* ☎ *702/733–7373* ⊕ *www. sushiroku.com* ⏱ *No lunch Mon.–Thurs.*

★ Tea Lounge at the Waldorf Astoria

$$$$ | **CAFÉ** | The Tea Lounge may be right off the main lobby, but it's still a sea of serenity (with the addition of fabulous 23rd-floor views; this is the Waldorf Astoria, after all. Service is formal but not stuffy, and the afternoon tea is done in classic English style, with the recent addition of caneles, those characteristically caramelized pastries of Bordeaux. **Known for:** variety of fresh fruit Bellinis; wide selection of teas and tisanes; reservations necessary most days. $ *Average main: $45* ✉ *Waldorf Astoria Las Vegas, 3752 Las Vegas Blvd. S, 23rd fl., Center Strip* ☎ *702/590–8888* ⊕ *www.waldorfastorialasvegas.com* ⏱ *No dinner. Closed Mon.-Thurs.*

Twist by Pierre Gagnaire

$$$$ | **FRENCH** | The 23rd floor of the Waldorf Astoria is the only place in the United States to experience food from renowned French chef Pierre Gagnaire. He pioneered the "fusion" movement in cooking, and every dish blends flavor and texture in surprising ways. **Known for:** Pierre Gagnaire's only U.S. restaurant; fusion-dominated menu; expansive views. $ *Average main: $65* ✉ *Waldorf Astoria, 3752 Las Vegas Blvd. S, Center Strip* ☎ *888/881–9367* ⊕ *www.waldorfastorialasvegas.com* ⏱ *Closed Mon. No lunch.*

☕ Coffee and Quick Bites

Bellagio Patisserie

$$ | **CAFÉ** | Chocolate—dark, white, and milk—flows from a tall glass fountain at the entrance of this stunning pastry shop just off the Bellagio's iconic conservatory. This artful homage to chocolate has decadent desserts, including cakes, cookies, gelato, hand-dipped chocolate candies, and particularly memorable crepes (try the one filled with mango, coconut, passion fruit, and pineapple sorbets). **Known for:** three-tier chocolate fountain; indulgent pastries and chocolates; amusing seasonal sculptures. $ *Average main: $15* ✉ *Bellagio, 3600 Las Vegas Blvd. S, Center Strip* ☎ *702/693–8865* ⊕ *www. bellagio.com/restaurants.*

Hotels

The Center Strip is busy, conveniently located, and full of popular hotels and attractions. It stretches from CityCenter (an $8.5-billion city-within-a-city) and Planet Hollywood to The Mirage, including the Waldorf Astoria, The Cosmopolitan, Paris (and its half-size replica of the Eiffel Tower), Bally's, The Cromwell, Caesars Palace (and the Nobu Hotel), the Flamingo, and Harrah's along the way. Taken as a group, these properties represent some of the most storied on the Strip (Caesars Palace and the Flamingo) and the newer (The Cromwell).

The Center Strip also can be characterized by shopping. Lots and lots of shopping. The highest of the high-end stores are inside Crystals, the gateway to CityCenter. At Planet Hollywood, reputable brands dominate the Miracle Mile. Stores inside the astonishing Forum Shops, next to Caesars, fall somewhere in between. Outside Bally's, the Grand Bazaar Shops replicates an open-air mall. The Center Strip even is home to one of the largest Walgreens in the world. Another commonality among hotels here: great spas. Treatment options at the Waldorf Astoria, ARIA, The Cosmopolitan, and Caesars Palace could keep visitors busy (or is it relaxed?) for months. Some spas also offer hammams.

Rooms themselves in this area are all over the lot; some, like standard rooms at Bally's, are affordable and bare-bones; others, such as those inside The Cosmopolitan, with balconies, make all others appear plebeian. It pays to shop around.

★ ARIA Resort & Casino

$$$$ | **RESORT** | Unlike most casino hotels, ARIA has an abundance of light, even in standard guest rooms, and their modern style makes this one of the Strip's most contemporary-feeling options. **Pros:** high-tech rooms; natural light; excellent restaurants. **Cons:** shower setup soaks the tub; long walk to Strip; end rooms are a very long walk to the single elevator bank. $ *Rooms from: $540 ⊠ 3730 Las Vegas Blvd. S, Center Strip* ☎ *702/590–7111, 866/359–7757, 877/580–2742 Sky-Suites* ⊕ *www.aria.com* ⇄ *4004 rooms* ¶◎¶ *No meals.*

Bally's Las Vegas Hotel & Casino

$ | **RESORT** | An old-school property with contemporary rooms in its Jubilee Tower make the reasonably priced Bally's Resort, in the heart of the Strip, an underrated choice for a Vegas vacation. **Pros:** affordable rooms with a perfect Center-Strip location; tennis courts; has a monorail stop. **Cons:** rooms in Indigo tower could use an upgrade; casino floor can get smoky; some readers report poor service. $ *Rooms from: $102 ⊠ 3645 Las Vegas Blvd. S, Center Strip* ☎ *702/967–4111, 877/603–4390* ⊕ *www.ballyslasvegas.com* ⇄ *2814 rooms* ¶◎¶ *No meals.*

★ Bellagio Las Vegas

$$$$ | **RESORT** | The Grand Dame of Strip resorts is still as exquisite as ever, with snazzy rooms full of Italian marble and luxurious fabrics. **Pros:** centrally located; posh suites; classy amenities. **Cons:** pricey; can be difficult to grab a quick bite because of crowds; a very long walk out to the Strip. $ *Rooms from: $699 ⊠ 3600 Las Vegas Blvd. S, Center Strip* ☎ *702/693–7111, 888/987–6667* ⊕ *www.bellagio.com* ⇄ *3933 rooms* ¶◎¶ *No meals.*

Caesars Palace

$$$$ | **RESORT** | Caesars was one of the first properties in town to create rooms so lavish that guests might actually want to spend time in them, and all come standard with marble bathrooms and sumptuous beds. **Pros:** Arctic ice rooms at Qua; Garden of the Gods pool oasis; storied property. **Cons:** floorplan is difficult to navigate; small casino; limited on-site parking. $ *Rooms from: $530 ⊠ 3570 Las Vegas Blvd. S, Center Strip* ☎ *702/731–7110, 866/227–5938* ⊕ *www.caesars.com-caesarspalace* ⇄ *3992 rooms* ¶◎¶ *No meals.*

The ARIA Resort & Casino is the centerpiece of the City Center development and one of the largest LEED Gold certified buildings in the U.S.

The Cosmopolitan of Las Vegas

$$$$ | **RESORT** | Balconies make The Cosmopolitan's rooms stand apart: the vast majority have balconies or terraces, the only ones on the Strip. **Pros:** terraces; in-room technology; Yoo-hoo in minibar. **Cons:** kitchenettes seem random; walls paper-thin; queues for Marquee can get annoying. *Rooms from: $540* *3708 Las Vegas Blvd. S, Center Strip* *702/698–7000* *www.cosmopolitanlasvegas.com* *2995 rooms* *No meals.*

The Cromwell Hotel & Casino

$$$$ | **HOTEL** | Caesars has transformed Bill's Gambling Hall into the only small boutique hotel on the Las Vegas Strip. **Pros:** intimate, exclusive vibe; steam showers; stellar Giada restaurant. **Cons:** limited dining and entertainment options; thumping bass from Drai's upstairs; cramped rooms. *Rooms from: $409* *3595 Las Vegas Blvd. S, Center Strip* *702/777–3777, 844/426–2766* *www.caesars.com/cromwell* *188 rooms* *No meals.*

Flamingo Las Vegas

$$ | **RESORT** | This elaborately landscaped, pink, classic-era resort with a 15-acre pool complex is still one of the best choices in town, and "Go" rooms (which run about $50 to $100 more per night than standard rooms), with MP3 docking stations and 42-inch flat-screen TVs, are downright stylish. **Pros:** Margaritaville is a laid-back place for drinks and live music; heart-of-the-Strip location; terrific pool. **Cons:** entrance is difficult to navigate by car or taxi; standard rooms are pretty old; crowds near LINQ Promenade entrance. *Rooms from: $206* *3555 Las Vegas Blvd. S, Center Strip* *702/733–3111, 888/902–9929* *www.flamingolasvegas.com* *3460 rooms* *No meals.*

Harrah's Las Vegas Hotel & Casino

$$ | **RESORT** | Old-school Vegas is alive and well at this affordable Center-Strip property. **Pros:** throwback vibe with some modern touches thrown in; affordable, reliable rooms; ideal location. **Cons:** zero wow factor; small pool; lots and lots of mirrors. *Rooms from: $230* *3475 Las Vegas

Blvd. S, Center Strip ☎ 800/214–9110 ⊕ www.harrahslasvegas.com ⊐ 2530 rooms ❍ No meals.

The LINQ Hotel & Casino

$$$$ | RESORT | Rooms in The LINQ (which was briefly known as The Quad after a long stint as Imperial Palace) are small but have been recently renovated with a modern, clean design. **Pros:** Center-Strip location; High Roller; Hash House a Go Go is a great dining option. **Cons:** no-frills; many have complained that check-in can be very slow; the hotel's layout is winding and confusing. ⑤ Rooms from: $339 ✉ 3535 Las Vegas Blvd. S, Center Strip ☎ 800/634–6441 ⊕ www.caesars.com/linq ⊐ 2253 rooms ❍ No meals.

Mirage Las Vegas

$$$$ | RESORT | FAMILY | After a comprehensive makeover, rooms at the Mirage are decorated in a cosmopolitan style, with blacks, dark browns, and deep reds. **Pros:** classic Vegas; dolphins!; one of the best pools in town. **Cons:** smoky casino; rooms hard to get to; labyrinthine layout. ⑤ Rooms from: $459 ✉ 3400 Las Vegas Blvd. S, Center Strip ☎ 702/791–7111, 800/374–9000 ⊕ www.mirage.com ⊐ 3044 rooms ❍ No meals.

★ Nobu Hotel at Caesars Palace

$$$$ | HOTEL | The hotel from celebrity chef Nobu Matsuhisa and partner Robert DeNiro is a sleek foodie haven tucked inside the Centurion Tower of the Caesars Palace complex. **Pros:** foodie paradise; insider access and VIP treatment; quiet haven in central Vegas. **Cons:** view of air-conditioning units atop Caesars casino; hard to locate entrance; almost too much technology. ⑤ Rooms from: $515 ✉ 3570 Las Vegas Blvd. S, Center Strip ☎ 702/785–6677 ⊕ www.nobucaesarspalace.com ⊐ 181 rooms ❍ No meals.

Paris Las Vegas

$$$ | RESORT | Life is *magnifique* at this French-theme hotel, but some find the heavy-handed decor a little busy.

Pros: campy decor; spacious rooms; views. **Cons:** some rooms are tired; lack of standout restaurants; big crowds and long lines. ⑤ Rooms from: $284 ✉ 3655 Las Vegas Blvd. S, Center Strip ☎ 877/796–2096 ⊕ www.parislasvegas.com ⊐ 2916 rooms ❍ No meals.

Planet Hollywood Las Vegas Resort & Casino

$$$ | RESORT | Everything at Planet Hollywood is designed to make ordinary people feel like stars, and the spacious rooms are no exception. **Pros:** classic Hollywood vibe; incredible views; posh suites. **Cons:** relatively small casino; in-room bath products are nothing special; extremely noisy at times. ⑤ Rooms from: $244 ✉ 3667 Las Vegas Blvd. S, Center Strip ☎ 702/785–5555, 866/919–7472 ⊕ caesars.com/planet-hollywood/hotel ⊐ 2496 rooms ❍ No meals.

Vdara Hotel & Spa at ARIA Las Vegas

$$$$ | RESORT | This low-key property is actually a hotel-condo, with beautiful, independently owned suites that have efficiency kitchens, pull-out sofas, and lots of extra space. **Pros:** quiet retreat right in the middle of the action; efficiency kitchens; nice spa. **Cons:** lacks the excitement of splashy resort properties; no casino; underwhelming pool. ⑤ Rooms from: $399 ✉ 2600 W. Harmon Ave., Center Strip ☎ 702/590–2111, 866/745–7111 ⊕ www.vdara.com ⊐ 1495 suites ❍ No meals.

Waldorf Astoria Las Vegas

$$$$ | HOTEL | The former Mandarin Oriental was transformed to the Waldorf almost overnight, and has retained many of the same features, such as Pierre Gagnaire's Twist restaurant and a 23rd-floor bar and Tea Lounge. **Pros:** location in center of the action; attentive service; lots of expansive windows for great views. **Cons:** rooms on the small side; doesn't quite have its own identity yet; a little pricey. ⑤ Rooms from: $795 ✉ 3752 Las Vegas Blvd. S, Center Strip ☎ 702/590–8888 ⊕ waldorfastoria.hilton.com ⊐ 389 rooms ❍ No meals.

✶ Nightlife

BARS AND LOUNGES

Alibi Ultra Lounge

PIANO BARS/LOUNGES | Who knew you could have an alibi all night long in Las Vegas? This cocktail lounge offers up that—it's open until 5 am most days—along with bottle service, but you don't have to go all out. You can order creative cocktails as well. Alibi is perhaps best suited for those who want a VIP-style experience without waiting in a long line or shelling out extravagant prices. ✉ *ARIA Resort & Casino, 3730 Las Vegas Blvd. S, Center Strip* ☎ *702/590–9777* ⊕ *alibiloungelv.com.*

Bound

PIANO BARS/LOUNGES | The inventive cocktails snag the spotlight at this hidden gem tucked away at the back of The Cromwell. Try a breakfast martini with orange marmalade, or explore the Aristocrats Spirits Cabinet of rare tastes from all over the world. ✉ *The Cromwell, 3595 Las Vegas Blvd. S, Center Strip* ☎ *702/777–3777* ⊕ *www.caesars.com/cromwell.*

★ The Chandelier

BARS/PUBS | True to its name, this swanky lounge sits in a chandelier with 2 million crystal beads, making it the largest chandelier in town (and, perhaps, the world). The bar is separated into three separate levels, and each has a different theme. The ground floor—dubbed "Bottom of The Chandelier," for those of you scoring at home—is dedicated to intricate specialty drinks, the kinds of cocktails you'll find only here. The second floor (non-smoking!) pays homage to molecular gastronomy in cocktail form; spiked sorbets and dehydrated fruits are common in drinks here. Finally, at the top of The Chandelier, everything's coming up floral, with rose and lavender syrups and violet sugar. If you're particularly adventuresome (and you can get a seat on the first floor), try the off-menu

Verbena cocktail with a "Szechuan button." This desiccated flower from Africa numbs your mouth to make flavors more potent; it also prompts you to down your cocktail in mere seconds. All three levels offer excellent people-watching opportunities. Open 24/7. ✉ *The Cosmopolitan of Las Vegas, 3708 Las Vegas Blvd. S, South Strip* ☎ *702/698–7000* ⊕ *www.cosmopolitanlasvegas.com/lounges-bars/the-chandelier.*

★ Drai's After Hours

PIANO BARS/LOUNGES | All hail Victor Drai, classiest of Vegas nightlife sultans. The wild scene inside this after-hours titan is closer to a dance club or a rave than to a lounge, even though its four rooms with two music formats are as gorgeous as any lounge in town. The vibe of decadence can reach an extraordinary pitch, but this, of course, is exactly how an after-hours club *should* be, right? Besides, you'll be hard-pressed to find a more beautiful insider crowd anywhere within the city limits. ✉ *The Cromwell, 3595 Las Vegas Blvd. S, Center Strip* ☎ *702/777–3800* ⊕ *www.caesars.com/cromwell.*

Drai's Beach Club and Nightclub

DANCE CLUBS | The innovations continue in Las Vegas, and this incarnation includes full concerts from hip-hop stars such as Nelly, Future, Fat Joe, Trey Songz, Jeremih, G-Eazy, and even Chris Brown. The 70,000-square-foot venue sits on top of the resort replete with a pool with some pretty amazing views of the Strip. ✉ *The Cromwell, 3595 Las Vegas Blvd. S, Center Strip* ☎ *702/737–0555* ⊕ *www.draislv.com.*

★ Ghost Donkey

BARS/PUBS | You'll need to access a hidden door in the back of the Block 16 food hall at The Cosmopolitan of Las Vegas (■**TIP→ Look for the small donkey on the otherwise plain door**), but employees will help you find it if you get stuck. Once inside, you'll find yourself in a tiny space with a gigantic collection of mezcal and tequila. The food menu's limited to nachos, but they're quite creative, with choices like black truffles with white cheddar, and carrot chili with carrot pickles and carrot habanero hot sauce. ⊠ *The Cosmpolitan of Las Vegas, 3708 Las Vegas Blvd. S, Center Strip* ⊹ *In Bloc 16 Food Hall* ☎ *702/698–7000* ⊕ *www. cosmopolitanlasvegas.com.*

Koi Lounge

PIANO BARS/LOUNGES | Circles are a big theme at this lounge that fronts Koi restaurant. More than 20 Tibetan hand-carved prayer wheels are positioned around the room, interspersed with circular banquettes that are great for big groups and lousy for small ones. Be sure to visit during happy hour, when mixologists oblige by offering signature drinks for reasonably discounted prices. Unlike other lounges around town, this joint's happy hour runs seven days a week, with a discounted food menu, too. ⊠ *Planet Hollywood, 3667 Las Vegas Blvd. S, Center Strip* ☎ *702/454–4555* ⊕ *koirestaurant.com.*

Lily Bar & Lounge

PIANO BARS/LOUNGES | This colorful (hence the name) ultralounge is quite literally at the center of the action in Bellagio; it's smack-dab in the middle of the casino floor, which you can view through windows on two sides. Community-style ottomans lend themselves to conversation. At the bar, expert mixologists pour cocktails made with seasonally fresh ingredients. DJs spin most nights until the venue closes around 3. ⊠ *Bellagio, 3600 Las Vegas Blvd. S, Center Strip* ☎ *702/693–8384* ⊕ *lilybarlv.com.*

Mayfair Supper Club

PIANO BARS/LOUNGES | Whatever the name—and past incarnations include Hyde and Fontana Bar—this posh ultralounge is prime real estate inside the Bellagio, famous for its front-and-center view overlooking the Bellagio fountains. As the new name suggests, the latest incarnation hearkens back to an earlier era, with dinner and live entertainment offered in the same room that drips with the chic atmosphere of a black-and-white movie from the 1930s. ⊠ *Bellagio, 3600 Las Vegas Blvd. S, Center Strip* ☎ *702/693–8700* ⊕ *www.bellagio.com.*

Parlor Lounge

PIANO BARS/LOUNGES | Be serenaded by a piano while imbibing creative cocktails at this little lounge on the casino floor. The Typhoon is a tropical drink that comes in a custom, limited-edition, Mirage souvenir tiki mug. ⊠ *Mirage Las Vegas, 3400 Las Vegas Blvd. S, Center Strip* ☎ *702/791–7111* ⊕ *www.mirage.com.*

★ Petrossian Bar

PIANO BARS/LOUNGES | Leave your designer handbags on the bar; this is a place to see and be seen. Sophisticated clientele frequent this piano lounge with experts tickling the ivories of a one-of-a-kind, art deco–style Steinway grand while patrons sup on three refined versions of the gin and tonic. Whether you're catching your breath or going for full elegance at this 24-hour lounge overlooking the grandiose entrance to Bellagio, you can sip on sublime cocktails such as the Beluga vodka martini with a cube of namesake Petrossian caviar at the bottom of the glass or pair up your vodkas with caviar in a tasting of three of each. ⊠ *Bellagio, 3600 Las Vegas Blvd. S, Center Strip* ☎ *702/693–7111* ⊕ *www.bellagio.com.*

Skybar

PIANO BARS/LOUNGES | Few views of the Strip are as breathtaking as the one you'll get from this uber-chic lounge on the 23rd floor of the Waldorf Astoria in CityCenter. The room is wrapped with floor-to-ceiling windows, meaning just about every one of the plush banquettes is a winning seat. Mixologists have concocted cocktails themed to southern Nevada ("The Paiute," "The Meadows"), and it's easy to pay a dollar for every floor of that view in a single cocktail. There's also a small menu of bite-size appetizers and "luxurious experiences" that include vodka and caviar pairings. Business-casual dress is recommended. ⊠ *Waldorf Astoria, 3452 Las Vegas Blvd. S, Center Strip* ☎ *702/590–8888* ⊕ *www. waldorfastorialasvegas.com.*

Vesper Bar

PIANO BARS/LOUNGES | The Chandelier Bar may be The Cosmopolitan's bar of the moment, but you shouldn't overlook the sleek Vesper Bar, the true mixologist space here. Name an ingredient, any ingredient, and the talented staff behind the bar can come up with a drink for you. Long-forgotten cocktail recipes are a specialty at this very modern square bar sitting alongside hotel registration. ⊠ *The Cosmopolitan of Las Vegas, 3708 Las Vegas Blvd. S, Center Strip* ☎ *702/698– 7969* ⊕ *www.cosmopolitanlasvegas.com.*

Vista Cocktail Lounge

PIANO BARS/LOUNGES | Different city-scapes ranging from sunset in Hong Kong to night in Dubai to evening in New York City change on huge screens that make up the background at this lounge. ⊠ *Caesars Palace, 3570 Las Vegas Blvd. S, Center Strip* ☎ *702/731–7852* ⊕ *www. caesars.com.*

CIGAR BARS

Casa Fuente

BARS/PUBS | This full-service cigar shop reproduces the decor and atmosphere of El Floridita, Ernest Hemingway's favorite Havana watering hole. Its sophisticated lounge, which obviously specializes in rum drinks, is a great place to enjoy your smoke. ⊠ *The Forum Shops, 3500 Las Vegas Blvd. S, Center Strip* ☎ *702/731–5051* ⊕ *www. casafuente.com* Ⓜ *Center Strip.*

Montecristo Cigar Bar

BARS/PUBS | Cigars team up with whis-keys and small bites at this respite in the center of the resort. Find more than 1,000 cigars housed in a climate-con-trolled humidor, one of the largest in the city. Head to the library, out on the courtyard, in the vault room, or to the bar.

⊠ *Caesars Palace, 3570 Las Vegas Blvd. S, Center Strip* ☎ *866/733–5827* ⊕ *www. caesars.com.*

DANCE CLUBS AND NIGHTCLUBS

Chateau Nightclub and Rooftop

DANCE CLUBS | A staircase leads revelers straight from the Paris casino floor up to this French-inspired nightclub. The space itself offers two distinct experiences: a main dance room or the open-air terrace, for the rooftop portion of the name ready for Instagram-worthy photos. In the main room, house DJs spin from a booth atop a 10-foot-high fireplace, and go-go dancers in French maid costumes abound. If you're looking for something different, don't miss the chandeliers made of globes near the bar; with LED screens in every nightclub these days, the handmade fixtures are wonderfully unique. ⊠ *Paris Las Vegas, 3655 Las Vegas Blvd. S, Center Strip* ☎ *702/776–7777* ⊕ *www. chateaunights.com.*

Drai's

DANCE CLUBS | Victor Drai wants your business day and night, and he nabs it with his multiuse space 11 stories up at The Cromwell. Drai's boasts a roof-top day- and nightclub with pools and cabanas for basking in the sun or dancing to the beats under the moon. It's huge, too, clocking in at 65,000 square feet with a monster-size 7,000-square-foot LED screen and every imaginable seating option. Go ultraswanky at one of 150 VIP tables. ⊠ *The Cromwell, 3595 Las Vegas Blvd. S, Center Strip* ☎ *702/777–3800* ⊕ *draislv.com.*

Marquee

DANCE CLUBS | This cavernous joint boasts three different rooms spread across two levels, as well as 50-foot ceilings. In the main area, stadium-style seating surrounds the dance floor, and four-story LED screens and projection walls display light and image shows customized for every performer. For a more intimate experience, check out the Boom Box, a smaller room (usually featuring something other than house music) with windows overlooking the Strip. On the top level, the Library provides a respite from the thumping downstairs with dark wood, books (actual books!), and billiard tables. In spring and summer, the hot spot opens Marquee Dayclub, which features two pools, several bars, a gaming area, and DJs all day long. A dome even permits the pool party to rage on in colder months. ✉ *The Cosmopolitan of Las Vegas, 3708 Las Vegas Blvd. S, Center Strip* ☎ *702/333–9000* ⊕ *marqueelasvegas.com.*

Omnia
DANCE CLUBS | Las Vegas nightlife is always looking for the next big thing, and in the case of Omnia, that means a 75,000-square-foot behemoth of a club with an ultralounge dubbed Heart of Omnia tucked to the side. This monster features liquid-crystal display portals embedded in black one-way mirrors on all four sides as you walk in and a 65-foot-tall ceiling dome anchored by a 22,000-pound chandelier with eight rings that dance with light to the music. The lines to enter stretch through the casino floor with gaggles of trendy girls and dapper guys hoping to attract the ladies. ✉ *Caesars Palace, 3570 Las Vegas Blvd, S, Center Strip* ☎ *702/785–6200* ⊕ *omnianightclub.com.*

PIANO BARS
Napoleon's Lounge
BARS/PUBS | This baroque Paris piano bar can get loud, but it's all good fun. Free performances nightly from 5 to 1. Tip the dueling piano players even more if you really want to hear your favorite song. ✉ *Paris Las Vegas, 3655 Las Vegas Blvd. S, Center Strip* ☎ *702/946–7000* ⊕ *www.caesars.com/paris-las-vegas.*

🛍 Shopping

CHILDREN'S CLOTHING
Though the casino-hotel malls and area shopping centers have the usual children's clothing stores such as Gap Kids and Gymboree, you can find some great gifts for kids at the shops below.

Kids Kastle
CLOTHING | **FAMILY** | For the fashionistas-in-training, Marc Jacobs, Lipstick, and Sister Sam ensembles await you. The boys can dress themselves in equally impressive duds from True Religion and Diesel. ✉ *The Forum Shops at Caesars Palace, 3500 Las Vegas Blvd. S, Center Strip* ☎ *702/369–5437.*

Vilebrequin
CLOTHING | **FAMILY** | If there's a daddy's boy in the family, this is the place to shop for him. Vilebrequin specializes in matching father-son swim trunks with a stylish aesthetic and speedy drying technology. A second location is at Fashion Show mall and a discount store is at the Las Vegas Premium Outlets—North. ✉ *The Forum Shops at Caesars Palace, 3500 Las Vegas Blvd. S, Center Strip* ☎ *702/894–9460* ⊕ *www.vilebrequin.com.*

FOOD AND DRINK
La Cave
FOOD/CANDY | Take your pick of decadent delights and gifts for the gourmand such as French-imported wines and Godiva chocolate. ✉ *Paris, 3655 Las Vegas Blvd. S, Center Strip* ☎ *702/946–4339.*

GIFTS AND SOUVENIRS
Curios
GIFTS/SOUVENIRS | This little gem of a store carries more than just alcohol, snacks, and everything you may have left at home. Gifts for him and her with a British theme pepper the shelves here. Snap up a top hat from Christy's (made for the royals, so why not you?), clever men's products, including shaving brushes and mustache wax, Union Jack–emblazoned knickknacks,

and even decorative pieces for your bathroom at home. ✉ *The Cromwell, 3595 Las Vegas Blvd. S, Center Strip* ☎ *702/777–3777* ⊕ *www.caesars.com/ cromwell.*

JEWELRY

Most malls and shopping centers on and off the Strip have jewelry stores, including national chains such as Ben Bridge, Gordon's, Lundstrom, Whitehall Co., and Zales. More-exclusive jewelers can be found in several of the Strip hotels, most notably Bellagio, The Shops at Crystals, and The Venetian.

Cartier

JEWELRY/ACCESSORIES | There are three outposts of this venerable jeweler in Las Vegas: at The Forum Shops, Wynn, and The Shops at Crystals. You'll find a fine collection of jewelry, watches, leather goods, accessories, and fragrances. ✉ *The Forum Shops at Caesars Palace, 3500 Las Vegas Blvd. S, Center Strip* ☎ *702/418–3904* ⊕ *www.cartier.us.*

Harry Winston

JEWELRY/ACCESSORIES | Celebrities continually turn to this exclusive jeweler for red-carpet-worthy diamonds and rare gemstones. There are locations at Via Bellagio and The Shops at Crystals. ✉ *The Shops at Crystals, 3720 Las Vegas Blvd. S, Level 2, Center Strip* ☎ *702/262–0001* ⊕ *www.harrywinston.com.*

Richard Mille

JEWELRY/ACCESSORIES | Make like tennis star Rafael Nadal and shop for high-end Swiss watches that can reach six figures. Chichi surroundings swaddled in macassar wood, steel, and leather help soften the sticker shock, but the museumlike setting makes Richard Mille worth at least a walk-through. ✉ *The Shops at Crystals, 3720 Las Vegas Blvd. S, Center Strip* ☎ *702/588–7272* ⊕ *www.richard-mille.com.*

Tiffany & Co.

JEWELRY/ACCESSORIES | Browse through a full selection of Tiffany's timeless merchandise as well as the exclusive jewelry designs of Elsa Peretti, Paloma Picasso, and Jean Schlumberger. Cleaning and repair services are also offered. Additional store locations include The Forum Shops at Caesars Palace, The Shops at Crystals, and Fashion Show mall. ✉ *Via Bellagio, 3600 Las Vegas Blvd. S, Center Strip* ☎ *702/697–5400* ⊕ *www.tiffany.com.*

Van Cleef & Arpels

JEWELRY/ACCESSORIES | French jewelry, watches, and perfume find a home at this boutique founded in 1896. Even royalty turn to this jewelry maker; Prince Rainier of Monaco gave Grace Kelly a Van Cleef & Arpels pearl and diamond necklace and earrings. There's another location in The Forum Shops. ✉ *The Shops at Crystals, 3720 Las Vegas Blvd. S, Center Strip* ☎ *702/560–6556* ⊕ *www. vancleefarpels.com.*

MALLS

Appian Way Shops

SHOPPING CENTERS/MALLS | FAMILY | A majestic replica of Michelangelo's *David* in Carrara marble marks the entrance to the Appian Way Shops, where a dozen stores sell wares such as luggage, home goods, gifts, eyewear, skin-care products, cigars, condiments, and apparel. King Baby has a wealth of rock-and-roll handcrafted sterling silver pieces with elements of precious stones. Take home olive oils and vinegars from around the world at Olive & Beauty. Carina can spiff up your wardrobe with brands such as Joseph Ribkoff, True Religion, Betsey Johnson, Jessica Simpson, and Vince Camuto. And Roberto Coin, an Italian jeweler, focuses on sleek designs, each of which contains a signature hidden ruby. ✉ *Caesars Palace, 3570 Las Vegas Blvd. S, Casino floor near Forum Tower elevators, Center Strip* ☎ *866/227–5938* ⊕ *www.caesars.com/caesars-palace.*

Did You Know?

In case you can't make it to Rome, you'll find a replica of the Trevi Fountain outside The Forum Shops at Caesars Palace.

★ The Forum Shops at Caesars Palace

SHOPPING CENTERS/MALLS | Amazing ambience, architecture, and design means visitors won't have to drop a single dime to enjoy touring this highly accessible mid-Strip mall. Leave the high heels at home to better roam three levels of restaurants and retail—some paths cobblestoned—that resemble an ancient Roman streetscape, with scattered statuary, immense columns and arches, two central piazzas with ornate fountains, and a cloud-filled ceiling-sky that changes from sunrise to sunset over the course of three hours (to subconsciously spur shoppers to step up their pace of acquisition, perhaps?). ■TIP➔ **The Mitsubishi-designed freestanding Spiral Escalator is a must-ride for the view.**

Of course, shopaholics will rejoice at the selection of designer shops and traditional standbys, from high-end heavy hitters such as Elie Tahari, Brooks Brothers, Gucci, Fendi, Michael Kors, Christian Louboutin, Jimmy Choo, Salvatore Ferragamo, Louis Vuitton, and Balenciaga, to more casual labels like Abercrombie & Fitch, Nike, Guess, and Gap/Gap Kids. Armani fans will find an Exchange for menswear, along with John Varvatos, Hugo Boss, and Canali. Gaze at stunning jewelry, watches, and crystal works at Baccarat, Cartier, Hearts on Fire, Tourneau, Tiffany & Co., Pandora, and David Yurman. Apple offers a whole host of electronics. Cosmetics queens will keep themselves busy at Chanel Beauty, Dior Beauty, and Lush. And don't miss the flagship Victoria's Secret for lingerie and swimwear, or Agent Provocateur and La Perla, for that matter.

When all this walking/shopping brings on the inevitable hunger, head to the renovated The Palm or Carmine's Italian. The Cheesecake Factory is popular, as are Sushi Roku, and Joe's Seafood, Steak & Stone Crab. ⊠ *Caesars Palace, 3500 Las Vegas Blvd. S, Center Strip* ☎ *702/893–4800* ⊕ *www.simon.com.*

Grand Bazaar Shops

SHOPPING CENTERS/MALLS | In front of Bally's Las Vegas, a "21st-century bazaar" inspired by the world's great outdoor markets showcases 150 shops over 2 acres. A giant crystal starburst by Swarovski re-creates Times Square, New York's New Year's Eve nightly while the booths feature glowing, mosaic, undulating rooftops over a broad selection of retail covering apparel, footwear, accessories, electronics, jewelry, and beauty. Black Clover, Alex & Ani, Lindbergh, Superdry, and Havaianas take up the front of the market, and smaller boutiques line four alleys stretching back to the resort along with Wahlburgers from the Wahlberg brothers and Giordano's deep-dish pizza. ⊠ *Bally's Las Vegas, 3645 Las Vegas Blvd. S, Center Strip* ☎ *702/967–4111* ⊕ *www.grandbazaarshops.com.*

Le Boulevard

SHOPPING CENTERS/MALLS | Petite by Vegas standards, this Parisian-style shopping lane is chock-full of Gallic delights. Le Journal stocks sundries and that jaunty French beret you know you're longing for. La Cave offers Godiva chocolates and wines. Premium cigars and international cigarettes are sold at Davidoff Boutique (until 2 am). Les Elèments keeps a stock of nice gifts and children's toys. ⊠ *Paris Las Vegas, 3655 Las Vegas Blvd. S, Center Strip* ☎ *702/946–7000* ⊕ *caesars.com/paris-las-vegas.*

The LINQ Promenade

SHOPPING CENTERS/MALLS | FAMILY | The focal point of Caesars Entertainment's 300,000-square-foot entertainment district is the High Roller, the world's tallest observation wheel at 550 feet. There's also a zip line (the only one on the Strip) but there's also shopping. A boutique specializing in Harley-Davidson merchandise brings the iconic American brand to the Strip. Chilli Beans brings sunglasses and Brazil's largest eyewear brand. Goorin Bros. fulfills all your headgear needs.

Pick up some sweets at I Love Sugar, Sprinkles, or Honolulu Cookie Co. Open 24/7. ⊠ *3545 Las Vegas Blvd. S, Center Strip* ☎ *702/322–0560* ⊕ *www.caesars. com/linq/things-to-do.*

Miracle Mile Shops

SHOPPING CENTERS/MALLS | The shops here line an indoor sidewalk built around the circular Zappos Theater, where the Backstreet Boys and Gwen Stefani have had their resident shows. Along the way, you'll find such notable and diverse fashion names as Tommy Bahama, Urban Outfitters, H&M, and Lululemon. Beauty lovers will enjoy Bath & Body Works and Sephora, the authority in beauty retail stores, which are well worth the walk on the cobblestone flooring. Miracle Mile does an admirable job of balancing fashion designer boutiques with modestly priced shops. Many of the stores are at your local mall, but you still may discover a treasure here. ⊠ *Planet Hollywood Resort & Casino, 3663 Las Vegas Blvd. S, Center Strip* ☎ *702/866–0703, 888/800–8284* ⊕ *www.miraclemileshopslv.com.*

★ The Shops at Crystals

SHOPPING CENTERS/MALLS | Two levels of opulent boutiques, restaurants, and artistic flourishes are housed within the dramatic steel-and-glass structure that envelops The Shops at Crystals shopping venue at CityCenter. True to its gleaming facade, scads of swanky designer apparel and accessories from fashion's crème de la crème line the clean, minimalist confines within. Touch-screen directories guide you to brands such as Prada, Bulgari, Lanvin, Balenciaga, Bottega Veneta, Stella McCartney, Bally, and Tom Ford. Come dressed to impress if you intend to do anything more than ogle the latest and greatest offerings; some of the salespeople here can be more haughty than the couture.

One of Louis Vuitton's largest locations in North America is here, with two levels that extend beyond leather goods to include men's and women's ready-to-wear, shoes, jewelry, textiles, ties, and more.

Among the places to dine are Bobby Flay's Bobby's Burger Palace; Mastro's Ocean Club (sitting inside a tree house); and Cucina by Wolfgang Puck. Afterward, stroll outdoors to cross the CityCenter Sky Bridge to Gallery Row (near the Waldorf Astoria and giant, 4-ton sculpture of a blue-and-red typewriter eraser by Claes Oldenburg and Coosje van Bruggen), where three galleries feature the work of Seattle glass master Dale Chihuly, bronze sculptures by Richard MacDonald, and wilderness photography by Rodney Lough Jr. ■**TIP**➜ **For a fun way to access The Shops at Crystals, ride the sleek and silent Aria Express, CityCenter's free electric tram with a fantastic elevated view of the complex.** ⊠ *CityCenter, 3720 Las Vegas Blvd. S, adjacent to ARIA, Center Strip* ⊕ *By car: cross Las Vegas Blvd. via E. Harmon Ave. to enter ARIA's South Parking garage. Park on its southwestern side for closest elevator access to Monte Carlo's casino level. Once inside, turn right on Monte Carlo's shopping walkway, Street of Dreams, for short walk to tram's boarding platform. Board and travel one stop to Crystals Station; downward escalator deposits you onto Level 2 of Crystals* ☎ *866/754–2489* ⊕ *www.simon.com.*

Via Bellagio

SHOPPING CENTERS/MALLS | Steve Wynn spared no expense to create the Bellagio, so be prepared to spare no expense shopping at its exclusive boutiques. Elegant luxury stores, such as Prada, Chanel, Gucci, Harry Winston, and Tiffany & Co., line a long passage. When you're ready to cool your heels, dine on the balcony at Spago right in the promenade, to snag the best patio seat (first-come, first-served) for watching the Fountains of Bellagio (aka dancing waters). ⊠ *Bellagio, 3600 Las Vegas Blvd. S, Center Strip* ☎ *702/693–7111, 888/987–6667* ⊕ *www. bellagio.com.*

MEN'S CLOTHING

You can't walk into the shopping areas of Strip hotels without encountering high-end men's clothing stores. If the price tags on the Strip are too out of reach, the outlet malls have brand names for less, such as Tommy Hilfiger, Perry Ellis, Hugo Boss, Van Heusen, Polo Ralph Lauren, and DKNY. Streetwear and high-end sneaker stores also abound; you just have to know where to find the boutiques.

Berluti

SHOES/LUGGAGE/LEATHER GOODS | Parisian luxury brand Berluti brings luxe shoes and leather accessories for men. Find oxfords, derbies, and loafers in alligator skin, kangaroo leather, and calfskin, as well as business portfolios, wallets, belts, and bags. ⊠ *The Shops at Crystals, 3720 Las Vegas Blvd. S, Center Strip* ☎ *702/795–1542* ⊕ *store.berluti.com.*

Ermenegildo Zegna

CLOTHING | You'll find the finest in Italian men's suits on this store's racks. High-quality craftsmanship, superior fit, and impeccable style dominate here. Made-to-measure service, small leather goods and accessories, and a selection of apparel from fashion lines Z Zegna and Zegna Sport are also available. Additional locations are at The Shops at Crystals and Fashion Show Mall. ⊠ *The Forum Shops at Caesars Palace, 3500 Las Vegas Blvd. S, Center Strip* ☎ *702/369–5458* ⊕ *www.zegna.com.*

Giorgio Armani

CLOTHING | Italian designer Armani cuts a cloth like nobody's business. Clean lines, high-quality fabrics, expert stitching—all are evident in the luxury formalwear displayed throughout this elegant store. The maestro's signature spiffy sportswear, shoes, handbags, and accessories are sold here, too, as well as fragrances and cosmetics. ⊠ *The Forum Shops at Caesars Palace, 3500 Las Vegas Blvd. S, Center Strip* ☎ *702/893–4800* ⊕ *www.armani.com/giorgioarmani.*

Hugo Boss

CLOTHING | Browse men's fashions straight from European and New York runways, also at two additional local branches (The Venetian and Fashion Show mall), plus two factory store outlets. ⊠ *The Forum Shops at Caesars Palace, 3500 Las Vegas Blvd. S, Center Strip* ☎ *702/696–9444* ⊕ *www.hugoboss.com.*

John Varvatos

CLOTHING | Casual-chic men's clothes and a slew of shoes, belts, and messenger bags make up the offerings here. The Forum Shops location also carries formalwear. The version at the Hard Rock Hotel is a boutique store modeled after their New York City Bowery location (former site of the iconic rock club CBGB). There's also a local outlet store. ⊠ *The Forum Shops at Caesars Palace, 3500 Las Vegas Blvd. S, Center Strip* ☎ *702/939–0922* ⊕ *www.johnvarvatos.com.*

Stitched

CLOTHING | Men who want the best of the latest and greatest fashions will be right at home here. Jacks & Jokers, Zachary Prell shirts, and the XXXX Stitched collection of suits and sports coats are carried here. An on-site tailor can personalize garments. Made-to-measure suits are a specialty. Hang out in the Scotch lounge while you pick out your new wardrobe. ⊠ *The Cosmopolitan of Las Vegas, 3708 Las Vegas Blvd. S, Center Strip* ☎ *702/698–7630* ⊕ *www.stitchedlifestyle.com.*

Tom Ford

CLOTHING | The designer put his stamp on the fashion world when he brought Gucci back from the dead. Since then the outstanding craftsmanship of his modern menswear line has suited Brad Pitt, George Clooney, and Jay-Z on the red carpet. Men's eyewear, accessories, and fragrances are offered, as well as women's ready-to-wear. Neiman Marcus in Fashion Show has an impressive counter of Tom Ford Beauty products for both men and women. ⊠ *The Shops at*

Crystals, 3720 Las Vegas Blvd. S, Level 1, Center Strip ☎ 702/740–2940 ⊕ www.tomford.com.

SPORTING GOODS AND CLOTHING

Nike

SPORTING GOODS | FAMILY | This multilevel Nike theme park features attractive displays, inspirational slogans, and giant swoosh symbols amid the latest cool technology in athletic shoes. Flashy and crowded, it's full of "Nike athletes" yelling into two-way radios. ⊠ The Forum Shops at Caesars Palace, 3500 Las Vegas Blvd. S, Center Strip ☎ 702/650–8888 ⊕ www.nike.com.

WOMEN'S CLOTHING

Vegas shopping will impress the most jaded of shoppers. Prepare to find an abundant selection of women's wear at area hotel-casino malls and outlet centers. Go ahead, name a designer. The odds are high that you'll find a signature shop in this town.

AllSaints Spitalfields

CLOTHING | The British brand uses vintage themes as its inspiration for graphic tees and embellished dresses that cater to a youthful demographic. Celebrities like Vanessa Hudgens, Jessica Alba, and Dakota Fanning have been known to wear the edgy styles here. The flagship location at The Forum Shops features two levels of shopping for men and women. Also located at The Cosmopolitan, and there's an outlet store at Las Vegas Premium Outlets North. ⊠ The Forum Shops at Caesars Palace, 3500 Las Vegas Blvd. S, Center Strip ☎ 702/893–4800 ⊕ www.us.allsaints.com.

Balenciaga

CLOTHING | The highly stylish Italian fashion house brings an architectural approach to men's and women's ready-to-wear fashions, handbags, and accessories. Additional location at The Shops at Crystals. ⊠ The Forum Shops at Caesars Palace, 3500 Las Vegas Blvd. S, Center Strip ☎ 702/732–1660 ⊕ www.balenciaga.com.

Bottega Veneta

CLOTHING | Renowned for its modern, sophisticated take on the classics, this Italian fashion house melds elegant style with leather fabrics. The line appeals to the woman with a taste for timelessness. Additional locations at Via Bellagio and Wynn. ⊠ The Shops at Crystals, 3320 Las Vegas Blvd. S, Center Strip ☎ 702/369–0747 ⊕ www.bottegaveneta.com.

CH Carolina Herrera

CLOTHING | Chic sophistication is the name of the game at this fashion boutique where you can find the acclaimed designer's bridge collection. There's also a store at Las Vegas Premium Outlets North. ⊠ The Forum Shops at Caesars Palace, 3500 Las Vegas Blvd. S, Level 2, Center Strip ☎ 702/894–5242.

Fendi

CLOTHING | The Italian designer offers elegant garments, furs, shoes, and handbags that transcend trends. The boutique at The Shops at Crystals features a replica of Rome's Trevi Fountain inside, and The Forum Shops at Caesars boutique features a jewel box of a glass-enclosed store with its handbags and shoes as well as a traditional shop across the aisle. There are additional locations at The Shops at Crystals, and Via Bellagio. ⊠ The Forum Shops at Caesars Palace, 3500 Las Vegas Blvd. S, Center Strip ☎ 702/732–9040 ⊕ www.fendi.com.

Gucci

CLOTHING | The Italian luxury designer features the men's and women's clothing and shoe collections as well as leather goods, luggage, jewelry, timepieces, silks, and eyewear. Additional locations at Via Bellagio and The Shops at Crystals. ⊠ The Forum Shops at Caesars Palace, 3500 Las Vegas Blvd. S, Center Strip ☎ 702/369–7333 ⊕ www.gucci.com.

H&M

CLOTHING | The crème de la crème of fast fashion, this Swedish retailer features affordable apparel and accessories that rival what you'll see on high-profile runways. Diffusion lines from acclaimed designers are also prevalent here, and generally make an appearance only at this location. The store contains three floors, three checkout stations, an elevator, and a cut-open facade. ■TIP➔ **The location at The Forum Shops is the second-biggest H&M in the country.** Find men's and children's attire as well. There are additional locations at the Miracle Mile Shops, Downtown Summerlin, and Town Square. ⌖ *The Forum Shops at Caesars Palace, 3500 Las Vegas Blvd. S, Center Strip* ☎ *702/207–0167* ⊕ *www.hm.com.*

Lanvin

CLOTHING | The creative decor in the windows alone is reason enough to check out this boutique that carries men's and women's fashions and accessories. Inside you'll be dazzled by the bold, sophisticated fashions. ⌖ *The Shops at Crystals, 3720 Las Vegas Blvd. S, Center Strip* ☎ *702/982–0425* ⊕ *www.lanvin.com.*

Louis Vuitton

SHOES/LUGGAGE/LEATHER GOODS | Stash your winnings in a designer bag from one of six Vegas branches of this famous French accessories maker. Hot-stamping services are offered at all branches. The store at The Shops at Crystals is the largest in North America and houses James Turrell's *Akhob*, a walk-in light installation, the artist's largest Ganzfeld exhibit to date; it's accessible by reservation only, so call ahead. There are additional locations at Wynn, The Forum Shops at Caesars, Via Bellagio, Palazzo, and Fashion Show Mall. ⌖ *The Shops at Crystals, 3720 Las Vegas Blvd. S, Center Strip* ☎ *702/262–6262* ⊕ *www.louisvuitton.com.*

Stella McCartney

CLOTHING | Sharp tailoring and feminine lines mark Stella McCartney's clothing. The lifelong vegetarian does not use any leather or fur in her collections for women and children. The centerpiece of this flagship store is a horse sculpture made from 8,000 Swarovski crystals dubbed *Lucky Spot*. McCartney commissioned the sculpture in 2004 and named it for a horse once owned by her late mother. There's another store in the new Wynn Plaza. ⌖ *The Shops at Crystals, 3720 Las Vegas Blvd. S, City Center* ☎ *702/798–5102* ⊕ *www.stellamccartney.com/us.*

Tory Burch

CLOTHING | Rich textures, zippy colors, perky prints, and Bohemian spirit infuse the stylish, wearable clothing and accessories at Tory Burch. The handbags, pumps, and ballet flats are staples here. Additional locations are at Palazzo and Fashion Show Mall, and there's an outlet at Las Vegas Premium Outlets North. ■TIP➔ **The Forum Shops branch is the largest and carries a wider selection.** ⌖ *The Forum Shops at Caesars Palace, 3500 Las Vegas Blvd. S, Center Strip* ☎ *702/369–3459* ⊕ *www.toryburch.com.*

Versace

CLOTHING | This boutique features a body-conscious, seductive line of ready-to-wear clothes that speak to a confident woman. Additional location at The Shops at Crystals. ⌖ *The Forum Shops at Caesars Palace, 3500 Las Vegas Blvd. S, Center Strip* ☎ *702/932–5757* ⊕ *www.versace.com.*

⛹ Activities

BOWLING

Brooklyn Bowl

BOWLING | This 32-lane bowling alley on the LINQ Promenade doubles as a live music venue, sometimes simultaneously. Bowlers can lounge on Chesterfield sofas and enjoy food from New York City's Blue Ribbon between frames. If you'd rather just watch, there's an elevated bowler's lounge from where you can observe the action. The biggest downside to this spot is the acoustics; oddly, for a music venue, they're incredibly poor. Be prepared to lose your voice if you want to converse with your pals. ✉ *LINQ Promenade, 3545 Las Vegas Blvd. S, Center Strip* ☎ *702/862–2695* ⊕ *www.brooklynbowl. com* 🎳 *Bowling from $20; shoe rental $5.*

SPAS

ESPA at Vdara

FITNESS/HEALTH CLUBS | British skin-care line ESPA brings a slice of tranquillity to the clamorous Strip. With it comes a line of products with natural ingredients that ties in with Vdara's commitment to organic and natural spa treatments and skin-care products. Try the Desert Rose, a 110-minute body treatment that includes a welcoming foot bath, body scrub, shower, and massage with body butter. On the Rocks uses a body brush followed by a massage using hot stones. ESPA takes care of the men with treatments such as a purifying facial and a fitness massage. ✉ *Vdara, 2600 Harmon Ave., Center Strip* ☎ *702/590–2474* ⊕ *www.vdara.com.*

★ Qua Baths & Spa

FITNESS/HEALTH CLUBS | This behemoth of a spa at Caesars Palace bases its philosophy on the calming properties of water. Many of the treatments and special features here draw heavily on this element, beginning with the Roman Baths. Qua's social spa-ing concept of encouraging guests to verbally interact comes naturally when indulging in these three soothing baths. For guests suffering from heat exhaustion, the Arctic Room offers the perfect solution: snow falling from a glass sky. If traditional treatments bore you, consider visiting the Crystal Body Art Room. Qua also has Men's Zone, a salon for men, and the Tea Lounge, where an in-house tea sommelier blends you a cup. Color, a phenomenal hair salon from colorist-to-the-stars Michael Boychuck, is right next door. ∎ **TIP→ The Nobu Hotel flexes its influence with a whole series of treatments including the Nagomi Ritual with a welcoming foot bath, aroma nectars, and massage.** ✉ *Caesars Palace, 3570 Las Vegas Blvd. S, Center Strip* ☎ *866/782–0655* ⊕ *www.caesars. com/caesars-palace/things-to-do/qua.*

Sahra Spa and Hammam

FITNESS/HEALTH CLUBS | Omnipresent slot machines and neon lights can make you forget that you're in the desert, but Sahra Spa is designed to return you to the peace and solitude of the Southwest. It starts with the Space Between, the serenity lounge that makes you feel transported to the peak of a canyon, and stretches all the way to the metallic ceilings that twinkle like only a nighttime desert sky can. Highlights here include the extensive skin-care treatments, special baths, and hammam, one of only three in Las Vegas. Two of the "transformations," the Sahra Journey and the Sahra Select, incorporate the heat-infused hammam to address the body's needs and all its senses. At the center of the hammam is a heated slab of stone that feels like it's been sitting in the warm sun for hours. Follow this up with the Red Flower Bathing Ritual, which exfoliates and moisturizes your desert-dried skin. ✉ *The Cosmopolitan of Las Vegas, 3708 Las Vegas Blvd. S, Center Strip* ☎ *855/724–7258* ⊕ *www.cosmopolitanlasvegas.com.*

The Spa at ARIA

FITNESS/HEALTH CLUBS | ARIA provides a contemporary way to spa, starting with the design, which is all about clean lines and modern furniture. Some of the furniture is even functional to your pampering, like the Japanese *gabanyoku* beds. Made up of warm stones, the beds are designed to balance metabolism, circulation, and muscle movement. The services are just as innovative, like the ashiatsu massage that has therapists using ceiling bars to balance as they walk on your back. The Shio Salt Room uses lamps and a brick wall to emit salt to improve breathing as guests lounge. A customized men's menu includes the Man Tan and extensive barber services. A Vichy rain bar enhances certain body treatments, and facial add-ons include a firming system for décolletage, an eye mask, and hand and feet massages. ✉ *ARIA Resort & Casino, 3730 Las Vegas Blvd. S, Center Strip* ☎ *702/590–9600* ⊕ *www.aria.com.*

Spa Bellagio

FITNESS/HEALTH CLUBS | Besides the calming reflecting pools and the Reflexology Pebble Walk, this swank Zen sanctuary has treatments such as Thai yoga massage and a hydrotherapy bath. The 6,000-square-foot fitness center has a gorgeous view of the Mediterranean gardens and the pool. There's even a candlelit meditation room with fountain walls. If overindulging and the dry climate have gotten to you, try the Thermal Seaweed Body Wrap for a seaweed- and water-based detoxifying and hydrating treatment. Water-based treatments such as the Watsu Massage, which combines Zen shiatsu and stretching while gently floating in a private 94-degree pool, and the Aquastretch, which increases flexibility and releases tension, are specialties here. The massages can even be done poolside or in a hotel room. ■**TIP→ Spa services are exclusive to Bellagio guests Friday through Sunday.** ✉ *Bellagio, 3600 Las Vegas Blvd. S, Center Strip* ☎ *702/693–7472* ⊕ *www.bellagio.com.*

Chapter 5

NORTH STRIP

Updated by
Steven Bornfeld

👁 **Sights**
★★★★☆

🍴 **Restaurants**
★★★★☆

🛏 **Hotels**
★★★★☆

🛍 **Shopping**
★★★★☆

🍸 **Nightlife**
★★★★☆

NEIGHBORHOOD SNAPSHOT

TOP EXPERIENCES

- **Adventuredome:** Most of the kid-friendly things that popped up in the 1990s are gone; this is one place for the small set to burn off some energy.

- **Carlo's Bakery:** Fans of Food Network Cake Boss Buddy Valastro stand in long lines for the treats of this offshoot of the Hoboken original.

- **Shopping:** If browsing is your thing, you won't find better opportunities than at Fashion Show, the Grand Canal Shoppes, and Wynn.

- **The Venetian:** There's no denying the charm of these indoor (and outdoor, in good weather) canal rides on imported gondolas.

- **Wynn:** The place is just beautiful from top to bottom, with flowers, plants, and aquatic accents everywhere you look.

GETTING HERE

The North Strip is far enough from the airport (up to 30 minutes) that your taxi driver may take the interstate (though it's the same $27 flat fare). A pedestrian bridge between The Palazzo and Wynn makes exploring these two properties easy. The journey from Trump and Encore to SLS, Circus Circus, and the Strat is deceptively long; on hot days, it pays to take a cab or public transportation. Be warned: on foot from the Strat, it's still 20 to 30 minutes to Downtown. And it's not the best neighborhood.

Las Vegas Monorail stations here include the Harrah's/LINQ station, the Las Vegas Convention Center station, the Westgate station, and the SLS Vegas station. RTC services this part of the Strip with public buses and double-deckers.

QUICK BITES

- **Goodies on Demand.** Wynn routinely attracts the best pastry chefs, and their skills are on display in this shop near the Encore registration desk. ⊠ *Wynn Las Vegas, 3131 Las Vegas Blvd. S* ⊕ *www.wynnlasvegas.com*

- **Luke's Lobster.** This New York City import serves lobster, crab, and shrimp rolls, including seasonal specials. ⊠ *Fashion Show Mall, 3200 Las Vegas Blvd. S* ⊕ *www.lukeslobster.com*

- **Tasti D-Lite.** Choose from over 100 flavors of creamy, dairy desserts as a delish breather in between everything else to occupy your attention at Circus Circus. ⊠ *Circus Circus, 2880 Las Vegas Blvd. S*

PLANNING YOUR TIME

- As is the case with most of Las Vegas, how much time you want to spend here depends on how much time you have. If you're an avid shopper, plan to spend hours in the various shopping centers. A trip to the top of the Strat—complete with a thrill ride or two—won't take more than two hours, but if you plan to ride the Venetian gondolas, be sure to plan ahead to get a timed ticket.

Like the best nights out, the North Strip is the perfect mix of luxury, fun, and debauchery—a blend of the very best that Vegas has to offer in high-end, low-brow, and laugh-out-loud diversion. Wynn, Encore, The Palazzo, and The Venetian are posh celebrity favorites. Carnival acts at Circus Circus and thrill rides at the Strat entertain the masses.

Sister properties dominate the landscape in this part of town—resorts that complement each other wonderfully. One pair, The Venetian and The Palazzo, whisks visitors to Italy, where they can ride gondolas and marvel at indoor waterfalls. Another pair, Wynn and Encore, offer a different kind of luxury. Encore in particular is a one-of-a-kind blend of classic (authentic antiques pervade the property) and modern (windows in the casino). Also not to be missed: the Encore Beach Club, a thumping day-lounge experience.

Farther north, this part of the Strip embraces the circus. In the Adventuredome, behind Circus Circus, visitors can participate in an actual carnival, complete with cotton candy and midway games. On top of the Strat tower the attractions aren't for the faint of heart, considering that they suspend you about 900 feet over the ground.

The North Strip has improved on a number of familiar Vegas experiences, too. Circus acts at Circus Circus are as campy as ever. The North Strip presents a number of familiar sights; it just does them better.

👁 Sights

Adventuredome Theme Park
AMUSEMENT PARK/WATER PARK | FAMILY
If the sun is blazing, the kids are antsy, and you need a place to while away a few hours, make for the big pink dome behind Circus Circus. The 5-acre amusement park has more than 25 rides and attractions for all age levels, and is kept at a constant 72°F. The newest attraction is a roller-skating rink, with skate rentals available. The El Loco roller coaster includes a barrel roll and a number of G-force drops. Also check out the Canyon Blaster, the world's only indoor double-loop, double-corkscrew roller coaster, a huge swinging pirate ship, bumper cars, several kiddie rides, a minigolf course, two Bank Heist Laser Challenges, a rock-climbing wall, and much more. There are even attractions with computer-generated iterations of the Angry Birds and SpongeBob SquarePants. And Neon Nights on Friday and Saturday give everything a whole new glow. ✉ *Circus Circus, 2880 Las Vegas Blvd. S, North Strip* ☎ *702/794–3939, 866/456–8894* ⊕ *www.adventuredome.com* 💲 *From $6 per ride, all-day pass $34 for those 48 inches and taller, $20 for under 48 inches.*

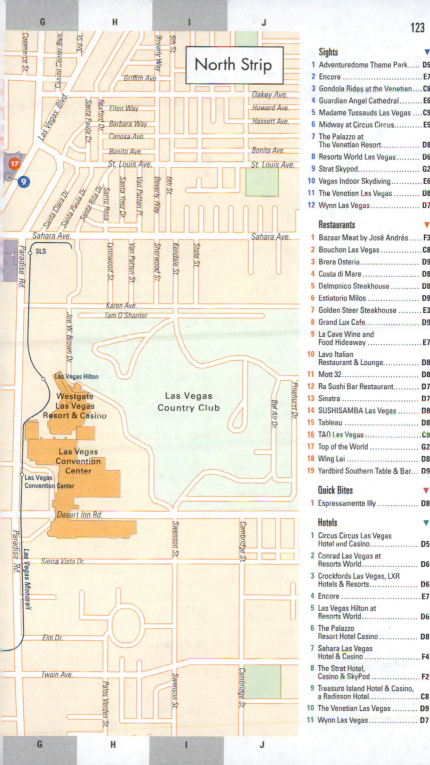

North Strip

Sights ▼

#		
1	Adventuredome Theme Park	D5
2	Encore	E7
3	Gondola Rides at the Venetian	C9
4	Guardian Angel Cathedral	E6
5	Madame Tussauds Las Vegas	C9
6	Midway at Circus Circus	E5
7	The Palazzo at The Venetian Resort	D8
8	Resorts World Las Vegas	D6
9	Strat Skypod	G2
10	Vegas Indoor Skydiving	E6
11	The Venetian Las Vegas	D8
12	Wynn Las Vegas	D7

Restaurants ▼

#		
1	Bazaar Meat by José Andrés	F3
2	Bouchon Las Vegas	C8
3	Brera Osteria	D9
4	Costa di Mare	D8
5	Delmonico Steakhouse	D8
6	Estiatorio Milos	D9
7	Golden Steer Steakhouse	E3
8	Grand Lux Cafe	D9
9	La Cave Wine and Food Hideaway	E7
10	Lavo Italian Restaurant & Lounge	D8
11	Mott 32	D8
12	Ra Sushi Bar Restaurant	D7
13	Sinatra	D7
14	SUSHISAMBA Las Vegas	D8
15	Tableau	D8
16	TAO Las Vegas	C9
17	Top of the World	G2
18	Wing Lei	D8
19	Yardbird Southern Table & Bar	D9

Quick Bites ▼

#		
1	Espressamente Illy	D8

Hotels ▼

#		
1	Circus Circus Las Vegas Hotel and Casino	D5
2	Conrad Las Vegas at Resorts World	D6
3	Crockfords Las Vegas, LXR Hotels & Resorts	D6
4	Encore	E7
5	Las Vegas Hilton at Resorts World	D6
6	The Palazzo Resort Hotel Casino	D8
7	Sahara Las Vegas Hotel & Casino	F4
8	The Strat Hotel, Casino & SkyPod	F2
9	Treasure Island Hotel & Casino, a Radisson Hotel	C8
10	The Venetian Las Vegas	D9
11	Wynn Las Vegas	D7

★ Encore

RESORT—SIGHT | Though smaller than its neighbor Wynn, Encore pulls together some of the best touches from all of Wynn. For that we owe thanks to designer Roger Thomas, who invested in antiques from all over the world to decorate the resort. The other notable design element: sunlight, which streams in through window-lined corridors (a relative rarity in Vegas). Most people come to Encore for the partying, specifically the partying at Encore Beach Club, Intrigue, and XS. A modest but beautiful shopping strip, the Esplanade at Encore, features Hermès, Chanel, and Christian Louboutin. ✉ *3131 Las Vegas Blvd. S, North Strip* ☎ *702/770–7000, 888/320–7123* ⊕ *www.wynnlasvegas.com.*

Gondola Rides at The Venetian

AMUSEMENT PARK/WATER PARK | **FAMILY**
Let a gondolier "o sole mio" you down Vegas's rendition of Venice's Grand Canal. We love this attraction because it's done so well—owner Sheldon Adelson was obsessed with getting the canals *just right*: he had them drained and repainted three times before he was satisfied with the hue, and the colossal reproduction of St. Mark's Square at the end of the canal is authentic right down to the colors of the facades. The gondoliers who ply the waterway are professional entertainers and train for two weeks to maneuver the canals. It all makes for a rather entertaining way to while away an hour on the Strip. Outdoor gondola rides along the resort's exterior waterway are also available, weather permitting. Photo packages are available with all rides. ✉ *The Venetian Las Vegas, 3355 Las Vegas Blvd. S, North Strip* ☎ *702/414–4300* ⊕ *www.venetian.com* ✉ *From $29; photo packages from $22.*

Guardian Angel Cathedral

RELIGIOUS SITE | The Roman Catholic cathedral often has standing-room only on Saturday afternoon, as visitors pray for luck—and sometimes drop casino chips into the collection cups during a special tourist mass. Periodically, a priest known as the "chip monk" collects the chips and takes them to the respective casinos to cash them in. ✉ *302 Cathedral Way, North Strip* ☎ *702/735–5241* ⊕ *www.gaclv.org.*

Madame Tussauds Las Vegas

MUSEUM | **FAMILY** | Audition in front of Simon Cowell or stand toe-to-toe with Muhammad Ali as you explore the open showroom filled with uncanny celebrity wax portrayals of people from the worlds of show business, sports, politics, and everywhere in between. Crowd-pleasers include Khloe Kardashian, Will Smith, Steve Aoki, Lady Gaga, Miley Cyrus, and *The Hangover Bar.* An interactive segment lets you play golf with Tiger Woods or shoot baskets with Shaquille O'Neill. The new Virtual Room even gives you a chance to save the world. Discount tickets are available online. ✉ *The Venetian Las Vegas, 3377 Las Vegas Blvd. S, North Strip* ⊹ *Outside main hotel entrance* ☎ *866/841–3739* ⊕ *www.madametussauds.com/lasvegas* ✉ *From $37.*

Midway at Circus Circus

AMUSEMENT PARK/WATER PARK | **FAMILY**
If you can't win the jackpot at the casino, try winning your sweetheart a teddy bear instead. Here you can play 200 old-time fair and newly popular games like the dime toss, milk can, bushel basket, Skee-Ball, and Pop-A-Shot for the chance to win cuddly prizes. Beginning at 11:30 am daily, acrobats, high-wire walkers, jugglers, and trapeze artists perform free shows on the circus stage. ✉ *Circus Circus, 2880 Las Vegas Blvd. S, North Strip* ☎ *702/734–0410* ⊕ *www.circuscircus.com* ✉ *From $1 per game.*

The Palazzo at The Venetian Resort

RESORT—SIGHT | The Palazzo certainly feels palatial. Wide, cavernous corridors give way to an expansive casino, which, in turn, fronts escalators to the Grand Canal Shoppes, a mall with nearly 200 stores. Music lovers flock to the property to experience Human Nature Jukebox or for short-term residencies by artists such as ZZ Top and Earth, Wind & Fire. With a top-quality energy conservation program and other green amenities, The Palazzo has received LEED-Gold distinction from the U.S. Green Building Council. ⊠ *3325 Las Vegas Blvd. S, North Strip* ☎ *702/607–7777, 866/263–3001* ⊕ *www. palazzo.com.*

★ Resorts World Las Vegas

HOTEL—SIGHT | When it opened in June 2021, the first new casino resort on the Las Vegas Strip in more than a decade came at a time when the city needed something to cheer about. The 3,500-room property was bankrolled by Genting Corp., a Singaporean outfit, and it features two hotel towers that comprise three separate Hilton brands: Hilton, Conrad, and Crockfords. The resort has more than 50 food outlets, including a hawker-style food court that brings together delicious morsels from all over the world. Hotel guests can get room service from any restaurant on-site. The 5.5-acre pool complex (the largest in all of Vegas) includes seven pools and trees from the Stardust, which sat on the site many years ago. Headliners such as Katy Perry, Carrie Underwood, and Celine will pack theaters for years to come. ⊠ *3000 Las Vegas Blvd. S, North Strip* ☎ *702/676–7000* ⊕ *rwlasvegas.com.*

Strat Skypod

AMUSEMENT PARK/WATER PARK | FAMILY High above the Strip at the tip of the Strat (now officially shortening its original name, the Stratosphere Tower, to its longtime nickname) are four major thrill rides that will scare the bejeezus out of you, especially if you have even the slightest fear of heights. Don't even think about heading up here if you have serious vertigo. People have been known to get sick just watching these rides. But if you are of the less adventurous sort, you can just visit the **Observation Decks** on Levels 108 and 109.

The **Big Shot** starts from the 112th floor, shooting four riders 160 feet up into the air at 45 mph and climaxing at more than 1,000 feet above the Strip with very little warning (it may be better that way). The whole thing is over in less than a minute, but your knees will wobble for the rest of the day.

The **X Scream** tips passengers 27 feet over the edge of the tower like a giant seesaw again and again. From the very front, you get an unobstructed view of the Strip, straight down.

Insanity hangs you out 64 feet from the edge of the tower; then it spins you faster and faster, so you're lifted to a 70-degree angle by a centrifugal force that's the equivalent of 3 G-forces.

The newest ride, **SkyJump Las Vegas,** is a controlled free fall that sends you careening off the side of the 108th floor.

Sharing the space is the Top of the World restaurant and 107 Skylounge. ⊠ *The Strat, 2000 Las Vegas Blvd. S, North Strip* ☎ *702/380–7777* ⊕ *www. stratospherehotel.com* ⊠ *Skypod admission only from $25; Skypod and ride packages from $34 (for a single thrill ride); Skyjump from $130.*

★ Vegas Indoor Skydiving

SPORTS—SIGHT | This attraction, just north of Encore Las Vegas, provides the thrill of skydiving without a plane. After 20 minutes of training you enter a vertical wind tunnel that produces a powerful stream of air. You'll float, hover, and fly, simulating up to five minutes of free fall, with more time for large parties. Airspeeds reach 120 mph. Plan to reserve at least two hours in advance, making payment in full. The place closes for private parties from time to time, so it's wise to call ahead. ⊠ *200 Convention Center Dr., North Strip* ☎ *702/731–4768, 877/588–2359* ⊕ *www.vegasindoorskydiving.com* ⊠ *From $85.*

The Venetian Las Vegas

RESORT—SIGHT | This theme hotel re-creates Italy's most romantic city with meticulous reproductions of Venetian landmarks. As such, this gilded resort is a hit with foodies, shoppers, and high rollers alike. From the Strip you enter through the Doge's Palace, which stands on a walkway over a large lagoon. Inside, Renaissance characters roam the public areas, singing opera, performing mime, jesting, even kissing hands (but that was prepandemic, of course). Walking from the hotel lobby into the casino is one of the great experiences in Las Vegas: overhead, reproductions of famous frescoes adorn the ceiling; underfoot, the geometric design of the flat marble floor provides an Escher-like optical illusion of climbing stairs. On a lake in front of the casino visitors can take gondola rides and look out on the Strip; gondola rides also are available in the canals that adorn the Grand Canal Shoppes upstairs. The Venetian is known for its restaurant scene and the heralded bar project, Electra Cocktail Club, has gotten rave reviews for its rum, agricole, and mezcal specialty cocktails. ⊠ 3355 Las Vegas Blvd. S, North Strip ☎ 702/414–1000, 866/659–9643 ⊕ www. venetian.com.

★ Wynn Las Vegas

RESORT—SIGHT | In a city that keeps raising the bar for sheer luxury, Wynn Las Vegas—monolithic in both name and appearance—offers a discreet turn for the tasteful. The resort is a best-of-everything experience—a playground for jet-setters, high rollers, or anyone who wants to feel like one. This excellence starts with the gardens near the front entrance; though smaller than Bellagio's, they are just as exquisite. It continues with the waterfall that pours from (man-made) rocks into a interior lake, both visible from the Parasol Up and Parasol Down lounges. Instead of booking another Cirque du Soleil show, Wynn created Le Reve, which closed during the pandemic, and a replacement show has not yet been announced. On-site restaurants are just as appealing, with Wing Lei holding firm as one of the best Chinese restaurants in the entire city. High-end shopping options at Wynn Esplanade include Alexander McQueen, Brioni, and Chopard, and the new Wynn Plaza includes Breitling, Kenzo, and Cipriani restaurant, birthplace of the Bellini. ⊠ 3131 Las Vegas Blvd. S, North Strip ☎ 702/770–7000, 888/320–7123 ⊕ www. wynnlasvegas.com.

🍴 Restaurants

Bazaar Meat by José Andrés

$$$$ | **ECLECTIC** | This restaurant, the crown jewel of the Sahara Las Vegas, is decorated in a subtle jungle motif and is clearly all about meat. Choose from the steaks sold by the pound to suckling pig (by the quarter or whole, which you'll have to order ahead), and every other type you can imagine. **Known for:** meat in every form possible; whole suckling pig; jungle-theme atmosphere. ⑤ Average main: $70 ⊠ Sahara Las Vegas, 2535 Las Vegas Blvd. S, North Strip ☎ 702/761–7610 ⊕ www.thebazaar.com ⊘ No lunch. Closed Mon.–Wed.

Bouchon Las Vegas

$$$$ | **FRENCH** | When chefs name their idol, more than a few will cite French Laundry chef Thomas Keller, the star behind this stunning, capacious French bistro and oyster bar in The Venezia Tower. Soaring Palladian windows, antique lighting fixtures, a pewter-topped bar, and painted tile lend a sophisticated take on French country design, a fitting setting in which to dine on savory, rich cuisine. **Known for:** Thomas Keller's bistro interpretations; classic French-bistro atmosphere; patio overlooking Venezia Pool. ⑤ Average main: $35 ⊠ The Venetian, 3355 Las Vegas Blvd. S, Venezia Tower, 10th fl., North Strip ☎ 702/414–6200 ⊕ www.bouchonbistro.com.

Family Fun

Wild Times

This may be Sin City, but there are plenty of great family-oriented activities. There's wildlife galore, starting with exotic birds at **Flamingo** and fish and reptiles at **Shark Reef at Mandalay Bay.** Next, head to **The Mirage** to see the white tigers of the **Secret Garden** and the eponymous mammals of the **Dolphin Habitat.**

Fast Times

If your family prefers adrenaline-based bonding, scream your way up the Strip, starting at the **Big Apple Coaster** at **New York–New York.** Continue north along the Strip (via the Monorail to Sahara Las Vegas Station), stopping at **Circus Circus**'s indoor theme park **Adventuredome** on your way to the **Strat Tower.** Here the Big

Shot, X Scream, and Insanity–The Ride fly high above the Strip at 1,149 feet. Can't decide between wild animals and wild rides? Go Downtown for both at the Tank at **Golden Nugget**, where a three-story waterslide includes a ride through a glass tube into the heart of a 200,000-gallon shark tank.

Downtime

For a mellower afternoon, head to The Venetian's **Madame Tussauds Wax Museum.** After posing next to Miley and J-Lo, check out the exploding volcano at **The Mirage.** Since you're at The Mirage, grab last-minute tickets for ventriloquist **Terry Fator**'s one-of-a-kind musical puppet act. You can minimize your kids' sinful intake by staying at the **Waldorf Astoria**, posh accommodations that are unusual for being casino-free.

Brera Osteria

$$$ | **ITALIAN** | **FAMILY** | The latest entry in the *Viva Italiano!* culinary scene, Brera Osteria at the Grand Canal Shoppes (replacing Sixth + Mill) is a Milan-inspired creation sitting on the Venetian's replica of St. Mark's Square. Taking its name from the Brera neighborhood of Milan, the menu focuses on Milanese favorites. **Known for:** braised pork shank; nice Italian wine list; good pizza. Ⓢ *Average main: $26 ⊠ 3355 Las Vegas Blvd. S, North Strip ☎ 702/414–1227 ⊕ www.venetian.com.*

Costa di Mare

$$$$ | **MEDITERRANEAN** | Longtime Wynn chef Mark LoRusso was given a new showcase in this Mediterranean seafood spot in the space formerly occupied by Bartolotta Ristorante di Mare. Costa continues the tradition of freshly flown-in Mediterranean fish sold by weight, plus dishes such as cuttlefish, shrimp, and lobster with cuttlefish-ink pasta, and

several raw-fish appetizers. **Known for:** fish flown in daily from Mediterranean; many choices sold by weight; private cabanas overlooking lagoon. Ⓢ *Average main: $60 ⊠ Wynn Las Vegas, 3131 Las Vegas Blvd. S, North Strip ☎ 702/770–3305 ⊕ www.wynnlasvegas.com ⊗ No lunch. Closed Sun.–Wed.*

Delmonico Steakhouse

$$$$ | **STEAKHOUSE** | Chef Emeril Lagasse gives a New Orleans touch to this big city–style steak house at The Venetian. Enter through 12-foot oak doors to find a sedately decorated, modern room in which to relax and enjoy your Taste of Japan, made with two Japanese spirits, along with appetizers such as truffle and Parmesan potato chips; Lagasse's signature barbecue shrimp, served with a fresh-baked rosemary biscuit; or the Caesar salad, prepared table-side for two. **Known for:** Emeril's steak interpretations; Japanese whiskey selection;

contemporary decor. $ *Average main: $55* ✉ *The Venetian, 3355 Las Vegas Blvd. S, North Strip* ☎ *702/414–3737* ⊕ *www.emerilsrestaurants.com.*

Estiatorio Milos

$$$$ | **MEDITERRANEAN** | The first Greek restaurant on the Las Vegas Strip certainly doesn't disappoint, although you'll pay well for the experience. Though the eatery has relocated from The Cosmopolitan to The Venetian, the great basics are the same: chef Costas Spiliadis flies in fresh fish from the Mediterranean; you pick out the piece of fish at market price and select how you'd like it prepared. **Known for:** fish from the Mediterranean; updated Greek classics; evocative Greek atmosphere. $ *Average main: $31* ✉ *The Venetian, 3355 Las Vegas Blvd. S, North Strip* ☎ *702/414–1270* ⊕ *www.venetian.com.*

Golden Steer Steakhouse

$$$$ | **STEAKHOUSE** | In a town where restaurants come and go almost as quickly as visitors' cash, the longevity of this steak house, which opened in 1958, is itself a recommendation. Both locals and visitors adore this classic steak house with red-leather seating, polished dark wood, and stained-glass windows for the huge slabs of well-prepared meat. **Known for:** Rat Pack–era vibe; dark, opulent atmosphere; table-side preparations. $ *Average main: $55* ✉ *308 W. Sahara Ave., North Strip* ☎ *702/384–4470* ⊕ *www.goldensteersteakhouselasvegas. com* ☾ *No lunch. Closed Sun. and Mon.*

Grand Lux Cafe

$$$ | **AMERICAN** | Warm earth tones, soft music and lighting, cloth napkins, and marble-topped tables are an elegant milieu in which to enjoy a glass of wine and mélange of appealing, freshly cooked flavors and textures—Asian nachos, double-stuffed potato spring rolls, stacked chicken quesadilla—24 hours a day. Located right off the main casino floor, this convenient chain eatery offers eclectic menu items and familiar crowd-pleasers: pizza, pastas, barbecue ribs, burgers,

BLTs, and even wood-grilled filet mignon or rib eye. **Known for:** varied, eclectic menu; Cheesecake Factory desserts; open 24/7. $ *Average main: $25* ✉ *The Venetian, 3355 Las Vegas Blvd. S, North Strip* ☎ *702/414–3888* ⊕ *www.grandluxcafe.com.*

La Cave Wine and Food Hideaway

$$$ | **MEDITERRANEAN** | This intimate, casual restaurant focuses on wine and Mediterranean-inspired small plates such as sweet and salty bacon-wrapped dates with blue-cheese fondue and beef carpaccio with mushrooms and truffle aioli. The remarkable wine list reflects global selections, with an emphasis on Europe. **Known for:** innovative, varied menu; cozy spot; scenic view from patio. $ *Average main: $30* ✉ *Wynn Las Vegas, 3131 Las Vegas Blvd. S, North Strip* ☎ *702/770–7100, 877/321–9966* ⊕ *www. wynnlasvegas.com.*

Lavo Italian Restaurant & Lounge

$$$$ | **ITALIAN** | The food at this Roman-styled see-and-be-seen restaurant/nightclub often is overshadowed by the roaring club scene, but it's worth a stop—especially if you go early to avoid the *thump thump* of the music upstairs. Many of the dishes are meant to be shared. **Known for:** celebrity sightings; funky atmosphere; menu far beyond red-sauce choices. $ *Average main: $40* ✉ *The Palazzo, 3325 Las Vegas Blvd. S, North Strip* ☎ *702/791–1800* ⊕ *www.lavolv.com* ☾ *No lunch. Closed Mon.–Wed.*

★ Mott 32

$$$$ | **CHINESE** | Hong Kong street food comes to life at this lively and architecturally stunning restaurant inside the Palazzo Tower at The Venetian Resort Las Vegas. The eatery, which opened in December 2018, is the first U.S. outpost of a Hong Kong restaurant by the same name. **Known for:** smoked Peking duck; excellent dim sum; lobster ma po tofu. $ *Average main: $55* ✉ *The Venetian Las Vegas, 3325 Las Vegas Blvd. S, North Strip* ☎ *702/607–3232* ⊕ *www.mott32. com/lasvegas* ☾ *No lunch.*

Ra Sushi Bar Restaurant

$$$ | JAPANESE | FAMILY | Take a break from shopping at the Fashion Show mall and step into this dimly lighted restaurant and lounge that's part of a growing chain. The menu has both sushi and cooked entrées. **Known for:** plenty of classic sushi; far-from-classic rolls; contemporary decor. ⑤ *Average main: $22 ⊠ Fashion Show Mall, 3200 Las Vegas Blvd. S, Suite 1132, North Strip ☎ 702/696–0008 ⊕ www.rasushi.com.*

Sinatra

$$$$ | ITALIAN | Encore recalls the panache of vintage Vegas by dedicating one of its fine-dining venues to Frank Sinatra. Expect simple, elegantly presented Italian cuisine, such as Frank's spaghetti and clams and Ossobuco "My Way." Framed photos of Ol' Blue Eyes (as well as his Academy Award for *From Here to Eternity*) adorn the ivory-and-ruby-hue indoor dining room. **Known for:** menu includes Frank's favorites; Ol' Blue Eyes decor and music; outdoor seating with fireplaces. ⑤ *Average main: $55 ⊠ Encore, 3131 Las Vegas Blvd. S, North Strip ☎ 702/770–3463 ⊕ www.wynnlasvegas.com/restaurants ⊗ No lunch. Closed Mon.–Wed.*

SUSHISAMBA Las Vegas

$$$$ | ASIAN | Come to this trendy, tricolor restaurant for its fresh sushi and sashimi, beautifully prepared and presented, with delightful dipping sauces and edible garnish. Dim lighting, hip music, voluptuous decor, and excellent cocktails complement the exotic fusion of flavors from Japan, Brazil, and Peru. **Known for:** Japanese-Peruvian fusion; extensive cocktail selection; lively atmosphere. ⑤ *Average main: $37 ⊠ The Palazzo, 3325 Las Vegas Blvd. S, North Strip ☎ 702/607–0700 ⊕ www.sushisamba.com.*

Tableau

$$$ | AMERICAN | Isolated from the busier parts of Wynn, this bright, airy breakfast-and-lunch restaurant overlooks a serene pool and well-manicured garden off the gleaming Tower Suites lobby. It also offers a splurge-worthy weekend brunch. **Known for:** quiet refuge; opulent breakfasts and brunches; view of resort pool. ⑤ *Average main: $25 ⊠ Wynn Las Vegas, 3131 Las Vegas Blvd. S, North Strip ☎ 702/770–3463 ⊕ www.wynnlasvegas.com/restaurants ⊗ No dinner.*

TAO Las Vegas

$$$$ | ASIAN | The tunneled vestibule of this nightclub-cum-bistro is lined with stone tubs filled with water and rose petals, leading patrons—including lots of celebrities, some of them hired to host—into the dim, lavishly decorated space. The pan-Asian menu is almost endless, with dishes from sushi to dim sum and everything in between, but you don't necessarily come for the food. **Known for:** celebrity-sighting hot spot; dramatic Asian decor; lots of offbeat dishes. ⑤ *Average main: $33 ⊠ The Venetian, 3355 Las Vegas Blvd. S, North Strip ☎ 702/388–8338 ⊕ taolasvegas.com ⊗ No lunch. Closed Mon. and Tues.*

Top of the World

$$$$ | EUROPEAN | Reserve a window-side table at twilight to see sunset melt into sparkling night while savoring updated Continental cuisine. From a height of 844 feet, the restaurant's floor-to-ceiling windows offer 360-degree views of the Vegas Valley as the entire 106th-floor dining room makes a complete revolution every 80 minutes. **Known for:** expansive, continually changing views; menu mix of classic and innovative; romantic atmosphere. ⑤ *Average main: $55 ⊠ The Strat Hotel, Casino & Skypod, 2000 Las Vegas Blvd. S, 106th fl., North Strip ☎ 702/380–7711 ⊕ www.topoftheworldlv.com.*

★ Wing Lei

$$$$ | CHINESE | With all the panache of an Asian royal palace, this fine-dining restaurant serves some of the choicest Chinese food on the Strip. Chefs present contemporary French-inspired cuisine that blends the Cantonese, Shanghai, and Sichuan traditions. **Known for:** fine Chinese food; Peking duck; elegant atmosphere.

Cheap Eats

Don't forget about Sin City's terrific hole-in-the-wall dives, inexpensive regional chains, and cheap-and-cheerful take-out counters that serve tasty treats at rock-bottom prices.

Fatburger. There are about a dozen branches of this popular California chain around Las Vegas, but only one on the Strip: across from the Park MGM. ⊠ *3763 Las Vegas Blvd. S, South Strip.*

In-N-Out Burger. Visitors no longer need a car or taxi for an In-N-Out fix, now that there's a location at The LINQ on the Strip. ⊠ *3545 Las Vegas Blvd. S, Center Strip.*

Jason's Deli. Jason's offers all manner of deli food, and free ice cream for dessert! And there's a convenient location Downtown. ⊠ *100 N. City Pkwy., Downtown.*

L&L Hawaiian Barbecue. With 15 of these in the valley, you don't have to go far to go Hawaiian, but there's no location on the Strip. ⊠ *Sahara Square, 4030 S. Maryland Pkwy., University District.*

---

⑤ *Average main: $40* ⊠ *Wynn Las Vegas, 3131 Las Vegas Blvd. S, North Strip* ☎ *702/248–3463* ⊕ *www.wynnlasvegas. com/restaurants* ⊙ *No lunch.*

Yardbird Southern Table & Bar
$$$$ | AMERICAN | A craft-ice program may seem a bit much, but that's indicative of Yardbird's attention to detail, as first evidenced at the Miami original. Go for the artisanal beverages but stay for Southern-leaning favorites. **Known for:** fare like chicken, watermelon, and waffles; upscale cocktails program with artisanal ice; fun, countrified decor. ⑤ *Average main: $32* ⊠ *The Venetian, 3355 Las Vegas Blvd. S, North Strip* ☎ *702/297–6541* ⊕ *runchickenrun.com.*

☕ Coffee and Quick Bites

Espressamente Illy
$$ | ITALIAN | Swoop into this authentic, cozy Italian coffee bar, at the entrance to The Shoppes at The Palazzo, for richly brewed premium beverages, flaky pastries, and warm paninis. This smart, colorful nook offers 36 flavors of glorious, creamy gelatos, as well as fresh dessert crepes, soups, and salads. **Known for:** fine

Illy coffees; fresh pastries and paninis; dozens of gelatos. ⑤ *Average main: $15* ⊠ *The Palazzo, 3325 Las Vegas Blvd. S, North Strip* ☎ *702/869–2233* ⊕ *www. palazzo.com/restaurants.html.*

🛏 Hotels

Luxury reigns supreme in the top third of the Las Vegas Strip. There aren't as many resorts here, but spacious rooms, exquisite details, and deep-sleep-inducing beds make four of them among the most luxurious in the world. This part of town is about a 30-minute ride from the airport and at least 20 minutes to the South Strip, so visitors often stay put once they're here. Then again, when you're staying at resorts that have just about everything, who wants to leave?

The cluster of hotels that make up this section include The Venetian, Palazzo, Treasure Island, Wynn, Encore, Sahara Las Vegas, and Circus Circus. Of particular interest: pools. Swanky, ultra-exclusive day-lounge areas surround the pools at North Strip properties; The Palazzo's Azure Pool is one of the newest, and Encore Beach Club is by far the most popular. As with most pools in Vegas, these offer European-style sunbathing sections, too. Bikini tops optional.

Other amenities are worth raves as well. Wynn, for instance, has a men's barbershop. The Venetian's spa is operated by none other than the world-renowned Canyon Ranch. Factor in additional amenities such as high-end shopping, indoor gardens, and breathtaking design, and it's no wonder the North Strip is seen as the spot where Vegas meets high fashion, year after year.

Circus Circus Las Vegas Hotel and Casino

$$ | RESORT | FAMILY | The hotel at the "Big Top" has renovated all of its rooms in the last decade, giving some much-needed TLC to some of the oldest rooms on the Strip (the resort opened in 1968). **Pros:** Adventure Dome Theme Park; pet-friendly; old-school. **Cons:** gaming atmosphere isn't nearly as elegant as most Strip properties; not close to any other casinos; only one good restaurant (The Steak House). ⑤ *Rooms from: $188* ✉ *2880 Las Vegas Blvd. S, North Strip* ☎ *702/734–0410, 800/634–3450* ⊕ *www. circuscircus.com* ⇨ *3632 rooms* ⑩ *No meals.*

Conrad Las Vegas at Resorts World

$$$$ | HOTEL | The largest Conrad in the world takes the basic Hilton vibe and enhances it considerably with spacious rooms, in some cases topping out around 1,200 square feet. **Pros:** curated art pieces for guest rooms; private check-in lobby; all keyless entry. **Cons:** very busy carpeting; views of a construction site; small VIP lobby. ⑤ *Rooms from: $369* ✉ *111 Resorts World Ave., North Strip* ☎ *702/676–7000* ⊕ *www.rwlasvegas. com/stay/conrad-las-vegas* ⇨ *1496 rooms* ⑩ *No meals.*

Crockfords Las Vegas, LXR Hotels & Resorts

$$$$ | HOTEL | Lavish accommodations and highly personalized service characterize this brand, the most upscale of the three Hilton brands on-site, offering a spectacular private lobby right off the high-limit room of the casino. **Pros:** dedicated 24-hour concierge services; ultra-private gaming in the Sky Casino; palatial bedrooms. **Cons:** pretty expensive for the isolated location; bathrooms are so big as to seem cavernous; high level of service bordering on invasive. ⑤ *Rooms from: $529* ✉ *333 Resorts World Ave., North Strip* ☎ *702/676–7000* ⊕ *www.rwlasvegas.com/stay/crockfords-las-vegas* ⇨ *236 rooms* ⑩ *No meals.*

★ Encore

$$$$ | RESORT | As far as luxury is concerned, Las Vegas simply doesn't get much better than Encore. **Pros:** huge suites; glorious pools; casino is fun and intimate. **Cons:** cab ride to South Strip; pricey rates; check-in can be very slow. ⑤ *Rooms from: $842* ✉ *3131 Las Vegas Blvd. S, North Strip* ☎ *702/770–7000, 888/320–7123* ⊕ *www.wynnlasvegas. com* ⇨ *2034 suites* ⑩ *No meals.*

Las Vegas Hilton at Resorts World

$$ | HOTEL | The Las Vegas Hilton (which once existed as the property now known as Westgate) returned to Sin City with fanfare in June 2021, with modern but sparse rooms. **Pros:** spacious bathrooms; epic pool area; proximity to casino. **Cons:** it's a schlep to other properties in town; rooms are on the smaller side; spotty Wi-Fi. ⑤ *Rooms from: $189* ✉ *999 Resorts World Ave., North Strip* ☎ *702/676–7000* ⊕ *rwlasvegas.com/stay/las-vegas-hilton* ⇨ *1774 rooms* ⑩ *No meals.*

★ The Palazzo Resort Hotel Casino

$$$ | RESORT | The $1.8-billion, all-suites Palazzo offers downright huge suites, almost exactly the same as those of the nearby Venetian. **Pros:** state-of-the-art amenities; spacious suites; sumptuous linens. **Cons:** thin walls; deserted on weekdays; long walk to Venetian. ⑤ *Rooms from: $275* ✉ *3325 Las Vegas Blvd. S, North Strip* ☎ *702/607–7777, 866/263–3001* ⊕ *www.palazzo.com* ⇨ *3064 suites* ⑩ *No meals.*

The 5.5-acre pool deck at the new Resorts World Las Vegas is the largest in the city, with 7 different pools and even some older trees rescued from the old Stardust property, which used to be at this spot.

Sahara Las Vegas Hotel & Casino

$$ | HOTEL | Minus Michael J. Fox and a weird DeLorean, this resort is as close as you'll get to a *Back to the Future* experience in Las Vegas, one that literally reinvents a reinvention (in this case the Sahara, whose ill-fated rebranding as the SLS has now been rolled back). **Pros:** easygoing boutique-hotel atmosphere; genuinely friendly staff; good variety of on-site restaurants. **Cons:** far from the center-Strip action; fairly small rooms; unreliable Wi-Fi reception. $ *Rooms from: $161* ✉ *2535 Las Vegas Blvd. S, North Strip* ☎ *702/761–7000* ⊕ *saharalasvegas.com* 🛏 *1600 rooms* ⦿ *No meals.*

The Strat Hotel, Casino & SkyPod

$ | RESORT | The Strat (now officially shortening its former name, the Stratosphere Tower, to its longtime nickname) is synonymous with the 1,149-foot observation tower that soars over every other building in town, an iconic part of the Las Vegas skyline. **Pros:** Top of the World restaurant and observation deck; Radius Pool; value for the rooms. **Cons:** surrounding neighborhood sketchy; nondescript casino; rides and Tower cost more than a movie. $ *Rooms from: $120* ✉ *2000 Las Vegas Blvd. S, North Strip* ☎ *800/998–6937* ⊕ *www.stratospherehotel.com* 🛏 *2427 rooms* ⦿ *No meals.*

Treasure Island Hotel & Casino, a Radisson Hotel (*T.I.*)

$$ | RESORT | FAMILY | Whether you call it Treasure Island or T.I., what sets this resort apart is a dash of elegance mixed with a decidedly unpretentious vibe. Whereas other properties boast of a branch of Tiffany, this one features a jewelry store that specializes in cubic zirconia. **Pros:** fairly modest price point; convenient location; giant CVS on-site. **Cons:** no real nightlife or stand-out amenities; tiny poker room; no in-room coffee. $ *Rooms from: $230* ✉ *3300 Las Vegas Blvd. S, North Strip* ☎ *702/894–7111, 800/944–7444* ⊕ *www.treasureisland.com* 🛏 *2885 rooms* ⦿ *No meals.*

★ The Venetian Las Vegas

$$ | **RESORT** | It's no secret that this theme hotel re-creates Italy's most romantic city with meticulous reproductions of Venetian landmarks, and the large suites aren't too shabby, either. **Pros:** excellent re-creations of Italian sights; modern amenities; tremendous rooms. **Cons:** sometimes difficult to navigate to rooms; poker room action can be aggressive; a big, busy hotel that is always crowded with toursts. $ *Rooms from: $190* ⊠ *3355 Las Vegas Blvd. S, North Strip* ☎ *702/414–1000, 866/659–9643* ⊕ *www. venetian.com* 🛏 *4028 suites* ⦿ *No meals.*

★ Wynn Las Vegas

$$$$ | **RESORT** | Decked out with replicas of former chairman Steve Wynn's acclaimed art collection, the princely rooms here, averaging a whopping 650 square feet, offer spectacular views through wall-to-wall, floor-to-ceiling windows. **Pros:** opulence throughout casino and hotel; access to gorgeous pool; top-notch restaurant collection. **Cons:** cramped casino walkways; slow elevators; artificial lawns. $ *Rooms from: $842* ⊠ *3131 Las Vegas Blvd. S, North Strip* ☎ *702/770–7000* ⊕ *www.wynnlasvegas.com* 🛏 *2716 rooms* ⦿ *No meals.*

⏣ Nightlife

BARS AND LOUNGES

Encore Players Lounge

PIANO BARS/LOUNGES | Blackjack, roulette, and craps mingle with a Las Vegas nightlife vibe in an effort to capture the elusive millennial dollar across from Encore Beach Club at Night. Play pool or shuffleboard, hang out at interactive tables, or watch the sports on one of 23 56-inch HDTVs. A live DJ keeps the beats going. ⊠ *Encore Las Vegas, 3121 Las Vegas Blvd. S, North Strip* ☎ *702/770–7300* ⊕ *wynnsocial.com.*

107 SkyLounge

PIANO BARS/LOUNGES | The Strat might be downscale compared with other Vegas hotels, but there ain't nothing "down" about the high-in-the-sky experience to be had here. From this sleek, attractive room, the view of Sin City is truly amazing (if slightly remote). For an even bigger thrill, head upstairs and outside (to Level 108, of course). ⊠ *The Strat, 2000 Las Vegas Blvd. S, North Strip* ☎ *702/380–7777* ⊕ *www.thestrat.com.*

★ Parasol Up

PIANO BARS/LOUNGES | Not to be confused with sister lounge "Parasol Down," this exquisite-looking—and exquisitely tranquil—setting near the entrance of Wynn ensures you can indulge in that most endangered of all pleasures: a good conversation. Tufted leather chairs and an extensive menu of house martinis certainly contribute to the vibe. Best of all, the menu features a handful of snacks, and the place stays open all night. ⊠ *Wynn Las Vegas, 3131 Las Vegas Blvd. S, North Strip* ☎ *702/770–7000* ⊕ *www. wynnlasvegas.com.*

★ Peppermill's Fireside Lounge

PIANO BARS/LOUNGES | Pining for a genuine taste of retro Las Vegas? This kitschy and shagadelic lounge remains one of the town's truly essential nightspots. Just north of Encore, this evergreen romantic getaway serves food, but what you're really here for is the prismatic fire pit and signature cocktails such as the Key Lime Pie Martini and the lethal, 64-ounce Scorpion. ⊠ *2985 Las Vegas Blvd. S, North Strip* ☎ *702/735–4177* ⊕ *www. peppermilllasvegas.com.*

DANCE CLUBS AND NIGHTCLUBS

Intrigue Nightclub

DANCE CLUBS | Leave your cell phones in the room and head to this nightclub that colors itself a bit different than the rest. Inside, a private club-within-a-club is designated as a social media–free zone so revelers can concentrate on the here and now. ⊠ *Wynn Las Vegas, 3131 Las Vegas*

Blvd. S, North Strip ☎ *702/770–7300*
⊕ *intriguevegas.com.*

★ Tao

DANCE CLUBS | Nowhere else in Vegas furnishes you with the four Ds—dining, drinking, dancing, and drooling—in quite as alluring a mix as this multilevel (and multimillion-dollar) playground. The ground floor and mezzanine levels are exquisite enough (you almost tumble into rosewater baths with women bathing inside before you're in the door), but once you get off the elevator at the top floor, where an army of dramatically lighted stone deities greets you, the party truly begins. Chinese antiques, crimson chandeliers, and a so-called Opium Room set the mood. It's still one of the best dance clubs in Vegas. In spring and summer, Tao Beach opens with daytime pool parties. ✉ *The Venetian, 3355 Las Vegas Blvd. S, North Strip* ☎ *702/388–8588* ⊕ *taolasvegas.com.*

★ XS

DANCE CLUBS | This club backs up onto a pool that converts into one of the most spacious open-air dance floors in town. Steve Wynn's signature attention to detail shines through with touches such as a chandelier that doubles as a psychedelic disco ball, light fixtures that turn into stripper poles, and walls imprinted with golden body casts (the waitresses modeled for them). At the pool are cabanas, another bar, and outdoor gaming, where the sexiest croupiers in town ply their trade. *Excess* is a pretty good word for all of this. ✉ *Encore, 3121 Las Vegas Blvd. S, North Strip* ☎ *702/770–7300* ⊕ *www. xslasvegas.com.*

🛍 Shopping

BOOKS

Bookstores aren't exactly as ubiquitous in Las Vegas as video-poker machines, but if you venture out into the greater metro area, you inevitably find them. They're stashed among the many strip malls and neighborhood shopping centers. The more rarified, albeit pricier, offerings are found on the Strip.

Bauman Rare Books

BOOKS/STATIONERY | **FAMILY** | Housing an exquisite collection of first-edition titles in pristine condition, this antiquarian bookstore carries an ever-changing selection that might include such classics as Dr. Seuss's *The Cat in the Hat,* Truman Capote's *Breakfast at Tiffany's,* and *A Farewell to Arms,* inscribed by Hemingway himself. A large-folio 1679 edition of the King James Bible contains meticulous engraved-plate illustrations, as does Ellen Willmott's rare first-edition printing of *The Genus Rosa,* with its full-page color pages of roses. Historical documents showcase the original signatures of Jung, Edison, and presidents Lincoln and FDR, among other notables. Special binding services are also offered. You may have seen this bookshop on the History Channel's *Pawn Stars.* ✉ *Grand Canal Shoppes, 3377 Las Vegas Blvd. S, North Strip* ☎ *702/948–1617, 888/982–2862* ⊕ *www.baumanrarebooks.com.*

CANNABIS

Planet 13 Cannabis Dispensary

SPECIALTY STORES | It's a pot of fun—literally. This cannabis superstore not only has the goods—smokables, cannabis extracts, and all manner of cannabis-infused products, including edibles—but it's also framed in a good-time vibe unlike other dispensaries. Resembling another planet that could live in your imagination (especially if you partake of their stock), the creative atmosphere includes selfie spots and interactive art elements. When it comes to matching the ambience to the product, Planet 13's dispensary has it down to a science. And, most importantly, the budtenders know their stuff, so you can feel well guided through everything you need to know before making the right (and safe) purchase. ✉ *2548 W. Desert Inn Rd., North Strip* ☎ *702/815–1313* ⊕ *www. planet13lasvegas.com.*

GIFTS AND SOUVENIRS
Bonanza "World's Largest Gift Shop"

LOCAL SPECIALTIES | Okay, so it may not, in fact, be the world's largest, but at more than 40,000 square feet, it's Vegas's largest souvenir store. And although it carries most of the usual junk, this peddler of pop-culture kitsch also stocks some most unusual junk. A pair of fuzzy pink dice? Check. Blinking "Welcome to Fabulous Las Vegas" sign? Check. Elvis aviator sunglasses complete with black sideburns? Check. How about a battery-operated parrot with a potty mouth or a 3-inch plastic slot machine that squirts water? They're all here, seven days a week, open until 10:30 pm. Check out an area of the store that contains Elvis and Marilyn Monroe gifts. As the store likes to say, "If it's in stock, we have it." ⊠ *2440 Las Vegas Blvd. S, North Strip* ☎ *702/385–7359* ⊕ *www.worldslargestgiftshop.com.*

JEWELRY
Chopard

JEWELRY/ACCESSORIES | This Swiss watchmaker is known particularly for its ladies' timepieces but creates an astonishing collection of diamond pieces of jewelry as well. ⊠ *Wynn Esplanade, 3131 Las Vegas Blvd. S, North Strip* ☎ *702/862–4522* ⊕ *www.chopard.com.*

Rolex

JEWELRY/ACCESSORIES | Many other authorized stores sell Rolex, but the standalone boutique at Wynn Esplanade showcases the entire line from the Swiss luxury watchmaker. ⊠ *Wynn Esplanade, 3131 Las Vegas Blvd. S, North Strip* ☎ *702/770–3560* ⊕ *www.rolex.com.*

MALLS
★ Fashion Show

SHOPPING CENTERS/MALLS | The frontage of this fashion-devoted mall is dominated by The Cloud—a giant, oblong disc that looms high above the entrance. Ads and footage of the mall's own fashion events are continuously projected across the expanse of this ovoid screen. Inside, the mall is sleek, spacious, and airy—a nice change from some of the claustrophobic casino malls. The mall delivers on its name: fashion shows are staged in the Great Hall on an 80-foot-long catwalk that rises from the floor (on select weekends, every hour from noon to 5). Although you can find many of the same stores in the casino malls, there's a smattering of different fare, such as Drybar, which specializes in blowouts, and Lolli & Pops, "purveyors of sweetness." Neiman Marcus, Saks Fifth Avenue, Nordstrom, and Dillard's serve as the mall's anchors. Along with an airy food court, dependable chains including Benihana and California Pizza Kitchen offer sit-down dining. ⊠ *3200 Las Vegas Blvd. S, North Strip* ☎ *702/784–7000* ⊕ *fslv.com* ☞ *Free valet and self-parking.*

★ Grand Canal Shoppes

SHOPPING CENTERS/MALLS | This is one of the most unforgettable shopping experiences on the Strip. Duck into shops like Field of Dreams, Sephora, or Peter Lik's rustic gallery of fine-art photography. Amble under blue-sky ceilings alongside the Grand Canal. All roads, balustraded bridges, and waterways lead to St. Mark's Square, an enormous open space filled with Italian opera singers and costumed performers. Watch for the living statues, who will intrigue and amuse. If you need to take a load off, hail a gondola.

Closer to The Palazzo, find powerhouse names such as Michael Kors and Tory Burch. Shoe lovers will swoon over the Jimmy Choo boutique. ⊠ *The Venetian, 3377 Las Vegas Blvd. S, North Strip* ☎ *702/414–4525* ⊕ *www.grandcanal-shoppes.com.*

MEN'S CLOTHING
Brioni

CLOTHING | High rollers can have an impeccably tailored suit made to order for a cool six grand. Or splurge on a crocodile watch case for $11,000. ⊠ *Wynn Esplanade, 3131 Las Vegas Blvd. S, North Strip* ☎ *702/770–3440* ⊕ *www.brioni.com.*

Suitsupply

CLOTHING | Suits, blazers, shirts, shoes, and accessories can be purchased and fitted on the spot at the tailoring bar situated front and center. ✉ *Grand Canal Shoppes, 3327 Las Vegas Blvd. S, South Strip* ☎ *702/359–6100* ⊕ *us.suitsupply.com.*

WOMEN'S CLOTHING

Alexander McQueen

CLOTHING | The British designer's store on the Wynn Esplanade features men's and women's attire as well as shoes and handbags, including the coveted brass knuckle clutches. ✉ *Wynn Esplanade, 3131 Las Vegas Blvd. S, North Strip* ☎ *702/369–0510* ⊕ *www.alexandermcqueen.com.*

Burberry

CLOTHING | The luxury British brand features its famous trench coats and rain gear as well as hot fashion accessories. Additional location at The Forum Shops at Caesars Palace. ✉ *Grand Canal Shoppes, 3377 Las Vegas Blvd. S, North Strip* ☎ *702/382–1911* ⊕ *us.burberry.com.*

Chanel

CLOTHING | The boutiques for this fine French couturier at Bellagio and Wynn Esplanade stock the latest women's ready-to-wear fashions, accessories, sunglasses, leather goods, shoes, jewelry, cosmetics, and fragrances. The boutique at Encore carries a smaller, ultralux selection and is home to Chanel's Fine Jewelry Collection. The Forum Shops at Caesars now has the first Chanel boutique dedicated to beauty and fragrances only. ✉ *Wynn Esplanade, 3131 Las Vegas Blvd. S, North Strip* ☎ *702/765–5055* ⊕ *www.chanel.com.*

Chloé

CLOTHING | This high-end French fashion house sports a large selection of women's ready-to-wear collections, as well as gorgeous handbags, shoes, and accessories for the bohemian in every woman. ✉ *Wynn Esplanade, 3131 Las Vegas Blvd. S, North Strip* ☎ *702/675–9998* ⊕ *www.chloe.com.*

Dior

CLOTHING | Clothes from this storied fashion house appeal to the sophisticated woman who still wants to stand out in a crowd. The Wynn and The Shops at Crystals locations also carry the collection of Dior Homme menswear. There's an additional location at Via Bellagio. ✉ *Wynn Esplanade, 3131 Las Vegas Blvd. S, North Strip* ☎ *702/735–1345* ⊕ *www.dior.com.*

Forever 21

CLOTHING | This two-level store-worthy location features all the fast fashion you can imagine for young women, men, and children. Shoes, jewelry, and even games make an appearance here. ✉ *Fashion Show Mall, 3200 Las Vegas Blvd. S, North Strip* ☎ *702/735–1014* ⊕ *www.forever21.com.*

Givenchy

CLOTHING | No longer in the Holly Golightly style of Audrey Hepburn, Givenchy's whimsical looks have nevertheless made it a fashion forerunner. The brand's first U.S. boutique brings its entire collection of men's and women's lines to a store that looks like one of its coveted boxes. ✉ *Wynn Las Vegas, 3131 Las Vegas Blvd. S, South Strip* ☎ *702/737–1091* ⊕ *givenchy.com.*

Hermès

CLOTHING | The Parisian brand's iconic Birkin bags are so exclusive, you could be on a waiting list for several years—yes, years—before securing one. The fine silk scarves and well-crafted clothes carry the same prestige without the waiting game. Additional locations at Via Bellagio and The Shops at Crystals. ✉ *Encore Esplanade, 3121 Las Vegas Blvd. S, North Strip* ☎ *702/650–3116* ⊕ *hermes.com.*

⊛ Activities

SPAS

★ Canyon Ranch SpaClub at The Venetian and The Palazzo

FITNESS/HEALTH CLUBS | Vegas's largest spa—one of the best day spas in the country—is this outpost of Tucson's famed Canyon Ranch connected to The Venetian and The Palazzo. The extensive treatment menu here covers any desire, including an ayurvedic herbal rejuvenating treatment. The real treat here is the Aquavana, a European-inspired space that offers a host of water-related experiences. The Hydrospa introduces a pulsating massage from a variety of fountains. The Finnish sauna infuses colored light into a dry heat sauna; and the Igloo cools guests off with three arctic mist experiences and sparkling fiber optics. Weekend warriors love the health club, the Strip's largest, with its 40-foot climbing wall and frequent fitness and yoga classes. The nutrition, wellness, and exercise physiology departments also offer free lectures, Lifetime Nutrition Consultation, and acupuncture. An adjoining café serves healthy cuisine and smoothies. ⊠ *The Venetian, 3355 Las Vegas Blvd. S, North Strip* ☎ *877/220–2688* ⊕ *www. canyonranch.com.*

The Spa at Encore

FITNESS/HEALTH CLUBS | The opulent Spa at Encore feels like a splendid outdoor retreat, with natural sunlight, limestone, and water features. Try the Nalu Body Ritual with its relaxing Polynesian fusion massage, full-body exfoliation, and scalp treatment with coconut oil, or the Encore Escape, a massage that incorporates a multitude of techniques. Claude Baruk provides the hair services, including Kérastase treatments. Perhaps the only drawback is the spa's exorbitant prices. ⊠ *Encore Las Vegas, 3121 Las Vegas Blvd. S, North Strip* ☎ *702/770–4772* ⊕ *www.wynnlasvegas.com.*

★ The Spa at Wynn

FITNESS/HEALTH CLUBS | Designed according to feng-shui principles and set away from the bells and jangles of the Strip, this spa exudes an elegant Zen calm while remaining very cozy. There's a fireplace and flat-screen TV in the lounge areas, and the hot and cool plunge area is naturally lighted and lush with thriving palms and orchids. Treatments, such as the Thai oil fusion massage, are Asian-inspired. The Good Luck Ritual is based on the five elements of feng shui, and includes a fusion massage, an ultramoisturizing hand therapy, and a wild lime botanical scalp treatment. For the ultimate in combating the drying desert clime, try the Hydrating Collagen Booster Therapy facial, which infuses phytonutrients, ceramides, and plant-based minerals. Claude Baruk Salon provides the latest styles and techniques, including Kérastase treatments. ⊠ *Wynn Las Vegas, 3131 Las Vegas Blvd. S, North Strip* ☎ *702/770–3900* ⊕ *www.wynnlasvegas.com.*

Chapter 6

DOWNTOWN

Updated by
Steven Bornfeld

◉ Sights   **🍴 Restaurants**   **🛏 Hotels**   **🛍 Shopping**   **🍸 Nightlife**
★★★★☆   ★★★☆☆   ★★★☆☆   ★★☆☆☆   ★★★☆☆

NEIGHBORHOOD SNAPSHOT

TOP EXPERIENCES

■ **Las Vegas Arts District:** Soak up the quirk and creativity of the city's most lively new neighborhood, especially on the first Friday of every month.

■ **Fremont Street East:** Sample one-of-a-kind bites and drinks at the restaurants and bars.

■ **Historic Casinos:** The El Cortez and the Golden Nugget offer lively nightlife and a living look at Vegas history over time.

■ **Live Music and Theater:** Las Vegas now offers good options for both in the art deco–style Smith Center for the Performing Arts.

■ **Outdoor Party Games at the Gold Spike:** It's like a day camp for adults.

GETTING HERE

Taxi and public transportation are the easiest ways to get to Downtown from the South, Central, and North Strips, but be warned that city buses must stick to Las Vegas Boulevard and often get stuck in terrible traffic around rush hour. Both the Deuce and the Strip and Downtown Express routes connect the Strip with Downtown, but the express is the faster option since it makes fewer stops. Once you're Downtown, everything is walkable, but there is a free Downtown Loop bus that connects the Bonneville Transit Center with several of the most important sights in the Downtown area. On foot, don't stray from populated areas, and travel in pairs at night. And if you've had too much to drink, it's admirable but not advisable to attempt to walk back to the North Strip: it's more than an hour on foot and isn't where you want to be walking late at night. Best to take a taxi or a ride-share.

PLANNING YOUR TIME

The best thing about Downtown is the history. Plan to spend at least a few hours at a museum (either the Mob Museum or the Neon Museum), and grab a meal or hit the bars after. However, it's a different atmosphere at night.

QUICK BITES

■ **Donut Bar.** The Las Vegas outpost of this West Coast chain offers more than a dozen different doughnut varieties daily, as well as strong coffee drinks made to order. ⊠ *124 S. 6th St., #140* ⊕ *donutbar.com*

■ **Evel Pie.** Pizza and rock-n-roll come together at this tiny restaurant/bar that pays homage to Evel Knievel. Promoters book live music on the back patio every weekend. ⊠ *508 Fremont St.* ⊕ *evelpie.com*

■ **Luv-It Frozen Custard.** This ramshackle-looking ice-cream shop has been serving thick and creamy frozen treats for more than 50 years. Check the website for special flavors. ⊠ *505 E. Oakley Blvd.* ⊕ *www.luvit-frozencustard.com*

There was a time not so many years ago when Downtown Las Vegas was filled with little more than tired casinos and hotels. Well, that's just not the case any longer. With neon lights—actually, make that a quarter-mile canopy with 12.5 million synchronized LED modules—single-deck blackjack, legitimately cool bars, and a host of new attractions that spotlight yesteryear (not to mention an influx of new businesses), old Vegas is alive and well Downtown.

This neighborhood still revolves around Fremont Street, a covered pedestrian walkway through the heart of the Downtown gambling district. Originally, this attraction was nothing more than a place to stroll; today, however, the canopy sparkles with millions of lights, and outfitters have set up everything from zip lines to band shells on street level down below. Use Fremont Street to access resorts such as the Golden Nugget (our fave in this neighborhood), Four Queens, and the Plaza Hotel and Casino. Just be prepared for sensory overload.

Old is new again all over Downtown. The Mob Museum, which opened in 2012, pays homage to Las Vegas's Mafia years. Also on 3rd Street, the Downtown Grand has brought back some of the 1950s-era swagger. The Smith Center, a world-class performing arts center that opened in 2012, was designed to invoke the same art deco style that inspired the Hoover Dam. Then, of course, there's the Neon Museum, where visitors can behold the greatness (and, in a few cases, the glow) of original Las Vegas neon signs.

With the Downtown Container Park, SlotZilla and its zip lines, and the Zappos.com headquarters in the (renovated) old City Hall, Downtown is undergoing an extended renaissance. A vibrant arts-and-mixology scene is emerging—the "First Friday" walkabout celebrates local art and artists on the first Friday of every month, and a burgeoning Arts District attracts fans of the avant-garde from all over the world.

No visit to Downtown Vegas would be complete without a pilgrimage to one of the neighborhood's most lasting legacies: Luv-it Frozen Custard. Flavors here change regularly, but cinnamon and almond chip are mainstays in the rotation. Try some in a homemade waffle cone with chocolate sauce on top.

The swath of suburbia north of Downtown Las Vegas that stretches out past Nellis Air Force Base is vast and largely faceless. The highlight is probably the Las Vegas Motor Speedway. Because the region is so expansive, you'll need a car if you head this way.

⊙ Sights

★ The Arts Factory

MUSEUM | FAMILY | An intriguing concentration of antiques shops and galleries is found on East Charleston Boulevard and Casino Center Drive, anchored by the Arts Factory. This former warehouse with a colorful mural on the front houses studios and galleries for art of all types, including painting, photography, and sculpture. There's also a bistro on-site and a drop-in yoga studio. The Arts Factory comes alive on "First Friday" with gallery openings, exhibits, receptions, and special events. "Preview Thursday," the day before First Friday, offers the same artwork with fewer crowds. Guided tours are available on request (and with a reservation). ⊠ *107 E. Charleston Blvd., Downtown* ☎ *702/383–3133* ⊕ *www. dtlvarts.com* ☒ *Free.*

DISCOVERY Children's Museum

MUSEUM | FAMILY | The DISCOVERY Children's Museum is one of the most technologically sophisticated children's museums in the entire country. The facility comprises nine theme exhibition halls, all of which are designed to inspire visitors—both children and adults—to learn through play. The star of the show: a 12-story exhibit dubbed "The Summit," with education stations on every level and a lookout that peeks through the building's roof. Parents of the smallest visitors will also love "Toddler Town," an area designed for those who are still crawling or just learning how to walk. And since this particular author has been in the news lately, stop in at "Young at

Art," which asks: "Have you wondered what it would be like walking into a Dr. Seuss book?" While you're at an institution of both fun and learning, remember the good doc's immortal words: "The more that you read, the more things you will know. The more that you learn, the more places you'll go." ⊠ *360 Promenade Pl., Downtown* ☎ *702/382–3445* ⊕ *www. discoverykidslv.org* ☒ *$15 for nonlocals; $13 for locals with valid Nevada ID* ⊘ *Closed Mon. Aug.–May.*

Downtown Container Park

STORE/MALL | FAMILY | It turns out shipping containers—the same kinds you see on cargo ships and tractor trailers—can be pretty versatile. At this open-air mall, for instance, on the outskirts of the Fremont East neighborhood, the structures have been repurposed into food stalls, boutiques (38 of them), offices, and even a three-story "tree house" complete with grown-up-friendly slides. The place also has an amphitheater stage fronted by real grass. Although the tree house is fun (especially with young kids), the highlight of the attraction is the large, fire-spewing praying mantis, which was originally constructed for use at the Burning Man festival in northern Nevada. ⊠ *707 E. Fremont St., Downtown* ☎ *702/359–9982* ⊕ *www.downtowncontainerpark.com.*

Fremont Street Experience

PEDESTRIAN MALL | The Experience was originally the name for the 1,450-foot arched canopy that was built 90 feet above "Glitter Gulch," downtown's main drag, to revive its sadly fading epicenter. The plan worked, slowly but spectacularly—now the whole street is an "experience." The Viva Vision synchronized light shows, which run the length of the canopy, got a $32-million makeover in 2019 and now sparkles with LED lights (officially touted as "16.4 million brilliant pixels") to create displays that are seven times brighter and four times sharper than previous versions. The brief shows are themed, such as the salutes to homegrown rockers The Killers, or Las Vegas–based music producer Steve Aoki. They play five to seven times a night, depending on the time of year, and the six-minute presentations change regularly. The upgrades to the overhead show were necessary to keep up with the carnival atmosphere on the street. Costumed characters and street performers vie for attention with the bands playing on two stages, and outdoor bars now line the fronts of the historic casinos, the bartops doubling as stages for dancing showgirls. Thrill-seekers can ride one of two zip lines ($) beneath the length of the canopy; the zips emerge from the face of the world's largest slot machine, appropriately dubbed SlotZilla. ⊠ *Fremont St. from Main St. to 4th St., Downtown* ⊕ *www.vegasexperience.com* ⊠ *Free.*

Gold Spike

AMUSEMENT PARK/WATER PARK | Once a (seedy) casino, the Gold Spike was resuscitated as part of the late Tony Hsieh's $350 million Downtown Project. In this case, that means gambling is out and free gaming is in. Gaming, as in shuffleboard, giant versions of Connect Four, and, on the back patio, life-size Jenga and beer pong with soccer balls and garbage pails. There's also a restaurant, multiple bars, and a tiny house that visitors can rent for parties or spend the night in. Sure, at times (especially on Thursday after dark) it feels like the former casino floor is now a clubhouse for employees of Zappos.com. But the hot spot that bills itself as an "adult playground" is open to the public and is becoming a popular place for locals, visitors, and hipsters to hang, too, especially during weekday Happy Hour. ⊠ *217 Las Vegas Blvd. N, Downtown* ☎ *702/476–1082* ⊕ *www.goldspike.com* ⊠ *Free* ⊙ *Closed Mon.–Wed.*

Las Vegas Arts District

NEIGHBORHOOD | The emergence of the offbeat Las Vegas Arts District (which comprises 18 blocks bounded by South 7th, Main, Bonneville, and Charleston Streets on Downtown's southeastern corner) continues to generate excitement in the city's arts community and, increasingly, among visitors. With a number of funky, independent art galleries in its confines, the area is a growing, thriving cultural hub—think of it as the Anti-Strip. In addition to the galleries—some of which contain impressive collections of locally known and world-famous artists— you'll find interesting eateries and dive bars to serve the alternative artists, musicians, and writers who have gravitated to the neighborhood. Each month the district hosts a First Friday gallery walk from 5 to 11 pm with gallery openings, street performers, and entertainment. It's an excellent time to come check out the still-nascent but steadily improving scene for yourself. ⊠ *Downtown.*

Las Vegas Natural History Museum

MUSEUM | FAMILY | If your kids are into animals (or taxidermy), they'll love this museum, where every continent and geological age is represented. You're greeted by a 35-foot-tall roaring T. rex in the dinosaur gallery that features Shonisaurus, Nevada's state fossil. From there, you can enjoy rooms full of sharks (including live ones, swimming in a 3,000-gallon reef tank), birds, cavemen, and scenes from the African savanna. Kids especially enjoy the various hands-on exhibits; the Young Scientist Center offers youngsters the opportunity to investigate fossils and animal tracks up close. After that, tour the Wild Nevada Gallery, where kids can see, smell, and even touch Nevada wildlife. Two-for-one ticket coupons are available online. ⊠ *900 Las Vegas Blvd. N, Downtown* ☎ *702/384–3466* ⊕ *www. lvnhm.org* ⊠ *$12.*

Downtown

Sights ▼

1 The Arts Factory C6
2 DISCOVERY
   Children's Museum C4
3 Downtown Container Park F4
4 Fremont Street Experience E3
5 Gold Spike F4
6 Las Vegas Arts District C6
7 Las Vegas Natural
   History Museum G2
8 The Mob Museum E3
9 Neon Museum G2
10 Old Las Vegas Mormon
    Fort State Historic Park G1
11 SlotZilla E4
12 Springs Preserve A5
13 Vegas Vic D3

Restaurants ▼

1 Andiamo Steakhouse E4
2 Carson Kitchen F4
3 Doña Maria Tamales D6
4 Eat F5
5 Esther's Kitchen C7
6 Eureka! F4
7 Hugo's Cellar E4
8 Jammyland Cocktail Bar
   & Reggae Kitchen C7
9 La Comida F4
10 Le Thai F4
11 Pizza Rock E3
12 Soulbelly BBQ G5
13 Triple George Grill E3

Quick Bites ▼

1 Luv-It Frozen Custard C8

Hotels ▼

1 Circa Resort & Casino E3
2 The D Las Vegas E4
3 Downtown Grand E3
4 Four Queens
   Hotel & Casino E4
5 Golden Nugget Las Vegas
   Hotel & Casino D4

★ The Mob Museum

MUSEUM | It's fitting that the $42-million Mob Museum sits in the circa-1933 former federal courthouse and U.S. Post Office Downtown where the Kefauver Committee held one of its historic hearings on organized crime in 1950. Today the museum pays homage to Las Vegas's criminal underbelly, explaining to visitors (sometimes with way too much exhibit text) how the Mafia worked, who was involved, how the law brought down local mobsters, and what happened to gangsters once they were caught and incarcerated. Museum highlights include bricks from the wall of the St. Valentine's Day Massacre in 1929, and a mock-up of the electric chair that killed a number of mobsters (as well as spies Julius and Ethel Rosenberg). In 2018 the museum converted its basement into The Underground, which comprises a working distillery and an open-to-the-public "speakeasy" that has become a separate draw for locals in its own right. ⊠ *300 Stewart Ave., Downtown* ☎ *702/229–2734* ⊕ *www.themobmuseum.org* ⊠ *$30.*

★ Neon Museum

MUSEUM | FAMILY | Consider this Downtown museum the afterlife for old neon signs. The facility, which displays more than 150 signs that date back to the 1930s, opened to the public in 2012. The old La Concha motel's iconic lobby was renovated and now serves as the museum's entry point. The sign collection includes the original signs from the Stardust, the Horseshoe, and other properties. To get up close, visitors must take an educational and informative one-hour guided tour. Daytime tours, especially in summer, can be scorching. For an alternative, try one of the nighttime tours, where you can see four of the signs illuminated the way they were intended to be. In 2018 the museum added "Brilliant," a separate experience in the North Gallery where a laser-light show set to music appears to reanimate some of the signs. The result is, well, illuminating. ⊠ *770 Las Vegas Blvd. N, Downtown* ☎ *702/387–6366* ⊕ *www. neonmuseum.org* ⊠ *From $20* ☞ *Reservations essential.*

Old Las Vegas Mormon Fort State Historic Park

HISTORIC SITE | FAMILY | Southern Nevada's oldest historic site was built by Mormons in 1855 to give refuge to travelers along the Salt Lake–Los Angeles trail, many of whom were bound for the California goldfields. Left to Native Americans after the gold rush, the adobe fort was later revitalized by a miner and his partners. In 1895 it was turned into a resort, and the city's first swimming pool was constructed by damming Las Vegas Creek. Today the restored fort contains more than half the original bricks. Antiques and artifacts help to re-create a turn-of-the-20th-century Mormon living room. ⊠ *500 E. Washington Ave., Downtown* ☎ *702/486–3511* ⊕ *parks.nv.gov/parks/old-las-vegas-mormon-fort* ⊠ *$3* ⊘ *Closed Sun. and Mon.*

SlotZilla

SPORTS—SIGHT | It wouldn't be Vegas enough to build the world's largest slot machine and just leave it there. Now thrill-seekers can take off from a platform atop the 11-story slot machine and soar over Fremont Street. There are two options to zip: one that averages 70 feet above the ground and a second line that averages 110 feet. If you'd rather just play the big slot machine, you can do that, too. It is Vegas, after all. ⊠ *425 E. Fremont St., Downtown* ⊕ *vegasexperience. com/slotzilla-zip-line* ⊠ *From $39.*

Springs Preserve

MUSEUM VILLAGE | FAMILY | This 180-acre complex defies traditional categories, combining botanical gardens, hiking trails, live animal exhibits, an ultramodern interactive museum, and a playground. The overarching theme of the facility is the rich diversity and delicate balance of nature in southern Nevada's deserts. Kids love the simulations of the flash-flood ravine, the re-created Southern

Did You Know?

You can see relics of Las Vegas past at the fascinating Neon Museum, including the famous "Las Vegas Vic" and also signs from long-gone resorts, including the Stardust.

Paiute Indian village (complete with grass huts!), and the trackless train, aboard which an engineer explains the role trains played in settling the West. The NV Energy Foundation Sustainability Gallery teaches about eco-friendly living, and a 2016 addition, Boomtown 1905, re-creates a streetscape designed to evoke turn-of-the-20th-century Vegas. There are also a few miles of walking trails that swing you by archaeological sites and may—if you're lucky—bring you face-to-face with some of the local fauna such as bats, peregrine falcons, and Gila monsters. The Divine Café provides famished eco-explorers with sustainable choices, like ethically raised cheeseburgers and environmentally mindful salads. The **Nevada State Museum**, with its famous fossil Ichthyosaur and a number of exhibits on local mining, is on the site (and included with admission) as well. ⊠ *333 S. Valley View Blvd., Downtown* ☎ *702/822–7700* ⊕ *www.springspreserve.org* ✉ *$5; reservations required online; tickets not available on-site* ⊙ *Closed Tues.–Thurs.*

Vegas Vic

PUBLIC ART | The 50-foot-tall neon cowboy outside the Pioneer Club has been waving to Las Vegas visitors since 1947 (though, truth be told, he was actually replaced by a newer version in 1951). His neon sidekick, Vegas Vicki, went up across the street in 1980, was retired in 2017, then unretired—complete with her own lounge—in Downtown's new Circa Resort & Casino. ⊠ *Fremont St. at N. 1st St., Downtown.*

⚭ Restaurants

Even during its heyday as the city's casino-gaming hot spot, Downtown was never much of a haven for gourmets, but things have gotten better with the influence of the Downtown Redevelopment Project. Downtown's big revitalization over the past few years includes a budding restaurant scene with a few places that are on par with the big Strip properties, and some casual but very tasty spots in the Downtown Container Park.

Andiamo Steakhouse

$$$$ | **STEAKHOUSE** | This offshoot of Joe Vicari's numerous restaurants in the Detroit area is right at home in the loosely Detroit-theme D Las Vegas. The menu is evenly split between steak-house classics and Italian-American favorites. **Known for:** elegant, subdued atmosphere; steaks aged 30 days; polished, dignified service. ⑤ *Average main: $55* ⊠ *The D Las Vegas, 301 Fremont St., Downtown* ☎ *702/388–2220* ⊕ *www.thed.com* ⊙ *No lunch.*

Carson Kitchen

$$$ | **AMERICAN** | The late rock-and-roll chef Kerry Simon brought his fun, contemporary cuisine to this restored hotel in the Downtown redevelopment district, and his legacy continues. It's small and kind of rustic, with an airy (and kitschy) patio out back and one on the roof. **Known for:** seasonal—and surprising—cuisine; counter seating with a view of kitchen; rooftop patio. ⑤ *Average main: $25* ⊠ *John E. Carson Bldg., 124 S. 6th St., Downtown* ☎ *702/473–9523* ⊕ *www.carsonkitchen.com.*

Doña Maria Tamales

$$ | **MEXICAN** | **FAMILY** | You'll forget you're in Las Vegas after a few minutes in this relaxed and unpretentious Downtown cantina. All of the combinations and specials are good, but the best play here is to order the house-made tamales. **Known for:** house-made of tamales; well-prepared Mexican favorites; lively, colorful atmosphere. ⑤ *Average main: $15* ⊠ *910 Las Vegas Blvd. S, Downtown* ☎ *702/382–6538* ⊕ *www.donamariatamales.com.*

Eat

$$ | **MODERN AMERICAN** | **FAMILY** | Eat may serve only breakfast and lunch, but chef Natalie Young's food is so hearty (and so uniquely appealing), you may not feel the need for dinner. Among the specialties are cinnamon biscuits with warm strawberry compote, shrimp and grits with bacon, and the "DWBLTA" (thick toasted sourdough bracketing thick-sliced bacon, tomato, lettuce, and avocado). **Known for:** creative, indulgent fare; truly killer grilled cheese; tiny, intimate spot. $ *Average main: $20 ⊠ 707 Carson St., Downtown ☎ 702/534–1515 ⊕ eatdtlv.chefnatalieyoung.com ⊗ No dinner. Closed Tues. and Wed.*

★ Esther's Kitchen

$$$$ | **ITALIAN** | The best Italian food in Las Vegas these days might be at Esther's Kitchen, a hip and lively restaurant in the Las Vegas Arts District southwest of Downtown. Chef James Trees, a Las Vegas native, churns out house-made pastas such as rigatoni carbonara with guanciale, tagliatelle with braised duck, and black fettucine with lobster. **Known for:** house-made pasta; creative cocktails; long wait times for those without reservations. $ *Average main: $50 ⊠ 1130 S. Casino Center Blvd., Downtown ☎ 702/570–7864 ⊕ www.estherslv.com.*

Eureka!

$$ | **AMERICAN** | Inside Downtown's bohemian temple, the Emergency Arts Building, this restaurant features what they call a "scratch kitchen concept." It may sound rather pot-lucky, but this isn't the standard chain-food menu (despite being part of a California-based chain). How does this sound: skirt steak with broccolini, red chimichurri, chili flakes, Parmesan, and lemon zest; a cowboy burger nearly tipping over with shoestring onions, bacon, cheddar cheese, and a beer barbecue sauce; and a bourbon barrel cake. **Known for:** creative menu; an enticing array of beverages; arts-inspired atmosphere. $ *Average main: $17 ⊠ 520 E. Fremont St., Downtown ☎ 702/570–3660 ⊕ www.eurekarestaurantgroup.com.*

★ Hugo's Cellar

$$$$ | **AMERICAN** | This venerable restaurant dates to the Rat Pack era. The "cellar" aspect (it's about a half-flight below ground) gives it a cozy feel, as do old Vegas touches like table-side salad preparation with every dinner (you choose what you want from the cart), a red rose for each woman, and formal, impeccable service. **Known for:** cozy, semi-underground location; lots of table-side service; menu of old Las Vegas classics. $ *Average main: $60 ⊠ Four Queens, 202 Fremont St., Downtown ☎ 702/385–4011 ⊕ www.hugoscellar.com ⊗ No lunch.*

Jammyland Cocktail Bar & Reggae Kitchen

$$$$ | **JAMAICAN** | The Caribbean meets Las Vegas at this hip bar/restaurant in the Arts District downtown. Cocktails are bold and boozy, mixing liquors such as rum and cachaca with tropical flavors in new, exciting, and counterintuitive ways. **Known for:** hipster scene, especially around the open-air fire pits; strong rum drinks; jerk chicken. $ *Average main: $35 ⊠ 1121 S. Main St., Downtown ☎ 702/800–9098 ⊕ jammy.land ⊗ Closed Sun.–Tues.*

La Comida

$$$ | **MEXICAN** | **FAMILY** | This rustic restaurant and lounge is brought to you by Michael and Jenna Morton, late of the N9NE Group. The menu focuses on updated Mexican food served on what looks like Abuelita's old china with mismatched furniture and plenty of depictions of the Virgin of Guadalupe. **Known for:** updated versions of Mexican classics; creative margaritas; rustic, fun atmosphere. $ *Average main: $25 ⊠ 100 6th St., Downtown ☎ 702/463–9900 ⊕ lacomidalv.com ⊗ Closed Mon. and Tues.*

★ Le Thai

$$ | THAI | FAMILY | Noodles are the house specialty at this intimate restaurant in the Fremont East district of Downtown. Although most of the dishes are Thai (try the Awesome Noodles; the name isn't hyperbole), others lean more toward Chinese and Japanese influences. **Known for:** tiny spot with expansive patio; some other Asian influences; Awesome Noodles really are. $ *Average main: $15* ⊠ *523 Fremont St. E, Downtown* ☎ *702/778–0888* ⊕ *www.lethaivegas. com* ⏱ *Closed Tues. No lunch Sun.*

Pizza Rock

$$$ | PIZZA | FAMILY | Eleven-time world pizza champion Tony Gemignani installed four ovens in this heavily renovated, industrial-chic space in the Downtown Third district so he could produce all styles of pizza: Neapolitan, Romano, American, New York, classic Italian, Californian, New York/New Haven, Sicilian, and Chicago. Don't neglect the starters, though; the fried green beans with garlic and olive oil and beer-battered fried artichokes are worth the trip alone. **Known for:** all styles of pizzas; don't-miss appetizers; hipsterish quasi-industrial vibe. $ *Average main: $25* ⊠ *Downtown Grand, 201 N. 3rd St., Downtown* ☎ *702/385–0838* ⊕ *www.pizzarocklasvegas.com.*

Soulbelly BBQ

$$$ | BARBECUE | FAMILY | The soul in the belly here comes courtesy of James Beard–nominated Chef Bruce Kalman, who might be recognizable on sight to viewers of foodie faves *Top Chef, Chopped,* and *Beat Bobby Flay.* Bringing the barbecue flavors of Central Texas to Vegas, this atmospheric venue adds cocktails, local beers, and live entertainment to the mix to turn what might have been just a barbecue dinner into a barbecue experience and a night on the (Down)town. **Known for:** authentic barbecue flavors from Central Texas; both combos and meat by the pound; "Belly of the Soul" sandwich with brisket, cheese sauce, and a fried egg. $ *Average main: $26* ⊠ *1327 S. Main St., Downtown* ☎ *702/483–4404* ⊕ *www.soulbellybbq. com* ⏱ *Closed Mon.*

Triple George Grill

$$$$ | AMERICAN | You won't find too much in the way of nouvelle flourishes or ultramod decor at this San Francisco–style restaurant, and that's just how both visitors and locals prefer it—the elegant dining room is a favorite haunt for power-lunching and hobnobbing. Triple George is known for its commendably prepared traditional American fare such as oysters on the half shell, classic "wedge" salad, oh-so-tender pot roast, and truly stellar sourdough. **Known for:** eclectic menu, including vegan choices; San Francisco food and decor; intimate, semi-enclosed booths. $ *Average main: $35* ⊠ *Downtown Grand, 201 N. 3rd St., Downtown* ☎ *702/384–2761* ⊕ *www.triplegeorgegrill.com* ⏱ *No lunch weekends.*

☕ Coffee and Quick Bites

Luv-it Frozen Custard

$ | CAFÉ | Walking distance from the Strat, this tiny take-out stand offers unbelievably delicious, velvety smooth frozen custard. The flavors change daily (check the website for the schedule), and sundaes are a popular offering. **Known for:** fun flavors of frozen custard; daily changing availability; Western sundae with hot fudge, caramel, and pecans. $ *Average main: $5* ⊠ *505 E. Oakey Blvd., Downtown* ☎ *702/384–6452* ⊕ *www.luvitfrozencustard.com.*

The Golden Nugget, whose entrance sits right along the Fremont Street Experience, is one of the top hotels downtown.

🛏 Hotels

★ Circa Resort & Casino

$$ | **HOTEL** | Downtown's newest big hoo-hah comes from Downtown's newest big pooh-bahs—the brothers Stevens, owners Derek and Greg—is a major boost to the Vegas aesthetic and the first downtown hotel built from the ground up since the 1980s. **Pros:** world's biggest sports book; a pool "amphitheater" that defies the imagination; the cachet of being Las Vegas's latest hotpost. **Cons:** you haven't experienced noise until you've heard it in here; long lines to show driver's license for proof of age for admittance (including some guests who could have flashed an AARP card instead); no bedside plugs to charge phones in rooms. $ *Rooms from: $177* ✉ *8 Fremont St., Downtown* ☎ *833/247–2258* ⊕ *circalasvegas.com* ⇌ *777 rooms* ⦿ *No meals.*

The D Las Vegas

$ | **HOTEL** | The "D" may be for eccentric owner Derek Stevens—or perhaps "Downtown"—but the 34-story resort has established itself in recent years as the liveliest of the area's hotels. **Pros:** live music out front; casino has the only Sigma Derby machine left in town; bitcoin ATMs. **Cons:** small rooms and pool; few restaurant options; can be very loud. $ *Rooms from: $89* ✉ *301 Fremont St., Downtown* ☎ *702/388–2400* ⊕ *www.thed.com* ⇌ *629 rooms* ⦿ *No meals.*

Downtown Grand

$ | **HOTEL** | The venerable Lady Luck, built in 1964, was reimagined as the Downtown Grand in 2013 and is characterized by industrial-chic decor in its public spaces and surprising modern and affordable rooms; it was greatly expanded in 2020, now boasting a "grand" total of 1,124 rooms A new 495-room tower has added three 1,500-square-foot penthouse suites, as well as 47 studios rooms and

20 one-bedroom suites, among other offerings. **Pros:** excellent pool; great restaurants; bargain-basement rates. **Cons:** small rooms; noise from nearby Fremont street hard to block out; lots of construction nearby. $ *Rooms from: $69* ✉ *206 N. 3rd St., at Ogden, Downtown* ☎ *855/384–7263, 702/337–2494* ⊕ *www. downtowngrand.com* ⇥ *1124 rooms* ○ *No meals.*

Four Queens Hotel & Casino
$ | **HOTEL** | Named after former owner Ben Goffstein's four daughters, the circa-1966 Four Queens is what Vegas regulars would consider an "oldie but goodie," one of the most iconic casinos on Fremont Street. **Pros:** no resort fees; kitsch factor; Hugo's Cellar steak house. **Cons:** rooms need a remodel; pool off-site; outdated gaming floor. $ *Rooms from: $69* ✉ *202 Fremont St., Downtown* ☎ *702/385–4011, 800/634–6045* ⊕ *www.fourqueens. com* ⇥ *690 rooms* ○ *No meals.*

Golden Nugget Las Vegas Hotel & Casino
$ | **RESORT** | The Golden Nugget has long reigned as Downtown's top property since the mid-1970s, evolving with the times but maintaining classic appeal. **Pros:** legendary Vegas property; one-of-a-kind pool; great poker room. **Cons:** small sports book; table games change frequently; too many room options. $ *Rooms from: $99* ✉ *129 E. Fremont St., Downtown* ☎ *702/385–7111, 844/468–4438* ⊕ *www.goldennugget. com* ⇥ *2345 rooms* ○ *No meals.*

ⓨ Nightlife

BARS AND PUBS

The Underground
BARS/PUBS | Since it's part of the Mob Museum, you may wish to think of The Underground as an immersive and interactive exhibit on Prohibition-era speakeasies. Memorabilia from the 1920s abounds. Period music plays all night long. But it also functions as a working bar, with hand-crafted cocktails, drink specials, and serious bartender sass. There's even a distillery in a back room—The Underground distills and serves its own special-edition moonshine, and visitors can take guided tours. Admission to the museum gets you in for free, but if you aren't visiting the museum, check the bar's Instagram account for the nightly password to give the bouncer at the back door. And be sure to check out some of the secret meeting rooms; one is hidden behind a big painting. ✉ *The Mob Museum, 300 Stewart Ave., Downtown* ☎ *702/229–2734* ⊕ *themobmuseum.org/basement.*

LIVE MUSIC

JAZZ AND CLASSICAL

★ The Smith Center for the Performing Arts
CABARET | Las Vegas got its very own ($150-million) world-class performing arts center in 2012, and what a spot it is. The multibuilding complex (complete with a bell tower) was designed to invoke 1930s-era art deco construction, the same motif you'll find at the Hoover Dam. Here, this elegance graces the main concert hall, which anchors its calendar around a season of touring Broadway musicals and Las Vegas Philharmonic concerts, filling the in-between dates with touring concert acts and other attractions. ■**TIP→ Myron's Caberet Jazz across the breezeway hosts live jazz or cabaret singers every weekend.** ✉ *361 Symphony Park Ave., Downtown* ☎ *702/749–2000* ⊕ *www.thesmithcenter. com.*

ROCK

Bunkhouse Saloon
MUSIC CLUBS | Offering raucous rock in a raucous Downtown saloon, this is where the most clued-in locals go to shake, rattle, headbang, and roll. Brandon Flowers, Bob Mould, and Local H are some of the bigger names to play the tiny stage. It's closed on Sunday. ✉ *124 S. 11th St., Downtown* ☎ *702/854–1414* ⊕ *www. bunkhousedowntown.com.*

LOCAL HANGOUTS

Outside the realm of the big casinos, the Las Vegas bar scene is dominated by so-called video-poker taverns, named after the 15 video-poker machines they're legally allowed to have. Most Vegas bars are generic, but there are exceptions—in some cases, glorious exceptions—scattered about town and clustered in the Downtown area. Despite the touristy "Fremont Street Experience," Downtown is the gritty birthplace of Las Vegas. It can be quite dangerous if you stray from the tourist circuit at night, but visiting its nightspots is essential if you want to claim you've truly experienced Vegas.

★ Atomic Liquors

BARS/PUBS | This Downtown bar is the oldest freestanding bar in Las Vegas and owns the first liquor license in the state (literally, No. 00001). It takes its name from the custom of patrons in the '50s, who would buy drinks, head to the roof, and watch atomic blasts in the desert in the distance. The Rat Pack and Barbra Streisand drank here. Fast-forward to now, and it's become the place to hang out, with 20 microbrews on tap and an inventive menu that specializes in fancy beer cocktails. There's even a restaurant next door, but the bar is closed on Monday and Tuesday. ⊠ *917 Fremont St., Downtown* ☎ *702/982–3000* ⊕ *atomic.vegas*.

Commonwealth

BARS/PUBS | As urban renewal continues Downtown, the one-block stretch of Fremont east of Las Vegas Boulevard (dubbed Fremont East) remains the hottest of the hot spots, and Commonwealth arguably is the epicenter. Inside, wrought-iron railings, chandeliers, and a tin ceiling create a feeling of old-school opulence without being excessive. Drink options range from handcrafted cocktails to microbrews; there's also good live music in the evening. The atmosphere changes as evenings progress, from quiet happy hours conducive to conversation to full-on dance craziness for a younger crowd. Venture upstairs to the rooftop bar, or try to secure an invite to the private Laundry Room speakeasy. It's closed on Monday and Tuesday. ⊠ *525 Fremont St., Downtown* ☎ *702/445–6400* ⊕ *www.commonwealthlv.com*.

Downtown Cocktail Room

BARS/PUBS | Hiding from your creditors? Seeking a good spot for a séance or a Spin-the-Bottle party? If so, then consider stepping—carefully—into the gorgeous gloom of this hipster hangout, which is just around the corner from The Griffin. The minimalist lounge glows from candle-filled tables and thumps with simmering house music, making the vibe mysterious and romantic. Happy Hour is 4 to 7 pm every night but Sunday, and everything on the menu is half-price. Locals love that deal, as well as the seasonal cocktail menus. Just beware: the front door is hard to find. It's closed Sunday and Monday. ⊠ *111 Las Vegas Blvd. S, Downtown* ☎ *702/880–3696* ⊕ *www.downtowncocktailroom.com*.

The Griffin

BARS/PUBS | As good as Vegas Bohemia gets, this Downtown bar, close to the Beauty Bar and the Downtown Cocktail Room, is an instant winner. Some wags have likened it to a Peppermill for the younger, looser set, but this description fails to account for the beauty of its hipster crowd as well as its decor, from the kitschy neon sign outside to the fire grills, the barrel-vaulted brick ceiling, the semicircular banquettes, and the griffin insignias on the bathroom walls. The best feature, though, is the back room, which resembles a study owned by King Henry VIII—in the 1950s. ⊠ *511 Fremont St., Downtown* ☎ *702/382–0577*.

★ Oak & Ivy

BARS/PUBS | Should you happen to be Downtown, head over to the Downtown Container Park and sit inside a shipping container to sip barrel-aged cocktails and whiskeys galore. Although tiny—it's sometimes tough to nab a spot at the bar—this little railroad car of a drinking spot packs a punch with a well-crafted menu of drinks. Can't decide on a whiskey? Order a flight. Want to try something truly special? Order a taste of one of the bar's barrel-aged bourbons. ✉ *Downtown Container Park, 707 Fremont St., Downtown* ☎ *702/553–2549* ⊕ *oakandivy.com.*

★ Velveteen Rabbit

BARS/PUBS | There's nothing better than a feel-good story in Las Vegas. Sisters Pamela and Christina Dylag saved and scrimped to open this great, velvet-lined cocktail lounge dotted with furniture they found at vintage shops and equipped with beer taps that look like hands. A great cocktail list with a vintage feel and punches are just some of the treasures behind the bar. Regular Wednesday specials mean a number of wines are available for $5 per glass. ✉ *1218 S. Main St., Downtown* ☎ *702/685–9642* ⊕ *velveteenrabbitlv.com.*

STRIP CLUBS

Palomino Club

THEMED ENTERTAINMENT | This is one of the oldest strip clubs in the area (the Rat Pack used to hang out here), as well as the most notorious; two separate owners have been accused of murders, and it was also owned briefly by a noted heart surgeon. Because the "Pal" was grandfathered into the North Las Vegas zoning codes, it's allowed to have both a full bar *and* full nudity. There's also a burlesque stage and the hip-hop, urban Club Lacy's next door. ✉ *1848 Las Vegas Blvd. N, North Las Vegas* ☎ *702/642–2984* ⊕ *www.palominolv.com.*

🛍 Shopping

BOOKS

Gamblers General Store

BOOKS/STATIONERY | This shop near Fremont Street sells everything gambling, from cards and casino tables to felts, cases, trays, and, of course, chips. It also is home to the Gamblers Book Club, an independent bookstore specializing in books about blackjack, craps, poker, roulette, and all the other games of chance. With more than 3,000 titles in stock, the place dubs itself the "World's Largest Gambling Bookstore." You'll also find novels about casinos, biographies of crime figures, and other topics that relate to Las Vegas history and gambling. Time your visit right, and you might even score autographed copies of some of your favorite tomes. ✉ *727 S. Main St., Downtown* ☎ *702/382–7555, 800/522–1777* ⊕ *www.gamblersgeneralstore.com.*

FOOD AND DRINK

The Beef Jerky Store

FOOD/CANDY | A few steps from Fremont Street you'll find every conceivable form of jerky, including bacon, ostrich, alligator, salmon, and even tofu, and adds hot and spicy choices to boot. Take home the Las Vegas specialty jerky shaped like all four suits in a deck of cards. It's not all jerky; there are candy and other products as well. ✉ *112-B N. 3rd St., Downtown* ☎ *702/388–0073* ⊕ *www.beefjerkystore.com.*

MALLS

★ Las Vegas North Premium Outlets

OUTLET/DISCOUNT STORES | The upscale mix at this racetrack-shape Downtown outlet mall includes 175 stores, all of which offer merchandise discounts of some sort. Some of the stores are fairly common, including Sketchers, Charlotte Russe, and Aeropostale. Others, such as Dolce & Gabbana, Brooks Brothers Factory Store, Kate Spade New York, Ted Baker London, Tory Burch, and Salvatore Ferragamo, are more high-fashion. Saks Off Fifth and a giant Nike store anchor the mall, and a Cheesecake Factory restaurant offers a good place to have lunch. This is one of the few outdoor malls in town, and it offers plenty of shade as well as misting towers help keep you cool in the Vegas heat. Three parking garages afford easy access to the mall but tend to fill up quickly; valet parking is available in the main garage. ✉ *875 Grand Central Pkwy. S, Downtown* ☎ *702/474–7500* ⊕ *www.premiumoutlets.com/outlet/las-vegas-north.*

CANNABIS

NuWu Cannabis Marketplace

SPECIALTY STORES | Nevada legalized recreational cannabis in 2018, and today about 80% of the state's dispensaries are located in Las Vegas. The largest of these, NuWu Cannabis Marketplace, is 16,000 square feet and sits just outside of Downtown. The facility is open 24 hours a day and boasts a drive-through for those who don't want to leave their limos or rideshares. Be prepared to fork over your ID when you buy, and remember that it's cash only, at least for now. It's also worth noting that you can't fly with cannabis

products, so it's best to use what you buy before you skip town. ✉ *1235 Paiute Circle, Las Vegas* ☎ *702/844–2707* ⊕ *www.nuwucannabis.com.*

JEWELRY AND COLLECTIBLES

★ Gold and Silver Pawn Shop

ANTIQUES/COLLECTIBLES | Home to the History Channel's *Pawn Stars*, Gold and Silver Pawn Shop has a little bit of everything. Shop for rare coins, first-edition books, and jewelry and watches galore, including Super Bowl rings or that special piece of history you saw on the show. With ever-changing stock, you never know what you will see. Because the shop doubles as a TV set, lines to get in can get long, and the store is open 24/7. The neighboring Pawn Plaza—a two-story shopping center made from shipping containers—features Rick's Rollin Smoke BBQ from Gold and Silver Pawn Shop co-owner Rick Harrison, along with other small stores. ✉ *713 Las Vegas Blvd. S, Downtown* ☎ *702/385–7912* ⊕ *gspawn.com.*

VINTAGE CLOTHING

Buffalo Exchange

CLOTHING | The local outpost of a national chain is a thrift store must-stop for the terminally hip. The store's extensive collection of trendy vintage and used clothing at reasonable prices makes for satisfying shopping. You also can find great recycled discards and, since we all could use the help, lots of suggestions from the staff. ✉ *1209 S. Main St., Downtown* ☎ *702/791–3960* ⊕ *www.buffaloexchange.com.*

🏃 Activities

AUTO RACING

★ Las Vegas Motor Speedway

AUTO RACING | The Las Vegas Motor Speedway is home to NASCAR and NHRA events throughout the year, and its Neon Garage, in the center of the infield, is a place where fans can watch drivers and crews work magic on their cars. But it also is a mecca for racing fans of all kinds, with a variety of experiences available year-round. For enthusiasts who want to be more hands-on, the NASCAR/Andretti puts laypeople behind the wheels of real-live (600 horsepower) NASCAR race cars or Indycars and gives them the chance to run the track (for 8, 18, or 30 laps) at speeds of more than 100 mph. Of course, visitors can always opt for track tours as well. Reservations are required for all experiences. Adult diapers are optional. ✉ *7000 Las Vegas Blvd. N, North Las Vegas* ☎ *800/644–4444* ⊕ *www.lvms.com* 🖃 *Prices vary by experience.*

Chapter 7

PARADISE ROAD AND THE EAST SIDE

Updated by
Mike Weatherford

◉ Sights	🍴 Restaurants	🛏 Hotels	🛍 Shopping	🍸 Nightlife
★★☆☆☆	★★★☆☆	★★☆☆☆	★☆☆☆☆	★★★☆☆

NEIGHBORHOOD SNAPSHOT

TOP EXPERIENCES

■ **Lotus of Siam:** One of the best restaurants in Las Vegas is not on the Strip and won't break the bank.

■ **Marjorie Barrick Museum of Art:** UNLV's museum offers a nice excursion if you're looking for a low-key art-viewing experience; the museum also has a lovely xeriscape garden.

■ **National Atomic Testing Museum:** You'll learn all about the history of the atom bomb at this off-the-beaten-path treasure, and if you plan far ahead (like a year), you can even visit a real atomic test site.

■ **Virgin Hotels Las Vegas:** The rock gods bailed and took their guitars with them, but the former Hard Rock Hotel now sports a sophisticated and oddly serene desert-theme interior. The atmosphere gets wilder as you head out back to the pool area or to the concert hall.

■ **Westgate:** The sprawling casino-resort is worth seeing for the sheer amount of glitz, its statue of Elvis Presley, and mind-boggling World's Largest Race & Sports Book.

GETTING HERE

Public transportation from the Strip to the East Side is actually pretty reliable, so long as you're not travel-ing in the middle of the night. Taxis know the area well, too, especially if you're heading from the Strip over to the Virgin or into the University District. As is the case with most of the Vegas suburbs, the best bets here are to opt for ride-sharing services or to rent a car.

PLANNING YOUR TIME

The East Side sprawls, so it's difficult to "do" this part of town, especially if you don't have a car. The points of interest are spread out, so it's better to just choose the activity or sight you wish to see and just go there. It's also worth noting that Paradise Road isn't a ridiculous walk from the hotels on the East side of the Strip. The walk from the MGM Grand to Virgin Las Vegas is the same as a mile on the Strip.

QUICK BITES

■ **Big Chicken.** Naming it the "Chicken Shaq" would've maybe been too obvious; Shaquille O'Neal's own restaurant specializes in crispy chicken sandwiches but also serves tenders, sliders, and more. ⊠ *4480 Paradise Rd.* ⊕ *www.bigchicken.com*

■ **Cugino's Italian Deli.** Right across the street from UNLV, Cugino's is known for its vast array of hot and cold sandwiches and pizzas. ⊠ *4550 S. Maryland Pkwy.* ⊕ *cuginositalian.com*

■ **Insomnia Cookies.** The company was started with college students in mind, but most of us would love warm cookies and cold milk in the wee hours. ⊠ *4480 Paradise Rd.* ⊕ *insomnia-cookies.com*

The East Side of Las Vegas, an area that includes Paradise Road and stretches to the University District and as far east as Boulder Highway, is as eclectic as it is convenient. Much of the area is residential, save for a handful of (older) resorts, and has become more Spanish-speaking in recent years.

Lacking a lot of recent tourism investments with a "wow" factor (with one major recent exception), it's a more ordinary, aging part of town layered with restaurants, extensive medical offices, and most of the area's collegiate athletic facilities; an area that shows what Las Vegas suburbia looked like in the 1960s and 1970s, before the city's explosive growth. Old-school entertainers such as Gladys Knight, and Liberace used to live near the Las Vegas National Golf Course, and "Mr. Las Vegas" himself, Wayne Newton, claims the area's most famous residence, Casa de Shenandoah.

Paradise Road itself is the Strip's sister street, catering to the city's convention trade. On the southern end, the new Virgin Las Vegas Hotel has made a splashy renovation of the former Hard Rock Hotel in an attempt to remain one of the most popular off-Strip resorts in town. A number of other resorts, such as the Platinum, qualify as nongaming, but are still within walking distance of larger casinos. This stretch also comprises the heart of the area affectionately known as "Fruit Loop," Vegas's gay-friendly neighborhood near the airport.

Though there aren't any resorts in the University District, UNLV (University of Las Vegas) and the Thomas and Mack Center provide plenty of things to see and do, from sporting events to (on-campus) museums and more. UNLV is mostly a commuter school lacking that "college town" vibe, but the campus is a pleasant stroll, and the neighboring Maryland Parkway does offer the cheap eats and shops (vintage clothing, comic book and now, legal marijuana) you'd expect to encounter in a college town.

◉ Sights

The Gun Store

SPORTS VENUE | Opened in 1988, the Gun Store puts you on the range with a machine gun of your choice. When you walk in, you're greeted with a wall full of weapons, most of which are available to rent. Pick your era; hose the target a steady diet of lead Cagney-style with a Thompson. World War II buffs might go for an MP40 Schmeisser. Have a flair for the international? Grab an Uzi or Sten. They've got handguns, rifles, and shotguns, too. ✉ *2900 E. Tropicana Ave., East Side* ☏ *702/454–1110* ⊕ *www.thegunstorelasvegas.com* 💲 *From $90.*

Paradise Road and the East Side

Haunted Vegas Ghost Hunt

LOCAL INTEREST | Things start with a not-so-scary pizza party at the Tuscany Resort. Then with ghost-hunting equipment provided by your guide, you ride through the streets of Las Vegas on this three-hour tour to hear the tales of Sin City's notorious murders, suicides, and ghosts (including Bugsy Siegel, Elvis, and Tupac Shakur). Organizers stress that this isn't a theatrical show, but a "guided paranormal investigation." It's open to kids 13 and older, although those younger than 18 must be accompanied by an adult. Make reservations in advance. ⊠ *Tuscany Resort, 255 E. Flamingo Ave., East Side* ☎ *702/677–9015, 866/218–4935* ⊕ *www.hauntedvegastours.com* ⊡ *$100.*

Marjorie Barrick Museum of Art

MUSEUM | This museum on the University of Nevada Las Vegas campus, formerly the Marjorie Barrick Museum of Natural History, has a growing collection of works by artists with ties to Southern Nevada, many of them from the former Las Vegas Art Museum. It hosts rotating exhibitions, including touring shows, as well as lectures focused on art. The Xeric Garden in front of the museum, which dates to 1988, was the first xeriscape demonstration garden in town and contains pathways and benches that are great places to observe native fauna. ⊠ *4505 S. Maryland Pkwy., University District* ☎ *702/895–3381* ⊕ *www.unlv. edu/barrickmuseum* ⊡ *Free; suggested contribution $5.* ⊙ *Closed weekends.*

National Atomic Testing Museum

HISTORIC SITE | FAMILY | Today's Las Vegas is lighted by neon and LED, but during the Cold War, uranium and plutonium illuminated the area from time to time as well in the form of a roiling mushroom cloud in the distance. This museum, in association with the Smithsonian, commemorates southern Nevada's long and fascinating history of nuclear weapons research and testing with film footage and photographs of mushroom clouds; testimonials; and artifacts (including a deactivated bomb, twisted chunks of steel, and bomb-testing machinery from the Nevada Test Site).

The museum is home to virtual tours of the 1,375-square-mile **Nevada National Security Site** and is the starting point for monthly group tours of the area larger than the state of Rhode Island, which used to be the spot in the desert where the government tested atomic bombs. The site is 65 miles northwest of Downtown, and each tour usually covers a total of 250 miles. There are plenty of restrictions, and live tours book as much as a year ahead, so plan well ahead if you're interested. Make reservations with the National Nuclear Security Administration (⊕ *www.nnss.gov/pages/publicaffairsoutreach/nnsstours.html*). ⊠ *Desert Research Institute, 755 E. Flamingo Rd., East Side* ☎ *702/409–7366 museum, 702/295–0514 Nevada National Security Site tour reservations* ⊕ *www.nationalatomictestingmuseum.org* ⊡ *$22.*

🍴 Restaurants

The venerable Hard Rock Hotel reopened in March 2021 after a six-month makeover into Virgin Hotels Las Vegas. Several restaurants in the Hard Rock had become Las Vegas mainstays. Nobu is a holdover, and fans of the old place will recognize its coffee shop and Mexican restaurant, albeit with new names and menus.

Blueberry Hill

$$ | DINER | FAMILY | This local minichain feels a bit like Denny's with an old-fashioned, family-owned vibe. And it serves far superior food, including hearty Mexican specialties, fruit-topped pancakes and waffles, and a number of "diet delight"–type platters. **Known for:** varied breakfast specialties; most meals available all day; casual, diner-esque

atmosphere. $ *Average main: $12
⊠ 1505 E. Flamingo Rd., East Side
☎ 702/696–9666 ⊕ www.blueberryhill-
restaurants.com.*

Casa Calavera

$$ | MEXICAN | Fans of the bygone Pink
Taco will still smile in recognition when
they see its replacement. The layout is
much the same, including the convivial
center bar. **Known for:** lively, party atmosphere; outdoor seating; taco Tuesdays.
$ *Average main: $20 ⊠ Virgin Hotels Las
Vegas, 4455 Paradise Rd., Paradise Road
☎ 702/693–5000 ⊕ virginhotelslv.com.*

Crown & Anchor British Pub

$$ | BRITISH | With 24-hour service and
graveyard specials, Crown & Anchor
is uniquely Las Vegas (and a favorite
haunt of students from nearby UNLV).
Most of the food is British, including the
steak-and-kidney pie, bangers and mash,
and authentic fish-and-chips. **Known for:**
classic English foods; live "football" from
across the pond; open 24/7. $ *Average
main: $20 ⊠ 1350 E. Tropicana Ave., Uni-
versity District ☎ 702/739–8676 ⊕ www.
crownandanchorlv.com.*

Ferraro's Italian Restaurant & Wine Bar

$$$$ | ITALIAN | Like time-traveling to
Vegas's vintage days when upscale
restaurants were quiet and atmospheric,
venerable Ferraro's features a dark and
decidedly romantic dining room with
candles on every table, and a pricey
menu stocked with steaks, fresh-made
pastas, and Mediterranean-styled
seafood. Around since 1985 and in this
location—directly across the street
from Virgin Hotels Las Vegas—since
2009, this fine Italian eatery offers small
plates nightly from 5 to 7 pm and bigger
feasts throughout the evening. **Known
for:** 6,000-bottle wine cellar; osso buco;
stewed rabbit served on polenta. $ *Aver-
age main: $56 ⊠ 2840 Paradise Rd., East
Side ☎ 702/364–5300 ⊕ Ferraroslasve-
gas.com ☾ Closed Mon. No lunch.*

Firefly* Tapas Kitchen & Bar

$$$ | MEDITERRANEAN | As the name
suggests, this hip bistro focuses on small
plates (few of which cost more than $10),
reflecting most of the world's cuisines.
Order several and you've got a meal,
made even better with one of Firefly's
signature sangrias or mojitos, available
by the glass or pitcher. **Known for:** tapas
from multiple cuisines; quick, friendly
service; funky decor. $ *Average main:
$25 ⊠ 3824 Paradise Rd., Paradise Road
☎ 702/369–3971 ⊕ www.fireflylv.com.*

Hofbräuhaus Las Vegas

$$$ | GERMAN | Enjoy a loud dose of kitsch
at this gargantuan offshoot of Munich's
most famous brewery. The interior beer
garden can make you feel like a tourist
within a tourist town. **Known for:** raucous
beer hall front room; quieter indoor beer
garden; menu of German classics. $ *Av-
erage main: $25 ⊠ 4510 Paradise Rd.,
Paradise Road ☎ 702/853–2337 ⊕ www.
hofbrauhauslasvegas.com.*

India Palace

$$ | INDIAN | The surrounding neighbor-
hood has been on the decline for years,
so don't walk here—but also don't be
deterred from this clean and solid Indian
establishment, which has weathered the
changes. The Palace has been known for
decades for its all-you-can-eat lunch buffet
(11:30 to 3) and as an evening refuge for
conventioneers who *aren't* on an expense
account. **Known for:** popular lunch buffet;
good service; modest prices for the
convention corridor. $ *Average main: $18
⊠ 505 E. Twain, East Side ☎ 702/796–
4177 ⊕ indiapalacevegas.com.*

L&L Hawaiian Barbecue

$ | HAWAIIAN | This growing chain of
zero-ambience fast-food eateries serves
Hawaiian-style barbecue to a heavily
Hawaiian clientele (Las Vegas is known
as the "ninth island" to Hawaiians).
The plate lunch is the draw here, and
considering that it comes with two
scoops of rice and one of macaroni salad
(along with whatever protein you'd like;

the choices naturally include Spam), it's no surprise that there are so many guys walking around calling themselves the Big Kahuna. **Known for:** plate lunch with various meats; island-favorite Spam; quick and inexpensive. $ *Average main: $9* ⊠ *4030 S. Maryland Pkwy., University District* ☎ *702/880–9898* ⊕ *www.hawaiianbarbecue.com* ▭ *No credit cards.*

Lindo Michoacán

$$ | **MEXICAN** | **FAMILY** | Javier Barajas, the congenial owner and host of this colorful cantina group, named it for his home in Mexico. He presents outstanding specialties that he learned to cook while growing up in the culinary capital of Michoacán. **Known for:** specialties from Michoacán region; table-side guacamole; colorful, lively atmosphere. $ *Average main: $20* ⊠ *2655 E. Desert Inn Rd., East Side* ☎ *702/735–6828* ⊕ *www.lindomichoacan.com.*

L2 Texas BBQ

$$ | **BARBECUE** | **FAMILY** | Taking its name from two owners (both named Larry), this barbecue joint moved to inherit the smoked meat addicts left stranded when Memphis Championship Barbecue abandoned the same location. The atmosphere is unchanged, and they didn't have to worry about the delicious smell of smoke that saturated the sheet-metal accented interior. **Known for:** big barbecue platters; all-you-can-eat special; diverse choices beyond smoked meat. $ *Average main: $20* ⊠ *2250 E. Warm Springs Rd., East Side* ☎ *702/260–6903* ⊕ *www.l2texasbbq.com.*

★ Lotus of Siam

$$$$ | **THAI** | This simple Thai restaurant has attained near-fanatical cult status, leaving some to wonder what all the fuss is about. It's simply that everything is so very good. **Known for:** spicy Issan Thai cuisine; garlic prawns; cult following. $ *Average main: $33* ⊠ *953 E. Sahara Ave., Suite A5, East Side* ☎ *702/735–3033 phone for both locations* ⊕ *lotusofsiamlv.com* ☾ *No lunch at Flamingo location.*

Marrakech Mediterranean Restaurant

$$$$ | **MOROCCAN** | Sprawl out on soft floor cushions and feel like a pampered pasha as belly dancers shake it up in a cozy Middle Eastern–style "tent" with a fabric-covered ceiling and eye-catching mosaics. The prix-fixe feast is a six-course affair that you eat with your hands. **Known for:** exotic decor; fun atmosphere; great for groups. $ *Average main: $70* ⊠ *3900 Paradise Rd., Paradise Road* ☎ *702/737–5611* ⊕ *www.marrakechvegas.com* ☾ *No lunch.*

Nobu

$$$$ | **JAPANESE** | Executive chef Nobu Matsuhisa helped fuel the popularity of the original Hard Rock Hotel in Las Vegas, so it would have just seemed wrong for the restaurant not to be the one carry-over when the hotel transitioned into Virgin Hotels Las Vegas. Although there's now an entire Nobu subhotel within Caesars Palace, this restaurant reflects the decor and menu of the Manhattan Nobu original, with bamboo and wood accents. **Known for:** Nobu classics such as black cod miso; plenty of sushi and sashimi; quiet, efficient service. $ *Average main: $55* ⊠ *Virgin Hotels Las Vegas, 4455 Paradise Rd., South Strip* ☎ *702/693–5090* ⊕ *noburestaurants.com* ☾ *No lunch.*

One Steakhouse

$$$$ | **STEAKHOUSE** | Brothers David and Michael Morton, restaurateurs whose father founded the Morton's the Steakhouse chain back in the day, maintain the tradition of a Morton steak house at the new Virgin Hotel. This one is quite a bit different than their MB Steak, dividing its seating between the front bar with a bit of a retro vibe, and its rear dining room. **Known for:** 32-ounce tomahawk steak; table-side carving; de-stigmatizing "we'll just sit in the bar". $ *Average main: $55* ⊠ *Virgin Hotels Las Vegas, 4455 Paradise Rd., Paradise Road* ☎ *702/522–8111* ⊕ *virginhotelslv.com* ☾ *No lunch.*

Table 34

$$$$ | **AMERICAN** | Run by Wes Kendrick, a well-known local chef who's dedicated to local ingredient sourcing, this intimate, modern restaurant with clean lines, blond-wood floors, and high ceilings looks like something you'd find in California wine country. Especially good among the reasonably priced, outstanding bistro creations are the fresh pastas and thin-crust pizzas (try the one topped with bacon, Gouda, wilted spinach, and mushrooms). **Known for:** fresh, farm-to-table creations; house-made pastas; contemporary decor. ⑤ *Average main: $32* ✉ *600 E. Warm Springs Rd., East Side* ☎ *702/263–0034* ⊕ *table34lasvegas. com* ⊗ *Closed Sun. No lunch Sat.*

🛏 Hotels

Boulder Station Hotel & Casino

$$ | **HOTEL** | The story of how Station Casinos came to dominate the Las Vegas "locals casino" scene—and divide that dominance into regions—is exemplified by Boulder Station, which opened in early 1994, cementing what's now the Stations formula with its attached Regal movie theater, Feast Buffet, Guadalajara Mexican Restaurant, and The Broiler steak house for living-it-up occasions. **Pros:** solid values throughout; Railhead concert attractions; plenty of free parking. **Cons:** restaurants duplicated at other Station properties; bleak surrounding neighborhood; distance from other Las Vegas attractions. ⑤ *Rooms from: $150* ✉ *4111 Boulder Hwy., East Side* ☎ *702/432–7777* ⊕ *boulderstation.com* ⇄ *299 rooms* ⍩ *No meals.*

Oyo Hotel & Casino

$ | **HOTEL** | Hooters Hotel has become part of a fast-growing Indian chain, though things look much the same, and there is still even a Hooters Restaurant inside. **Pros:** location near top-tier resorts; fun pool area; budget-minded in a high-rent district. **Cons:** hand-me-down atmosphere; compact rooms; scary garage. ⑤ *Rooms from: $80* ✉ *115 E. Tropicana Ave., East Side* ☎ *866/584–6687, 702/739–9000* ⊕ *oyolasvegas.com* ⇄ *696 rooms* ⍩ *No meals.*

The Platinum Hotel and Spa

$$ | **RESORT** | This swank, nongaming, and LGBT-friendly condo-hotel has become a fashionable hideaway for Vegas regulars who prefer top-notch amenities but don't need to stay on the Strip. **Pros:** cocktail menu at STIR Lounge; lavish rooms with comfy sofas and beds; popularity with LGBTQ community. **Cons:** no casino; off-Strip location; quieter than Strip hotels. ⑤ *Rooms from: $229* ✉ *211 E. Flamingo Rd., Paradise Road* ☎ *702/365–5000, 877/211–9211* ⊕ *www.theplatinumhotel. com* ⇄ *255 suites* ⍩ *No meals.*

Renaissance Las Vegas Hotel

$$ | **HOTEL** | Everything is intimate at this nongaming hotel off the Strip on Paradise Road, a favorite of business travelers because it's located right next to the Las Vegas Convention Center. **Pros:** ENVY steak house; fresh, stylish rooms; no casino. **Cons:** rooms a bit small; pool can get overcrowded; geared more to business travelers than vacationers. ⑤ *Rooms from: $200* ✉ *3400 Paradise Rd., Paradise Road* ☎ *702/784–5700, 800/750–0980* ⊕ *www.marriott.com* ⇄ *578 rooms* ⍩ *No meals.*

Sam's Town Hotel & Gambling Hall

$ | **HOTEL** | The pioneering "locals casino" has anchored Boulder Highway since 1979 as a pure example of the casino as a mall-meets-community center: Locals flock to the movie theater, huge sports book, and sprawling underground bowling center, and (in prepandemic times) line up in queues rivaling Disneyland for a crack at the enormous Firelight Buffet. **Pros:** Mystic Park area; "locals" prices throughout; something for the whole family. **Cons:** smoky, old-school casino floor; unappealing neighborhood; distanced from other Las Vegas attractions. ⑤ *Rooms from: $85* ✉ *5111 Boulder Hwy., East Side* ☎ *702/456–7777, 800/634–6371 reservations*

⊕ *samstownlv.com* 🛏 *645 rooms* ⦿ *No meals.*

Virgin Hotels Las Vegas

$$ | RESORT | "Virgin" may be a curious name for Las Vegas, but Sir Richard Branson's brand hopes to sell a completely made-over version of the original Hard Rock Hotel—replacing the guitars and rock memorabilia with a tranquil yet sophisticated desert vibe. **Pros:** tranquil resort atmosphere; great, if pricey, restaurants; no "resort" fee or parking charges for self-parking (yes, that's correct...zero). **Cons:** not directly on the Strip, and the hotel no longer has a Strip shuttle; hotel guests must be 21 (no under-agers allowed, even with their parents); early reopening inconclusive on whether it becomes a convention hotel or if "the party" returns. ⑤ *Rooms from: $200* ✉ *4455 Paradise Rd., Paradise Road* ☎ *702/693–5000, 800/693–7625* ⊕ *www.virginhotelslv.com* 🛏 *1500 rooms* ⦿ *No meals.*

Westgate Las Vegas Resort & Casino

$ | RESORT | Convention attendees have loved the convenience of this hotel for decades, as it's adjacent to the Las Vegas Convention Center, but converting some of its hotel rooms to a time-share strategy also has helped the hotel stay in the game as the Strip exploded with bigger and bolder properties. **Pros:** great location for convention-goers; classic sports book; world's largest Benihana. **Cons:** small poker area; away from much of the action; reputation for top entertainment has faded. ⑤ *Rooms from: $110* ✉ *3000 Paradise Rd., Paradise Road* ☎ *702/732–5111, 888/796–3564 reservations* ⊕ *www.westgateresorts.com* 🛏 *3000 rooms* ⦿ *No meals.*

ⓨ Nightlife

BARS AND LOUNGES

Paymon's Fresh Kitchen and Lounge

PIANO BARS/LOUNGES | The hookah is an elaborate Middle Eastern water pipe

used to smoke exotic tobacco. It also happens to be a point of distinction (or perhaps gimmick) for this Mediterranean favorite overseen by local entrepreneur Paymon Rouf. Instead of the bare-bones set-up or kitschy Greek murals in most gyro joints in the Valley, Paymon's conjures a sexy, chill-out experience, with a contemporary, red-velvet laden, incense-filled environment that draws a diverse crowd. Prices are a bargain, and the extensive menu offers plenty of dinner options if you want to eat as well as smoke and lounge. (Those who remember the original, University-district location, which has closed, will find the new, larger location worth the drive.) ✉ *8955 S. Eastern Ave., East Side* ☎ *702/333-4622* ⊕ *www.paymons.com.*

GAY AND LESBIAN

Las Vegas was never really known for gay tourism, but things have changed rapidly in the past few years; the major resorts include gay-oriented events in their marketing. But there are still a number of bars and nightclubs catering to different segments of the community.

One area of town particularly reflects the more segregated days when gay and lesbian nightlife were concentrated in certain areas. The so-called Fruit Loop—which wins our award for best nickname for a North American gay neighborhood—is near the intersection of Naples Drive and Paradise Road, just north of the airport and close to Virgin Hotels Las Vegas (formerly the Hard Rock Hotel). And some gay-oriented establishments are still in the struggling Commercial Center, one of the city's oldest shopping centers, on East Sahara Avenue, just west of Maryland Parkway. If there are cover charges at all, expect them to be around $10 for dance clubs on weekends.

Unfortunately, there are no all-out lesbian bars in Vegas, although many of the gay bars (most prominently FreeZone) host special nights for their sapphic sisters.

The new Virgin Hotels Las Vegas is expected to become a hot off-Strip nightlife destination with such drinking spots as The Bar at Commons Club, and The Shag Room.

These parties, like so much in Sin City, change frequently, so it's best to consult a copy of *Q Life* (⊕ *gay.vegas*), the city publication.

Badlands Saloon

BARS/PUBS | Consider the Badlands a 24-hour haven for local gay cowboys. It's decorated with a mock-log-cabin façade and offers cubbyholes in which regulars can store their beer steins. There's also a jukebox crammed to the coin slot with country-and-western hits. Plus, the Nevada Gay Rodeo Association hosts its fund-raisers here. Perhaps the only downside is the smoke. ⊠ *Commercial Center, 953 E. Sahara Ave., East Side* ☎ *702/792–9262.*

★ FreeZone

BARS/PUBS | An egalitarian mix of (straight and gay) men and women congregates at this 24-hour bar with a dance floor, pool tables, karaoke, and video-poker machines. Special promotions such as ladies night (currently Tuesday) appeal to both conventioneers and locals, while live drag shows are more raucous than the tame ones on the Strip. ⊠ *610 E. Naples Dr., University District* ☎ *702/794–2300* ⊕ *freezonelv.com.*

Piranha Nightclub & Ultra Lounge

DANCE CLUBS | Revelers pack this gorgeous spot every night of the week—and with good reason, given that each night of the week offers a different drink promotion or special theme. Although the dance floor at Piranha is legendary, the best spot in the house is the spacious, fireplace-ringed open-air patio out back. Head here for a Latin night on Sunday and partake in the fun. ⊠ *4633 Paradise Rd., Paradise Road* ☎ *702/379–9500* ⊕ *www.piranhavegas.com.*

LIVE MUSIC
ROCK
Piazza Lounge

CABARET | A lot of people ask, Where do Las Vegas entertainers hang out and perform for one another? One of the best and most consistent answers is found in this appealing and easily accessed lounge at The Tuscany (an attractive, convention-oriented hotel that is otherwise unremarkable). Kenny Davidson's Celebrity Piano Bar is a Friday-night fixture for local performers, and other nights features singers on the level of *America's Got Talent* winner Michael Grimm. ✉ *Tuscany Suites & Casino, 255 E. Flamingo Rd., East Side* ☎ 702/893–8933 ⊕ *tuscanylv.com/entertainment*.

The Railhead

MUSIC CLUBS | This comfortable venue is versatile enough to be closed off for ticketed concerts, or opened up to host free lounge acts and casino promotional events. Sight lines are great, and it's really the only game on this side of town for a diverse range of local and mid-level concerts that range from rock to country and just about everything in between. ✉ *Boulder Station Hotel and Casino, 4111 Boulder Hwy., Boulder Strip* ☎ 702/432–7777 ⊕ *www.stationcasinosevents.com*.

The Theater at Virgin Hotels Las Vegas

MUSIC CLUBS | The concert hall long known as The Joint is now just The Theater as Virgin Hotels Las Vegas. During the makeover, the 4,000-plus capacity venue was entrusted to concert promoter AEG Presents, and the room was spruced up with new seating and some changes, such as moving a VIP area to the ground-floor level. Upgrades were welcome, as the venue was always better known for the big names it hosted than for the room itself, a big box, which jammed seated fans into folding chairs and put the versatility of its seating configurations ahead of comfort, aesthetics, or design. Acts already scheduled to perform include Lady A, Christina Aguilera, Primus, and Little Big Town. ✉ *Hard Rock Hotel, 4455 Paradise Rd., Paradise Road* ☎ 702/693–5000 ⊕ *www.hardrockhotel.com*.

Tiki Di Amore

PIANO BARS/LOUNGES | You get two kinds of retro-hip nostalgia at Casa Di Amore, a durable Italian restaurant. Inside, vintage photos of Las Vegas line the walls where a live pianist often entertains diners. Except for the limited bar seating, the indoor area is primarily for those with dinner reservations. Out back, however, the outdoor Tiki Di Amore is more for the walk-up crowd of those in shorts and flip-flops, with a separate menu of bar food, and often live bands amid the kitschy thatched-roof surroundings. ✉ *Casa Di Amore, 2850 E. Tropicana Ave., East Side* ☎ 702/433–4967 ⊕ *tikidiamore.com*.

LOCAL HANGOUTS
Double Down Saloon

BARS/PUBS | The grand poo-bah of Vegas dive bars, the Double D is a short walk from the Virgin Las Vegas and a long, long way from Paradise—a sign inside says it nicely: "Shut Up and Drink." Delicious decadence prevails here 24 hours a day; no wonder it was a fave of the late food celebrity Anthony Bourdain and anyone else adventurous enough to enjoy a bacon martini. For the boho crowd, this deliberately downscale bar awash in cleverly obscene graffiti has everything from great local bands to a satisfying jukebox with truly eclectic selections. Our advice: go late, choke back the cigarette smoke, and try the (fabled) Ass Juice cocktail. ✉ *4640 Paradise Rd., Paradise Road* ☎ 702/791–5775 ⊕ *www.doubledownsaloon.com*.

STRIP CLUBS
Centerfolds Cabaret

THEMED ENTERTAINMENT | The lone topless club in the convention corridor is smaller than the splashy ones to the west, but has long benefited from its location: across the street and literally within stumbling distance of the Virgin Hotel Las Vegas (formerly the Hard Rock Hotel). The location was grandfathered: the club was one of the first strip joints in town in the 1970s, and one of the first to embrace the upscaling to "gentlemen's club" in the 1990s. Beyond the industry-standard free limo rides and night-of-the-week liquor specials, the only other real novelty here is a hookah lounge. ✉ *4416 Paradise Rd., Paradise Road* ☎ 702/767–8757 ⊕ *centerfoldscabaretlv.com*.

🛍️ Shopping

MEN'S CLOTHING
Undefeated

SHOES/LUGGAGE/LEATHER GOODS | Las Vegas has its own branch of this store, the authority on premium sneakers and street wear. Look for classic brands sitting next to limited-edition pieces as well as Undefeated, their own label, which collaborates with the big boys to create lustful objects such as the Air Jordan IV Retro and Nike Dunk Hi Ballistic. ✉ *Paradise Esplanade, 4480 Paradise Rd., Suite 400, Paradise Road* ☎ *702/732–0019* ⊕ *undefeated.com.*

MUSIC
Zia Records

MUSIC STORES | **FAMILY** | This store is for the music lover who enjoys shopping for tunes the old-fashioned way—thumbing through title after title, hoping to get that lucky break. As streaming pummels compact discs into extinction, Zia's vinyl selection has re-emerged to claim at least an equal amount of floor space from CDs. With DVDs and Blu-Rays also disappearing from the big-box retailers, Zia—which bills itself as "The Last Record Store"—is now the rare place to find those obscure cult movies, which are now only remastered in small batches. Zia has responded to shrinking physical media by devoting more of its massive store space to games, books, T-shirts and novelties; not unlike a bigger, hipper Spencer Gifts. But the place still feels like the basement where the ol' band once practiced. In fact, you might get lucky on your visit and enjoy local talent performing live. Take advantage of the knowledgeable staff, who can test your music trivia or offer recommendations based on your current collection. There's also a newer, more compact location in west Las Vegas on Rainbow Boulevard. ✉ *4225 S. Eastern Ave., East Side* ☎ *702/735–4942* ⊕ *www.ziarecords.com.*

SHOPPING CENTERS
Boulevard Mall

SHOPPING CENTERS/MALLS | **FAMILY** | Like many an indoor mall, Las Vegas's first (it opened in 1968) was in danger of becoming a "ghost mall" before new owners began a transformation. Bygone anchor stores such as Sears and Dillards were replaced with more activity- and entertainment-oriented draws: a Galaxy cineplex touting the city's largest indoor movie screen, a SeaQuest Aquarium, and John's Incredible Pizza, overflowing with rides and bumper cars. Occupancy is rising and Boulevard Mall's new additions are developing a funky charm of their own. The latest addition plays to the changing demographics of the neighborhood: the Mercado is a separately themed area styled like a street market, hosting small-business food and retail vendors. ✉ *3528 S. Maryland Pkwy., East Side* ☎ *702/735–7430 guest services and management* ⊕ *boulevardmall.com.*

🏃 Activities

BOWLING
Sam's Town Bowling Center

BOWLING | **FAMILY** | This is a 56-lane locals' alley where leagues and tournaments are taken seriously. The sprawling underground lanes offer a cocktail lounge and snack bar to eliminate changing shoes. The "Xtreme Bowling Experience" at 9 pm on Friday and Saturday night will allow you to "strike out" in a nightclub-like environment. Be sure to check for deals such as $1.25 games on early mornings. ✉ *5111 Boulder Hwy., Boulder Strip* ☎ *702/456–7777, 800/897–8696* ⊕ *www.samstownlv.com* 🎟 *From $4; shoe rental $5.*

GOLF

Las Vegas National Golf Club

GOLF | **FAMILY** | Built in 1961, this historic course has played host to Vegas royalty and golf's superstars over the years. Tiger shot 70 on the final round of his first PGA Tour win during the 1996 Las Vegas Invitational, and Mickey Wright won two of her four LPGA Championships here. You'll find five difficult par-3s and a killer 550-yard par-5 at the 18th. "Las Vegas National," as it's known, is about a $15 cab ride from most properties on the Strip. ⊠ *1911 E. Desert Inn Rd., East Side* ☎ *702/889–1000* ⊕ *www.lasvegasnational.com* ✉ *From $69 for nonresidents* 🏌 *18 holes, 6721 yards, par 73.*

Royal Links Golf Club

GOLF | **FAMILY** | Similar in concept to Bear's Best, Royal Links is a greatest-hits course, replicating popular holes from 11 courses in the British Open rotation. You can play the Road Hole from the famed St. Andrews, and the Postage Stamp from Royal Troon. Also on-site is Stymie's Pub. Tee times cost $134 per person; check for online specials as low as $99. ⊠ *5995 E. Vegas Valley Dr., East Side* ☎ *702/765–0484, 888/427–6678* ⊕ *www.royallinksgolfclub.com* ✉ *$134 for nonresidents* 🏌 *18 holes, 7029 yards, par 72.*

Chapter 8

HENDERSON AND LAKE LAS VEGAS

Updated by
Jason Bracelin

👁 Sights	🍽 Restaurants	🛏 Hotels	👜 Shopping	🍸 Nightlife
★★★★☆	★★☆☆☆	★★★☆☆	★★☆☆☆	★★☆☆☆

NEIGHBORHOOD SNAPSHOT

TOP EXPERIENCES

■ **City Parks:** Henderson is known for its multitude of parks, which include walking and biking trails, athletic fields, and dog parks (including a splash pad for canines).

■ **Clark County Museum:** Familiar to many because of its director's cameos on *Pawn Stars*, the 30-acre museum site has Heritage Street with historic buildings, a mining exhibit, and more.

■ **The District at Green Valley Ranch:** A mixed-use commercial/residential hub, The District draws crowds for its popular restaurants, shops, and special events.

■ **Lake Las Vegas:** Though it took a heavy hit in the recession that ended in 2009, this sprawling community is buzzing with new residential and commercial development, including restaurants and shops.

■ **Water Street District:** This original heart of the city, near City Hall and the Henderson Convention Center, is undergoing a revitalization, with new restaurants, bars and shops.

GETTING HERE

From the Strip, both Interstate 515 (also known as Highway 93/95) and Boulder Highway wind southeast toward Henderson, Lake Mead Parkway cuts due east toward the lake and Interstate 215 goes west. Public transportation serves this area, but the only practical way to get around is to rent a car. Once you're out by Lake Las Vegas, bicycles are actually a great method of transportation. If you're philosophically opposed to exercise in Las Vegas, fear not—taxis and ride-sharing services are readily available.

PLANNING YOUR TIME

Henderson, the second-largest city in the state, is a thriving bedroom community with plenty to explore, whether for a few hours (at Water Street, The District at Green Valley Ranch, or Lake Las Vegas) or days (to take in the city's parks and many recreational opportunities).

QUICK BITES

■ **Carlito's Burritos.** A longtime local favorite, Carlito's specializes in Hatch chile—red or green—in all-day breakfasts, stuffed *sopapillas*, and more. ⊠ *4300 E. Sunset Rd., Henderson* ⊕ *www.carlitosburritos.com*

■ **CRAFTkitchen.** A breakfast-and-lunch spot from a former Strip baker, this is a great place to pick up breads, pastries, cakes and more. ⊠ *10940 S. Eastern Ave., Henderson* ⊕ *www.craftkitchenlv.com.*

■ **Public Works Coffee Bar.** One of the first members of the revitalized Water Street District serves every type of coffee imaginable and a good selection of teas, and hosts occasional pop-ups. ⊠ *314 S. Water St., Henderson* ⊕ *www.publicworkscoffee.com*

Suburbia stretches to the east and southeast of the Las Vegas Strip, and it continues to spread; Henderson is one of the fastest-growing cities in the entire nation. Much of this area is residential, with only a smattering of casinos. Some travelers may just pass through on their way to Lake Mead or Hoover Dam, but the resorts in the area are also worth a look.

One of those casinos—the M Resort—has commanding views of the Strip. Because the property is uphill from town, it literally looks down on the rest of the Valley. Another casino resort, Green Valley Ranch, is adjacent to one of the best shopping malls in the area. Both are worthwhile destinations for a weekend or an afternoon.

Out near Lake Las Vegas, the vibe is much more luxurious. Resorts such as the Westin Lake Las Vegas Resort & Spa and the Hilton Lake Las Vegas Resort & Spa dot the shoreline of a man-made lake, providing the perfect backdrop for golf and a variety of other outdoor activities. Bicyclists, joggers, Rollerbladers, and walkers will love the River Mountains Trail, a 36-mile loop that links Henderson, Lake Las Vegas, and Boulder City to the south. Pedaling over the sometimes-for-midable mountains, it's hard to believe this deserted region is just a dozen miles from a major city.

Farther afield are the main attractions in this part of the Valley: Lake Mead National Recreation Area and Hoover Dam (⇨ see *Side Trips from Las Vegas*). If you've got the time, rent a houseboat for a multiday vacation on the lake; it's the best way to explore the body of water at your own pace. At the dam, take the tour for an inside look (literally) at one of humankind's greatest engineering feats. These icons are packed in summer, so it's best to plan your trip for a shoulder season.

👁 Sights

Clark County Museum
MUSEUM | FAMILY | Step into the past (quite literally) at this modest museum, a 30-acre site that features a small exhibit hall with a time-line exhibit about southern Nevada from prehistoric to modern times. The facility also offers a collection of restored historic buildings that depict daily life from different decades in Las Vegas, Boulder City, Henderson, and Goldfield. Other attractions include a replica of a 19th-century frontier print shop, and a 1960s wedding chapel that once stood on the Las Vegas Strip. There are also buildings and machinery dating from the turn of the 20th century, a nature trail, and a small ghost town. The museum also hosts a memorial to the 58 people killed in the Route 91 Harvest Festival shooting. If you can't get to the

Henderson and Lake Las Vegas

THE STRIP

PARADISE

McCarran International Airport

WHITNEY

Sunset Park

ENTERPRISE

HENDERSON

Henderson Airport

E. Desert Inn Rd.
Flamingo Rd.
Harmon Ave.
Tropicana Ave.
Tropicana Ave.
E. Patrick Ln.
E. Sunset Rd.
E. Warm Springs Rd.
Robindale Rd.
Windmill Pkwy.
E. Wigwam Ave.
Pebble Rd.
E. Serene Ave.
Silverado Ranch Blvd.
E. Pyle Ave.
E. Russell Rd.

Las Vegas Blvd.
Paradise Rd.
S. Eastern Ave.
S. Sandhill Rd.
S. Pecos Rd.
Mountain Vista St.
S. Nellis Blvd.
Cabana Dr.
North Boulder Hwy.
N. Stephanie St.
N. Gibson Rd.
Bermuda Rd.
Pollock Dr.
S. Maryland Pkwy.
Spencer St.
S. Eastern Ave.
S. Green Valley Pkwy.
Horizon Ridge Pkwy.
American Pacific Dr.
Saint Rose Pkwy.

582
515
215
146
604
15

0   2 mi
0   2 km

Sights ▼

1 Clark County Museum G5
2 Ethel M Chocolate Factory D3
3 Lake Las Vegas H1
4 River Mountains Loop Trail H4

Restaurants ▼

1 Anthony's Prime Steak & Seafood A7
2 Biscuits and Bourbon F4
3 Grimaldi's Green Valley B5
4 Hank's Fine Steaks C5
5 Juan's Flaming Fajitas & Cantina F4
6 Pasta Shop Ristorante & Art Gallery C5
7 Raiders Tavern & Grill A7
8 Todd's Unique Dining D3

LAKE LAS VEGAS

Las Vegas Bay Marina (Closed)

Desert Wetlands Park

Lake Las Vegas Parkway

Lake Mead National Recreation Area

Silver Bowl Sports Complex

E. Lake Mead Pkwy.

N. Major Ave.

S. Racetrack Rd.

North Boulder Hwy.

Water St.

S. Magic Way

W. Pacific Ave.

E. Horizon Dr.

Appaloosa Rd.

Boulder Airport

BOULDER

KEY

1	*Exploring Sights*
1	*Restaurants*
1	*Hotels*

Lake Las Vegas, a 320-acre artificial lake in Henderson, was finished in 1991.

Las Vegas Springs Preserve, west of the Strip, this is a worthwhile substitute. ✉ *1830 Boulder Hwy. S, Henderson* ☎ *702/455–7955* ⊕ *www.clarkcountynv. gov* 🎫 *$2.*

Ethel M Chocolate Factory

FACTORY | FAMILY | Ethel M celebrated its 35th anniversary in 2016 and renovated its Henderson factory to commemorate the occasion. Today, watching gourmet chocolates being made on one of the daily tours will make your mouth water; fortunately the self-guided tour is brief, and there are free samples at the end. You can buy more of your favorites in the store. There are also chocolate tasting experiences beginning at $20, where you will learn about how chocolate is sourced and produced and become an honorary chocolatier complete with certificate afterward. Randomly, the factory also happens to be home to the largest cactus garden in the southwestern United States, and hosts spectacular light displays at Christmas, Easter, and Halloween. ✉ *2 Cactus Garden Dr.,*

Henderson ☎ *702/458–8864* ⊕ *www. ethelm.com* 🎫 *Free.*

Lake Las Vegas

BODY OF WATER | FAMILY | This 320-acre, man-made lake outside of Henderson is regarded for its golf courses, boating, fishing, and hotels. Two resorts sit on the lake shore: Hilton Lake Las Vegas Resort & Spa and the Westin Lake Las Vegas Resort & Spa. The lake was created by an earthen dam in 1991. ✉ *29 Grand Mediterra Blvd., Henderson* ⊕ *www. lakelasvegas.com.*

River Mountains Loop Trail

TRAIL | FAMILY | Stretching 36 miles around the River Mountains, this mul-tiuse paved trail is perfect for hiking, biking, running, jogging, and horseback riding. For a stretch, the trail parallels the shores of Lake Mead, and connects with a historic spur that leads from the Lake Mead National Recreation Area to a parking lot just north of the Hoover Dam. The route runs through Boulder City, Henderson, and Lake Las Vegas. You can rent bikes at **McGhie's in Henderson**

(⊕ www.mcghies.com) or **All Mountain Cyclery** (⊕ allmountaincyclery.com) in Boulder City. The most popular trailheads are at the Alan Bible Visitor Center inside the recreation area and Bootleg Canyon Park, at the north end of Yucca Street in Boulder City. Access is also available at the eastern end of Equestrian Drive in Henderson, and the Railroad Pass Hotel & Casino, also in Henderson. ⊠ *Alan Bible Visitor Center trailhead, 8 Lake Shore Rd., Boulder City* ⊕ *www. rivermountainstrail.com.*

🍴 Restaurants

Anthony's Prime Steak & Seafood

$$$$ | **STEAKHOUSE** | Anthony's is the M Resort's version of the steak house that's de rigueur in every casino. The atmosphere is sleek and sophisticated, with the feel, food, and service of a Strip spot without the steep Strip prices. **Known for:** dry- or wet-aged steaks; oysters Rockefeller; quiet elegance. ⑤ *Average main: $55* ⊠ *M Resort, 12300 Las Vegas Blvd. S, South Las Vegas* ☎ *702/797–1000* ⊕ *www.themresort.com* ⊙ *No lunch.*

Biscuits and Bourbon

$$ | **BARBECUE** | **FAMILY** | What warms the blood more swiftly at this down-home hang: the fresh-from-the-oven biscuits or the 80-plus varieties of bourbon? Find out at this unique addition to the ongoing refurbishment of the Water Street District in downtown Henderson, where you will find drinks served in Mason jars and a menu of smoked meats, from pulled pork to apple-brined chicken, in big portions. **Known for:** gourmet biscuits served with a variety of flavored butters, honey, and jams; a wide selection of 80-plus bourbons; mouthwatering smoked meats. ⑤ *Average main: $15* ⊠ *109 S. Water St., Henderson* ☎ *702/986–0307* ⊕ *www. bandbonwater.com.*

Grimaldi's Green Valley

$$ | **PIZZA** | **FAMILY** | A branch of the legendary coal-fired pizza-baker nestled beneath the Brooklyn Bridge, this casual little joint in Henderson doesn't quite conjure up the atmosphere of the original, despite exposed-brick walls and red-checked tablecloths, but it does have a wine list and an extensive beer menu. What counts, of course, is the pizza, and in this regard, Grimaldi's deserves high praise. **Known for:** coal-fired pizza; specialty white pizza; monthly specials. ⑤ *Average main: $18* ⊠ *9595 S. Eastern Ave., Henderson* ☎ *702/657–9400* ⊕ *www.grimaldispizzeria.com.*

Hank's Fine Steaks

$$$$ | **STEAKHOUSE** | Start with a martini in the classy piano bar at this steak house at the much-loved Green Valley Ranch Resort (they're half-price during happy hour between 4 and 7). Then make your way into the ornately decorated dining room, with its marble floors and glittering chandeliers for a traditional Las Vegas steak-house dinner. **Known for:** steaks aged 28 days; broad seafood selection; onyx bar. ⑤ *Average main: $60* ⊠ *Green Valley Ranch, 2300 Paseo Verde Pkwy., Henderson* ☎ *702/617–7075* ⊕ *greenvalleyranch.sclv.com* ⊙ *No lunch.*

Juan's Flaming Fajitas & Cantina

$$ | **MEXICAN** | An anchor of the revitalization of Henderson's Water Street District downtown, Juan's is an offshoot of an established spot in southwest Las Vegas. Yes, the fajitas really are served flaming, on custom grills, and the variety extends from the usual beef, chicken, and shrimp to pork as well. **Known for:** fajitas and other familiar Mexican specialties; Jalisco-style plates; margaritas and mezcal. ⑤ *Average main: $17* ⊠ *16 S. Water St., Henderson* ☎ *702/476–4647* ⊕ *juansflamingfajitasandcantina.com.*

Pasta Shop Ristorante & Art Gallery

$$$ | **ITALIAN** | **FAMILY** | This house-made pasta pioneer (which sells to Strip resorts) is part restaurant and part art gallery, showcasing the owner's works. Pasta is, as you might expect, the specialty here, shown to advantage in dishes such as "Artisan Pasta Anne" (spinach pappardelle with grilled shrimp, feta, and tomatoes in a scampi sauce). **Known for:** house-made pasta; friendly, personable service; extensive options for vegans. $ *Average main: $23 ⊠ 2525 W. Horizon Ridge Pkwy., Henderson ☎ 702/451–1893 ⊕ pastashop.com.*

Raiders Tavern & Grill

$$ | **AMERICAN** | **FAMILY** | With spectators invited once again to Las Vegas Raiders games, fans of the Silver and Black will likely find this new sports bar and grill at the M Resort as intoxicating as the spirits on tap at one of two bars in this large, 3,400-square-foot room. Raiders helmets and footballs line the entry way, while framed jerseys of past gridiron greats and a gift shop loaded with Raiders gear make this a must-stop for team diehards. **Known for:** Raiders-theme atmosphere; 45 TVs for plenty of sports viewing; all-night menu of stadium food favorites. $ *Average main: $20 ⊠ 12300 Las Vegas Blvd. S, Henderson ☎ 702/797–1000 ⊕ www.themresort.com/dining/raiders-tavern-and-grill.*

Todd's Unique Dining

$$$$ | **AMERICAN** | What's really unique (for Vegas) about this intimate spot a short drive southeast of the airport is that artful, creative contemporary cuisine is served in an easygoing space with an unpretentious vibe. This place, from a former Strip executive chef, used to be something of a sleeper, but it's becoming better known. **Known for:** innovative dishes; former Strip chef; cozy suburban spot. $ *Average main: $45 ⊠ 4350 E. Sunset Rd., Henderson ☎ 702/259–8633 ⊕ www.toddsunique.com ☼ Closed Sun. No lunch.*

🛏 Hotels

Green Valley Ranch Resort, Spa & Casino

$$$ | **RESORT** | **FAMILY** | Locals have long known that Green Valley is a low-key, refined resort that prefers style over bustle (the Strip is a 25-minute drive away). **Pros:** sophisticated casino; proximity to malls that offer great shopping; newer sports book. **Cons:** 25 minutes from the Strip; not much in the immediate area; can be overrun with locals. $ *Rooms from: $235 ⊠ 2300 Paseo Verde Pkwy., Henderson ☎ 702/617–7777, 866/782–9487 ⊕ greenvalleyranch.com �}} 496 rooms ⦿ No meals.*

Hilton Lake Las Vegas Resort & Spa

$$ | **RESORT** | **FAMILY** | After previous lives as the Ritz-Carlton Lake Las Vegas and Ravella, this property was rebranded yet again in 2013, retaining its Mediterranean vibe and resplendent pool complex. **Pros:** relaxing ambience; complimentary shuttle; golf nearby. **Cons:** still has a lack of identity; far from Strip; disappointing restaurants. $ *Rooms from: $209 ⊠ 1610 Lake Las Vegas Pkwy., Henderson ☎ 702/567–4700 ⊕ www3.hilton.com ➽ 349 rooms ⦿ No meals.*

M Resort Spa Casino

$ | **RESORT** | Built by the Marnells, the same family that created the Rio, this resort is 6 miles south of McCarran Airport and is a destination unto itself. **Pros:** huge rooms; convenient yet removed from hubbub; views of Strip. **Cons:** cab ride to other casinos; planes roaring overhead; location in the middle of nowhere. $ *Rooms from: $115 ⊠ 12300 Las Vegas Blvd. S, Henderson ☎ 702/797–1000, 877/673–7678 ⊕ www.themresort.com ➽ 390 rooms ⦿ No meals.*

The Westin Lake Las Vegas Resort & Spa

$ | **RESORT** | This lavish resort with a Moroccan vibe sits on the shore of Lake Las Vegas and has richly appointed rooms with arched windows that offer sweeping views of the glittering lake and desert. **Pros:** lake vistas; Marssa

Green Valley Ranch, an elegant resort that rivals many big Strip properties, is a great place to explore in Henderson.

restaurant; activity center on beach rents kayaks and paddleboats. **Cons:** no casino nearby; manic design; 30 minutes from Strip. $ *Rooms from: $131* ✉ *101 Montelago Blvd., Lake Las Vegas, Henderson* ☎ *702/567–6000* ⊕ *www. westinlakelasvegas.com* ⇥ *447 rooms, 46 suites* ⦿ *No meals.*

ⓨ Nightlife

Hostile Grape

WINE BARS—NIGHTLIFE | Despite what the name implies, there's nothing hostile about this upscale wine bar in the M Resort downstairs, away from the casino floor. Instead, with over 450 wines by the bottle, the place offers visitors a welcoming and intimate environment in which to sample some new vino. The collection includes fine American, Italian, and French wines, as well as selections from Spain, South Africa, and Germany (to name a few). Visitors can taste as much as they like, thanks to the venue's innovative dispensing system that doles out prepaid tasting cards to allow guests

to enjoy pours of 1, 3, or 5 ounces at a time. Guests also enjoy buy one, get one appetizers from 7 to 8 from Wednesday through Saturday. ✉ *M Resort Spa Casino, 12300 Las Vegas Blvd. S, Henderson* ☎ *702/797–1000* ⊕ *www.themresort. com* ⦿ *Closed Sun.–Tues.*

🛍 Shopping

FOOD AND DRINK

Ethel M Chocolates Factory and Cactus Garden

FOOD/CANDY | **FAMILY** | The *M* stands for Mars, the name of the family (headed by Ethel in the early days) that brings you Snickers, Milky Way, Three Musketeers, and M&M's. Come here for two special reasons: one, to watch the candy making, and two (more important), to taste free samples in the adjoining shop that was recently renovated. As for the other half of this place's name, yes, there is, indeed, a cactus garden—Nevada's largest—with more than 300 species of succulents and desert plants. It's at its peak during spring flowering but also takes on a holiday spirit when it's lit up during the Christmas, Easter, and Halloween seasons. ■TIP➜ **The factory tour and gardens are free, but if you forget to go, McCarran International Airport features branches at all gates after airport security.** ⊠ *2 Cactus Garden Dr., Henderson* ☎ *702/435–2608* ⊕ *www.ethelm.com.*

HOME FURNISHINGS

Williams-Sonoma

HOUSEHOLD ITEMS/FURNITURE | FAMILY Many of the cleverly designed and stylish cooking tools, gourmet goodies, and home-decor items at Williams-Sonoma are suitcase-friendly for the gourmand in your life. Of course, looking through the shelves upon shelves of cookbooks, dishes, and utensils also makes a pleasant way to pass an hour before going to lunch. Call the branch for a rundown on its monthly cooking demos, hands-on workshops, or other technique classes. There's an additional location on the west side of Las Vegas. ⊠ *The District at Green Valley Ranch, 2255 Village Walk Dr., Suite 129, Henderson* ☎ *702/897–2346* ⊕ *www.williams-sonoma.com.*

MALLS

Galleria at Sunset

STORE/MALL | FAMILY | This enclosed mall in northwest Henderson boasts dozens of stores and boutiques, a large food court, sit-down restaurants such as Rodizio Grill the Brazilian Steakhouse and Gen Korean BBQ House, and seasonal carnivals. There's also a children's play area and a kiddie train to keep the little ones entertained. ⊠ *1300 W. Sunset Rd., Henderson* ☎ *702/434–0202* ⊕ *www. galleriaatsunset.com.*

🏃 Activities

BIRD-WATCHING

Henderson Bird Viewing Preserve

NATURE PRESERVE | FAMILY | More than 200 bird species have been spotted among the system of nine ponds at the 140-acre Henderson Bird Viewing Preserve. The preserve's ponds, at the Kurt R. Segler Water Reclamation Facility, are a stop along the Pacific flyway for migratory waterbirds, and the best viewing times are winter and early spring. The earlier you get there, the better if you want to fill your bird checklist. The ponds also harbor hummingbirds, raptors, peregrine falcons, tundra swans, cormorants, ducks, hawks, and herons. The office will lend out a pair of binoculars if you ask. Keep the bags of bread crumbs at home; the preserve doesn't allow the feeding of wildlife, and bikes and domestic pets are not allowed. ⊠ *350 E. Galleria Dr., Henderson* ☎ *702/267–4180* ⊕ *www. cityofhenderson.com* ⊠ *Free.*

GOLF

SouthShore Country Club

GOLF | Technically, the Jack Nicklaus–designed Signature Course at this Lake Las Vegas golf club is members-only, but a relatively new change in the bylaws allows guests at some of the local resorts to play with limited access. Hardcore enthusiasts say the layout is challenging; there are nearly 90 bunkers in all. Still, with views of Lake Las Vegas and the surrounding River Mountains, the experience is second to few others in the Las Vegas Valley. ⊠ *100 Strada di Circolo, Lake Las Vegas* ☎ *702/856–8402* ⊕ *www.southshoreccllv.com* ⊠ *$250 for nonmembers (prices vary by season; cheaper in summer months)* 🏌 *18 holes, 6917 yards, par 71.*

WEST SIDE

Updated by
Mike Weatherford

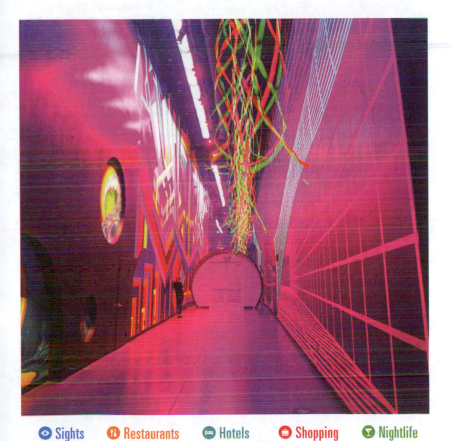

👁 **Sights** ★★☆☆☆ 🍴 **Restaurants** ★★★☆☆ 🛏 **Hotels** ★★☆☆☆ 🛍 **Shopping** ★☆☆☆☆ 🍸 **Nightlife** ★★★☆☆

NEIGHBORHOOD SNAPSHOT

TOP EXPERIENCES

■ **Area 15:** Burning Man meets Silicon Valley in a black-light indoor playground full of high-tech surprises. Its anchor attraction is the Omega Mart, an interactive funhouse from the Meow Wolf arts collective in Santa Fe, NM.

■ **Chinatown:** This pan-Asian enclave with shopping, restaurants, and a wide variety of businesses continually grows, and lately some top-notch non-Asian restaurants have sprung up for further diversification.

■ **Orleans Arena and Showroom:** The Orleans Arena regularly hosts large-scale shows such as rodeos and concerts, and smaller acts regularly appear in its showroom.

■ **Pole Position Raceway:** This go-kart track is adaptable to any kind of experience, from families to bachelor or bachelorette parties to corporate team-building.

■ **Rio Zip Line:** For a phenomenal view of the city and a huge adrenaline rush, glide along nearly 500 feet above the ground.

GETTING HERE

The Palms and the Rio are within a quick taxi ride from the Strip; they're even walkable from the Center Strip—about 20 minutes west on Flamingo. As you venture beyond the Palms, you approach rental-car territory. Because the West Side is home to thousands of casino employees, public transportation blankets the area.

PLANNING YOUR TIME

The West Side offers whatever you're looking for, from down-and-dirty activities like Dig It to fine dining in the casinos; figure out what you want to do rather than trying to randomly wander around. Beyond the Chinatown area, Las Vegas becomes a more typical automobile-age city that's fully spread out, not a master-planned, pedestrian-focused tourist zone.

QUICK BITES

■ **Capriotti's.** Want to feel like a busy local? Check out one of many Capriotti's numerous outlets around town, for a Bobbie ("Thanksgiving on a bun!") or any of the submarine sandwiches that have made this Nevada-based mini-chain a local phenomenon.. ✉ *4983 W. Flamingo Rd.* ⊕ *fomoeats.com*

■ **Halal Guys.** This New York cult favorite was one of the first non-Asian restaurants behind the recent diversification of Chinatown. ✉ *3755 Spring Mountain Rd.* ⊕ *fomoeats.com*

■ **Wine Cellar & Tasting Room at the Rio.** This impressive cellar's more than 3,000 bottles include numerous hard-to-find labels, and more than 100 wines by the glass. ✉ *Rio All-Suite Hotel & Casino, 3700 W. Flamingo Rd.* ⊕ *www.caesars.com/ rio-las-vegas*

The West Side of Las Vegas is a fascinating mix of urban city and 1970s-era suburbia colliding in the same place; an overspill of the tourist corridor blending into neighborhoods full of the grand ranch houses that carved out the area in the 1970s.

Housing developments lie behind just about every strip mall. Resorts such as the Palms and the Rio do double duty as locals' joints and major tourist draws with vibes just as swanky as their on-Strip counterparts. But for the most part, the locals in these neighborhoods gravitate to the more modest locals' casinos, including the Gold Coast, Orleans, Palace Station, and way to the north, Santa Fe Station.

The (deliberately) grungy industrial section that falls in the shadows of Interstate 15, a stone's throw (west) from the Strip, has become home base for the booming topless club industry, and filled in with visitor-oriented attractions such as Machine Guns Vegas, a decidedly upscale shooting range, or Pole Position Raceway Las Vegas, an indoor go-kart facility. This former no-man's land even hosts two of the city's most heralded arrivals: Allegiant Stadium, home of the transplanted NFL team Las Vegas Raiders, and Area 15, an indoor amusement park with a Burning Man vibe.

The West Side also has an ever-expanding Chinatown. This area, which started with one strip mall and street signs optimistically proclaiming a Chinatown, now sprawls a couple of miles in different directions, and offers everything from ramen to vegan doughnuts to world-class Thai food. The ground-up construction of a new center, Shanghai Plaza, was a 2019 testimony to investment in the area. It brought several new restaurants, including the revolving sushi bar Kura. Restaurants in the primary stretch of strip malls along Spring Mountain Road are known for their unpretentious and authentic dining scene. Not surprisingly, this is where many Strip chefs come to eat when they're not on the clock, and some stellar non-Asian restaurants have sprung up here as well. New apartments and condominiums popping up in the area fuel talk that Chinatown could be the next "downtown" in terms of gentrification and hipster appeal.

👁 Sights

★ Area 15

ARTS VENUE | FAMILY | Those who love hi-tech art served with a Burning Man or Electric Daisy Carnival vibe—and with the addition of air-conditioning—will gravitate to this indoor amusement park inside a giant warehouse next to Interstate 15 (the name is a play on both the highway and the mysterious Area 51). The very fluorescent interior (the black-light averse may feel like they are trapped in a giant Spencer Gifts) even features two big Burning Man art installations: a giant skull covered in video graphics and the fantasy

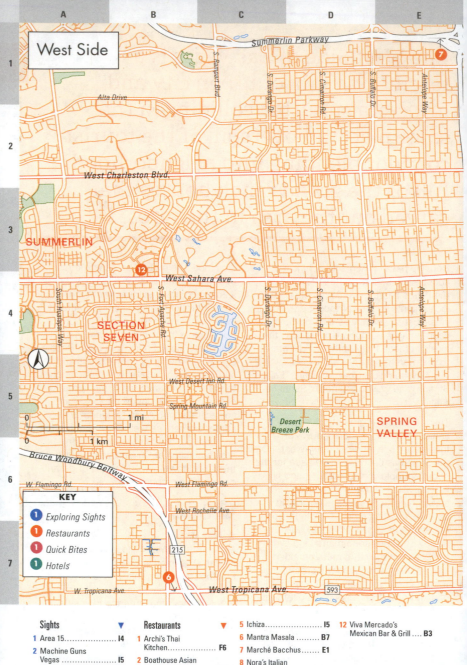

West Side

SUMMERLIN

SECTION SEVEN

SPRING VALLEY

Desert Breeze Park

hot rod known as Flux Capacitor. No one in the target demographic will remember when Disneyland had free admission and separate tickets for the rides, but that's the business plan here. Each of the three big attractions is a separate admission: **Omega Mart** is an otherworldly convenience store, which leads into a walk-through funhouse full of immersive art from the Santa Fe–based arts collective Meow Wolf; **Winkworld** is full of art and tech surprises courtesy of Chris Wink, a co-founder and original member of the Blue Man Group; **Museum Fiasco** is an immersive, disorienting clublike bombardment of light and sound. Peripheral attractions include axe-throwing and rides on ski-lift chairs suspended from a ceiling track. Chill out with a cocktail in the "Digital Forest" or maximize this new era of carnival midway with a Korean Corn Dog from the Todd English restaurant The Beast. The complex also has both indoor and outdoor entertainment spaces. The Portal is a 7,000-square-foot indoor venue where projection mapping augments everything from a Van Gogh exhibit to drag shows. The outdoor A-Lot hosts electronic music masters such as Paul Oakenfold. ■ **TIP→ Admission is free, but online reservations let you skip lines out front and may be required on busy nights.** ✉ *3215 S. Rancho Dr., West Side* ☎ *702/846–1900* ⊕ *area15.com* ⌂ *Entry free; Omegaworld $45, Winkworld $15, Museum Fiasco $17.*

Machine Guns Vegas

SPORTS—SIGHT | Swanky nightclub meets gun range in this only-in-Vegas addition to the scene. In an industrial neighborhood just west of the Interstate, "MGV" (as it's known) offers 10 indoor shooting lanes, including 2 in an ultra-exclusive VIP area, as well as a number of outdoor lanes. Many of the instructors are attractive women. Visitors have dozens of firearms to choose from, everything from "miniguns" and .22-caliber handguns up to an M-60 fully automatic machine gun. Package deals include multiple guns.

Guests can select their targets; among the options are evil clowns and Osama bin Laden. ✉ *3501 Aldebaran Ave., West Side* ☎ *800/757–4668, 702/476–9228* ⊕ *www.machinegunsvegas.com* ⌂ *From $100.*

Pole Position Raceway Las Vegas

SPORTS—SIGHT | FAMILY | This is no putt-putting lawn-mower-engine powered go-kart. These miniature racers are electric (think: souped-up golf carts) and reach up to 45 mph. You and up to 12 competitors zip around the ¼-mile indoor track full of twists and turns. The Pole Position computers track your overall performance from race to race, and over multiple visits. You'll get a score sheet giving a detailed score breakdown to compare with your friends. Signing up for "membership" cuts the fees by about 20%. There's also a second location out near Summerlin. ✉ *4175 S. Arville, West Side* ☎ *702/227–7223* ⊕ *www.polepositionraceway.com/las-vegas* ⌂ *$18* ☞ *Adults must be 56 inches tall to ride; kids must be 48 inches.*

Rio Zip Line

LOCAL INTEREST | FAMILY | For those who really want to see Las Vegas like a bird, the Rio Zip Line, which extends between two of the hotel's towers, will let them glide along almost 500 feet in the air—nearly half the height of the Strat. Riders can experience it alone or in tandem with a friend or loved one. ✉ *Rio All-Suite Hotel & Casino, 3700 W. Flamingo Rd., West Side* ☎ *702/388–0477* ⊕ *voodoozipline.com* ⌂ *$28.*

Sin City Smash

LOCAL INTEREST | This West Side attraction offers what is called a "rage room" experience—essentially, the place lets customers pay to smash stuff to smithereens. You sign up for a particular length of time in a room of certain size and are given bats and sledgehammers to destroy everything in sight. All participants also must wear safety gear such as goggles and helmets. The place cites

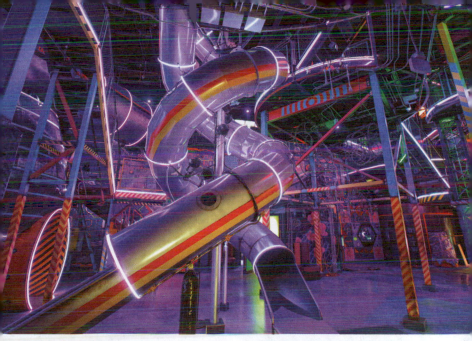

Behind the facade of Meow Wolf's Omega Mart is a whole new world in the city's newest big attraction, Area 15.

"destruction therapy" as a great way to cure stress. Whatever your perspective, you certainly will be sore in the morning. The shortest session is 15 minutes, and prices go up from there. And they now have the new trend of axe-throwing to diversify the catharsis. ✉ *2004 S. Rancho Dr., West Side* ☎ *702/912–1344* ✉ *From $39.*

🍴 Restaurants

Archi's Thai Kitchen

$$ | THAI | FAMILY | Fans of Thai food flock here for spot-on exceptional chow with few surprises—just expertly prepared curries, tom yum soups, fish cakes, and pad Thais. In particular, the shrimp "ginger ginger ginger" (or you can choose it with meat or tofu) has drawn raves; yes, it really is that gingery. **Known for:** carefully executed Thai classics; Thai iced tea; lovely interiors. ⑤ *Average main: $15* ✉ *6360 W. Flamingo Rd., West Side* ☎ *702/880–5550* ⊕ *www.archisthai.com.*

Boathouse Asian Eatery

$$ | MODERN ASIAN | This pan-Asian spot from a brother-and-sister team from California's Sonoma County is a lively, colorful, and contemporary anchor for the renovated and expanded Palace Station. Boathouse specializes in some large-format seafood, such as whole live lobster and whole live crab, as well as sushi, rolls, small plates such as crispy crab wontons, and hard-to-find foods like abalone. **Known for:** clay pot salmon; whole striped bass and branzino, steamed or fried; lots of colorful art. ⑤ *Average main: $20* ✉ *Palace Station, 2411 W. Sahara Ave., West Side* ☎ *702/367–2411* ⊕ *palacestation.sclv.com.*

Hash House A Go Go

$$ | AMERICAN | FAMILY | Hearty appetites and a dash of patience will be richly rewarded at this quirky purveyor of so-called twisted farm food. Heaps of savory comfort food are cooked to order in this spacious restaurant done up in industrial, urban-farmhouse decor. **Known for:** oversize servings; "twisted

farm food"; lively atmosphere. $ *Average main: $18* ✉ *6800 W. Sahara Ave., West Side* ☎ *702/804–4646* ⊕ *www.hashhouseagogo.com* ⊗ *No dinner Sun.–Thurs.*

Hot N Juicy Crawfish

$$ | SEAFOOD | FAMILY | This busy eatery has developed a loyal following for its delicious, fresh seafood, where crawfish from Louisiana is delivered regularly and available with five seasoning choices at five heat levels. But other choices can be just as good. **Known for:** crawfish and other seafood; messy, pound-it self-service; lively atmosphere. $ *Average main: $15* ✉ *4810 W. Spring Mountain Rd., West Side* ☎ *702/891–8889* ⊕ *www.hotnjuicycrawfish.com.*

Ichiza

$$ | JAPANESE | Modest little Ichiza has developed a cult following for serving sublimely delicious, authentic Japanese food and drink in a casual social environment that borders on controlled chaos. Located on the second floor of a shopping center in the city's Chinatown section, this boisterous pub is crammed with tourists, students, and local hipsters who love a good value and the chance to chow down on a variety of tasty small-plate offerings (aka "Japa tapas") until the wee hours. **Known for:** pub-style Japanese food; daily specials; service into the wee hours. $ *Average main: $19* ✉ *4355 Spring Mountain Rd., Suite 205, West Side* ☎ *702/367–3151* ⊗ *No lunch.*

Mantra Masala

$$ | INDIAN | FAMILY | Indian-food purists insist it's no big deal to drive 15 minutes from the Strip to the back of a bland strip mall for exceptionally authentic cuisine. While meat and fish make notable appearances, a dozen vegetarian dishes are on the menu as well. **Known for:** authentic Indian food; healthy emphasis; soothing environment. $ *Average main: $19* ✉ *Durango Springs Plaza, 8530 W. Warm Springs Rd., West Side* ☎ *702/598–3663* ⊕ *www.themantramasala.com* ⊗ *Closed Mon. No lunch.*

Marché Bacchus

$$$$ | FRENCH | This French bistro-cum-wineshop is in a quiet master-planned neighborhood that winds around its own lake (!), a remnant of the era when Las Vegas cared even less about running out of water. The tranquil setting and view are rivaled by a wine list nearly 1,000 bottles deep, and tastings and wine dinners are held regularly. **Known for:** serene view of lake and swans; updated French classics; nearly 1,000 wines. $ *Average main: $33* ✉ *2620 Regatta Dr., Suite 106, West Side* ☎ *702/804–8008* ⊕ *www.marchebacchus.com.*

Nora's Italian Cuisine

$$$ | ITALIAN | Independent restaurants in Las Vegas have such a struggle that Nora's is a refreshing success story. It's so popular with locals that it was able to build a new home, ground up, within walking distance of the old storefront location (now the equally worthwhile Monzu Italian Oven, owned by a family member) that fueled its 24-year reputation. **Known for:** osso buco; rack of lamb; easygoing atmosphere. $ *Average main: $25* ✉ *5780 W. Flamingo Rd., West Side* ☎ *702/873–8990* ⊕ *norascuisine.com.*

★ The Oyster Bar

$$$ | SEAFOOD | Palace Station has for years flown under the radar of most visitors, although a recent refurbishment has given it new life, especially its restaurants. One holdover is the justly popular Oyster Bar, which has a cult following among the cognoscenti, not to mention long waits during peak hours (reservations aren't taken for the limited seating area). **Known for:** Palace pan roast with shrimp, crab, chicken, and andouille; cioppino; "Bouill-Roast" (like a bouillabaise), a former secret-menu item. $ *Average main: $23* ✉ *Palace Station Hotel & Casino, 2411 W. Sahara Ave., West Side* ☎ *702/367–2411* ⊕ *palacestation.sclv.com.*

Ping Pang Pong

$$ | **CHINESE** | **FAMILY** | Delicious regional (mostly Cantonese) fare includes marvelous dim sum made fresh daily (and available until 3 pm). The great food often compels discerning diners—many of whom hail from Vegas's large Asian community—to brave the smoky, low-rollers casino floor of the Gold Coast. **Known for:** dim sum plentiful and varied; authentic Chinese specialties; lots of Chinese expats. $ *Average main: $19* ⊠ *Gold Coast Hotel and Casino, 4000 W. Flamingo Rd., West Side* ☎ *702/247–8136* ⊕ *www.goldcoastcasino.com.*

★ Raku

$$ | **JAPANESE** | Seating is at a premium in this softly lighted strip mall *robata,* a favorite of almost every chef in town. At 6 pm sharp every day but Sunday, doors open for small-plate offerings of creamy house-made tofu, fresh sashimi (no sushi), and savory grilled meats, fish, and veggies (cooked over charcoal imported from Japan) that reflect the culinary mastery of its Tokyo-born owner-chef. **Known for:** agedashi tofu, robata foods; daily specials; cozy atmosphere. $ *Average main: $20* ⊠ *5030 W. Spring Mountain Rd., Suite 2, West Side* ☎ *702/367–3511* ⊕ *www.raku-grill.com* ☾ *Closed Sun. No lunch.*

Viva Mercado's Mexican Bar & Grill

$$ | **MEXICAN** | **FAMILY** | Although popular namesake and founder Bobby Mercado is enjoying his retirement, Bobby's sister Carolina is the new owner and operator of this Mexican restaurant that's been a steady draw with locals and visitors in one location or another since the early 1990s. This colorful, comfortable spot (with patio dining when the weather's pleasant) features 10 house-made salsas and a well-executed, seafood-heavy menu. **Known for:** 10 house-made salsas; seafood-heavy menu; friendly, efficient service. $ *Average main: $18* ⊠ *9440 W. Sahara Ave., West Side* ☎ *702/454–8482* ⊕ *vivamercadoslv.com.*

☕ Coffee and Quick Bites

Capriotti's Sandwich Shop

$ | **AMERICAN** | **FAMILY** | This East Coast transplant with nearly 40 locations in the Valley satisfies Sin City's cravings for giant sub sandwiches, including a Philly-style cheese steak, a hot pastrami sandwich, and a divine creation called the Bobbie—basically Thanksgiving dinner on a bun. Numerous locations around town include outposts in a few outlying casinos, such as Red Rock, Aliante, Santa Fe, and Green Valley Ranch. **Known for:** turkey roasted in-house; the Bobbie sandwich; vegetarian offerings. $ *Average main: $10* ⊠ *4983 W. Flamingo Ave., Suite D, West Side* ☎ *702/222–3331* ⊕ *www.capriottis.com.*

Gabi Coffee and Bakery

$ | **BAKERY** | This is maybe the best example of a Las Vegas adage, "Never judge a place by its ugly strip-mall facade." In a shopping center you'd usually drive by lies a coffee and tea house that's about as beautiful as they come. An indoor greenhouse covers the central kitchen area, amid a well-appointed warehouse feel with plants, art, and cozy seating and a singular three-tiered reading and browsing area (shoes off, please) in back. **Known for:** fanciful atmosphere; fresh bakery temptations; vast coffee and tea menu. $ *Average main: $11* ⊠ *5808 Spring Mountain Rd., #104, West Side* ☎ *702/331–1144* ⊕ *gabicafe.com.*

Ronald's Donuts

BREAKFAST | **QUICK BITE** | Some of the best doughnuts in Vegas are sold at this tiny Chinatown storefront tucked in a strip mall along Spring Mountain Road. Locals rave about the apple fritters, but more traditional selections, such as Boston creme, are addictive, too. $ *Average main:* ⊠ *4600 Spring Mountain Rd., West Side* ☎ *702/873–1032* ▭ *No credit cards.*

🛏 Hotels

Palace Station Hotel & Casino
$$ | HOTEL | The Las Vegas success story synonymous with "locals casinos" began humbly with the former Bingo Palace at this location. **Pros:** makeover in 2018; plenty of parking; amazing choice of good restaurants. **Cons:** car ride from Strip; smoky, old-Vegas casino floor; lines or waits for popular eateries. *⑤ Rooms from: $120 ⊠ Palace Station, 2411 W. Sahara Ave., West Side ☎ 702/367–2411 ⊕ palacestation.com ⇆ 575 rooms ⦿ No meals.*

Rio Las Vegas Hotel & Casino
$$ | HOTEL | FAMILY | In Brazil, Rio is party central, and in Las Vegas so is this sprawling resort with spacious rooms just west of the Strip. **Pros:** pioneering Carnival buffet; three shows in-house; Rio Zip Line. **Cons:** just off-Strip enough to be inconvenient; big house advantage for gaming; rooms need a refresh. *⑤ Rooms from: $205 ⊠ 3700 W. Flamingo Rd., West Side ☎ 702/777–7777, 866/746–7671 ⊕ www.caesars.com ⇆ 2522 suites ⦿ No meals.*

🍸 Nightlife

BARS AND LOUNGES

The Artisan Lounge
PIANO BARS/LOUNGES | This not-yet-well-known favorite of ours is in the slightly out-of-the-way Artisan Hotel and is sort of an upscale version of the Peppermill. The vibe is relatively chill even on weekends, so it can serve as a tonic to the usual Vegas lunacy. The interior is filled with gilt-framed paintings (and sometimes frames without the paintings), which are even on the ceiling. Ordinarily, a crazy ceiling stunt like this one would seem silly, but the muted romantic ambience here (candlelight, soft music, dark wood, comfy leather couches) makes it work. On Friday and Saturday night DJs spin electro, house, and techno from 10 pm until dawn, but you can party 24

hours a day here. The Artisan's fate had been touch-and-go for a stretch, before it came under the umbrella of the Siegel Group, which is known for sprucing up troubled properties. *⊠ The Artisan Hotel, 1501 W. Sahara Ave., West Side ☎ 702/214–4000 ⊕ artisanhotel.com.*

VooDoo Rooftop Nightclub & Lounge
DANCE CLUBS | Take in great views of the city at this indoor/outdoor club 51 floors atop the Rio. DJs, great dance bands, and well-trained flair bartenders, serving concoctions such as the rum-packed Witch Doctor with dry ice, keep things lively. Faux-primitive voodoo paintings on the walls of the dance rooms maintain a tenuous thematic connection. The crowd tends to be slightly older and less, shall we say, sophisticated than at similar clubs. The party starts at 8 pm daily; the cover charge starts at 10. *⊠ Rio, 3700 W. Flamingo Rd., West Side ☎ 702/777–7800 ⊕ www.caesars.com.*

GAY AND LESBIAN

Flex Cocktail Lounge
BARS/PUBS | A small, neighborhood-oriented club for men, this 24-hour dive bar sometimes has floor shows, banana-eating contests, and entertainment (think male strippers, folks, sometimes in drag). Of course, the strong and inexpensive drinks don't hurt. *⊠ 4371 W. Charleston Ave., West Side ☎ 702/385–3539 ⊕ flex-lasvegas.com.*

LOCAL HANGOUTS

Frankie's Tiki Room
BARS/PUBS | You want Polynesian tiki-bar culture, Vegas-style? You want grass huts, carved wooden furniture, and cocktails such as the Green Gasser, the Thurston Howl, the Lava Letch, and the Bearded Clam? You'll get it all here, and more, 24 hours a day in this small, windowless but thoroughly charming tiki bar that is utterly committed to its theme. The tiki mugs are all original, and if you love yours (and trust us, you will), there's a "merch hut" where you can buy one to bring the spirit of aloha

home with you. ✉ *1712 W. Charleston Blvd., West Side* ☎ *702/385–3110* ⊕ *www.frankiestikiroom.com.*

The Golden Tiki

BARS/PUBS | This classic midcentury tiki bar might remind you of Don the Beachcomber and Trader Vic's. It's tucked inside a strip mall in Chinatown with a cocktail menu spilling over with nostalgic classics. Sip a cautious Dole Whip, line up a ride share before a Navy Grog with three rums, or splurge for a special treasure chest VIP experience. The roomy decor is full of surprises if you look around, including such treasures as an animatronic skeleton of the mythical privateer and legend behind The Golden Tiki, William Tobias Faulkner. There's a tiny stage and dance floor that hosts occasional DJs or live bands with a retro-lounge or Rat Pack vibe. ✉ *3939 Spring Mountain Rd., West Side* ☎ *702/222–3196* ⊕ *www.thegoldentiki.com.*

Herbs & Rye

BARS/PUBS | Classic cocktails are the name of the game at this bar off the Strip and worth the cab ride. Each cocktail comes with a story and quite a show while it's being made. Crack open the menu to learn the history behind each libation from the Prohibition era. This is the place to rub elbows with bartenders from other joints who often visit when finished with their shifts on the Strip. ✉ *3713 W. Sahara Ave., West Side* ☎ *702/982–8036* ⊕ *www.herbsandrye.com.*

STRIP CLUBS

It's not called Sin City for nothing. "Exotic dancing" clubs are a major industry here, but they do have some quirks. Zoning laws restrict most clubs to industrial areas not far off the Strip. And whatever the advertising may lead you to believe, if a club sells alcohol it's not "fully nude"; such venues can't carry liquor licenses. (The Palomino Club in North Las Vegas, is the one exception.) With new draws such as Resorts World and Allegiant Stadium conveniently landing near the traditional strip-club zone, the industry continues to explode, both in the number of clubs and the size of some of them. The difference between Las Vegas and the gentlemen's clubs you might be used to in your hometown is a trade-off. On the plus side: only in Las Vegas are you likely to see the industry done on this staggering scale, with multiple stages and literally dozens of dancers everywhere you look (the big conventions and, now, NFL weekends, bring dancers from out of town as well as their customers).

The downside might well be sticker shock: the biggest clubs, such as Sapphire and Hustler, can charge as much as $50 for a cover to walk inside, where beers can run $17 or $18 and mixed drinks up to $35. Wherever you go, be prepared to shell out some serious cash. The real money's made on the table dances continuously solicited inside. The long-standing rate is still $20 per song, but the hard-sell from the dancers is for the out-of-sight back rooms where a negotiable number of VIP dances usually starts with a C-note.

Crazy Horse III

THEMED ENTERTAINMENT | The builders of this club might have never anticipated the windfall headed its way in the form of Allegiant Stadium, which turns out to be within walking distance. The pandemic postponed the answers to how crazy the club would be on NFL weekends, but Crazy Horse was already in the top tier of the local skin game. The name that stuck (after previous incarnations as Sin and the Penthouse Club) is an homage to the bygone Crazy Horse II, which long ruled in the industry's smaller more downscale era. This version now has a center stage in-the-round and the more typically plush trappings of the modern era, as well as a kitchen to serve up pizzas and a "Taco Tuesday" promotion. Checking the website in advance might pay off with package deals that include limo transportation and drink credits. ✉ *3525 W. Russell Rd., West Side* ☎ *702/673–1700* ⊕ *www.crazyhorse3.com.*

Déjà Vu Showgirls

THEMED ENTERTAINMENT | Both the name and the scale of this one might be familiar to those who visit topless clubs in their home towns. Déjà Vu is part of a national chain, and the single-stage club is small compared to its increasingly grandiose competitors. But this branch has been spruced up with new carpet and the like. It also stays competitive with its $20 cover (compared to $50 at the splashier clubs) and is arguably within walking distance of the Strip—at least from the Fashion Show mall. The place is absolutely packed on Tuesday when all drinks are $2, and Sunday brings a uniquely popular "Sunday School" promotion in which the gals wear naughty schoolgirl outfits and bottles are $99. ⊠ 3247 S. Sammy Davis Jr. Dr., West Side ☎ 702/894–4167 ⊕ dejavuvegas. com.

Larry Flynt's Hustler Club

THEMED ENTERTAINMENT | The late porn mogul Larry Flynt's name is displayed prominently on this massive (70,000-square foot) three-story den of iniquity, allowing the whole second floor to be a VIP area with sky boxes. The main floor, lined with discretely curtained lap-dance areas, has a circular main stage, a pod stage, and even two (covered) dancers on top of the main bartop. There's an attached Hustler Hollywood store with all manner of exotic clothing and sundry sexual accessories. The high-profile location—it's right alongside Interstate 15 with its name in giant lights—may also help explain cover charges as high as $50 a person. A creative idea born of necessity in the pandemic (when the dancers had to be "covered") proved popular enough that it may stick around: "Sexxy After Dark" is a ticketed dinner show like you find on the Strip, which moved here from the Westgate Las Vegas to give the club an early-evening attraction. Friday and Saturday also bring a male revue up on the rooftop deck, where "girls night out" parties can watch male dancers in g-strings against a panorama of the Las Vegas skyline. ⊠ 6007 Dean Martin Dr., West Side ☎ 702/795–3131, 866/983–4279 ⊕ vegashustlerclub.com.

Sapphire

THEMED ENTERTAINMENT | Sapphire is billed as "the world's largest gentlemen's club," and until willing volunteers comb the globe to verify the claim, there's no disputing it here. After all, Sapphire was once a gym, which explains the 70,000 square-foot sprawl and the adjacent swimming pool, which operates seasonally as Sapphire Day Club (it's not topless, but there's plenty of indoor-outdoor commerce if you find a dancer you like outside working on her tan). There are no bargains here beyond the usual free-transportation and VIP-upgrade promotions, but the sheer spectacle when you first walk in may well justify the inflated drink prices and $50 cover. The adjacent El Dorado Cantina shares an owner and many customers but is a worthy enough 24-hour Mexican restaurant in its own right. The long-awaited arrival of neighboring Resorts World—either a solid walk or very short ride-share to the east—is only more likely to keep Sapphire at the top of the jiggle-joint heap. ⊠ 3025 Sammy Davis Jr. Dr., West Side ☎ 702/869–0003 ⊕ www.sapphirelasvegas.com.

★ Spearmint Rhino

THEMED ENTERTAINMENT | At the Rhino, as everyone calls it, you can expect a veritable onslaught of gorgeous half-clad women and an international name brand trusted by both dancers and customers alike. The place got a late start in Vegas, but it grew fast, expanding its original space to more than 20,000 square feet in 2019. In prepandemic times it was also the rare topless club that offers lunch, including steak sandwiches. There's an adjoining shop for lingerie, sex toys, and various other implements of physical naughtiness. A return to full operations

The Zoltar fortune-telling machine made popular in the movie *Big* is now built in Boulder City, and machines can be found all over Las Vegas.

also was likely to bring back the male g-string show "Men of Vegas" on Friday and Saturday. ✉ *3340 S. Highland Dr., West Side* ☎ *702/796–3600* ⊕ *www. spearmintrhinolv.com.*

🛍 Shopping

BOOKS
Psychic Eye Book Shop
BOOKS/STATIONERY | Behind the innocuous strip-mall facade are all sorts of esoteric books, lucky talismans, tarot cards, and candles. Get a psychic reading or an astrological chart on where to place your bets. This store for the metaphysically minded is part of a chain, with additional locations near McCarran International Airport and in Henderson. ✉ *6848 W. Charleston Blvd., West Side* ☎ *702/255–4477* ⊕ *www.pebooks.com.*

ONLY IN VEGAS
Houdini's Magic Shop
LOCAL SPECIALTIES | **FAMILY** | Magicians are hot tickets in Vegas, so it's no surprise that Houdini's corporate headquarters are in town. Find replicas of some of Harry Houdini's favorite illusions as well as volumes of books on how to perform magic, complete with costumes. Smaller branches can be found in the Grand Canal Shoppes at The Venetian, and next to Circus Circus. ✉ *Peterson Center, 6455 Dean Martin Dr., Suite L, Airport* ☎ *702/798–4789* ⊕ *www.houdini.com* ⊙ *Closed weekends* ☞ *Free parking.*

Serge's Wigs
LOCAL SPECIALTIES | If you've always wished for the sleek tresses of the stunning Vegas showgirls (or female impersonators), or if you want to try a daring new look for the clubs, head to this bright and spacious Vegas institution. You'll find an expansive selection of natural-hair and synthetic wigs and

hairpieces available in many styles, lengths, and colors, as well as accoutrements such as Styrofoam heads, hair adhesives, shampoos, scarves/turbans, and eyelashes. ■TIP➡ **A hair covering must be worn (scarf, bandana, nylon stocking) or purchased ($2) before trying on wigs. Allow additional time for cutting, styling, and proper fitting of your hairpiece if you plan to wear it on the same day of purchase.** ✉ *4515 W. Sahara Ave., West Side* ☎ *702/207–7494* ⊕ *www.sergeswigs. com* ⊗ *Closed Sun.*

🏃 Activities

BOWLING

The Orleans Bowling Center

BOWLING | FAMILY | This 70-lane bowling center is tucked inside the Orleans Resort and Casino, an all-purpose locals casino in a working-class neighborhood. Be sure to check out the pro shop, as well as the video arcade, which can get rocking on weekend nights. ✉ *4500 W. Tropicana Rd., West Side* ☎ *702/365– 7400* ⊕ *www.orleanscasino.com* 🍴 *From $4; shoe rental $5.*

Santa Fe Station Bowling Center

BOWLING | FAMILY | This 60-lane facility at Santa Fe Station Casino is a traditional bowling center, with video arcade, bar, and top-of-the-line Brunswick electronic scoring system. Cosmic Bowling with a DJ is held every Wednesday, as well as Friday through Sunday. ✉ *4949 N. Rancho Dr., West Side* ☎ *702/658–4988* ⊕ *www. stationcasinoslanes.com* 🍴 *From $5; shoe rental $5.*

FOOTBALL

Allegiant Stadium

FOOTBALL | Suppose they built a $2 billion NFL stadium and nobody came? That was the weird pandemic story of the Las Vegas Raiders' first season, with the transplanted Oakland team playing games with no fans in their sparkling new Las Vegas home. Everyone was counting on the fall of 2021 to answer key questions about parking, restrooms, and beer lines (did going cashless speed up the latter?). But no one can say they didn't have time to get ready. Fans will finally get underneath the translucent roof to see the signature 93-foot Al Davis Memorial Torch that became familiar on television, and some gain access to the 127 VIP suites, or just how concerts and sporting events were going to interface with an 11,000-square-foot nightclub, the Wynn Field Club, complete with DJs and bottle service. The 65,000-seat stadium also plans to host nonfootball events: both Garth Brooks and DJ Illenium have played the venue. Food vendors include local favorites such as Ferraro's Italian restaurant and Holsteins, the fancy burger joint also at The Cosmopolitan. The easiest access for pedestrians from the Strip is to start from Mandalay Bay and hoof it over a bridge that spans I–15 on West Hacienda Avenue; the bridge will be closed to cars on game days. ✉ *Allegiant Stadium, 3333 Al Davis Way, West Side* ✛ *near intersection of Polaris Ave. and W. Hacienda Ave.* ☎ *725/780–2000, 800/724–3377* ⊕ *www.allegiantstadium. com.*

GOLF

Rhodes Ranch Golf Club

GOLF | One of the better courses in the Las Vegas Valley, the Rhodes Ranch course was designed by renowned architect Ted Robinson to provide enough challenges for any skill level—numerous water hazards, difficult bunkers, and less-than-even fairways. Twilight rates can drop to $59. ✉ *20 Rhodes Ranch Pkwy., West Side* ☎ *702/740–4114, 888/311–8337* ⊕ *www.rhodesranchgolf. com* 🍴 *From $110 for nonresidents* 🏌 *18 holes, 6909 yards, par 72.*

Chapter 10

SUMMERLIN AND RED ROCK CANYON

Updated by
Jason Bracelin

👁 Sights	🍴 Restaurants	🛏 Hotels	🛍 Shopping	🍸 Nightlife
★★★★☆	★★★☆☆	★★☆☆☆	★★☆☆☆	★★☆☆☆

NEIGHBORHOOD SNAPSHOT

TOP EXPERIENCES

■ **Catch a Las Vegas Aviators Game:** The city's minor-league baseball team plays at Las Vegas Ballpark, which opened in the spring of 2019 adjacent to City National Arena.

■ **Cheer at a Las Vegas Golden Knights practice:** The Golden Knights practice at City National Arena, which also hosts many community hockey teams. During Knights' games, a pub on the second floor of the rink opens to serve food while locals follow along on the big screens.

■ **Hike Red Rock Canyon:** Save time to meander off-trail and scan the rocks for petroglyphs. If you're a rock climber, be sure to stretch before you go; the open space offers some of the best climbing in the area.

■ **Shopping in downtown Summerlin:** The burgeoning and bustling retail center is adjacent to Red Rock Casino.

■ **Take in the View of the Strip:** Especially if you're up high, the buildings glisten in the sun, and the city has a skyline all its own.

GETTING HERE

Public transportation to Summerlin exists from the Strip, but considering how long it would take you to get out there, the best bet is to rent a car. Interstate 215 winds around the outskirts of the Las Vegas Valley and ends in Summerlin; another option is to take service roads such as Charleston Boulevard and Spring Mountain Road.

PLANNING YOUR TIME

Since most of the best parts of Summerlin are right around Red Rock Casino, make the casino your base and walk from there.

QUICK BITES

■ **The Baking Cup.** This mobile artisan bakery focuses more on quality than quantity, making sure every cake, cookie, and pie is as delicious as possible. The bakery is known for its macarons, which are the size of a small child's head. ✉ *Summerlin Farmers' Market, 1600 N. Rampart Blvd.* ⊕ *thebakingcup.com*

■ **Makers & Finders.** The Downtown Summerlin outpost of this Arts District favorite replicates the downtown experience pretty thoroughly, down to the stiff coffee drinks and Latin-infused cuisine. ✉ *2120 Festival Plaza Dr., Suite 140, Downtown Summerlin* ⊕ *www. makerslv.com*

■ **Nittaya's Secret Kitchen.** Regulars swear by this tiny Thai restaurant, which boasts a plethora of curry dishes and the cult-favorite pineapple fried rice. ✉ *2110 N. Rampart Blvd.* ⊕ *www.nittayassecret-kitchen.com*

There's a master plan behind the western suburb of Summerlin, and it shows. The town—which was founded by movie legend Howard Hughes—has been developed and built out according to a written-on-paper strategy, a "planned community" through and through. Today the neighborhood comprises dozens of gated communities, as well as a handful of epic golf courses and casino resorts such as the JW Marriott and Red Rock Casino, Resort & Spa.

Although the Red Rock Casino is hip and fun, the highlight of the region is the casino's namesake, the Red Rock National Conservation Area. This area, managed by the Bureau of Land Management (BLM), is an expansive open space that heads from civilization into the ocher-rock wilderness of the Spring Mountains beyond. Canyon walls boast some of the best rock climbing in the world. There are also petroglyphs, rock drawings by Native Americans who first inhabited this area more than 1,000 years ago.

One of the best ways to explore the wilderness outside Summerlin is, without question, on horseback. A number of outfitters run half- and full-day guided trips; some even include dinner. Just about every ride brings visitors up-close-and-personal with native flora and fauna, including Joshua trees, jackrabbits, and more. If possible, ask your guide to lead you to the top of the canyon for a one-of-a-kind glimpse of the Strip.

👁 Sights

City National Arena
SPORTS VENUE | FAMILY | Indoor ice rinks don't usually grab your attention, but City National Arena, a few blocks north from Downtown Summerlin, is worth a closer look. This is the practice facility for the Las Vegas Golden Knights, who are here daily (when they're home) from 10 am to 1 pm (practices are open to the public and free). The rink also is the center of the region's amateur hockey scene, meaning ice-time is hard to come by on weekends. There are skating and hockey skill classes offered as well. On the second floor, a pub shows Knights games and offers food and drink specials. During big games, the scene up here can get pretty raucous. ✉ *1550 S. Pavilion Center Dr., West Side* ☎ *702/902–4904* ⊕ *www.citynationalarenavegas.com.*

The West Side of Las Vegas is the gateway to the Red Rock Canyon National Conservation Area at the base of the Spring Mountains.

Downtown Summerlin

SHOPPING CENTERS/MALLS | **FAMILY** | This open-air shopping mall with more than 125 stores and restaurants sits at the center of the Summerlin planned community, and, since it opened in 2014, has become the very heart of town. Locals are delighted to have name-brand stores such as Lululemon and Sur la Table around the corner, and on-site restaurants, including the suburban outpost of Downtown standard MTO Cafe, are always packed. On Saturday, the mall hosts a farmers' market from 9 am to 2 pm; other events are scheduled throughout the year. The mall has its own movie theater with luxury seats and a full bar, and is a short walk from Red Rock Casino, Resort & Spa. In spring 2019, Downtown Summerlin welcomed another tenant: the Las Vegas Ballpark, home to the Las Vegas Aviators, the AAA affiliate of the Oakland Athletics. ⊠ *Sahara Ave. and 215 Beltway, Summerlin South* ⊕ *summerlin.com/downtown-summerlin.*

Las Vegas Ballpark

SPORTS VENUE | The newest addition to downtown Summerlin is also the home of the Las Vegas Aviators, the Class-AAA affiliate of the Oakland Athletics. The 10,000-seat stadium opened in time for the 2019 season and was named the best Triple-A Minor League park in 2019 by *Baseball Digest*. Amenities include breathable mesh seats to keep fans cool during summer, a kids' zone, and a pool beyond the outfield wall (to name a few). General admission tickets go for as low as $10 a pop, and there are two tiers of seats with prices that include two beers and all-you-can-eat food. There's also the Home Run BBQ tofu bowl and other vegetarian menu options. The stadium replaces Cashman Field, a circa-1983 downtown ballpark that was home to the team under its previous name, the Las Vegas 51s. ⊠ *1650 S. Pavilion Center Dr., Summerlin South* ☎ *702/943–7200* ⊕ *www.thelvballpark.com.*

★ Red Rock Canyon National Conservation Area

NATURE PRESERVE | **FAMILY** | Red sandstone cliffs and dramatic desert landscapes await day-trippers and outdoors enthusiasts at Red Rock Canyon National Conservation Area. Operated by the BLM, the 195,819-acre national conservation area features narrow canyons, fantastic rock formations, seasonal waterfalls, desert wildlife, and rock-art sites. The elevated Red Rock Overlook provides a fabulous view of the cream-and-red sandstone cliffs. For a closer look at the stunning scenery, take the 13-mile, one-way scenic drive through the canyon, open from dawn to dusk. Other activities including hiking, mountain biking, rock climbing, canyoneering, picnicking, and wildlife-watching. A developed campground, 2 miles from the visitor center, has 66 campsites (including RV and group sites), pit toilets, and drinking water for visitors wanting to extend their stay. A modest visitor center, operated by the Red Rock Canyon Interpretive Association and open on weekdays, contains an informative history of the region, as well as a number of exhibits on local flora and fauna. ⊠ *1000 Scenic Loop Dr., Summerlin South* ☎ *702/515–5350, 702/515–5367 programs and guided hikes* ⊕ *www. redrockcanyonlv.org* 🎫 *$15 per car, $10 per motorcycle, $5 per individual on bicycle or foot.*

Spring Mountains Visitor Gateway

INFO CENTER | **FAMILY** | About an hour from Downtown—and about halfway up Kyle Canyon Road to the Spring Mountains National Recreation Area—you'll find this eco-friendly visitor center, which opened in 2015 and welcomes those heading to Mt. Charleston. Spend some time perusing the educational exhibits about the ecosystems and microclimates in the region's tallest mountains. Then hike one of the short interpretive trails for a sense of what the cactus- and bristlecone pine–strewn landscape is like. In winter, a modest ski resort operates at the top of Lee Canyon. ⊠ *2525 Kyle Canyon Rd., Las Vegas* ☎ *702/872–5486* ⊕ *www. gomtcharleston.com.*

🍴 Restaurants

Echo & Rig Butcher & Steakhouse

$$$$ | **AMERICAN** | This Tivoli Village standout is all about meat. The menu offers a healthy list of options and cuts, from skirt steak, tri-tip, and hangar steak to a rib-eye cap and more. **Known for:** working butcher shop; modern spin on classic steak-house options; hipster vibe. 💲 *Average main: $40* ⊠ *Tivoli Village, 440 S. Rampart Blvd., Las Vegas* ☎ *702/489–3525* ⊕ *www.echoandrig.com.*

El Dorado Cantina

$$$ | **MEXICAN** | **FAMILY** | Every day is Día de los Muertos at this chic, skull-festooned cantina in Tivoli Village, where a pair of brightly colored calacas guard the entryway. Once inside, prepare to encounter a different kind of spirit: namely, a vast selection of tequila, with over 100 varieties available in this eye-popping, high-end Mexican eatery. **Known for:** vast tequila selection; high-end Mexican cuisine; chic decor. 💲 *Average main: $25* ⊠ *Tivoli Village, 430 S. Rampart Blvd., Suite 110, Summerlin South* ☎ *702/ 333–1112* ⊕ *www.eldoradocantina.com/ tivoli-village.*

Grape Street Cafe, Wine Bar & Grill

$$$ | **ITALIAN** | This smart neighborhood restaurant that relocated to the downtown Summerlin shopping district serves food intended to coordinate nicely with the restaurant's interesting, affordable, and plentiful (as in, nearly 30 selections by the glass) wine list and craft beer selection. The menu features salads, sandwiches, pizzas, pasta, and seafood, as well as traditional dishes such as short ribs and chicken Parmesan or marsala. **Known for:** varied menu; wines by the glass; romantic dining room. 💲 *Average main: $30* ⊠ *2120 Festival Plaza Dr., #160, Summerlin South*

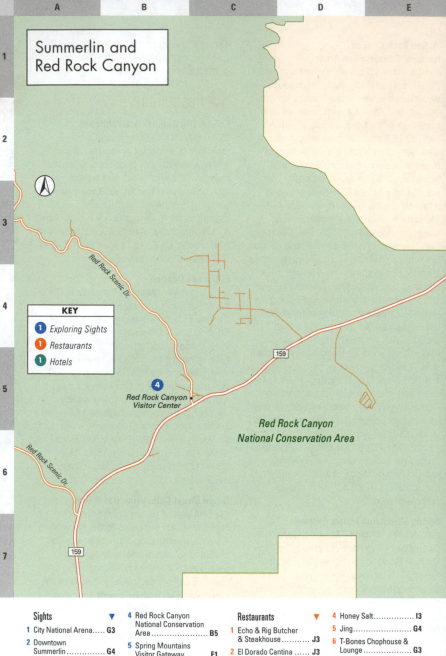

Summerlin and Red Rock Canyon

KEY

- ① Exploring Sights
- ① Restaurants
- ① Hotels

Red Rock Scenic Dr.

159

④ Red Rock Canyon Visitor Center

Red Rock Scenic Dr.

Red Rock Canyon National Conservation Area

159

Hotels ▼

1 JW Marriott
Las Vegas
Resort & Spa **I2**

2 Red Rock Casino
Resort & Spa **G3**

☎ 702/478–5030 ⊕ www.grapestreet-downtownsummerlin.com.

Honey Salt

$$$$ | **AMERICAN** | **FAMILY** | The brainchild of restaurateur Elizabeth Blau and chef Kim Canteenwalla, Honey Salt is, quite simply, a fun place to eat a meal. The atmosphere is convivial, dishes are designed for sharing, and a creative kids' menu encourages diners to bring the whole family. **Known for:** creative kids' menu; weekend brunch; open and festive decor. ⓈAverage main: $35 ⊠ 1031 S. Rampart Blvd., Summerlin South ☎ 702/445–6100 ⊕ www.honeysalt.com.

Jing

$$$$ | **ASIAN FUSION** | The luminous, color-changing, crescent-shape lighting above the bar glows like a jellyfish, a fitting visual motif for this seafood-heavy, upscale Asian restaurant and nightspot. The cuisine here ranges from noodle and rice and wok dishes to thick steaks and a deep, delectable sushi menu. **Known for:** chic, clublike decor; deep wine menu; popular upscale happy hour for local workers. ⓈAverage main: $35 ⊠ 10975 Oval Park Dr., Summerlin South ☎ 725/735–7172 ⊕ www.jingrestaurant.com.

T-Bones Chophouse & Lounge

$$$$ | **STEAKHOUSE** | Well-dressed local professionals are drawn in by the striking slabs of dragon onyx guarding the entrance to this upscale steak house inside Red Rock Casino. It's the perfect spot for a romantic or celebratory meal, especially since live music enhances the ambience after 5 on weekends (6 on Friday and Saturday). **Known for:** dry-aged steaks; "Seafood Jumbo Jackpot" cold platter with lobster, crab, and more; elegant atmosphere. ⓈAverage main: $50 ⊠ Red Rock Casino Resort & Spa, 11011 W. Charleston Blvd., Summerlin South ☎ 702/797–7576 ⊕ redrock.sclv.com ⊙ No lunch.

Vintner Grill

$$$ | **MEDITERRANEAN** | Once you get past the bland office-park setting, you'll find that this sumptuously decorated spot near Red Rock Resort has plenty to recommend in the way of contemporary Mediterranean fare. A Spanish- and Italian-influenced menu is enhanced by a large selection of wines by the glass. **Known for:** broad cheese selection; varied menu; outdoor dining area. ⓈAverage main: $30 ⊠ Summerlin Centre, 10100 W. Charleston Blvd., Suite 100, Summerlin South ☎ 702/214–5590 ⊕ www.vglasvegas.com ⊙ No lunch Sun.

🛏 Hotels

JW Marriott Las Vegas Resort & Spa

$$ | **RESORT** | If you have a penchant for pampering and personal service—or if your plans include golfing or hiking—this stunner in Summerlin is for you. **Pros:** proximity to golf and Red Rock National Conservation Area; terrific spa; large, nice rooms. **Cons:** a bit pricey for a Marriott; casino can fill up quickly during big conferences; far from the Strip. ⓈRooms from: $199 ⊠ 221 N. Rampart Blvd., Summerlin South ☎ 702/869–7777 ⊕ www.jwmarriottlv.com ➦ 548 rooms ⊙I No meals.

Red Rock Casino Resort & Spa

$$ | **RESORT** | Way out on the western edge of the Las Vegas suburbs, this swanky golden-age Vegas property looks out on the ocher-red Spring Mountains, just a stone's throw from Red Rock National Conservation Area. **Pros:** bowling alley and movie theater on-site; nice, expansive pool area; proximity to Red Rock Canyon. **Cons:** waitress service in gaming areas can be slow; long distance from Strip; summertime concerts by pool bring crowds. ⓈRooms from: $159 ⊠ 11011 W. Charleston Blvd., Summerlin South ☎ 702/797–7777, 866/767–7773 ⊕ redrock.sclv.com ➦ 813 rooms ⊙I No meals.

Did You Know?

Although far from the Strip, Red Rock Casino Resort & Spa is popular among both locals and visitors for its elegant lobby, modern rooms, and extensive pool area.

◉ Nightlife

BARS AND LOUNGES

Lucky Bar

PIANO BARS/LOUNGES | This circular bar's casual, lively atmosphere, comfy couchlike seats, sexy staff, and giant chandelier make it one of the best in town, and worth the trip to the impressive Red Rock Resort complex. What's more, the bar is steps away from Rocks Lounge, another hip spot that features live performers most nights of the week. ✉ *Red Rock Casino, Resort & Spa, 11011 W. Charleston Blvd., Summerlin South* ☎ *702/797–7777* ⊕ *redrock.sclv.com.*

McKenzie River Pizza, Grill & Pub

BARS/PUBS | **FAMILY** | Beer and pizza are in high demand at this lively sports bar on the second floor of City National Arena. The restaurant is open for lunch and dinner most days, and is particularly hopping during Las Vegas Golden Knights games, when locals turn out to watch on big-screen televisions and enjoy food and drink specials. The connection to the Knights here runs deep; City National serves as the team's practice facility, and you can watch practices for free on certain days. ✉ *City National Arena, 1550 S. Pavilion Center Dr., Summerlin South* ☎ *702/916–2999* ⊕ *www.mackenzieriver-pizza.com.*

LIVE MUSIC

Rocks Lounge

MUSIC CLUBS | This venue became famous hosting Zowie Bowie, a guy-and-gal, too-blond-for-words act with music that sounds like Eminem and Frank Sinatra getting together to groove. The intimate venue now welcomes a variety of other entertainers, mainly tribute bands. Not exactly worth a trip from the Strip in and of itself, but if you're already at the Red Rock Resort, it's a fun place to hang out. ✉ *Red Rock Resort, 11011 W. Charleston Blvd., Summerlin South* ☎ *702/797–7777* ⊕ *redrock.sclv.com.*

◉ Activities

BASEBALL

Las Vegas Aviators

BASEBALL/SOFTBALL | **FAMILY** | A westward move was a new beginning for minor league baseball in Las Vegas. The Aviators, the Class-AAA affiliate of the Oakland Athletics, saw attendance jump to more than 9,000 people per game when they moved from faded Cashman Field downtown into the Las Vegas Ballpark, an impressive new $150 million stadium in the Downtown Summerlin development. Because Class-AAA is one step from the majors, lucky fans might see some big-leaguers down with the minor league ball club to rehab injuries. In addition to upgraded food and beverage concessions at the new park, fans can even rent the popular outfield pool and watch the action from the water. ✉ *Las Vegas Ballpark, 1650 S. Pavilion Center Dr., Summerlin South* ☎ *702/943–7200* ⊕ *www.milb.com/las-vegas* ✉ *Tickets from $10.*

BOWLING

Red Rock Lanes

BOWLING | Are we in a bowling alley or the club? This 72-lane bowling alley has all the amenities, including TV screens over every lane, a deli snack bar, and Cosmic Bowling—glow-in-the-dark bowling with a DJ—until 2 am on Friday and Saturday night. Roll on through until morning—it's open 24 hours a day. If you've got the bankroll, you can live the full nightclub-plus-bowling dream with bottle service at your own VIP lanes. ✉ *Red Rock Casino Resort & Spa, 11011 W. Charleston Blvd., Summerlin South* ☎ *702/797–7467, 866/767–7773* ⊕ *redrock.sclv.com* ✉ *From $4; shoe rental $6.*

Suncoast Bowling Center

BOWLING | Reflecting its upscale Summerlin neighborhood, the bowling center at the Suncoast, with 64 lanes, is designed to provide every high-tech toy for bowlers. The alley has Cosmic Bowling on Saturday 9 pm–2 am and hosts a number of different leagues throughout the week. ⊠ *Suncoast Hotel & Casino, 9090 Alta Dr., Summerlin South* ☎ *702/636–7111, 877/677–7111* ⊕ *www.suncoastcasino.com* ⊠ *From $3; shoe rental $5.*

GOLF

Bear's Best Las Vegas

GOLF | Jack Nicklaus created this course by placing replicas of his 18 favorite holes (from the 270 courses he's designed worldwide) into a single course. There's also a short course that measures just over 5,000 yards. If all of these on-greens options don't make you reach for your ugly pants, then consider that the clubhouse has enough Nicklaus memorabilia to fill a small museum. A huge dining area doubles as a banquet hall, and an even bigger pavilion provides beautiful views of the mountains and the Strip. Midday tee times are available online for less than half-price. ⊠ *11111 W. Flamingo Rd., Summerlin South* ☎ *702/804–8500* ⊕ *www.clubcorp.com/clubs/bear-s-best-las-vegas* ⊠ *From $129 for nonresidents* ⅄ *18 holes, 7194 yards, par 74.*

Las Vegas Paiute Golf Resort

GOLF | You can play three Pete Dye–designed courses here: Wolf, Snow Mountain, and Sun Mountain. Snow Mountain fits most skill levels and has been ranked by *Golf Digest* as Las Vegas's best public-access course. Sun Mountain is a player-friendly course, but its difficult par-4s make it marginally more challenging than Snow. Six of those holes measure longer than 400 yards, but the best is the fourth hole, which is 206 yards over water. Wolf, with its island hole at No. 15, is the toughest of the three and the longest course in Nevada. If you want to play last-minute, all courses offer great twilight 9-hole rates. ⊠ *10325 Nu-Wav Kaiv Blvd., Summerlin South* ☎ *702/658–1400, 800/711–2833* ⊕ *www.lvpaiutegolf.com* ⊠ *From $89 for nonresidents* ⅄ *Snow Mountain: 18 holes, 7164 yards, par 72; Sun Mountain: 18 holes, 7112 yards, par 72; Wolf: 18 holes, 7604 yards, par 72.*

TPC Las Vegas

GOLF | The PGA manages this championship layout next to the JW Marriott Las Vegas Resort & Spa. The course, designed by Bobby Weed and Raymond Floyd, features a number of elevation changes, steep ravines, and a lake. It's also one of the venues for the Las Vegas Invitational, a stop on the PGA Tour. ⊠ *9851 Canyon Run Dr., Summerlin South* ☎ *702/256–2500, 888/321–5725* ⊕ *www.tpc.com/tpc-las-vegas* ⊠ *From $125 for nonresidents* ⅄ *18 holes, 7104 yards, par 71.*

HIKING

Sweeping vistas. Ocher-color rocks. Desert flora and fauna. These are just some of the reasons to love hiking in and around Las Vegas. Most pedestrian trails in the area are mixed-use, meaning they double as bicycle and equestrian trails. All of the trails offer respite from the bustle of the resorts. The very best trails in the region are in Red Rock National Conservation Area. Here, the Ice Box Canyon trail heads 2.6 difficult miles from the exposed desert up into a shady box canyon, where waterfalls appear after rainstorms, and La Madre Springs trail stretches 3.3 miles up an old fire road to a spectacular vista point. What's more, the Willow Springs Loop, which is only 1.5 miles, takes hikers past some pictographs that have adorned the rocks for hundreds of years.

Trails on the other side of the Spring Mountains, in the Spring Mountain National Recreation Area, are breathtaking in a different way; in winter, there's snow all over the place, and the shade of the canyon keeps temperatures about 15 degrees cooler than they are on the Valley floor. Popular tromps there include the 3-mile round-trip to Mary Jane Falls (a waterfall at the back of a pristine mountain bowl) and Bristlecone Trail, a strenuous 6-mile loop at the end of Lee Canyon that hugs the ridgeline and offers some of the most incredible vistas in the entire Las Vegas Valley. For more information about hikes in the Spring Mountains, check out the Spring Mountains Visitor Gateway on Kyle Canyon Road, about an hour outside of Downtown Las Vegas.

Before you lace up those hiking shoes, remember that trails at all the region's top spots dot the landscape across a variety of sites, and you'll need a car to get from one trailhead to the next. And, of course, this is the desert, so you'll need to bring plenty of water, especially if you plan to spend at least part of your hike in the heat of the day.

HORSEBACK RIDING
★ Cowboy Trail Rides
CITY PARK | The best way to explore the mountains of Red Rock National Conservation Area is by horseback, and Cowboy Trail Rides has it covered. The outfitter runs one-hour, half-, and full-day trips from a location just east of the Red Rock Visitor Center. Some of the trips include lunch or dinner. Scenic packages include the Sunset BBQ Ride (1 hour 45 minutes) and the Canyon Rim Ride (2 hours). Beautiful views of the Strip give way to desert wilderness. Keep your eyes peeled for jackrabbits, Joshua trees, and other notable desert life. The view of the Strip isn't too shabby either. ⊠ *Red Rock Canyon Stables, Red Rock Canyon National Conservation Area, 4053 Fossil Ridge Rd., Las Vegas* ☎ *702/387–2457* ⊕ *www.cowboytrailrides.com* ✉ *From $69.*

Chapter 11

GAMBLING AND CASINOS

Updated by
Matt Villano

If the sum total of your gambling experience is a penny-ante neighborhood poker game, or your company's casino night holiday party, you may feel a little intimidated by the Vegas gambling scene. We're here to tell you that you don't need to be a gambling expert to sit and play.

All you need is a little knowledge of the games you plan on playing, the gumption to step up to the table, a bankroll, and the desire to have a great time. It would also be wise to remember that other than a very few extreme cases, the odds are always with the house. There are no foolproof methods, miracle betting systems, lucky charms, or incantations that will change this fact. So if you feel as though you can brave the risk, handle the action, and want to have some fun, roll up your sleeves and pull up a chair—it's gambling time.

Gambling Primer

Casino Rules

Keep IDs handy. Dealers strictly enforce the minimum gambling age, which is 21 years everywhere in Nevada.

No kids. Children are allowed in gaming areas only if they're passing through on their way to another part of the resort.

No electronic distractions. As a general rule, casinos forbid electronic devices such as phones at table games. When you sit down at a table, make sure to remove any listening devices from your ears and set phones on silent mode. If you receive a call that you must answer during a hand, the dealer will generally allow you to finish the hand before asking you to step away from the table, and will hold your place while you take the call. For years cell phones and any two-way communication devices were prohibited in sports books, but most books have softened this position a bit in recent years, and some even allow gamblers to download apps they can use to place wagers in real-time (more on that in a bit). Another exception: poker rooms, where most phones, headphones, and other electronic devices are allowed.

Smoking. Smoke only in designated areas. Signs on the tables and around the casino will inform you whether it's OK to smoke in a specific area. Generally, smoking is permitted in all table games areas, but smoking marijuana is not permitted at all. In the slot machine/video poker and sports book areas, there are usually some nonsmoking-designated areas. (In the case of the MGM Grand, the entire sports book is smoke-free.) In almost every (live) poker room in Las Vegas, smoking is not permitted. If you're unsure, ask someone before lighting up.

Casino Strategy

The right mindset. There's nothing quite like the excitement you feel when you step into a Vegas casino for the first time. The larger-than-life sights and sounds draw you in and inspire fantasies of life-changing jackpots and breaking the bank on a game of chance. There's nothing wrong with dreaming about hitting it big. Plenty of folks win money every single day in Las Vegas, but most don't. Gambling should be entertainment, a pastime, a bonding activity with friends or family, and occasionally an intellectual challenge. It should never be an investment, a job, or a way of making a quick buck. If you approach gambling in this way, you may leave Las Vegas without a shirt (or thousands of dollars in debt).

The best approach. Learn enough about the games so that you aren't simply giving away your money. A little education will prevent you from making terrible bets or playing out of control. Bad bets (i.e., high-risk, high payout) can be some of the most exciting to play at the tables, and great fun if you like the action. Just remember that higher-risk games are much less likely to pay out over time.

Have fun! If you have reasonable expectations, set and keep to your financial goals, and play with proper strategy, you're bound to have a successful and enjoyable trip.

Notice how bets are advertised. A good rule of thumb for discerning good bets from bad bets at the tables is to look at how/ if the bet is advertised. Good bets generally aren't posted (e.g., odds in craps aren't even on the table, except for the long-shot proposition bets in the center of the table, such as the "Hardways" or "Any Seven" bets). Bad bets will be in flashing lights, and their big payouts will be prominently shown on the table or on large printed cards. Or they'll be "sold"

by the dealer (like insurance in blackjack, and proposition bets in craps).

HOW NOT TO GO BROKE

■ Create solid goals on what you're willing to lose, and what would be a satisfying amount to win.

■ Consider what you can afford to lose and stick to this number, *no matter what.*

■ Pace yourself when you play, so you don't spend all your money too early in your trip.

■ Break your play into sessions.

■ If you lose your allotted goal during a session, quit playing and accept the loss. Many gamblers get deep into debt trying to "chase" a loss, and end up betting more than they can afford.

■ Never gamble with money borrowed on your credit card! Check out this sobering math: Say you want a $500 cash advance. The casino will charge a fee (it varies but for our example, 5%), which makes the total $525. Then the (credit-card) bank will charge you for the cash advance (usually 3%). You're now $45.75 in the hole before you even start playing. And if you're carrying a balance on previous purchases, the long-term costs of the *separate* finance charges on the cash advance can be staggering.

■ Make sure your winnings goal is realistic. If you wager $10 a hand at blackjack, it's not reasonable to think you'll win $5,000 in a session—$50–$100 would be a more obtainable goal. If you're fortunate enough to reach your realistic goal during one of your sessions, end that session immediately. You can put half of your winnings away, and gamble with the profit during another session.

■ Most important is to exercise discipline and not exceed your goals. Sticking to these basic rules, regardless of whether you're up or down, will contain your losses and preserve your winnings.

■ Go easy on the alcohol and the edible cannabis. We understand you want to let loose and have fun while you play, but overindulging at the tables can impair your judgment and cause you to make unwise decisions with your hard-earned money on the line. The only thing worse than a hangover is a hangover with an empty wallet.

THE GOOD, THE BAD, AND THE UGLY

Games you can actually beat under the right circumstances: Poker, sports betting, and video poker.

Games where you can lose money slowly: Baccarat (bank), single-deck blackjack, craps (Pass/Don't Pass, Come/Don't Come), Pai Gow Poker/Tiles, Single-Zero Roulette, Three-Card Poker, and some slot machines.

The rest: There are many more games offered in Vegas casinos (such as Blackjack Switch, Free Bet, Casino War), and new ones seemingly pop up every day. We won't discuss many of these games in the following pages because they're not considered to be "core" games, and aren't carried in the majority of the casinos. These games were created to increase profits that the better odds games don't provide, so if you choose to play them, do so with caution.

Games with worst odds: Keno and the Big Six Wheel. Avoid these two like the plague.

The House Edge

Think of a coin-flip game paying you $1 on heads and taking $1 on tails. Over time, you'd win as much as you'd lose. But a *casino*-hosted game might pay only $0.98 on heads while still taking your $1 on tails. That difference is the "house edge." Two cents doesn't seem like much, but when enough people play, the casino earns millions over an extended period; it's a mathematical certainty.

Another example: The "true odds" of rolling double sixes in craps is 1 in 36, but they pay you only 30 to 1, instead of $36 on a $1 bet. The extra $6 that should be paid to you is, in essence, kept by the house, making it a very bad bet. The house edge varies from game to game, so if you know the odds for each game, you can minimize your losses.

Comps, Clubs, and Coupons

Nearly every establishment has a rewards program, or Players Club, used to identify and reward its loyal gamblers. Members of the casino's Players Club will get regular mailings advertising specials, discounts, contests, and other information. When you sign up, you receive a card to present whenever you play. You may also get a PIN number so you can check your comp totals at one of the kiosks (a comp ATM) on the casino floor. The card is used to track your play at table games and slot machines. The amount of comps you're entitled to is based on factors such as the amount you buy in for, overall time played, average bet, and expected losses. Comps can be used for restaurants, gifts, rooms, or even cash in some places. In many cases one card is accepted at multiple casinos with the same owner. Sign up for a card at Harrah's, and use it at all of the Caesars-owned properties. Present your card every single time you play at a table or slot machine, and every time you move to a new one. Remember that comps are based on play, so don't expect to get a free meal if you sit at a game for only 15 minutes, and bet $10 a hand.

FUNBOOKS

Discount "funbooks" are another perk of joining a Players Club. Many casinos will offer you a book of coupons for discounts in their hotels, shops, and restaurants when you sign up. These books—yes, they're often still actual printed books—offer some excellent discounts of real value, and occasionally even freebies for drinks, food, or gift items, so it pays to take advantage of those while you are in town. Some hotels will give you the funbooks without signing up for the Players Card, but in others you will have to ask for them. However, some "books" exist in virtual form, and are accessible through a casino's app. Many of the best funbooks can be found at places that are off the Strip. The smaller casinos usually offer better deals in an attempt to lure you away from the big guys. You may also find some good coupon books in taxis, magazines in your room, and hotel gift shops, and even from people handing them out on the Strip.

TIPS FOR COMPS

Get a Players Club card. You *might* get a comp without a club card, but it's highly unlikely.

Don't forget to ask. No one is going to come up and offer you a comp. Even if you're not sure you've played enough for a comp, you should ask the floor person, or pit boss. The worst they can do is politely say no.

Buy in often, buy in big. Your initial cash stake, and average bet at a table is often what gets you noticed by the casino supervisors. They'll usually log your average bet based upon your opening few bets at the table, so make your first bets larger when the supervisor is paying attention, then reduce them when he or she moves away from the table. When you're finished at one table, cash in your chips at the cashier, and use those bills to buy in at the next table.

Consider the value of the comp. Never increase what you intended to gamble just to earn comps. It'll cost you *much* less to pay for dinner than to risk losing enough money to get a comp for that same dinner.

Better Bettor Etiquette

Know a little before you play. Dealers are available for questions, but you should learn the basics. Watch for a while, or ask the casino host or supervisor about beginner's classes. Even better, find an empty table and ask the dealer if he or she would be willing to walk you through the game.

Understand betting minimums before you sit down. Each table has a plaque or digital display with table minimums, maximums, and specific gaming rules.

Sympathy for the dealer. Dealers can't take cash directly from your hand, so lay it down on the table when you buy in. Place your bet in the proper area, and stack your entire bet in one pile, with the largest denomination chips on the bottom, and the smallest on the top.

Tip kindly. Dealers, like servers in restaurants, rely on tips as part of their salary. If a dealer is being particularly nice, tip him or her by sliding a chip toward the rack or by betting for the dealer to the upper right of your betting circle.

Ask for change as you need it. The dealers have a limited number of chips in their rack for payouts and making change, so they prefer to give you enough small chips for ten to twenty minimum bets at a time. If you're at a $10 table and you buy in with $300, they'll give you twenty $5 chips and eight $25 chips. If you run out of $5 chips, just ask them to change your $25 chips as needed.

Best Beginner Classes

The whole gambling scene can seem intimidating for the first-timer. But casinos have worked hard to help newbies feel comfortable playing the games, in the hopes that once they get a taste of the excitement, they'll be back for more.

Las Vegas Lingo

Bank. A row or group of similar gaming machines.

Bankroll. The amount of money you have to gamble with.

Buy-in. The amount of cash you exchange for chips during a gaming session.

Cage. The casino cashier, where you can exchange your chips for cash.

Cheques (or Checks). The chips with money-equivalent values, used to place wagers at the tables.

Color Up. To exchange a stack of lower-denomination chips for a few high-denomination chips. Dealers will ask if they can "color you up" before you leave their table. Say yes.

Comp. Short for complimentary (i.e., a freebie). Can be a drink, room, dinner, or show tickets from the casino.

Cut. A ritual splitting of a deck of cards performed after shuffling.

Eye-in-the-Sky. The overhead video surveillance system and its human monitors in a casino.

Fill. When chips are brought to a table from the casino cage to refill a money rack that's low.

House. Another name for the casino's side of any bet, as in this sentence: "The house wins on any tie."

Layout. The printed felt covering of a particular table game, which states the game being offered, betting area, payout odds, and other pertinent information related to the playing of the game.

Marker. A player's IOU to the casino. Rather than buy in with cash, players who register for casino credit can sign a marker in exchange for chips.

Match Play. A one-time bet voucher for a table game, often given as a perk by casinos.

Pit. A subdivision of the casino floor, with several adjacent gaming tables.

Pit Boss. A senior casino employee who supervises the gaming tables in a casino pit, settles player disputes, and authorizes comps. The pit boss can usually be found at a computer console in the middle of the pit, or patrolling the entire pit they are assigned to.

Players Club Card. A card with a magnetic stripe on it used to track a gambler's activities in a casino.

Progressive. A special kind of jackpot, often available to multiple tables or game machines, that continues to grow until it's won.

Push. A tie bet, where you neither win nor lose.

Rake. In poker, it's an amount the casino takes out of each pot as compensation for running the game. Usually it's 10% of the total pot (up to a certain limit, such as "10% up to $4"), or a flat fee per hour, depending on the game or casino.

Shoe. A small box in a table game from which cards are dealt.

Sports Book. The casino area for sports betting.

Table Games. All games of chance such as blackjack and craps played against the casino with a dealer.

Toke. A tip (short for token of your esteem), given to the dealer.

Free lessons in Vegas are widely available. One place to look is in your hotel room; some resorts play a running loop of gaming lessons on TV. If you prefer the in-person format, most resorts offer free group lessons where would-be gamblers gather around a real table game while a dealer or supervisor explains how it works. Classes usually take place at scheduled times during low-traffic hours (just ask a casino host or one of the supervisors). Venues we like include these two:

Luxor offers craps, blackjack, and roulette lessons daily at noon.

Golden Nugget has daily lessons for the most popular games: poker and craps at 10 am, Pai Gow at 10:30 am, roulette at 11:30 am, and blackjack at noon.

HELPFUL WEBSITES

Perhaps the best time and place to learn how the games are played is before you leave for Las Vegas, on your home computer or tablet. There are tons of websites, and even phone and tablet applications that not only teach you how to play the games, but also provide simulations of the gaming experience. And unlike the brief lessons given at the casino, you can learn at your own pace and practice playing as much as you like, whenever you like.

Check your app store for free simulation game apps to download to your phone or tablet.

For roulette: **Roulette Edu** (⊕ *www.rouletteedu.com*).

For blackjack, Pai Gow Tiles, and video poker: **Wizard of Vegas** (⊕ *www.wizardofvegas.com/games*).

Easiest Games to Play

Roulette is considered the easiest table game, but it's also one with a high house edge. That's not a coincidence; players typically pay for easier games in the

form of a larger advantage for the house.
■ TIP ➡ Play a single-zero wheel. It'll cut the house edge almost in half.

You can play **keno** while you eat in many casino coffee shops. Keno carries the worst odds in the whole casino, but it's extremely easy to play. You just mark numbers on a betting slip, give it to the keno runner with a buck or two, and watch the board on the wall to see if your numbers come up.

Bingo is also a fun, simple casino game. It's played in specialized parlors, mostly in the Downtown casinos, or off-Strip casinos (such as those owned by Station Casinos), with a crowd of people sitting at tables in a large room listening for their lucky numbers to line up. The people you run into are often locals and casino workers, who like bingo's humble aesthetic after a long day filled with glitz and kitsch.

Newer **slot machines** are a little more complicated than traditional slots, but they still remain the easiest to play in the casino—put the money in (or bet your credits) and touch a button (or pull the handle if it's an older machine) and wait for the reels to stop spinning to see if you've won or lost.

A handful of casinos recently have added multiplayer, low-limit **stadium-style table games** such as baccarat and blackjack. In these setups, individual betting terminals are clustered around a table, where a live dealer deals cards. The hands appear via closed-circuit video on the individual terminals, and bettors can wager as they see fit. This is a great way to learn a new game.

Best Dealers

Dealers on the Strip keep the games moving fast and aren't prone to many mistakes, but they often don't go in for a lot of small talk. Many beginners feel more comfortable at tables that are social and lively. For that, try the folksy atmospheres of the locals' casinos off the Strip and away from Downtown, like Gold Coast or Sunset Station. Before you sit down, make sure the game's moving at a speed you're comfortable with. Do the dealer and players look happy? Do the players have big stacks of chips? Is there a friendly vibe? If you're feeling especially chatty, locate a dealer from a familiar or interesting city (their hometowns are often printed on their name tags) and strike up some friendly banter. Vegas dealers are trained, skilled professionals who run their games like clockwork, but they're also customer service experts. It's their job to make sure you have a good time whether you win or lose. Don't hesitate to ask questions or seek advice if you're unsure of the rules, aren't sure what to do on a particular hand, or even want to know the best place to get a bite to eat. If you don't feel comfortable with a dealer for whatever reason, "color up" your chips and move on to another table. Conversely, don't hesitate to throw the dealer a toke (tip) if he or she enhances your overall experience.

Electronic Gaming

So you feel like playing some blackjack, but it's a sunny day and you want to work on your tan? You can do both with the right technology. Many casinos, including **The Venetian, The Cosmopolitan,** and **Red Rock** now offer a number of real-money casino games through various apps you can download on your phone. The apps allow you to bet on sports and play certain games such as blackjack, baccarat, and video poker from places other than the casino floor. These apps are similar to computer games you play on your phone or tablet, with one major difference. Here, you're wagering real money in the form of credits that you deposit at any point. The technology works in most areas of the casino, and also allows you to wager pretty much anywhere around

town, so long as you're within the state of Nevada at the time you place your wager.

Blackjack

Blackjack, aka "21," anchors virtually every casino in America. It's one of the most popular table games because it's easy to learn, fun to play, and has potentially excellent odds for the player.

The object of this classic card game is simple. You want to build a higher hand than the dealer without going over 21—a *bust*. Two-card hands, from one deck of cards up to eight decks of cards, are dealt to everyone at the table, including the dealer, who gets one card facedown (the "hole" card) and one card faceup for all to see. Play then proceeds from gambler to gambler. You play out your hand by taking additional cards ("hitting") or standing pat ("staying"). When all the players have finished playing out their hands, the dealer then plays the house hand following preset rules. Once that's complete, the dealer pays winning players and rakes the chips of the losers.

Playing the Game

The value of a blackjack hand is the sum of all the cards; aces count as 1 or 11 (whichever is more advantageous to your hand), and face cards (jacks, queens, and kings) have a value of 10. Suit plays no role in blackjack. If you bust, you lose your bet immediately, no matter what happens with the dealer's cards. The dealer can also bust by going over 21, in which case all players remaining in the hand get paid off. If you're dealt a combination of a 10-valued card (a 10 or any face card) and an ace on your first two cards, it's called a *natural* blackjack. If this is the case, you're paid a bonus on your bet, unless the house also has a blackjack. The payout is either 3 to 2 on your original bet, or 6 to 5, depending on the house rules where you're playing. The dealers use a little mirror or other device at the table to check their hidden card for blackjacks before dealing out extra cards.

For those who aren't lucky enough to be dealt blackjack, play starts with the person sitting to the dealer's left. Everyone plays out his or her hand by motioning to the dealer whether they want to hit or stand. Players *must* make specific motions to the dealer about their intentions:

■ If the cards have been dealt faceup, which is the case at most casinos these days, you're not supposed to touch your cards, so you hit by tapping on the table with your finger(s) in front of your cards. To stand, you simply wave your hand side to side over your cards.

■ If the cards have been dealt facedown, pick them up and hold them (with one hand only!). To hit, you "scratch" on the table toward yourself with the corner of your cards. To stand, you slide the cards facedown under your chips. Don't

fret if you knock over your chips in the process. The dealer will restack them for you if necessary. As long as your hand is less than 21, you can continue hitting and taking cards. If you bust, you must expose your cards immediately (if you are holding them), and the dealer will take your bet and remove your cards. At that point the dealer turns to the next player, who repeats the same hit/stand process. If you get a blackjack, expose your cards. You also should expose your cards if you wish to double-down or split (which we'll talk about in a bit).

■ Once every player has a chance to act on his or her hand, the dealer reveals his or her hidden card and plays out the hand according to the following rules:

■ Dealer shows 16 or less: dealer must hit.

■ Dealer shows 17 or more: dealer must stand (in most casinos). Note: In most casinos, the dealer must hit a "soft" 17 (Ace,6) until the hand reaches a total of 17 or higher.

Once the dealer's hand is complete, the bets are either paid (if the player's hand is higher than the dealer's) or raked (if the dealer's hand is higher than the player's). If the dealer has busted, all players remaining in the hand win their bets. In the event a player's hand value is equal to that of the dealer, it's a *push* (the dealer will knock on the table in front of the bet; the bet is neither paid nor raked.

DOUBLING DOWN

If your first two cards total 10 or 11, your chances of hitting and drawing a 10-value card to create a great hand are very good. To take full advantage of that, you can double down. It's a special bet you place after the hand has started, whose value can be any amount up to your initial bet. Doubling down for an amount not equal to your original bet is called "doubling for less," and the dealer will usually announce this when you do it. This confirms that you did not

Push-22 Games

Blackjack Switch and Free Bet are two relatively new games to the Vegas scene. Both operate under slightly different rules from blackjack itself; namely, when the dealer gets 22, all bets push. With Blackjack Switch, instead of playing one hand, players are required to play two. Players can switch the second cards of their two hands to make two totally new hands. Standard splitting and doubling rules apply (though there is some strategy involved with switching into potentially lucrative hands). With Free Bet, players play one hand, but after the first two cards you have the option to receive tokens that amount to "free" double-downs on 9, 10, and 11, and free splits on certain doubles. Think these rule changes favor the players? Think again. That push-22 rule keeps the edge with the house, and double or split winners on Free Bet win one unit less than they would if players ponied up their own chips.

take the full amount of the double, so there are no discrepancies when you are paid. The upside of doubling is that you put more money in play for an advantageous situation. The downside is that you receive only a single card in lieu of the normal hit/stand sequence. Casino rules vary on which starting hands you can double down on, so ask the dealer before you slide a matching stack of chips beside your first bet. For years casinos let you double down on your first two cards; recently, however, the rules have changed to where you only can double when your first two cards total 9, 10, or 11.

SPLITTING

Splitting is another good way to raise your bet in a favorable situation. If your first two cards are of equal value (even two different face cards such as king and queen), you can split them apart and form two separate hands, then play each hand out separately as if it were a brand-new hand. When you want to split, push a stack of chips equal to your original bet into the betting circle, and tell the dealer your intentions. Never touch the cards yourself, unless you're playing a game that calls for it (like single deck), in which case you'll lay your cards down and place the extra bet. In some casinos you can re-split if you get another matching card for three or even four separate hands. You can draw as many cards as you want to make a hand when you split. In many casinos, you can't re-split aces and are allowed to draw only one card on each ace.

INSURANCE AND EVEN MONEY

When the dealer's up card is an ace, he or she will ask if anyone wants to buy insurance. You can take insurance for up to half of your original wager. If the dealer makes blackjack, the insurance bet pays off at 2 to 1 odds; if the dealer doesn't, the insurance bet is lost and the hand is played normally. If you draw a blackjack when the dealer's up card is an ace, the dealer may ask if you want "even money" in some casinos. Taking even money is exactly the same as taking the insurance. It's offered this way to entice you to take the insurance (exactly what the house wants) instead of risking a push if the dealer has blackjack also. If you take even money, the dealer will pay you 1 to 1 on your bet instead of the normal 3 to 2, and lock up your cards before he or she checks her hidden card for blackjack. Experts consider both insurance and even money bad bets. Always pass on them.

Strategy

Although it's easy to learn, blackjack has varying layers of complexity that can be tackled, depending on your interest level. With practice and the perfection of basic strategy, you can reduce the house edge to about 0.5% (as opposed to about 2.5% for the average uninformed gambler), making blackjack one of the best bets of table games.

Basic strategy is simply the optimal way for a player to play his or her cards, based on the dealer's exposed card and a particular set of casino rules. We'll discuss these rules below *(The House Hedges)*, because basic strategy changes as certain rules change.

At its *most* basic, basic strategy is the assumption that the dealer's hole card is a 10. If the dealer's up card is a 9, he or she likely has a 10 underneath to make 19. If the dealer shows a 4, he or she likely has a 14. You then act accordingly, standing pat or hitting, depending on whether you can beat the dealer's hand. Learning and memorizing basic strategy is a must for professional gamblers, who can't afford to give up anything more to the house edge. For the casual or beginning gambler, the rules are printed on small charts *(example chart in this chapter)* that you can buy in any casino gift shop, or find and print online at one of the websites listed earlier. You're allowed to use these cards at the table for reference at any time, and you should every time you're not sure of whether to hit, stand, split, or double down on any given hand. You should, however, try to come with some basic knowledge of the game and strategy before you start playing, so you don't have to consult the card on *every* hand, which considerably slows down the game and enjoyment for other players at the table.

■ **TIP➜ To practice basic strategy, try** ⊕ **www.hitorstand.net. If you make the wrong decision on a hand, the program will tell you.**

If you don't have the patience to practice or memorize, or don't want to refer to a chart, you can always ask the dealer, who should have knowledge of basic strategy from his or her experience. Or, you can follow these basic rules-of-thumb based on the dealer's up card:

■ Ace, 10, 9, 8, 7—assume the dealer has a made hand (i.e., a hand totaling between 17 and 21 and will therefore not need to draw). If your hand is 17 or higher, stand. If your hand is 16 or lower, you should hit.

■ 2, 3, 4, 5, 6—assume that the dealer has an easily busted hand, so there's no need to take any risks. If your hand is 13 or higher, stand and hope the dealer busts. If your cards total 11 or lower, take a hit and then reevaluate using the same set of rules. If your hand totals 12, only hit against a dealer's 2 or 3.

■ If you have a "soft" hand (an ace with a value card; for example A,7) that totals less than 8 (or 18), you should always hit. If it totals 18, only hit against a dealer's 9, 10, or ace, and always stand on a soft total of 19 or 20.

■ If your hand total equals 11, you should consider doubling down against everything but a dealer ace. If your hand totals 10, you should consider doubling down against everything but a dealer 10 or ace.

■ Always split A,A, and never split 5,5. Some experts advise also always to split 8,8 and never to split 10,10, but those rules are up for interpretation and argument.

THE HOUSE HEDGES

The casinos know that their edge in blackjack is very small, especially against those who employ basic strategy, so they have come up with ways to hedge their bets by adding certain rules, or restrictions to the once-standard rules. These things not only increase the house edge against you, but can distort the

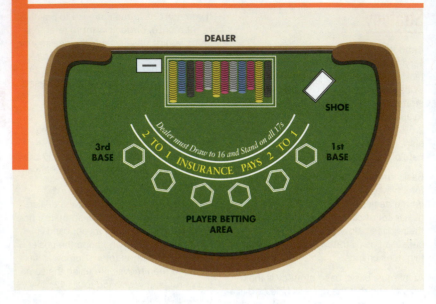

odds for basic strategy decisions and make your chart much less effective by changing some variables of the games. Because the variables change from game to game, and casino to casino, you must be sure your basic strategy card matches the game you're playing.

Here are some general rules for choosing a good blackjack table and keeping the house edge low. Chances are you won't find a game with all of the following things in your favor. The trick is to find one that uses a combination of as many as possible. Choose a table that:

■ Pays blackjack at 3 to 2, not 6 to 5 or anything else.

■ Uses a smaller number of decks in the game. The fewer decks, the better for you.

■ The dealer must stand on a soft 17 (A,6), instead of hitting.

■ Allows you to double down on any hand. Some casinos will let you double only on 10 or 11.

■ Allows you to split aces.

■ Allows you to double down after splitting.

■ Has surrender. This allows you to surrender a bad hand (usually a 15 or 16 against a dealer face-card) before drawing extra cards. The casino will charge you half your wager for this privilege. Sometimes it's a good idea, and basic strategy will let you know when.

THE SHUFFLE MATTERS

Some casinos now employ "continuous" shuffle machines at their blackjack tables. These machines recycle the used cards right back into the machine after every hand, where they're continuously shuffled and re-dealt nonstop directly from the machine, by the dealer. This should not be confused with an "automatic" shuffler, which uses a machine to shuffle the cards, but the cards are removed from the machine after the shuffle and placed in the shoe by the dealer. The difference? The continuous shuffler speeds up the game considerably, since

Sample Blackjack Basic Strategy Chart

Your Hand	Dealer's Up Card									
	2	3	4	5	6	7	8	9	10	A
5–8	H	H	H	H	H	H	H	H	H	H
9	D	D	D	D	D	H	H	H	H	H
10	D	D	D	D	D	D	D	D	H	H
11	D	D	D	D	D	D	D	D	D	D
12	H	H	S	S	S	H	H	H	H	H
13	S	S	S	S	S	H	H	H	H	H
14	S	S	S	S	S	H	H	H	H	H
15	S	S	S	S	S	H	H	H	H	H
16	S	S	S	S	S	H	H	H	H	H
17	S	S	S	S	S	S	S	S	S	S
18	S	S	S	S	S	S	S	S	S	S
19	S	S	S	S	S	S	S	S	S	S
20	S	S	S	S	S	S	S	S	S	S
21	S	S	S	S	S	S	S	S	S	S
A,2	H	H	D	D	D	H	H	H	H	H
A,3	H	H	D	D	D	H	H	H	H	H
A,4	H	H	D	D	D	H	H	H	H	H
A,5	H	H	D	D	D	H	H	H	H	H
A,6	D	D	D	D	D	H	H	H	H	H
A,7	S	D	D	D	D	S	S	H	H	H
A,8	S	S	S	S	S	S	S	S	S	S
A,9	S	S	S	S	S	S	S	S	S	S
A,A	SP	SP	SP	SP	SP	SP	SP	SP	SP	SP
2,2	H	SP	SP	SP	SP	SP	H	H	H	H
3,3	H	H	SP	SP	SP	SP	H	H	H	H
4,4	H	H	H	D	D	H	H	H	H	H
5,5	D	D	D	D	D	D	D	D	D	H
6,6	SP	SP	SP	SP	SP	H	H	H	H	H
7,7	SP	SP	SP	SP	SP	SP	H	H	H	H
8,8	SP	SP	SP	SP	SP	SP	SP	SP	SP	SP
9,9	SP	SP	SP	SP	SP	S	SP	SP	S	S
10,10	S	S	S	S	S	S	S	S	S	S

H-Hit, S-Stand, D-Double Down, SP-Split

there's no break for a shuffle, or a player cut. This increases the number of hands you'll play in your allotted session, and gives the house edge more chances to work against you. Remember, in blackjack, speed kills. If possible stick with the old-fashioned hand shuffle by the dealer, or even an automatic shuffler.

SIDE BETS AND VARIATIONS GAMES

Other strategies used by the casino to separate you from your money involve side bets and variation games. A side bet is a high-paying bet that's based on getting three 7s, a pair, a two-card 20, a three-card poker hand, and so on. This bet is usually placed before the cards are dealt, and isn't tied to the results of the main game—it's completely separate. Like the bonus bets in poker table games, these bets carry a hefty house edge and should be avoided.

Variation games like Double Attack Blackjack, Double Exposure Blackjack, or Spanish 21 use the rules of blackjack but change the dynamics of the game to stimulate more action and entice high-house-edge bets. For example, in Spanish 21 the deck has only 48 cards, because the 10s have been removed. Consequently, the rules allow players to do common blackjack things at strange times—you can surrender after your first two cards are dealt, or double down on any number of cards. Plus, hands like 6-7-8 and 7-7-7 pay automatic bonuses. There are many different variation games and side bets. If you're interested in learning them, you can take a course or ask the dealer, if he or she isn't busy. You should have a good understanding of how to play standard blackjack before attempting these games.

Shoe Break ♈

If you see a sign on a table that reads "No mid-shoe entry," you can't enter play in the middle of the shoe. You have to wait until the shoe ends to start play. Some players have the belief (unsupported by mathematics) that new people can bring bad luck or change the cards. Or they feel it just ruins the flow of the game. Casinos mostly put these signs at higher-limit tables to keep their highest-betting customers happy.

Where to Play

For the best odds: Check out the blackjack survey at ⊕ *wizardofvegas.com/guides/blackjack-survey* for the latest info. According to a recent update, **ARIA, Bellagio, The Cosmopolitan of Las Vegas,** and **Treasure Island** have 3-to-2 double-deck games with a house edge around 0.25, but you often must be willing to play $50 or $100 per hand.

To learn the game: Downtown casinos are your best bet for low minimums. On the Strip **Circus Circus** and a handful of other casinos have $5 games.

Poker

Even after the poker boom of 2006–10, folks still can't seem to get enough of poker. The top players are celebrities, and poker is on TV more than hockey. If you've played, you know why: it's an intellectual challenge to suit any size brain. And it has an egalitarian quality that beginners love; sometimes the cards fall just right for rookies and they win a tournament, or take home a huge pot.

Basic Rules

In poker you win by being the last player standing at the end of the hand. That happens one of two ways: by betting more than anyone else is willing to bet and forcing other players to "fold" (drop out until the next hand), or by having the best hand of all players remaining in the game after the final round of betting. The two twists that make poker great are that the hands of each player evolve as more cards are dealt or revealed, and that some or all of the cards are hidden from view, so you can only speculate on the hand values of other players.

The variations played in casinos—Seven-card Stud, Texas Hold'em, Omaha, and a smattering of others like Razz and Pineapple—all demand that the player create the best five-card hand from a deal that originates from a single standard deck of 52 cards. Five-card hands are valued in order of their statistical rarity:

Straight flush: Five cards of the same suit in consecutive rank. A 10-to-ace straight flush is called a "royal flush," the rarest and highest of all hands.

Four of a kind: Four cards of equal rank plus one nonmatching card.

Full house: Three cards of equal rank, and two of a different equal rank (e.g., 7-7-7-5-5). This hand is declared as "sevens full of fives." The value of the full house is dependent on the three equal cards, not the two. If two players both have full houses, the player whose three equal cards are higher value will win (e.g., A-A-A-2-2 is better than K-K-K-7-7).

Flush: Five cards of the same suit, regardless of order.

Straight: Five cards in consecutive order, regardless of suit.

Three of a kind: Three cards of equal rank, and two other nonmatching cards.

At a Glance

Format: Multiplayer card game, dealt by house dealer.

Goal: Bet your opponents out of the game, or have the highest hand in the final showdown.

Pays: Varies; each pot is determined by the amount of betting.

House Advantage: None. The house "rakes" a small percentage of the total money played.

Best Bet: Tournaments are a great way to stretch your poker dollar, even for novices.

Worst Bet: Underestimating your competition.

11

Gambling and Casinos **POKER**

Two pair: Two equal cards of one rank, two equal cards of a different second rank, with a fifth nonmatching card. Similar to the full house, the value of the highest-ranking pair wins (e.g., 10-10-4-4 beats 7-7-6-6).

Pair: Two cards of equal rank, and three other nonmatching cards.

High card: Any five cards that don't fit into one of the previous categories in which your highest card carries the value of your hand. If two hands have the exact same high card, the value of the next highest card is used, and so forth until the single largest-value high card is revealed.

The high card will also determine a winner when hands have the same value, such as a straight, flush, two pair, or a pair. For example, if two players have a pair of 9s, the player with the highest value of the remaining three cards wins (which is referred to as a "kicker," as in "I have a pair of 9s with an ace kicker"). Aces are the highest-ranked card with one exception: they can act as the low end of a straight (ace, 2, 3, 4, 5). The 5 card is considered the highest-ranked card for such a straight. In a final-round showdown that hand would lose to a 6-high straight (2, 3, 4, 5, 6). The suits are all equal in poker and totally identical hands split the pot.

The game starts when cards are dealt to all players at the table, who then take turns putting casino chips into a central "pot" during a predetermined number of betting rounds. When it's your turn to bet, you can decide to *check*, which means that you essentially pass your turn to the next player, or *fold*, which means you no longer participate in the hand. Any money you've already bet stays in the pot after you fold and will go to the winner of the hand. To stay in the game, each player must match, or *call*, the highest bet of that round to stay in the game. Players can also *raise*, which means that they are betting more than the round's current highest bet. After a raise, the betting round continues until everyone who wishes to stay in the game has contributed an equal amount to the pot.

Once all the betting rounds are over, if more than one player remains in the game, there's a *showdown* where all cards are revealed. In most games the highest-value hand wins, although some poker games pay players for having the lowest hand, as you will soon see.

Game Variations

TEXAS HOLD'EM

Hold'em is the most popular form of poker. Each player (up to 10 can play one game) is dealt two cards facedown, followed by a betting round. Then five community cards are dealt on the table in three groups, each followed by a betting round. First is a group of three cards (the *flop*), and then there are two more rounds of one card each (the *turn* and the *river*). You can use any combination

of your cards and community cards to create your best five-card hand.

Position is very important in Hold'em. The deal rotates around the table after every hand, and with it, the *blinds* (minimum opening bets used to stimulate the betting action). Depending on house rules, either one or two players must automatically bet in the first betting round, regardless of their cards (that's why they're called blinds; you have to bet without even seeing your cards). To stay in and see the three cards of the flop, the other players must match (or raise) the blind bet. This ensures that no player sees the flop for free, and adds heft to the pot. The later your position, the better—players have an advantage if they can see what the players before them decided to do, and can better judge whether the size of the pot justifies the risk of betting and staying in the game.

■ **TIP→ The dealer will hold your seat at a poker table for up to a half hour (for bathroom breaks, smoking, or just fresh air).** Upon returning, you'll have to post the small and big blinds if you want to play immediately, or wait until the deal comes around to you naturally. If you don't return in the allotted time, you'll lose your seat at the table and your cheques will be collected and stored in the cashier cage until you claim them.

OMAHA

Omaha is dealt and played exactly like Hold'em except the player is given four cards instead of two, and *must* use two, and *only* two of the four cards, plus three of the community cards, to make his or her final hand. This adds another dimension to the game, as you must base your strategy on using only two of the four cards in your hand, and this strategy may change drastically from flop to river, because of the extra cards you're holding. You should have some experience playing Hold'em before taking on Omaha, in which reading hands is more complicated.

Poker Betting Limits

Casino poker rooms list ongoing games and soon-to-start tournaments on a large video monitor at their entrance. Before you get into a game, you should understand the betting limit nomenclature. Here are the basics:

Limit Games. Also known as a "Fixed Limit" game, the amount you can bet is listed with two numbers, like "$3–$6." This means you must bet and raise $3 in the first two rounds of play and $6 in the third and fourth rounds. The amount of the "big" blind bet is equal to the low limit ($3).

Spread Limit. This type of game gives the player a range for betting and raising. An example would be a "$1–$4–$8" game, where your bets must be at least $1 and at most $4 for the first two rounds, and between $1 and $8 in the later rounds.

Pot Limit. Players are allowed to wager any amount up to the total of what's currently in the pot.

No-Limit. These games are exactly what they sound like; they usually have low betting minimums (they're listed as "$1–$2NL") designed to jump-start the betting action every hand. If you've got the chips on the table, you can bet them. This is the style of play you see on television, where players go "all in." Don't get involved in a No-Limit game if you don't know what you're doing.

SEVEN-CARD STUD

In Seven-card Stud there are no community cards; you're dealt your own set of seven cards over the course of five betting rounds: an initial batch of three cards (two down, one up); three more single up cards; and a final down card. By the showdown, every player remaining in the game has three down cards and four up cards from which to make his or her best five-card hand.

HI-LOW GAMES

Sometimes you'll see Omaha and Seven-card Stud listed with Hi-Low. These games are played with the same rules as their relatives with one big exception. To win the entire pot, you must have the best high hand *and* the best low hand. A low hand is basically the lowest value you can make for your five cards. For example 5, 4, 3, 2, A (or "wheel" as it's referred to) is the lowest possible hand. In a regular game of Omaha, this would be a straight, and a fairly high-ranked hand. In Hi-Low the straight rank used for the high hand isn't also assumed when determining the low hand. If one player has the high hand, and another has the low hand, the pot is split between them. If more than one player has an identical winning low, or high hand, then half of the pot is split between them and so forth.

Strategy

If you're a beginner, focus on learning how to play the game at low-stakes tables or tournaments before you invest any serious bankroll. The old adage "if you can't spot the sucker at the table, it's you" is never truer than at a Las Vegas poker table. Playing free poker online is a valuable tool for players who are trying to learn the game before a Vegas trip, but the style of play is different. Playing online ignores a lot of the subtleties of playing live, including the all-important *tells,* outward quirks that reveal the contents of your hand to observant opponents. Also, remember that you're not betting real money when you play online,

Poker Tournaments

Poker tournaments are an excellent way for beginners to learn the game of poker in a real-life setting without the risk of losing large sums of money to more experienced players. Most casino poker rooms run tournaments in most of the popular games at different times throughout the day. Schedules can be found in the poker rooms, your room, or at the front desk. The listings will contain the game offered, the limits of the bets, if any, the amount it will cost you to enter plus the amount you pay the casino to run the game (e.g., $60 + $15), if you can rebuy any more chips when your first amount runs out (or add on any more chips when the rebuy period has ended), the time start, and any other pertinent information. The entry fees of all the players who play in the tournament are put into a prize pool that pays out to a top number of finishers, which is determined by how many players enter (e.g., the top 10 finishers out of 100 that entered will get prize money). The tournament is played just like the live game except the players use fake poker chips instead of real ones, and the blinds increase at fixed time intervals to speed the game along. When you've lost all your chips and rebuys, you're out of the tournament. The one left with all the chips is the winner of the tournament, and wins the top money prize out of the pool.

and may be inclined to play bad hands that you would be ill-advised to play in real money games.

Although bluffing and big showdowns are part and parcel of the TV poker phenomenon, casino poker success in limit games and small tournaments comes with a steady, conservative approach. The most important thing to learn is how to calculate *pot odds*. You compare the amount of money likely to be in the pot—your potential win—with the relative odds that your hand will be improved as more cards are dealt or revealed. As with everything in life, if the payoff is big enough, the price you pay to stay in the game is worth the risk.

There are no shortcuts to learning poker strategy. Each variation of the game has its nuances. Part of learning the game is to understand how good your hand has to become in order to win a hand, given a certain pot size and number of opponents. You can get lucky, but it takes study and repetition to become consistently good at poker over the long haul.

Poker Derivatives

All of the following games are played like traditional casino table games that use the elements of poker at their core. These games are found in the main casino area with the other table games instead of the poker room. Although there are other variations of poker games around Vegas, these five are the most common. Most of these games carry high house advantages, but move at a slower, more relaxed pace, so you won't lose as quickly as you might at blackjack or craps. Most of them also have a jackpot or bonus bet that can carry a very high payout for rarer hands, which makes the hefty house advantage seem worth it to many players. The bonus hands and payouts are always clearly listed at the table, and you can always ask the dealer how to play these bets if you're feeling frisky.

THREE- AND FOUR-CARD POKER

Three- and Four-card Poker are two of the most popular poker table games, and at least one table of either can be found in virtually every casino in Vegas. Because you have fewer than the standard five cards to make your final poker hand in both of these games, the odds of making certain hands change. As a result, the ranking system of hands is adjusted. For example, in Three-card Poker, a straight beats a flush. The hand rankings will be listed clearly right on the table layout in front of you for your convenience. As always, if you're not sure of something, ask the dealer.

Three-card Poker. First, place a bet in the "Ante" spot. You and the dealer get three cards facedown. After seeing your cards, you have the option to fold and surrender your Ante, or to play and make the "Play" wager (directly beneath the Ante). The Play will always be equal to your Ante. The dealer will then reveal his or her cards. If the dealer doesn't have a total hand value of queen-high or better, he or she doesn't *qualify*. If this is the case, the dealer will return your Play bet to you and you'll get paid even money on your Ante, *no matter what you have*. If you have a straight or better, you'll also get a bonus on your Ante for having a rare hand. If the dealer qualifies for the hand with a queen-high or better, and has a hand that's better than yours, he or she collects your Ante and Play bets. If he or she qualifies and your hand is better, you'll be paid even money on both your Play and Ante bets (and an Ante bonus if your hand qualifies).

Four-card Poker. You start with an "Ante" wager and are dealt five cards, which you must use to make your best four-card hand. The dealer, however, will be dealt six cards to make his or her best four-card hand. Because of this extra card, there's no minimum hand needed for the dealer to qualify, as in Three-card Poker, so you'll always have to beat the dealer

to get paid. If you fold, you lose your Ante. If you decide to play, you can wager from 1 to 3 times your Ante wager in the spot marked "Play" (directly beneath the Ante). If your hand beats the dealer's when it's revealed, you'll be paid even money on both Ante and Play bets. You'll be paid a bonus on your Ante if your hand is three of a kind or better. If your hand isn't better than the dealer's, you lose both bets. Because the house has a large advantage by receiving an extra card in this game, it'll pay you if you push, or tie, the dealer's hand.

BONUS BETS

Both of these games have a stand-alone bet that has nothing to do with whether you win the hand or not. These bets are the real reason that these games are so popular, and even though they're optional, they're placed by most people who play the game. They pay high odds for rare hands, adding the excitement of potentially hitting a small jackpot. In Three-card Poker it's called Pair Plus (above the Ante). If you choose this bet and get any hand that has a rank value of a pair or better, you get paid a bonus of up to 40 to 1 on your initial bet, depending on what the hand is. In Four-card Poker the same bet is called Aces Up (also above the Ante). It pays if you get a hand that's at least a pair of aces or better, and like the Pairs Plus bet in Three-card, it's paid at increasing odds, depending on how rare your hand is, up to 50 to 1. In both games the bonus hands, and what they pay, will be clearly marked on the table layout.

CARIBBEAN STUD

Caribbean Stud has waned in popularity as more exciting games like Three-card Poker have emerged, so you might not find this game in every casino anymore. Each player places an initial Ante bet. You and the dealer are then dealt five cards facedown. The dealer will expose one of his or her cards to entice you to play. You must then decide whether to remain

Pai Gow Tiles

Many Vegas casinos offer Pai Gow Tiles, a distant cousin to poker. You'll recognize it right away because it's the only game in the house that uses a set of 32 dominoes (or "tiles") along with three dice. The goal of the game is to assemble a hand that beats the banker.

The dice are used to determine order of play, which begins with each player being given a stack of four tiles. The player then arranges them into two hands of two. Once everyone has set their pairs, the banker reveals the house hands and the players who beat both hands win even money,

the players who win one and lose the other push, and the players who lose both hands lose their wager. There's also a 5% commission involved and a bank option for the players.

The twist, and what makes Pai Gow so addictive according to its adherents, is that there are different approaches to arranging your pairs. Because of this, and whether you bank the hand, the house edge can vary. What makes it a difficult game to learn is that the tile pairs have a specific—and nonintuitive—ranking system, which determines when hands win and lose.

in the game, in which case you place an additional wager in the "Bet" square equal to double your Ante, or fold, in which case you lose your Ante.

After you've placed your additional bet, or folded, the dealer reveals the rest of his or her hand. If the dealer's hand isn't better than a minimum value of ace-king high, he or she doesn't *qualify,* and you're paid even money on your Ante wager, and push on your Bet wager, even if the dealer's nonqualifying hand is better than yours. If the dealer has a hand that's better than a value of ace-king high, it qualifies. If it's better than your hand, you lose both bets. If your hand is better than the dealer's *qualifying* hand, you're paid even money on your Ante wager, and your additional wager will get paid at even money, or at increasing odds, depending on what the hand is (e.g., two pair pays 2 to 1, a straight pays 4 to 1). This game also offers a hard-to-resist $1 side bet for a progressive jackpot that pays bonuses for any hand better than a straight, and the jackpot (advertised in flashing lights) for a royal flush. This bet offers terrible odds, but adds to the excitement factor.

LET IT RIDE

You're dealt three cards; the dealer lays down two community cards. If your three cards plus the community cards make a five-card hand that's a pair of 10s or better, you win. You start by placing three bets of equal size. On the first two bets you have the option to take them back or let them ride, as the community cards are revealed. When the second community card is revealed, the dealer turns over your cards. If you don't have a pair of 10s or better, you lose your remaining bets. If you have the 10s or a better hand, you're paid even money, or at increasing odds based on what hand you have, on all the bets you let ride during the betting rounds. Like Caribbean Stud, there's a $1 bonus bet that will pay out if you get a hand that's three of a kind or better.

PAI GOW POKER

In this game you're dealt seven cards from which you make one five-card and one two-card poker hand. The two-card hand can *never* have a better rank value than the five-card hand, so set your cards carefully. There's a joker, which can be used as an ace in either hand, or a wild card to complete a straight or flush in your five-card hand. You play against the dealer, who also makes two hands from seven cards, and will always set them according to a strict set of house rules. If both of your hands are beat by the dealer's hands, you lose. If you lose one and win one, you push. If you win both hands, you win even money on your bet, minus a 5% commission to the casino. Some casinos now offer a "commission-free" version of the game, which is a slightly worse bet for the players.

ULTIMATE TEXAS HOLD'EM

In this table version of the popular poker room game, you place your Ante bet and are dealt two cards along with the dealer. If you decide not to fold, you must place the "flop" bet, which will always be double your Ante. The dealer will then place three cards faceup in the middle of the table. You now have the option to pass (or "check"), or bet on the next two community cards as each is revealed. The amount you're allowed to bet on these is always equal to your Ante bet. When all the community cards are revealed, the dealer will reveal his or her cards. Your best five-card hand must beat his or hers. If it does, you'll be paid even money on your flop bet, and also the turn and river bets, if you didn't check them. The Ante bet gets paid only if you have a flush or better. It's what creates the house edge. The bonus bet will pay you odds if your two hole cards are a pair, or an ace and any face card.

Where to Play

With the big boys: Bellagio, one of the oldest and most storied poker rooms on the Strip; and **The Venetian,** where the poker room is an semi-open pit in the middle of the busy casino.

Best all-around poker room: ARIA, without question the most popular room in town among visitors, locals, and professionals alike.

Slots

Slot machines are the lifeblood of the Vegas casino, earning mountains of cash (roughly 80%–85% of the total gambling handle on an average year). There's a reason why there are what seems like zillions of slot machines compared with table games—they guarantee a fixed rate of return for the casino with no risk. Some gamblers can't get enough of the one-armed bandits, and if you're one of them (a gambler, not a bandit), set yourself a budget and pray for those three 7s to line up.

Basic Slot Play

Playing slots is basically the same as it's always been: insert money, see what happens. Over the years the look and feel of the games have changed dramatically. Machines that dispense a noisy waterfall of coins have all but given way to machines that pay with printed, coded tickets—gone are the one-arm-bandits of yore. Tickets are inserted like cash and redeemed at the cashier's cage or at ATM-like machines that dispense cash. If you're a historian, or sentimental, you may still find a few coin-dispensing relics in some of the Downtown or off-Strip casinos. Nearly all games are digital. The mechanical spinning reels that physically revolved have been replaced by video touch-sensitive screens that are interactive. These screens offer fun bonus games for big bucks and excitement and make you feel like you played some role in the outcome. No matter which format you prefer, the underlying concept is still the same: you're looking for the reels—real or virtual—to match a winning pattern of shapes.

Each reel may have a few dozen shapes, creating an enormous number of possible patterns. The payout varies, depending on how rare the pattern is. The payout tables for each shape are usually posted above or below the "play" area of the machine. On some of the newer digital machines, there's a button marked "Payout Table."

Strategy

All slot machines, including every mechanical reel game, are run by onboard computers. The machine's computer brain generates a new random number thousands of times a second, which then determines where each reel will come to rest.

Although the casino can set the percentage an individual machine will retain for the house over the long term, each individual spin is an independent, random event. That means that if a jackpot reel pattern appears and pays a huge amount, the next jackpot is equally likely (or unlikely) to appear the very next spin. There's no such thing as an overdue machine, or a machine that's "tapped out."

Slot "payout" ranges can vary between 80% and 98%. A machine that pays out at 98% will, in the long run, pay back 98 cents out of every dollar you put in, as opposed to the paltry 80 cents you'll get back on the 80% machine. Picking the right machine can make the biggest difference in how fast you lose. Of course, information on which slot machines are the loosest (the ones that pay out the most) is hard to obtain, and can change often. Play the games you enjoy, but never lose sight of the fact that the payout percentage of that machine will usually determine how much you win or lose.

■TIP➡ **Make sure you always insert your player card into the appropriate slot before you insert cash or tickets. Slot players often enjoy lucrative promotions and comps that table-game players don't.**

CHOOSING A MACHINE
■ Higher-denomination machines tend to have higher payback percentages.

At a Glance ⓨ

Format: Bill- and ticket-operated electronic/mechanical machines.

Goal: Line up winning symbols on machine's reels according to payout schedule.

Pays: Varies by machine and casino.

House Advantage: Varies widely, depending on how the machine is set.

Best Bet: Playing "looser" higher-limit machines at the maximum coin bet.

Worst Bet: Playing "tight" machines at noncasino locations.

■ Look for machines that advertise a higher payout, but beware of the fine print. The machines with the high progressive jackpots are usually the tightest. Resist the temptation, and avoid them.

■ If you want to take a shot at the jackpot, you need to play the *maximum* coins with *every play*. If that means stepping down to a lower-denomination machine (e.g., from dollars to quarters) so you can afford it, then do it. After all, we know that hitting the jackpot is the "reel" reason you're in Vegas.

Video Poker

Video poker attracts a large following. Many gamblers enjoy the solo play of a slot machine, but prefer a slightly more complex set of rules, like to have a say in the outcome, and can't get enough of that feeling when that fifth card completes a full house. Make no mistake, video poker is not "live poker on training wheels." People love video poker because it's fun and convenient, and because the house advantage can be relatively low under the right circumstances.

Basic Rules

Casino visitors will find video poker in long rows of machines just like slot machines. And many casino bars feature video-poker consoles for patrons to play as they sip. To play, just feed in bills or tickets to buy credits, then play the game until those credits run out or you decide to take the money and run.

Unlike regular poker, with its multiple betting rounds, bluffs, and competing players, video poker is all about you making the best possible five-card hand as the computer deals. Video poker comes in many different flavors like "Jacks or Better," "Double Bonus," and "Deuces Wild." Each game has a slightly different gimmick but follows the same basic sequence. After your bet (usually from one to five credits), you get dealt five cards, faceup. You then have to choose which of the five cards to keep by either touching the card on the screen or by activating the appropriate button underneath each card. The cards you didn't keep are replaced with new cards. If it contains a winning combination, you get paid. It's that simple.

Or is it? Imagine you've bet one coin on a Jacks-or-Better game and you're dealt four hearts and one spade. Holding your four hearts and discarding your spade gives you a decent chance at making a flush (five cards of the same suit), which pays six coins. But before you throw it away, you realize the spade you hold is an ace, which matches your ace of hearts to make a pair. A pair pays only one coin, but it's a guaranteed payout, versus the possible payout of the flush. That dilemma—and others like it—is at the heart of video poker and is what makes it so much fun for so many.

UNSPOKEN RULE

Veteran players can be territorial about their machines and often play several at one time. If you're unsure whether a machine is "occupied," politely ask before you sit down. Casino personnel can direct you to open machines.

At a Glance

Format: Bill/coin/ticket-operated solo video consoles.

Goal: To assemble the best possible poker hand.

Pays: Fixed odds depending on the game and your final hand.

House Advantage: Varies, but is very low or even in your favor, if you play perfect strategy.

Best Bet: Playing on full-pay machines, betting the maximum.

Worst Bet: Playing on less than full-pay machines.

Strategy

The first priority for any video poker player is finding the best machines. That's because even though two machines may be identical in the game or games they offer, slight variations in the payoff table make one far more advantageous to play than the other. Note: Most machines pay out with tickets instead of actual coins, and are multidenominational (that is, the machine will allow you to choose how much each "credit" is worth, from 1 cent all the way up to many dollars per credit).

■ **TIP→** In the following Payouts section, you can interchange the words "coins" or "quarters" with "credits," and it will mean the same thing.

PAYOUTS

Video poker enthusiasts identify games by certain key amounts in their payout tables (displayed on the machine). For example, with Jacks-or-Better (JOB) games, the important values to look for are those for the payout on a full house

Video Poker Rules

You'll find many video-poker variations in Vegas casinos, and a single machine can sometimes host several different game types, allowing the player to pick their poison from a menu. Here's a quick primer on the most popular:

Jacks-or-Better: The most common video poker game, and the basis for many variations. The player must have at least a pair of jacks to be in the money.

Deuces Wild: Players must have three of a kind to be in the money, but 2s are wild; that is, they become whatever card you need them to be to make your poker hand. Got two jacks, two queens, and a 2? The 2 can act as a jack or queen, so you've got a full house!

Double Bonus: Requires a pair of jacks or better to be in the money, but offers varied payouts on four of a kind hands, with a bonus for getting four aces.

and flush. Put simply, what you want are what's known affectionately as full-pay machines, and for JOB that means a 9/6 payout. If your game pays nine coins on a full house and six coins on a flush, you've found a 9/6 machine (that is "nine six" machine, not "nine-sixths" machine) and it's the most advantageous you'll find. So if the JOB game you just bellied up to pays less than 9/6 on a full house and flush, you should take your coins elsewhere.

Full pay for Double Bonus games are 10 coins to 1 on a full house and 6 coins on a flush. So if that's your game, look for 10/6 machines (if you're very lucky, you might find a rare 10/7 machine). Full pay for a Deuces Wild game is 9/5, but these numbers actually refer to the single coin payout for a straight flush and a four of a kind. If that seems low for such stellar poker hands, remember that the presence of wild cards makes the likelihood of an outstanding hand quite a bit higher. In fact, some experts go so far as to list the five of a kind payout and define full-pay Deuces Wild as 15/9/5. Such machines are rare these days on the Strip, and when they're found, it's often for higher bet denominations. Why? Read on.

Certain video poker games are considered positive advantage games, meaning the potential exists for players to actually win money over the long term (unlike just about every other game in the casino).

■ **TIP→ To make the house edge negative, though, the player must bet the maximum coins and make the statistically optimum choice during every single hand.** In a 25¢ game, you can choose to play any multiple of 25¢ up to five times that amount (five quarters or $1.25) per hand. If you examine the payout schedule for most video poker games, you'll see that the payout on the highest-value hands is inflated for maximum bet games. This is the casino urging you to bet more per hand.

For example, if you get a royal flush with four quarters in a common Jacks-or-Better game, the payout is 1,000 quarters. Bump your bet up to five quarters per hand and your royal flush is worth 4,000 quarters. The occasional windfall of a royal flush can boost the game's return up over 100%. The casino is betting on human behavior here—expecting that many royal flush winners will have inserted less than the full bet. Nevertheless, the positive payout expectation is what makes video poker such an attractive game. However, the time and bankroll necessary to invest before hitting the full-pay royal flush can be prohibitive, so don't count on paying for your kid's college with video poker proceeds.

Roulette

Roulette is an easy way to cut your teeth on the whole table game experience. You select and bet on numbers, groups of numbers, or a color (red or black); watch the dealer drop a ball on a spinning wheel; and hope that the ball lands on your space. It doesn't get more straightforward than this.

Basic Rules

Most wheels are divided into red and black slots numbered 1 through 36 along with two green slots labeled 0 and 00 (zero and double-zero). The dealer (or croupier) drops a little white ball onto the spinning wheel, and as it loses momentum, it falls onto a series of randomizing obstacles until it settles into one of the numbered slots. You place your bet on a layout filled with numbers; the main betting area has 12 rows of three squares each, alternating red and black and covering numbers 1 through 36. There are also two green spaces for betting on 0 or 00. You can put chips on single numbers, or the lines that connect two, four, five (if 0/00 is involved), or six numbers together. You can also bet on entire categories of numbers, such as red/black, odd/even, and 1 through 18/19 through 36, or one of six different ways to bet on one-third of the numbers at one time.

INSIDE AND OUT

When you buy into roulette, you're issued specialty chips so that each player at the table has his or her own color. When you want to stop, trade your roulette chips for regular casino chips. ■ TIP→ **Roulette chips are good only at the roulette table you bought them from. If you try to play at another table, or visit the cashier cage with them, you will be told to return them to the table you got them from.** As in any other game, you have to meet the table minimums when you're betting, but it gets a little confusing with roulette because the rules are different depending on what you want to bet on. Outside bets and inside bets are separate, and if you choose to bet on either or both, the table minimum rules apply independently. An "outside" bet is made anywhere but on the actual area of the layout that contains the numbers 0, 00, and 1–36. Even, Odd, Black, and Red would be outside bets. An "inside" bet is any bet placed within the numbered area. Betting the 1, 22, and 36 would be considered inside bets. A $5 minimum roulette table means you must bet $5 per bet if you bet on the outside, and $5 total if you bet inside. You may bet in smaller denominations on inside bets, but all inside bets must add up to the minimum (even if you placed outside bets that make your total amount wagered over the table minimum).

So $5 on a single outside bet (like "Red") is legal, whereas five different $1 bets on the outside aren't. And regardless of whether you've placed an outside bet or not, a $1 inside bet is legal only if there are other inside bets that bring the total amount wagered inside to $5. So you could place $2 on your birth month, $2 on your birthday, then $1 on No. 21 in honor of your favorite movie.

Once betting is closed and the ball lands in its spot, the croupier places a marker on the winning number, on top of the stack of winning chips (if there are any). All the losing chip areas, inside and outside, are raked, and the croupier pays out each winning bet. Never reach for your winnings or start to make new bets until *all* the winning bets have been paid and the dealer has removed the marker from the table.

Roulette Table

	Bet	Payoff
A	Single number	35 to 1
B	Two numbers	17 to 1
C	Three numbers	11 to 1
D	Four numbers	8 to 1
E	Five numbers	6 to 1
F	Six numbers	5 to 1
G	12 numbers (column)	2 to 1
G	1st 12, 2nd 12, 3rd 12	2 to 1
H	1-18 or 19-36	1 to 1
H	Odd or Even	1 to 1
H	Red or black	1 to 1

Strategy

Roulette is as simple a game as you'll find in the casino. The only complexity is in learning exactly where to place bets to cover the numbers you like. The odds, though, aren't good. The casino keeps more than 5% of the total amount wagered on American (or double-zero) roulette.

The best plan, if you're going to get serious about it, is to seek out the handful of "European" wheels in Las Vegas. The Euro wheel has only a 0, and no 00. Also, if the 0 is hit, you will lose only half of your even money bets. This will lower the house edge to 1.3% for even money bets, and 2.7% for all the rest. Unfortunately the few Euro wheels on the Strip usually reside behind the velvet ropes of the high-limit areas, so be sure to weigh the advantages of playing this type of wheel against what you can afford to bet, and lose. Another option is the single-zero wheel. Like the Euro wheel, this wheel has only a 0, and no 00, but you lose 100% of your money on even money bets (unlike the Euro wheel). This wheel has a much better house edge (2.7%) than the double-zero wheel, and you can find these wheels in a few casinos on the main floor, with lower minimums.

RAPID ROULETTE

Rapid Roulette is an automated version of roulette. Instead of standing around a table, you sit at your own video terminal or a cluster of virtual terminals. Players give live dealers cash for credits, and make bets via the video screen. The ball is then spun on a live wheel, and the winning number is input into the machine. You're paid by credits for your winnings at your own terminal. When you cash out, the live dealer will give you chips for your winnings. You can find Rapid Roulette at many Strip casinos, including Luxor, Caesars, and MGM Grand.

At a Glance

Goal: Place bet on the number or group of numbers that come up on the wheel.

Pays: From 36 to 1 on single numbers to even money on odd/even and red/black bets.

House Advantage: 5.26% for almost every bet on double-zero tables; 7.69% for almost every bet on triple-zero tables.

Best Bet: Playing at a European or single-zero table.

Worst Bet: The five-way bet (0, 00, 1, 2, 3), which is close to an 8% house advantage.

Where to Play

For low-limit games: Try **Sam's Town** (✉ *5111 Boulder Hwy., Boulder Strip* ☎ *800/897–8696* ⊕ *www.samstownlv.com*).

For single-zero games: Most of the tables in town have disappeared, but **The Venetian** still offers single-zero games, both on the main casino floor and through its handheld electronic gaming device.

To go all night: Golden Nugget's croupiers will hold your spot while you run to the 24-hour Starbucks in the South Tower for a jolt of gambling gasoline.

Craps

Even if you've never played this game, you may have heard the roar of a delighted crowd of players from across the casino floor. Craps is a fun and fast-paced game in which fortunes can be made or lost very quickly, depending on how smart you play.

It can look intimidating or complicated to the beginner, because there are so many bets that can be placed on every roll, but this shouldn't deter you from stepping up to the table to play. Craps offers a couple of the best odds bets in the casino.

Basic Rules

At its core, craps is a dice game. A dice thrower—a "shooter"—tosses two dice to the opposite end of a table and people bet on what they think the outcome or future outcome of the dice will be. It's the job of the "stickman" (the dealer with the stick) to keep the game moving, and to call out the dice totals so everyone knows them no matter what their vantage point at the table is. Two other dealers place bets for you, pay the winners, and collect from the losers. A "box man" sits or stands in the middle and supervises the action. The main layout is duplicated on the right and left sides of the table, although the middle section (the betting area in front of the stickman) is common to both wings of the craps table.

To play, step up to the table wherever you can find an open space. You can start betting casino chips immediately, but you have to wait your turn to be the shooter. If you don't want to "roll the bones" (throw the dice) when it's your turn, motion your refusal to the stickman and he or she will skip you. To roll the dice, you must place a bet first. Then choose only two of the five dice offered by the stickman.

DO'S AND DON'TS OF SHOOTING

Do: Use one hand to pick up the two dice you have chosen. Use the same hand to throw them.

Don't: Move the dice from one hand to the other before you shoot. It arouses suspicion of cheating.

Do: Throw both dice at the same time, and be sure to hit the far wall. A roll that

doesn't hit the far wall will not count, and the box man will make you retry.

Don't: Slide the dice during your toss.

Do: Follow table etiquette when someone else is shooting. Generally, this means that you should finish placing all of your bets before the dice is passed to the shooter.

Don't: Put your hands down into the table when someone else is shooting. If the dice hit your hand, it's considered bad luck. If a 7 "loser" is rolled after touching your hand, you may be blamed. To prevent this, again, make all of your bets before the dice are passed to the shooter.

PASS LINE BETS

The game starts with the "Come-out" roll. This is the first roll after someone rolls a 7, or if you happen to be the first one who comes to the table. The most common bet on the Come-out roll is the Pass/Don't Pass Line, which can only be placed on the Come-out roll, and which serves to illustrate the basic pattern the game follows.

RIGHT WAY

Pass Line bettors bet *with* the shooter, or *right way*. If the Come-out roll turns up a 7 or 11, it's an automatic win and they'll be paid even money on their Pass Line bet. If a total of 2, 3, or 12 (aka "craps") comes up on the Come-out roll, they lose. The exact opposite applies for the Don't Pass bettor, who bets *against* the shooter, or *wrong way* (the exception to this is if a 12 rolls, which is a push for the Don't Pass/Don't Come bettor). For learning purposes, we'll focus more on right-way bets, which is the majority of bettors. Wrong-way bets are covered below.

If a shooter rolls a total of 4, 5, 6, 8, 9, or 10 on the Come-out roll, it's known as hitting a "point." The point (e.g., 5) will be marked with a puck so everyone knows what it is. Once a point has been established, the players have the option to back up their Pass Line bets with "odds." The odds bet is probably the hardest bet for the beginner to understand. This is unfortunate because it's the best bet in the casino for the player, and it's not marked on the layout for this reason. The odds bet is placed directly behind the Pass Line bet. The maximum amount of odds you can take will be listed on the table, and it varies by casino. The term *5x odds* means you can bet up to 5 times your Pass Line bet. *The odds bet is so great because it's the only bet that has a 0% house edge.* Because of this, you should always play maximum odds, if you can afford to. Many other bets can be made at this point as well, but we'll cover them separately. Once all odds bets and any other bets are placed, the shooter keeps rolling the dice until he or she rolls the point again, or a 7. Any other rolls in the meantime won't affect the Line bets from winning or losing. If a point is hit before a roll of 7, it's called a *winner* and anyone who bet Pass will get paid even money on their Line bet, and the "true odds" on their odds bet. These are 2 to 1 for a roll of 4 or 10, 3 to 2 for a roll of 5 or 9, and 6 to 5 for a roll of 6 or 8. If the shooter rolls a 7 before he or she rolls the point, it's called a *loser,* and all Pass Line bets and the odds are lost. Once that happens, the dice are passed to the next player to "come out" and the sequence starts all over again.

OTHER BETS

In addition to Pass and Don't Pass bets, you can also make the following important wagers at craps:

COME BETS

Come bets can also be confusing for beginners, but if you understand how the Pass Line works, it's just as easy. The Come bet pays exactly the same as a Line bet and has the same great odds, so you should take the time to learn how to bet it. The main difference between a Line bet and a Come bet is that the

At a Glance

Format: Dice game played around a long, high-walled table.

Goal: Players bet that certain numbers or sequences of numbers will be rolled.

Pays: Even money on Pass/Don't Pass, Come/Don't Come, varies for other bets.

House Advantage: Varies according to what you bet.

Best Bets: Pass, Don't Pass/Come, Don't Come with full odds.

Worst Bets: Field bet, any proposition bet.

Come bet is placed *after* the come-out roll, once a point has been established. Try to think of a Come bet as being just like its own little private Pass Line bet for you only, that you can place at any time during the roll (which you can't do with a Pass Line bet). Put your Come bet in the area marked "Come." The next roll is now the come-out roll for your Come bet only, which will win on 7 or 11, or lose on 2, 3, or 12. If the next roll is any other number, the dealer will put your Come bet on that number, and that number will now be the point for your Come bet only, not the Pass Line point (which has already been established). Now that the point has been established for your Come bet, you can take odds on it, just like the Line bet. This is done by placing your chips in the "Come" area and stating to the dealer that you want odds on your Come bet. The dealer will stack your Come odds on top of your Come point bet and a little offset, so he or she knows the amount of your original Come bet as opposed to your odds bet. Now that your Come bet has a point, it's subject to the same rules as the Pass Line. If your Come point is rolled before a 7, you win and the dealer

Craps Table

will pay you in the "Come" area. If a 7 is rolled before your Come point, you lose.

PLACE BETS

If you want to bet on a number without subjecting to the rules of the Pass Line or Come, you can "place" it. The casino pays reduced odds for this bet, as opposed to true odds on the Line or Come. A Place bet can be wagered at any time on any number in the squared boxes. If that number is rolled before the 7, you win. Otherwise you lose. If you place the 4 or 10, it'll pay 9 to 5; the numbers 5 or 9 pay 7 to 5, and the numbers 6 or 8 pay 7 to 6. If you win the Place bet, the dealer will pay you your winnings only and leave your original bet on the number. Unlike a Come or Line bet, you can take down this bet at any time if you want. To make it easier for the dealers to figure the payouts, you should bet in multiples of $5 for the numbers 4, 5, 9, and 10, and multiples of $6 for the 6 or 8. The house edge is a very reasonable 1.52% for a Place bet on the 6 or 8 and a good option, but this isn't true for the other numbers. If you must place the 4 and 10, then "buy" them and you'll reduce the house edge on those bets. A "Buy" bet is a Place bet in which you pay a 5% commission to the house to get true odds on your money (in the case of 4 or 10, that's 2 to 1). Make this bet at least $20 or it won't be worth it. Never buy the 5, 9, 6, or 8.

■ **TIP→ Betting the Big 6 and 8 is exactly the same as placing the 6 and 8 with one important difference. Big 6 and 8 pays you only 1 to 1, as opposed to the 7 to 6 you'll get when you place them. This is the reason this bet is printed so huge and is closer to you on the table layout. The casino wants you to bet here, instead of making the better Place bet. Just say NO to the Big 6 and 8.**

ONE-ROLL BETS OR PROPOSITION BETS

One-roll bets are exactly that, bets that win or lose on one roll of the dice (e.g., Field, Eleven, or Double Sixes). Basically you bet what you think the next roll will be. If you happen to guess right, you will be paid the odds listed on the table for that bet. These bets are located in front of you or the stickman, and you toss your wager in to him and tell him what you want. He or she will place your one-roll bet for you (except the Field, which you place yourself). One-roll and hard-way bets are also considered "proposition bets," so named because well-trained dealers will try to entice you to make these bets after every roll. The only proposition bet that's not a one-roll bet is a hard-way bet. A "hard" number is basically an exact pair on the dice (e.g., 2-2, 4-4). This bet will remain on the layout until a "soft" version of your number comes up (say 5-3 instead of 4-4), or a 7 is rolled. In this case you'll lose your hard-way bet. Hard-way bets can't lose on the come-out roll. Note: Hard-way bets are always live, or "working" on the come-out roll unless the player specifically calls them "off" (this will be announced by the stickman before the come-out roll). If you want to wait until a point is established before you put the hard-ways in action (and avoid a winner 7 from wiping out all of your hard-way bets at the same time), be sure to tell the stickman that your hard-ways are "off coming out." He or she will then place an "off" button on your bets to indicate that your bets are "off" until a point has been established. Proposition bets carry an abysmal house edge (as much as 16.67% for some bets). Avoid these like the plague.

DON'T PASS BETTORS
WRONG WAY

Don't bettors, or wrong-way bettors, as they're called, are betting against the shooter. They win when the shooter rolls a 7 (once the point is established), when everyone else at the table will lose. The wrong-way bets are the Don't Pass and Don't Come, and they work exactly opposite to the Pass and Come. You can "lay" odds on the Don't bets also, but since you have the advantage once the point

Craps Sample Betting Sequence

Here's a sample sequence of bets, starting with a new shooter coming out. You begin by placing a $10 chip directly in front of you on the Pass Line:

Roll 1. Come-out: shooter throws a 7, a winner for the Pass Line. The dealer pays you $10. Since no point was established by this roll, the dice are still in the come-out phase.

Roll 2. Come-out: shooter throws a 2—craps. Dealer takes your $10 Pass Line chip, which you must replace to keep playing. There's still no point, so the dice are still "coming-out."

Roll 3. Come-out: shooter throws a 4—a point. Pass Line bets now win only if another 4 is thrown before a 7. You take $10 odds behind your Pass Line bet, and decide to place a $10 chip in the "Come" betting area.

Roll 4. Shooter throws a 12—craps. Your Pass Line bet is unaffected, but your Come bet loses because it's still in the come-out phase. You replace it with another $10 Come bet.

Roll 5. Shooter throws a 9. Your Pass Line bet is unaffected. Dealer moves your Come bet chips onto the 9 square. You take $10 odds on your Come bet, and the dealer stacks it on top of your original $10 Come bet that's now in square 9, so you're now rooting for either a 4 (Pass Line bet) or a 9 (Come bet) to appear before any 7.

Roll 6. Shooter throws a 3—craps. Both of your bets are unaffected.

Roll 7. Shooter throws a 9. Your Come bet is a winner. The dealer will pay you $10 for your original bet, and $15 (3 to 2) for your odds bet, and place your winnings, original bet, and odds in the "Come" area for you to pick up. You now have no more Come bet.

Roll 8. Shooter throws a 7. Your remaining bet on the Pass Line loses.

has been established (because 7 is the most common roll), the casino will compensate for this by making you bet $6 to get $5 on the point of 6 or 8, $7 to get $5 on the 5 or 9, and $2 to get $1 on the 4 or 10. Many people avoid wrong-way betting because they don't like the idea of betting more to get paid less, or they don't like to "go against" everyone else at the table. This is understandable, but wrong-way betting carries slightly better odds than right-way betting, and should be considered once you feel comfortable playing the game.

STRATEGY

Getting an education first is a good strategy for all the games, but it's essential for craps. Before you step up to a craps table, learn and understand the rules and mathematics of the game, as well as

table etiquette, betting procedures and placement, and which bets to stay away from. Craps is by far the most complicated game to learn in the casino, and if you throw money blindly into it without understanding how it works, you'll lose fast. Our advice is to use the basics given here as a starting point, then build on that by getting a more advanced book, taking a lesson at a casino, or learning and playing online for free. Playing craps offers too much fun and excitement to be ignored, so take the next step and do your homework. You won't regret it.

For those who don't mind playing "without a net" (you know who you are), or don't have the time or patience to sit for a class, you can enjoy the game using the basics above. Keep in mind that only

At the craps table, the dice thrower is called the "shooter" and the dealer is the "stickman."

a few bets carry a low house edge. They are:

- Pass/Don't Pass Line with maximum table odds.

- Come/Don't Come bet with maximum table odds.

- Place bet on the 6 or 8.

Stick to these bets. It's best to bet the minimum on the Pass/Don't Pass line and then make the odds bet for the maximum the table allows, or as much as you can afford to comfortably. If you feel you must bet proposition bets for some extra action, limit the amount you bet to single dollars. Even if you get lucky and hit some of these on occasion, rest assured that over time these bad bets will eat a big chunk of your potential winnings.

Where to Play

For the highest odds: Main Street Station Downtown offers up to 20-times odds and several $5 craps tables. On the Strip,

Casino Royale (✉ *3411 Las Vegas Blvd. S, Center Strip* ☎ *702/737–3500* ⊕ *www.casinoroyalehotel.com*) has low minimums and generous 100-times odds on certain craps bets.

For the friendliest dealers: The crews at **Harrah's** or **The Mirage** will help you learn and keep your bets on track.

Baccarat

Baccarat (pronounced bah-kah-rah) is a centuries-old card game played with an aristocratic feel at a patient rhythm. Baccarat is wildly popular around the world in all its varied forms and is gaining popularity in the United States. In fact, due to soaring popularity among high-rollers (sometimes called "whales" by casino insiders), in many Vegas casinos baccarat has replaced blackjack as the most profitable table game for the house.

Although it's an easy game to play, baccarat has an air of mystery about it—perceived by many as a game played only by James Bond and powerful tycoons, behind closed doors with special access. Not so. The big version of the game may be the game of choice for many wealthy gamblers who like to play in roped-off areas or private rooms, and have very high betting limits, but the mini version of the game is becoming increasingly common in Vegas, because it's extremely easy to play. Like the big game, it has reasonable betting limits and carries a very good house edge for the casual gambler.

Playing the "Big Bac"

Up to 14 players can squeeze into a baccarat table, but the game is played out with just two hands. Before play starts, you place your bet on one of three possible outcomes: the Player hand will win, the Bank hand will win, or that play will result in a Tie. The Tie bet can be placed along with a Bank or Player bet, or by itself. When it's your turn, you can either accept the responsibility of representing the Bank, or you can pass the shoe on to the next player in line.

The dealers, with an assist from the Bank player holding the shoe, start the game by dealing two two-card hands facedown. The Player hand is dealt first and is traditionally placed in front of the gambler with the largest Player bet, who then turns them over and slides them back to the dealer. The player holding the shoe does the same with the Bank hand. These rituals are really only for ceremony, and to keep the game lively. Everyone at the table is tied to these two hands, regardless of how they're dealt and who gets to turn them over.

Depending on the value of the initial two-card hands, an extra card may be added to each hand according to a complicated set of drawing rules. Ask your dealer where you can get a copy of the rules when you sit down so you can follow the action. The winner of the hand is determined by which side has the higher total after all cards have been drawn. If you win on the Bank side, you must pay the house a 5% commission. The dealers keep track of this in the numbered boxes in front of them, which correspond to the numbered seats the players are sitting in. You can pay down this commission at any time during the shoe, but must pay any remaining balance after the last hand of the shoe has been played.

UNDERSTANDING THE HANDS

■ Face cards and 10s equal zero.

■ For any total more than 9, the first digit is ignored.

So if the cards are 7, 7, and jack, the total would be 14: $7 + 7 + 0 = 14$. The first digit [1] in 14 is ignored, so the final total is 4.

If you draw a total of 9 (a 10 + 9, for example) on the first two cards, it's called a "natural" and is an automatic winner, unless the other side draws a natural 9 for a tie. A total of 8 is also called a natural, and can be beaten only by a natural 9 or tied with another natural 8. If a tie does occur, the Bank and Player bets push and the Tie wagers are paid at 8 to 1 (or more).

STRATEGY

There's no play strategy in the North American version of baccarat; the game is carried out according to immutable rules. In essence it's like choosing heads or tails, and flipping a coin to see who wins. Baccarat players enjoy looking for patterns in previously dealt hands that might give them a clue what will win next, by keeping track of them on little scorecards. But in the end your guess is as good as theirs as to who'll win the next hand. ■ **TIP➡ The Bank bet, at a 1.06% house advantage, has good odds for such a simple game. Always avoid the Tie bet, because it has an excessive house advantage.**

Baccarat Table

Mini-Baccarat and EZ-Baccarat

The popularity of the big version of the game has waned over the years, and many casinos are removing the large tables altogether in favor of the smaller, more accessible version known as mini-baccarat. If you want to try baccarat, but can't handle the high minimum bets, the glacial pace, and the odd superstitious rituals of the big game, look for a mini-bac table. They're usually in the main pit of any casino with the rest of the table games, or sometimes in a separate or Asian-theme room. Mini-bac follows the same rules as its blue-blooded cousin, but it's played at a much smaller blackjack-style table. The minimums are lower and a single dealer dispenses the hands, without the players ever touching the cards. The players merely place their bets for each new hand dealt. Midi-bac, or Macau-style mini-bac, is a hybrid of the big and mini-bac games. It's played at a slightly larger mini-bac table. In Midi, one dealer handles the shoe, but the players get to handle and reveal the cards as in the big game. These games sometimes employ an extra bet called "Dragon Bonus" or "Emperor Bonus." As with most side bets on table games, this one has a high house edge and should be ignored.

EZ-Baccarat is another version of mini-bac that plays the same, except there's no commission charged for winning Bank bets. In this game the casino makes its money on the "Dragon" bet. If the bank wins the hand with a three-card 7 total, it's called a "Dragon." When this occurs, the Player hand and Tie lose, and all Bank bets are pushes. If you bet on the Dragon, you'll be paid 40 to 1 if it hits. Another side bet on this game is called the "Panda." If you bet the Panda, you'll be paid 25 to 1 if a three-card 8 on the Player side wins.

At a Glance

Format: Multidealer card game usually played in roped-off areas.

Goal: Player bets that one of two hands of cards will be closest to 9.

Pays: Even money on Player and Bank bets; 8 to 1 (or more) on Tie bet. Bank bettors pay 5% fee.

House Advantage: 1.06% on Bank bets, 1.24% for Player bets, 14+% for Tie bets.

Best Bet: Bank bet.

Worst Bet: Tie bet.

Where to Play

Baccarat on a budget: Harrah's, the M Resort, and the Golden Nugget have tables with reasonable minimums.

With the whales: ARIA is baccarat nirvana.

To be alone: Try wireless handheld electronic baccarat at The Venetian. Find a comfortable chair and play for stakes so low it makes the high rollers giggle.

Sports Betting

For years, Nevada was the only place in America where you could physically, legally bet on sporting events. That all changed when federal law enabled other states to offer sports betting, but the experience of betting sports in Nevada still reigns supreme. The betting takes place in a sports book, a dedicated area of a casino that accepts wagers on upcoming games. Here you can try your luck on all the major team sports in America, plus a few individual sports. You can place a wide variety of wagers—from the outcome of a single game to a combination of events. You can even place "futures" wagers on a game that won't kick off for several months.

Sports books make money by taking a small percentage of the total amount bet on both sides of a game; this is called vigorish, or vig for short. Casinos adjust the odds they offer on a game to attract a similar amount to be bet on both teams. That ensures that they get their cut risk-free, regardless of who actually wins the game.

Basic Rules

Placing a bet in a sports book is simple. Pick a game where you like the betting odds, either in the form of a "point spread" or a "money line," *both of which will be explained below*. The sports book will have a betting window or counter with a cashier who'll take your wager (you have to pay up front) and issue you a ticket that states the details of your bet. Don't lose that ticket! If your wager is a winner, return to the betting window after the game, turn in your ticket, and you'll get your initial bet plus your winnings.

The most common bet in a sports book are 11-to-10 bets and involve a point spread. That means for every $11 you risk (or lay), you win a profit of $10. Place an $11 sports bet, and you get back $21 if your team beats the spread.

POINT SPREADS

An 11-to-10 bet indicates a nearly even-money bet. But if the two teams aren't evenly matched, the casino needs some way to prevent the public from betting heavily on the superior team. That's what a point spread is for; it provides a scoring "handicap" to make both teams equally attractive to a bettor.

When you read a point spread listing, one team is usually the favorite (denoted with a negative number), and one is the underdog (with a positive number). Consider this point spread listing:

Sooners

Longhorns-6.5

The spread on this game is 6½. They sometimes use half points to eliminate the possibility of ties. The sports books have determined that the public believes the Longhorns are more likely to win the game. To lure bettors to wager on the Sooners, the casino is effectively agreeing to take away 6½ points from the Longhorns' final score (or add 6½ points to the Sooners' score, depending on which way you look at it) when it evaluates bets placed on that game. Sports bettors will say that the spread on this game is "the Longhorns minus 6½" or "the Sooners plus 6½"—the two phrases mean the same thing. If you bet on the Longhorns, they'll have to have won by a margin greater than the point spread for you to win your bet. If you bet on the Sooners, your bet wins if the Longhorns win by less than the spread (for example, the Longhorns win 21–17, a margin of victory less than the point spread) or lose the game outright. If your point spread wager ends in a tie, the sports book will

Nevada is one of seven states where you can legally bet on sporting events. Bets must be placed in sports books, which you'll find in almost every casino on the Strip.

return your original bet, minus the vig, which it always takes.

OVER/UNDER

Here you're betting on whether the combined final score of the game will be either over or under a designated total. The total is determined by the sports book and usually appears in the point spread listing like this:

Giants 42.5

Eagles -7

The negative number is the point spread, and it has no effect on over/under bets. The other number, 42.5, is the total for this game. Bettors are welcome to bet on the point spread, the over/under, or both. Over/under bettors would try to predict whether the combined score of the Giants and Eagles will be higher or lower than the total (in this case, 42.5). If the Giants won 24–20, the combined score would be 44, so the over bets win and the under bets lose. An over/under bettor wouldn't care who won the game, as long as either lots of points were scored (over bettors) or few points were scored (under bettors).

■ TIP➔ Betting odds vary from sports book to sports book, and they can change over time right up to the moment a sporting event starts. Many books also now offer in-game wagering with lines that update constantly. But once you place your bet, the point spread, money line, and/or payout odds are locked in place for that wager. Your bet is evaluated and paid according to the odds on your betting ticket.

THE MONEY LINE

Money Line bets have no scoring handicap attached to them (such as a point spread). The bet wins if the team wins on the field. Sports books use money lines to entice you to bet on the underdog by increasing the payout in the event that team wins. And they discourage bettors from taking the better team by reducing the payout if they win. Let's take a look at an example:

Astros +150

Cubs -170

The two numbers represent money lines. The underdog has a positive number and the favorite has a negative number. For underdogs, the amount shown is the amount (in dollars) you'd win on a $100 bet. In this case, if the underdog Astros won and you bet $100, you'd win $150. On the other hand, the Cubs money line represents the amount you have to risk to win $100. Because the Cubs are seen to be more likely to win, the sports book asks a bettor to pay a premium to bet on them—to win $100, you'd have to bet $170.

Note: You don't have to bet $100 at a time. The money line just represents the proportions of amount risked to amount won (and vice versa). Most casinos require a $5 or $10 minimum bet.

PARLAYS

A parlay bet is a combination bet where two or more bets must win in order for your wager to pay off. A single parlay bet might include several different sports, as well as point spread, money line, and over/under bets. You can even parlay two games being played simultaneously. Standard parlay odds vary by casino, *but the table is a good example of what to expect:*

If you get all wins plus a tie on your parlay, the bet will still pay, just at the next lowest level of odds. For example, if you bet a four-team parlay and three of the bets beat the spread but the final game tied against the spread, you'd be paid 6 to 1 as if it were a three-teamer. If you get a win and a tie on a two-team parlay, it pays as if it were a straight 11-to-10 bet.

■ **TIP→ Parlay cards are a quick way to bet on multiple games, but they sometimes have reduced payouts relative to normal parlay bets; sports books do not take vigs on parlay bets.**

IN-GAME BETTING

In-game Betting is a relatively new and exciting way of making sports bets. The term *In-game Betting* describes a bet

Number of Teams	Parlay Betting Odds	Payout Odds
2	13–5	3–1
3	6–1	7–1
4	10–1	15–1
5	20–1	31–1
6	40–1	63–1
7	75–1	127–1
8	140–1	225–1
9	200–1	511–1
10	400–1	1,023–1

that you make on a game that's happening in real time. For example, you can make a bet on whether or not a player will make the next free throw in a basketball game that you're currently watching or which hockey team will score the next goal. Before this technology you had to make all of your final bets on a game before it started, and couldn't change or revise them once the game started. Players have two options for making In-game wagers. The first (and older) of the two revolves around a wireless, phone-size device known as an eDeck or PocketCasino; the second option comprises apps players can download to their mobile phones (but use only when they are in Nevada). Both of these iterations use similar technology to the software that runs the stock market; technology that can calculate and recalculate odds in real time. This enables the casino to change the odds tables, or lines, extremely quickly based on what's happening in the game being played at that time. How's this applied? Check out this scenario: You bet the "under" on a football game with an over/under of 40. At halftime the score is 27–10, which is already very close to the "over" of your original bet, and almost a certain loser. The computer has adjusted the over/under to 51 at halftime, enabling you to hedge (bet the other side to guard against a loss) your original bet, and now bet the "over." The benefit of this is that you have some information about how the game is being played because you're watching it as it's being played and can make better-educated guesses in the near future based on how the teams have already played in the past. The savvy bettor can also use information like momentum shifts, the resting of star players, and key injuries in real time to further enhance his or her chances. Of course, the downside is that you may still lose both bets and could get carried away placing too many bets to hedge your past losses as the game proceeds. Although this new type of betting may add some real excitement to watching and betting on sports, we recommend you have some knowledge and experience with sports betting, and know the sports you're betting on, before you try In-game Betting.

Tips

■ Betting against a team is just as valid—and profitable—as betting for a team.

■ Pick a few teams, become intimately acquainted with them, and be prepared to bet for and against them based on your expertise. Don't try to learn the habits of the entire league.

■ Be realistic. Sporting events include innumerable random events, so even the best sports bettors are thrilled to win 60% of their 11-to-10 bets over the long haul.

■ Avoid exotic bets. Casinos let you bet on almost anything; don't take them up on it. Stick with the bets listed in this chapter.

■ Beware of hype. It's often wrong. Do your own homework and draw your own conclusions, and take joy in being a contrarian. The sports media have a way of making certain teams look utterly unbeatable. No team ever is. History is littered with examples.

■ Become an NCAA hoops fan. With so many teams in play leading up to March Madness, it's easy for odds-makers to get a point spread wrong, especially when smaller schools are playing each other.

■ Take a pass sometimes. Remember that a losing bet not placed is a win.

Where to Play

For the best snacks: Every casino has plenty of eateries, but at Lagasse's Stadium, inside **The Palazzo**, the snacks are all gourmet and they're conceptualized by Emeril Lagasse. Reservations are required (usually with a $200 food-and-beverage minimum) for big events.

To watch the big game with your buddies: Hands-down it's **Caesars Palace,** followed by **The Mirage** and **Wynn.** If you're in the hinterlands, head to Red Rock.

Casinos

Vegas casino floors can vary dramatically in motif and interior design, but the basic play of the table games and slots, whether they're under decorative awnings, faux garden trellises, or mirrored ceilings, is the same. Odds, table limits, and machine "looseness" *(see the Blackjack and Video Poker sections)*, however, can vary greatly from casino to casino, so it pays (literally) to do a little research on the casino in which you wish to play.

Rewards and loyalty programs also vary. Of course, none of that may be as important to you as the overall setting and crowd. Here's the lowdown on some of Sin City's most popular casinos, and a few gamblers' choices, too.

South Strip

Luxor Las Vegas

CASINO—SIGHT | Although the casino at Luxor has lost almost all of its Egyptian flair, the new modern gaming floor delivers a vibe that's genuinely hip and exciting. The two main bars, Centra and Aurora, both open up to the casino, making them great spots to meet friends who'd rather not gamble. In the regular-limit area, table minimums are usually around $15 on weekends, but during the week you might find a $10 table or two as well. Free craps and blackjack lessons are offered daily at noon in the dice pit near the casino cage. ✉ *3900 Las Vegas Blvd. S, South Strip* ☎ *702/262–4444, 877/386–4658* ⊕ *www.luxor.com.*

Mandalay Bay Resort and Casino

CASINO—SIGHT | The casino floor here is better than ever. Table limits start around $15 during the week, but often rise to $25 on the weekends, when crowds descend and throw particularly absurd amounts of money around on roulette. Pits of table games are spread out across 135,000 square feet, and with rows and rows of slot machines, the casino floor is sprawling. Toward the entrance to Delano Las Vegas, the sports book has high ceilings but a noticeable dearth of seats. The poker room occupies a corner of the sports book with great views of the big screens. ✉ *3950 Las Vegas Blvd. S, South Strip* ☎ *702/632–7777, 877/632–7800* ⊕ *www.mandalaybay.com.*

MGM Grand Hotel & Casino

CASINO—SIGHT | The biggest of the Las Vegas casinos, the MGM has a staggering amount of gaming space, which includes more than 3,500 slot machines and 165 different table games. Table minimums on blackjack, craps, and roulette mostly start at $15; on weekends nearly all jump to $25. The Strip entrance is all about the sports book (unless you consider gambling on beer pong at Level Up). Slots and pits of table games fan out from there. The Mansion, the casino's high-roller area (with mostly baccarat), exists in a separate wing with its own bar, kitchen, and entrance. You don't have to play to hang here; so long as you're respectful (and quiet), this casino-within-a-casino is home to some of the best whale-watching in Vegas. ✉ *3799 Las Vegas Blvd. S, South Strip* ☎ *702/891–7777, 877/880–0880* ⊕ *www.mgmgrand.com.*

New York–New York Hotel & Casino

CASINO—SIGHT | The casino at New York–New York is just like New York City itself: loud, boisterous, and incessant. The gaming floor has a decor that can be described as art deco meets neon-futuristic. Table limits are a little lower than the high-end Strip casinos, with $10 blackjack available 24/7 and other table minimums starting at $15. Generally speaking, table games fan out from the Center Bar, and slot machines line the periphery of the casino. The oval-shape high-limit table games and slots area feature ornate Murano crystal chandeliers and wood paneling. Sports bettors will be disappointed by New York–New York's race and sports book—the area sits in a corner by Shake Shack and The Park, and barely has enough seats for a professional basketball team. ✉ *3790 Las Vegas Blvd. S, South Strip* ☎ *702/740–6969, 800/689–1797* ⊕ *www.newyorknewyork.com.*

★ Park MGM

CASINO—SIGHT | The property formerly known as Monte Carlo was reborn at the end of 2018 as Park MGM. This makeover included a complete overhaul of the casino floor, a refresh that made the old and stale gaming area hip and fun again. Table games are blackjack-heavy, and a black-walled high-limit room near the lobby of the NoMad Hotel Las Vegas (which occupies the top floors) feels like a gambling parlor out of Europe.

Perhaps the best addition to the casino is Moneyline, a sports book that now encompasses a rollicking sports bar complete with cornhole and duckpin bowling. ✉ *3770 Las Vegas Blvd. S, South Strip* ☎ *702/730–7777, 888/529–4828* ⊕ *www. parkmgm.com.*

Center Strip

ARIA Resort & Casino

CASINO—SIGHT | CityCenter's lone casino is at ARIA. Oddly, however, whereas the rest of the hotel is bathed in sunlight, the main gaming floor (especially the middle table games pits) can at times feel too dark. Brighter gaming experiences can be had in the high-limit salons; there are separate rooms for American games (blackjack and roulette) and Asian games (mostly baccarat). Poker fans rave about ARIA's spacious poker room, which has regular tournaments throughout the week. Perhaps the only disappointment is the sports book, which is oddly shaped and has sequestered horse betting in a closet-size satellite. ✉ *3730 Las Vegas Blvd. S, Center Strip* ☎ *702/590–7757, 866/359–7757* ⊕ *www.aria.com.*

★ Bellagio Las Vegas

CASINO—SIGHT | This roomy casino is luxurious and always packed. Under tasseled, orange canopies you can sometimes spot high rollers betting stacks of black chips ($100 apiece) per hand. In Club Privé, the high-roller's area (where they serve special top-shelf spirits), wagers climb even higher. There are games for more typical budgets, too. Low-denomination slots are tucked in the back corners for low rollers, and excellent blackjack games are offered for mid- to high-level players (table minimums usually start at $15). If you can find them, the $10-minimum craps tables also can get lively. The casino's epicenter remains its now-famous poker room, which rose to national notoriety as a key element of the TV poker fad. Players such

as Daniel Negreanu are regulars here, though they frequently hit Bobby's Poker Room, a private room behind a closed door. Elsewhere in the casino, the race and sports book is small but cozy; each leather seat is equipped with its own TV monitor. ✉ *3600 Las Vegas Blvd. S, Center Strip* ☎ *702/693–7111, 888/987–6667* ⊕ *www.bellagio.com.*

Caesars Palace

CASINO—SIGHT | Considering how huge Caesars Palace really is, the actual gaming area feels remarkably small. The Palace Casino retains its 1966 intimacy, with low ceilings and high stakes. The Colosseum Casino offers ShuffleMaster automated table games, and became home to the poker room in 2016. The Forum Casino boasts high ceilings, soaring marble columns, and graceful rooftop arches, and embraces the middle market with 25¢ slots and lower limits (but more stringent rules) on table games. The best place to gamble in Caesars Palace is in the race and sports book, which was refurbished in 2016 and now boasts the largest indoor big-screen in town. A bar at the back of the book has tightened the space a bit, but the area still has its signature armchairs for optimum viewing pleasure. ✉ *3570 Las Vegas Blvd. S, Center Strip* ☎ *702/731–7110, 866/227–5938* ⊕ *www.caesarspalace.com.*

Casino Royale

CASINO—SIGHT | The great odds are what make this no-frills casino (it's actually a Best Western!) across the street from The Mirage worth a visit. The place is famous for $3 craps (they used to have 100x odds!) and was the first casino in town to offer multiple Push-22 blackjack-derivative games, such as Blackjack Switch and Free Bet. Other options include $5 single-deck blackjack and a host of slot machines ranging in denominations from 1 penny to $5 a pull. With deals like these, Casino Royale isn't exactly known for top-shelf service; table-drink delivery can

The Cosmopolitan's glitzy gaming floor

be painfully slow. Also, dining options are limited; if you're not into the Outback Steakhouse or Denny's, you're better off walking to The Venetian next door. ✉ *3411 Las Vegas Blvd. S, Center Strip* ☎ *800/854–7666* ⊕ *www.casinoroyalehotel.com.*

The Cosmopolitan of Las Vegas

CASINO—SIGHT | Even with windows that look out to the Strip (rare for casino gaming floors), the casino at The Cosmopolitan feels cozy; a sense of intimacy is created by its long, narrow layout. The vast majority of the table games here are blackjack (with some tables that pay 3 to 2), and the craps pit, toward the back of the casino, often gets lively after dark. Also, most slot banks have their own television monitors. The belle of the ball here is the sports book, which debuted in a new space at the front of the casino in 2016. TV screens are everywhere, and a ticker that runs along the top of the bar provides up-to-the-minute scores and odds. ✉ *3708 Las Vegas Blvd. S, Center Strip* ☎ *702/698–7000* ⊕ *www.cosmopolitanlasvegas.com.*

The Mirage Hotel and Casino

CASINO—SIGHT | The casino at The Mirage can be described as old-school fun. Blackjack and craps tables with $10 minimums are alongside tables with $500 minimums, bringing low rollers and high rollers together on the same gaming floor. The poker room, which was relocated into an enclosed space in 2016, boasts some of the most active games in all of Vegas. Slots abound in just about every direction on the gaming floor. There's a high-limit lounge that offers blackjack, baccarat, and video poker. True gamblers come to The Mirage for its race and sports book. The book, to your left when you enter from the Caesars Palace end of the Strip, brags about 10,000 square feet of big-screen action and, well, it should—it resembles NASA's mission control. ✉ *3400 Las Vegas Blvd. S, Center Strip* ☎ *702/791–7111, 800/374–9000* ⊕ *www.mirage.com.*

Paris Las Vegas

CASINO—SIGHT | Dealers in this casino are trained to wish players *bonne chance*, which loosely translates into "good luck" in English. This catchphrase, coupled with the psychedelic sky-painted ceiling, conveys a dreamlike feeling that might distract you from the fact that some table rules are poor for the player. (Hint: stay away from those single-deck blackjack tables; they pay only 6-to-5 for natural blackjacks.) Livelier pits include the craps and baccarat sections; roulette is prevalent here, too—perhaps in keeping with the French theme. Slot machines are plentiful, though waitress service away from the tables can be spotty at best. The race and sports book is quaint but smoky. ✉ *3655 Las Vegas Blvd. S, Center Strip* ☎ *877/796–2096* ⊕ *www.parislasvegas.com.*

Planet Hollywood Resort & Casino

CASINO—SIGHT | Slots abound in the casino at Planet Hollywood; fittingly it was one of the first casinos on the Strip with Elvis-themed one-arm bandits. Table-game pits are clustered under Swarovski crystal chandeliers in the center of the main casino floor, and some feature scantily clad go-go dancers starting at 8 pm in the Pleasure Pit. On weekends the low-limit blackjack and Pai Gow tables stay busy for hours on end. The poker room, which sits on the main casino floor, is clean and spacious, and is outfitted with plenty of TVs to catch the big game when you're not staked in a pot. The Heart Bar, at the center of the casino, is a great spot from which to people-watch during breaks in the gambling action. ✉ *3667 Las Vegas Blvd. S, Center Strip* ☎ *702/785–5555, 866/919–7472* ⊕ *www.planethollywoodresort.com.*

North Strip

Encore

CASINO—SIGHT | Instead of occupying one giant space, Encore's gaming floor is broken up into tiny salons, separated by columns and exquisite red curtains. Thanks to floor-to-ceiling windows, each of the parlor-style casino areas has a garden or pool view. The gaming is surprisingly diverse, with a variety of low-minimum tables and slots (yes, you can play $10 blackjack here). The main-floor high-limit room features mostly baccarat; upstairs, an even more exclusive area named the Sky Casino features tables with betting limits in the stratosphere (keep dreaming; most of us regular folks will never see the inside of this salon). Encore has the poker room for the interconnected Wynn properties; to place sports bets, head to Wynn. Guest room keys double as players' cards and track play over the duration of each stay. ✉ *3131 Las Vegas Blvd. S, North Strip* ☎ *702/770–7000, 888/320–7123* ⊕ *www.wynnlasvegas.com.*

The Palazzo Hotel Resort Casino

CASINO—SIGHT | Whereas The Venetian's casino can be described as busy and buzzing, The Palazzo's has a more composed vibe. Higher ceilings and wider walkways create a much slower pace on the casino floor; people are always gambling, but there's just more space to absorb their exuberance. Table games include roulette, Pai Gow poker, and Caribbean Stud; a separate high-limit room houses baccarat tables, assuming the biggest bettors will go here. There's blackjack, too, but odds on blackjack payouts vary, so be careful were you sit. The Palazzo added stadium-style gaming in 2019; now you can play baccarat with 40 of your closest friends. Be sure to grab a cocktail at Electra or Rosina, two craft-cocktail bars on the casino floor. ✉ *3325 Las Vegas Blvd. S, North Strip* ☎ *702/607–7777, 877/283–6423* ⊕ *www.palazzo.com.*

★ Resorts World Casino

CASINO—SIGHT | Put simply, the newest casino in Las Vegas is a total game-changer. The 117,000-square-foot gaming floor is longer than two football fields strung together, and, unlike others in town, it is in one contiguous rectangle. All games are connected to a property-wide cashless gaming system that enables players to upload cash to an account at the cage and use the funds in real-time. At table games, this amounts to a virtual marker in everyone's pocket, regardless of bankroll. The floor also has a host of Electronic Table Games (ETGs), including some roulette installations with more than 40 seats apiece. A modest sports book is part of a Nashville-style sports bar. ⊠ *3000 Las Vegas Blvd. S, North Strip* ☎ *702/676–7000* ⊕ *www. rwlasvegas.com.*

Treasure Island Hotel & Casino

CASINO—SIGHT | T.I. has a reputation for being one of the best places to learn table games. Dealers are patient and kind, and just about every table game has an hour of free lessons every day. The best tutorials are in craps, where some pit bosses will go so far as to explain odds on certain bets. T.I.'s slot machines aren't nearly as enticing; despite machines at just about every denomination, the mix is oddly generic. Still, members of the casino's players club get huge deals on slots. The sports book was renovated in 2014. The casino added stadium-style blackjack and roulette in 2018. ⊠ *3300 Las Vegas Blvd. S, North Strip* ☎ *702/894–7111, 800/288–7206* ⊕ *www. treasureisland.com.*

★ The Venetian Las Vegas

CASINO—SIGHT | The Venetian's casino is a sprawling, bustling nexus of energy at just about every time of day. All told, the gaming floor boasts more than 120 games. Most table limits start at $25, though on weeknights you might find some with minimums of $15, and stadium-style gaming minimums start at $5 a hand. The blackjack tables in particular have very good odds for high-level players—3-to-2 payouts in some cases. What's more, the casino offers a higher-than-typical progressive jackpot, but you've got to buy in for $5 per hand instead of the usual $1. If you like slots, you're in luck—progressive machines abound. The Venetian also has Fortune Cup, a modernized version of the horse race–theme slot machine, Sigma Derby. The Venetian has kept up with the poker craze and has a tremendous poker room. ⊠ *3355 Las Vegas Blvd. S, North Strip* ☎ *702/414–1000, 866/659–9643* ⊕ *www.venetian.com.*

Wynn Las Vegas

CASINO—SIGHT | Wynn's casino is a gorgeous, inviting place to play (and a great place to spot celebrities). Table limits can be dauntingly high, most starting at $25, and it's not uncommon to spot $500-minimum blackjack tables on the regular casino floor. Lest you dismiss Wynn as exclusively opulent, rest assured that a healthy number of 1¢ slots are out in a prominent area, rather than relegated to some remote corner. It may also surprise you that the coin games have some of the best pay schedules in town. Wynn also offers a variety of push-22 blackjack-derivative games such as Blackjack Switch. There's a nice bar area next to the sports book, where plush chairs line individual viewing cubicles. The poker room for the interconnected Wynn properties now resides at Encore. ⊠ *3131 Las Vegas Blvd. S, North Strip* ☎ *702/770–7000, 888/320–7123* ⊕ *www. wynnlasvegas.com.*

Did You Know?

Wynn has one of the glitziest casinos on the Strip, not to mention some of the highest table minimums, including $500-minimum blackjack tables.

Downtown

The D Casino Hotel

CASINO—SIGHT | Old meets new on the gaming floor at The D. The old: an entire floor of vintage slot-machine games, including Sigma Derby, a quarter-powered contest in which plastic horses race around a plastic track. The new: points of sale around the casino that accept Bitcoin. The main gaming area is kitschy; female dealers tap out from behind table games and stand on tables to dance suggestively in lingerie. Thankfully, 3-to-2 payouts on blackjack and 10x odds at craps make the distractions worthwhile. Owner Derek Stevens has emerged as one of the most eccentric people in town; his newest resort, Circa, opened on the west end of Fremont Street in 2020. ⊠ *301 Fremont St., Downtown* ☎ *702/388–2400* ⊕ *www.thed.com.*

Downtown Grand Hotel & Casino

CASINO—SIGHT | In the olden days, the casino at the Lady Luck Hotel & Casino was considered one of the most happening spots in town. When the Downtown Grand opened on the same site in 2013, they sought to create a similar buzz. Results are mixed. The preponderance of low-minimum table games and low-denomination slot machines is a home run. Design, however, with exposed brick and HVAC ducts (they call it "industrial chic"), is curious and feels like just about any microbrewery in any city in the U.S. The small-but-swanky sports book is operated by William Hill. ⊠ *206 N. 3rd St., Downtown* ☎ *702/719–5100* ⊕ *www.downtowngrand.com.*

El Cortez Hotel & Casino

CASINO—SIGHT | It's fitting that one of the oldest casinos in Las Vegas (circa 1941, to be exact) still offers blackjack the way it should be played: with natural blackjacks paying 3 to 2. Elsewhere on the gaming floor, you'll find single-zero roulette and stickmen offering up to 10x odds on craps. Slots here are plentiful. The sports book, however, is cramped and in desperate need of the same kind of overhaul the Cortez gave its rooms in 2012. ⊠ *600 E. Fremont St., Downtown* ☎ *702/385–5200, 800/634–6703* ⊕ *www. elcortezhotelcasino.com.*

★ Four Queens Resort & Casino

CASINO—SIGHT | This isn't the fanciest casino in town, but locals and tourists (especially those from Hawaii, for some reason) love it for its approachable style and low table limits. At certain times of day, this means $3 blackjack (with single-deck games that pay 3 to 2 for blackjack), and 5x odds on craps. The casino also is home to a host of video poker options that pay out at 100%. The modest sports book is rarely crowded, making it a better option than some of the others in town. ⊠ *202 Fremont St., Downtown* ☎ *702/385–4011, 800/634–6045* ⊕ *www.fourqueens.com.*

★ Golden Nugget

CASINO—SIGHT | This is one of the most celebrated casinos in Downtown Vegas, and the place is as lively as ever. The biggest crowds tend to congregate in the older sections of the gaming floor, which are teeming with slot machines and lower-limit table games. This is also where companies such as ShuffleMaster like to pilot new games. The poker room, in a corner of the main casino floor, holds regular daily tournaments and offers free lessons daily at 10 am. You'll even find table games out by the pool. ⊠ *129 E. Fremont St., Downtown* ☎ *702/385–7111, 800/634–3454* ⊕ *www.goldennugget. com/lasvegas.*

Paradise Road and the East Side

Virgin Hotels Las Vegas

CASINO—SIGHT | A favorite among the young and wealthy crowd, this hip casino rebranded to Virgin from Hard Rock in early 2021. Since Virgin Hotels doesn't have experience running casinos, the parent company partnered with Mohegan Sun to run the gaming, which they have done with aplomb. (They've also brought their Momentum player's card program.) While the casino is outfitted with all the latest slots and table games, some aspects—the sports book, for instance— had not opened as of this writing but were expected to within weeks. Look for the casino floor at this exciting property to continue evolving. ⊠ *4455 Paradise Rd., Paradise Road* ☎ *800/693–7625* ⊕ *virginhotels.com/las-vegas.*

West Side

Palace Station Hotel & Casino

CASINO—SIGHT | The gaming floor at Palace Station got new life in 2018, part of a multimillion-dollar renovation that completely modernized and transformed the entire property. Now, as you walk past table games and slot banks, the inside feels a lot more like other Station Casinos properties, complete with rock columns, exposed wood beams, and high ceilings. The new floor has even more Asian games than in the past (the casino also offers a separate player's card for those who play Asian games exclusively). Palace Station also boasts a huge bingo hall and a lively poker room. ⊠ *2411 W. Sahara Ave., West Side* ☎ *702/367–2411* ⊕ *palacestation.sclv.com.*

Rio All-Suites Hotel and Casino

CASINO—SIGHT | The casino floor at the Rio is one of Vegas's liveliest places to play. The casino is perhaps best known for hosting the annual World Series of Poker, six weeks' worth of poker tournaments that culminate with the "Main Event" in which one pro takes home millions of dollars in cash. The Rio remains one of the only Vegas casinos to spread Mississippi Stud and a number of other difficult-to-understand table games. There are also more than 1,200 slot machines, including dozens of different statewide progressives. ⊠ *3700 W. Flamingo Rd., West Side* ☎ *702/777–7777, 866/746– 7671* ⊕ *www.riolasvegas.com.*

Summerlin and Red Rock Canyon

Rampart Casino

CASINO—SIGHT | The Rampart, as locals call it, is tiny but it packs a punch. Most of the slots and table games sit under a giant glass dome, making the casino seem even smaller than it is. In rooms off to the side, bettors can find more slots, a modest sports book, and restaurant options. The casino has become known across the Las Vegas Valley for its $5 blackjack, 3-to-2 odds on all blackjack games, and 10x odds on craps. There's also a bingo hall. The casino is connected to the JW Marriott Resort & Spa. ⊠ *The Resort at Summerlin, 221 N. Rampart Blvd., Summerlin South* ☎ *702/507– 5900* ⊕ *theresortatsummerlin.com/ las-vegas-casino.*

★ Red Rock Casino Resort & Spa

CASINO—SIGHT | Without question, this locals casino in Summerlin is one of the best-kept secrets in the entire Las Vegas Valley. Swarovski crystals sparkle over gamblers who wander around the circular gambling hall, creating a vibe of opulence and swank. There's even more bling inside the open-walled Lucky Bar, in the center of the casino. Despite all of these sparkles, betting minimums are low; it's not uncommon to stumble upon $5 craps and blackjack tables at peak hours. The real "gem" of the casino is the sports book, with its comfy chairs and giant big-screens. A cozy poker room, cavernous bingo hall, and ornate high-limit room (which promises blackjack as low as $50 per hand) also are worth a look. ✉ *11011 W. Charleston Blvd., Summerlin South* ☎ *702/797–7777, 866/767–7773* ⊕ *red-rock.sclv.com.*

Suncoast Hotel & Casino

CASINO—SIGHT | Bingo is the biggest draw at this Summerlin casino, which is just south of the JW Marriott Resort. With a 600-seat room and eight sessions daily, it's popular with locals, who swear by the slot offerings, rating the Suncoast one of the "loosest" casinos around. The rest of the casino grew up during a 2018 renovation that provided new design, new tables, and new carpets. The sports book is small and dated but it does the job. ✉ *9090 Alta Dr., Summerlin South* ☎ *702/636–7111* ⊕ *www.suncoastcasino.com.*

SHOWS

Updated by
Mike Weatherford

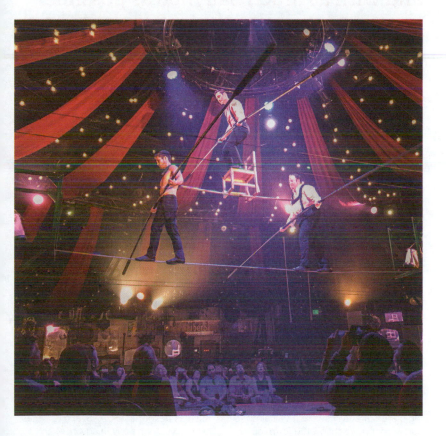

The very name "Las Vegas" has been synonymous with a certain style of showbiz ever since Jimmy Durante first headlined at Bugsy Siegel's Flamingo Hotel in 1946. Through the years this entertainment mecca has redefined itself a number of times, but one thing has remained consistent: doing things big, and with as much ballyhoo as possible.

The star power that made the old "supper club" days glitter with names like Frank Sinatra and Dean Martin is echoed in this decade's return of big names to the Strip, but this time primarily in large theaters devoted to recurring concert engagements, or "residencies," by everyone from Lady Gaga to Usher. Star magicians such as David Copperfield, Criss Angel, and Penn & Teller call Las Vegas home, and drive to work each day as commuters. Cirque du Soleil still dominates the Strip with spectacle and jaw-dropping acrobatics that present little or no language barrier to the city's large numbers of international tourists. Perennial pop stars such as Bruno Mars and younger-skewing production shows (such as the break-dancing Jabbawockeez) fight an ongoing battle to lure younger audiences that nightclubs have skimmed from the ticketed shows.

Shows are no longer treated as loss leaders for the gaming tables. Granted, a high credit line or enough points on a player's card can still work miracles for a hard-to-score ticket. But those who aren't big players are fully aware it will almost surely cost more than $100 for middle-of-the-house seats for the Cirque shows or star residencies. Meanwhile, the less-in-demand names and production shows that run year-round have become a confusing, "never pay face value" circus of discount outlets and offers.

The new generation of resident headliners is as likely to come from *America's Got Talent* as a recording studio, as evidenced by magicians Mat Franco or Piff the Magic Dragon. The names change, but there's something for everyone and still no other place in the world to find such a concentration of acrobats, singers, "dirty" dancers, magicians, and comedians—all continuing the razzle-dazzle tradition Las Vegas has popularized for the world.

Planning

Reserved-Seat Ticketing

Most hotels offer reserved-seat show tickets, and nearly all Las Vegas shows are available through ticketing networks such as Ticketmaster, AXS, and ⊕ *Vegas.com*. If you don't buy in advance, an old-fashioned visit to the show's box office is still your best bet for minimizing add-on charges. It's advisable to purchase tickets to concerts or the hotter shows, such as The Colosseum at Caesars Palace headliners, ahead of a visit. For smaller shows or spontaneous decisions, visit the various discount kiosks along the Strip; most producers "mark 'em up to mark 'em down" at these outlets anyway. Pay full face value only for a headliner name or a show you really want to see. Remember, too, that for the ongoing shows under their roofs, casinos make sure their big players are always taken care of. If advance tickets are no longer available, check for last-minute cancellations. Your chances of getting a seat are usually better when you're staying—and gambling—at the hotel.

If you plan on spending a fair amount of time at the tables or slots, call VIP Services or a slot host to find out what their requirements are for getting a comp, paid tickets that have been withheld for last-minute release, or perks such as premium seating or a line pass (it allows you to go straight to the VIP entrance without having to wait in line with the hoi polloi).

Ticket Agencies

AXS

TICKETS | AXS is the exclusive agency for some recurring headliners and ongoing shows, and for single-night concert (as well as sports events and Vegas Golden Knights games) in the T-Mobile Arena or MGM Grand Garden. ☎ *888/929–7849* ⊕ *www.axs.com.*

Showtickets.com

TICKETS | Showtickets.com, operated by Entertainment Benefits Group, sells tickets online and through machine kiosks at more than 35 locations around town. Most of them are at concierge desks, including those at The Venetian, The Cosmopolitan, and all Caesars Entertainment properties. The big point of distinction is also offering tickets for tours to regional attractions and backstage peeks at some of the shows. ✉ *Las Vegas* ☎ *800/838–8155* ⊕ *showtickets.com.*

Ticketmaster

TICKETS | Most Las Vegas performances are available on Ticketmaster; you can buy tickets through the website and choose to pick them up at a venue's "will call" window. More and more, even if you begin your purchase on a hotel or show's dedicated website, you will be routed to Ticketmaster to complete the purchase. ☎ *800/653–3000* ⊕ *www.ticketmaster.com.*

Tix4Vegas

TICKETS | With eight locations, Tix4Vegas (previously known as Tix4tonight) is the place to visit for most ongoing shows (but not the hot concert acts or headliners). There's a service charge for each ticket, and the majority of business is for same-day walk-up sales. Strip locations include the Grand Bazaar Shops in front of Bally's, the Fashion Show mall, the Showcase Mall (look for the giant Coke bottle), Planet Hollywood, and the Casino Royale. Another outlet is on Las Vegas Boulevard, way south of the pedestrian part of the Strip, in the popular Town Square shopping center. Originally, prices were half-price across the board and only for that day's performance. Now the percentage of discount varies, but you can buy through the show's website or over the phone, and some titles are available in advance. ☎ *877/849–4868* ⊕ *www.tix4tonight.com.*

Vegas.com

TICKETS | This major sales outlet for most Las Vegas shows is well organized by category, and clearly spells out the percentage of discount and associated fees before you hit the final button to place your order. ☎ *866/983–4279* ⊕ *www.vegas.com.*

Find Out What's Going On

Information on shows, including their reservation and seating policies, prices, and suitability for children (or age restrictions), is available by calling or visiting box offices. It's also listed in several local publications or websites.

The *Las Vegas Advisor* (✉ *3665 S. Procyon Ave., West Side* ☎ *800/244–2224* ⊕ *www.lasvegasadvisor.com*) is the bargain hunter and advantage player's guide to Las Vegas. News and information about shows, restaurants and casino promotions are updated almost daily on the website for anyone to view. Paid members get more discount offers and the option of a monthly printed newsletter. An online membership is $37.

The *Las Vegas Review-Journal* (⊕ *www.reviewjournal.com*), the city's morning daily newspaper, publishes a pull-out section each Friday called *Neon*, which includes showroom and lounge listings with complete time and price information.

The *Las Vegas Weekly* (⊕ *www.lasvegasweekly.com*) is distributed at retail stores and coffee shops around town. It's rich with nightclub ads and star DJ schedules, and a solid source for live music and cultural activities beyond the realm of the casinos.

What's New?

Star power is what drives the Strip again, with big names performing in everything from three sports arenas to several midsize concert halls and smaller theaters, ranging in capacity from 1,800 to 6,000 seats. The latter are particularly focused on booking stars for extended engagements that bring them to town several times a year. The 6,000-capacity Park Theater arrived in 2016, next to the 20,000-seat T-Mobile Arena, which hosts touring concerts as well as the Vegas Golden Knights hockey team. The two are connected by a lively plaza full of restaurants and bars between New York–New York and the Park-MGM. The long-awaited Resorts World (on the site of the old Stardust hotel) finally opened in the summer of 2021, bringing the delayed arrival of still another new 5,000-seat venue, one that hosts the return of **Celine Dion** and a roster of resident performers such as **Katy Perry** and **Carrie Underwood.** And those who look east past The Palazzo and Sands Convention Center will see the unique construction project known as MSG Sphere, which promises a new, fully immersed way to experience concerts inside a giant, yes, sphere, when the company behind Madison Square Garden finishes it in 2023.

"Residency" continues to be the casino buzzword for signing big names to some type of recurring engagement; anywhere from a multiyear commitment to a one-week stretch. They usually come with the promise of a big production or thematic material you won't see elsewhere. Divas from **Britney Spears** to **Christina Aguilera** created hybrids of old-Vegas spectacle and arena pop concerts. Classic rockers such as **Aerosmith** and **John Fogerty** offered deep album cuts or biographical career retrospectives. This new era started with **Celine Dion** and **Elton John** in the 4,300-seat Colosseum at Caesars Palace, and Celine is still opening new theaters with her residency at the new Resorts World. A few perennials such as **Donny Osmond** and **Barry Manilow** continue to notch up five decades or more on the Strip, even as Planet Hollywood expanded the palette by betting on younger-skewing stars such as **Pitbull** and **Gwen Stefani** in the Zappos Theater. Of course, the global pandemic put a temporary stop to all of it, including a residency by Sting, whose "My Songs" wasn't able to debut as planned in 2020. He's still due for The Colosseum at Caesars Palace whenever the path is clear, and postpandemic normalcy could include recurring engagements by the **Scorpions, Kelly Clarkson,** and **Shania Twain.** The off-Strip Virgin Hotel Las Vegas (formerly the Hard Rock Hotel) is keeping its concert hall as a primary attraction and planning smaller concerts in its outdoor pool area. While younger pop stars such as **Bruno Mars** and **Lady Gaga** have already become Vegas regulars, new headliners are announced all the time, including R&B trailblazer **Usher,** who was set to debut at Caesars Palace in July 2021.

The pandemic did put an unprecedented halt to all Las Vegas entertainment and claimed some permanent casualties. Cirque du Soleil's Las Vegas shows all went dark for more than a year, and during that time the company announced the long-running *Zumanity* would not reopen at New York–New York. Wynn Las Vegas similarly announced that its Cirque-like aquatic show *Le Rêve* was probably gone for good after 15 years. And just as the city was shedding its masks in May, Caesars Entertainment shuttered four of its small showrooms, displacing the likes of **Wayne Newton** and the long-running *Chippendales* and *Crazy Girls* adult revues. Other producers just couldn't wait to return, even braving severe restrictions to make shows such as the comedic *Absinthe* go on—even under profit-eating capacity limits. Gradually, Las Vegas entertainment began to reawaken in the spring of 2021, led by its home-based, "commuter" performers such as comic magician **Piff the Magic Dragon** and comedian **Carrot Top.** Magic in all forms continues to have a lopsided dominance in Las Vegas, from the biggest names—**Penn & Teller, David Copperfield,** and **Criss Angel**—to new stars such as **Mat Franco** and *America's Got Talent* winner **Shin Lim.** The NBC talent show has had such a synergistic relationship with Las Vegas that it's no surprise *America's Got Talent Live!* was set to replace the failed Cirque show *R.U.N.* in Luxor's big theater. But comedy is always high in the mix, too, and it never hurts that it comes without a lot of production expense. Late-night host Jimmy Kimmel put his name on a comedy club at The LINQ, following the lead of Brad Garrett over at the MGM Grand. The bigger names who are theater-level draws continue to play on any given weekend. The Mirage's Aces of Comedy series rotates the likes of Ray Romano, Ron White, and Daniel Tosh. When Las Vegas is running at full steam, any given weekend might bring as many as 100 different entertainment options. Professional sports, nightclubs, and signature restaurants all compete with the shows, but it seems the city isn't ready to surrender its self-appointed status of "The Entertainment Capital of the World" just yet.

Afternoon Shows

Las Vegas has become a wider-reaching and more family-friendly destination. But at the same time, evening show prices can be in the triple digits. These factors are sometimes at odds with one another and help explain a few afternoon shows that hold their ticket prices down or discount heavily with promotional coupons. The following are the most proven and popular.

South Strip

Legends in Concert

THEATER | FAMILY | The durable *Legends* has been on the Strip since 1983, which now makes it the longest-running show in Las Vegas. It inspired dozens of imitators over the years, but its production values and prominence on the Strip shrank as the big shows got bigger. In its latest home at the Tropicana, *Legends* adheres to the same basic formula of "miniconcerts" by a rotating lineup of celebrity impersonators, from Elvis to Lady Gaga. There's no lip-syncing and always a live band. Longtime Las Vegas visitors will find it symbolic and somehow natural

Raves and Faves

Splashiest opening: The beginning of *O* gets things off to an astonishing start when a regal curtain is whooshed away into the backstage recesses as though sucked into a giant vacuum cleaner. But when Lady Gaga is in town, nothing quite tops her descent from on high as she hangs from a wire to play keytar for the "Just Dance" show-opener of *Enigma*.

Best finale: The climactic scene of *LOVE* just had to be "A Day in the Life." Cirque du Soleil rises to the challenge of the famous orchestral buildup with a symbolic, moving scene featuring an angelic, floating mother figure. (Remember that both John Lennon and Paul McCartney's mothers died young.)

Best band in town: The blue baldies in the Blue Man Group never talk, so it's even more important that their silent antics be backed by a rocking sound track. The seven-piece band keeps the sound percussive and otherworldly.

Most words per minute: Penn & Teller discuss everything from "ocular hygiene" to "petroleum by-products" (meaning Solo cups), conveniently overlooking the fact that most Vegas shows push spectacle over words. What's even more amazing? Only one of them (Penn) talks.

Most deliberately provocative: Is a show offensive if everyone laughs not just at the jokes but at the very act of trying so hard to be offensive? It's the shared in-joke of the deliberately low-rent *Absinthe*, carried to even more juvenile extremes in the newer sister-show *Opium*.

Best guilty pleasure: The title says it all: *Zombie Burlesque*. The unlikely fusion of two hot trends is a smartly silly twist on *Cabaret*. As an opening video explains, a truce between zombies and humankind results in the undead entertaining us with original songs and a live band in a place called Club Z.

that drag star Frank Marino has been hosting the show of late; he showed up in town about the same time as *Legends*, so his tenure in shows such as *La Cage* is about the only thing that rivals its longevity. ⊠ *Tropicana Las Vegas—A DoubleTree by Hilton Hotel, 3801 Las Vegas Blvd. S, South Strip* ☎ *702/739–2222* ⊕ *legendsinconcert.com* ⌸ *From $60* ☞ *Dark Sun.–Wed.*

★ Mac King

THEATER | FAMILY | The reigning king of Las Vegas afternoons was set to celebrate his 20th anniversary at Harrah's Las Vegas before the pandemic hit the pause button on his show for a year. When shows started to reopen, Harrah's

had begun a shift into a more convention-minded property, so King relocated to the Excalibur. Though he shares his new home with the male revue *Thunder from Down Under*, the Excalibur overall is still better branded with the families and recreational travelers who have made the comedy magician popular for generations: he now greets the children of those who remember seeing his show when they were kids themselves. Onstage, King is ageless in his plaid suit and folksy "Howdy!" He's the perennial court jester rooted in vaudeville traditions of show business. He stands apart from the other magic shows on the Strip with a one-man hour of low-key, self-deprecating humor and the kind of close-up

Blue Man Group is a show for the whole family.

magic that's baffling but doesn't take the focus away from the running banter and audience participation. ✉ *Excalibur Hotel & Casino, 3580 Las Vegas Blvd. S, Center Strip* ☎ *702/597–7777* ⊕ *mackingshow. com* 🎟 *From $38* ☞ *Dark Sun. and Mon.*

Murray the Magician

THEATER | FAMILY | A knack for self-promotion—and an unimaginable outlay for hair products—made this comedy-magician a ubiquitous presence on YouTube, *Pawn Stars*, *America's Got Talent*... you name it. Instantly identifiable by his black-framed glasses and an exploding shock of vertical blonde hair, Murray (SawChuck) has become a Las Vegas mainstay with a relaxed, slow-burn stage presence, and a solid showcase of classic magic heavy on audience banter. ✉ *Tropicana Las Vegas—A DoubleTree by Hilton Hotel, 3801 Las Vegas Blvd. S, South Strip* ☎ *800/829–9034* ⊕ *murraymagic.com* 🎟 *$29 (plus fees)* ☞ *Dark Mon.–Wed.*

Center Strip

Nathan Burton Comedy Magic

THEATER | FAMILY | The likable magician had the good fortune to be on the very first, highly watched season of *America's Got Talent* in 2006, parlaying that national exposure into a durable career on the Strip. Burton puts a fun spin on familiar illusions and is family-friendly for those with older children. Mom and dad will like the fact that tickets are routinely discounted well below face value. ✉ *Planet Hollywood Resort & Casino, Saxe Theater, 3667 Las Vegas Blvd. S, Center Strip* ☎ *866/932–1818* ⊕ *www.nathanburton. com* 🎟 *From $50* ☞ *Dark Mon.*

Evening Revues

South Strip

★ Blue Man Group

THEATER | FAMILY | The three bald, blue, and silent characters in utilitarian uniforms have become part of the Las Vegas landscape. The satire of technology and information-overload merges with classic physical comedy and the Blue Man's unique brand of interstellar rock and roll. The group's latest home, a cozy theater at Luxor, brings the Blue dudes closer to their off-Broadway origins: paint splattering, mouth-catching marshmallows, and rollicking percussion jam sessions on PVC pipe contraptions. ⊠ *Luxor, 3900 Las Vegas Blvd. S, South Strip* ☎ *702/262–4400, 855/788–6755* ⊕ *www.blueman.com* ✉ *From $61* ☞ *Usually plays nightly.*

Fantasy

THEATER | *Fantasy* is a topless show (un)dressed up as a variety show, with power-pop singing by its female host and magic or acrobatic acts to widen its appeal beyond the topless choreography. It's the least strip club–like of the Las Vegas topless revues, so it's not uncommon to see couples in the audience at this durable show that's been around since 1999. ⊠ *Luxor Las Vegas, 3900 Las Vegas Blvd. S, South Strip* ☎ *702/262–4000* ⊕ *www.fantasyluxor.com* ✉ *From $39* ☞ *Plays nightly.*

Jabbawockeez JREAMZ

DANCE | FAMILY | The only Las Vegas performers who don't show their faces speak with their feet in a show that appeals to the younger nightclub demographic. The masked hip-hop dance collective has steadily improved its showmanship since it settled on the Strip in 2010. There's plenty of break dancing but also a contagious sense of fun, as comedy and warm-hearted themes of brotherhood and inclusiveness emerge from those blank masks. The troupe's latest home in a 300-seat theater allows only four to six of the dancers onstage at the same time, but video projections expand the sense of space in the down-the-rabbit-hole tale of a suburban "zombie" gradually shaken to life. ⊠ *MGM Grand Hotel, 3799 Las Vegas Blvd. S, South Strip* ☎ *866/740–7711* ⊕ *www.jbwkz.com* ✉ *From $50* ☞ *Dark Tues. and Wed.*

★ KÀ

THEATER | FAMILY | *KÀ*, Cirque du Soleil's biggest Las Vegas production, opened in 2006 and still stands as an amazing monument to the sky's-the-limit mentality that fueled Vegas in the go-go 2000s. The $165-million opus frees the stage itself from gravity, replacing a fixed stage with an 80,000-pound deck, maneuvered by a giant gantry arm into a near-vertical position for the climactic battle. Giant puppets also factor into the bold interpretation of live martial-arts period fantasies like *Crouching Tiger, Hidden Dragon* in the adventures of two separated twins. Though no other Cirque in Las Vegas rivals it for sheer spectacle, those not sitting close enough to see faces can be confused by the story, which is told without dialogue. ⊠ *MGM Grand Hotel & Casino, 3805 Las Vegas Blvd. S, South Strip* ☎ *855/788–6755* ⊕ *cirquedusoleil.com/ka* ✉ *From $75* ☞ *Dark Thurs. and Fri.*

Michael Jackson ONE

THEATER | FAMILY | After traveling the world as *The Immortal*, Cirque du Soleil's salute to Michael Jackson took on its second iteration in a remodeled Mandalay Bay theater. A partnership with Jackson's estate, it helps everyone remember why he became a worldwide phenomenon in his 1980s heyday. Amid the bombardment of video imagery, Jackson pops up now and then as the spirit guide to a quartet of misfit fans, who gain powers to defeat robotic paparazzi (don't ask) by harnessing the King of Pop's "agility, courage, playfulness, and love." Instead of a live band, the acrobatics and dance numbers unfold to remixes of Jackson's

Discount Tickets Vegas Style

Just as you learn not to ask people in your airline row what they paid for their plane tickets, don't bring up the question at a Las Vegas show. The answer might ruin your fun.

Internet discounting and "half-price" ticket booths on the Strip have made the standing Las Vegas shows a game of "mark 'em up to mark 'em down." While you will still pay face value (or more) for the big touring concerts, it pays to shop around for most of the titles here week in and week out. When the first Tix4Tonight discount booths (now known as Tix4Vegas) arrived on the Strip, they functioned more like their counterparts on Broadway, selling remaining seats at half-price once it appeared full-price sales had peaked for the day.

But with eight outlets in prominent locations—and now, online vendors such as Groupon as well—a middle-tier show such as *Fantasy* lists at $52 in order to get roughly half that. Any budget-minded person is almost forced to seek out the discount outlets for all but a handful of shows that still sell run close to capacity: Cirque du Soleil's *O*, usually, or headliners such as Lady Gaga, who offers a limited number of performance dates. By contrast, if you wonder how a magician such as Nathan Burton can sustain for years in such a crowded tourist market, check out his ticket prices on ⊕ *Vegas.com*: $13, advertised as a "79%" discount from the face value of $50 or $60.

The proliferation of discount vendors also changed what once used to be a simple, across-the-board pricing scheme—all seats half-price, plus a service charge—to offer discounts of less than 50% and some shows available in advance through telephone and online sales. "Half-price outlets are like crack," noted one veteran of the ticket wars. "You start with a few and get that easy sale, so you start doing more and more."

When you do start shopping online vendors such as ⊕ *Vegas.com* or Travel-Zoo—even the casinos themselves, who often offer room-and-show packages—it can get bewildering. The *Las Vegas Advisor* once experimented to see how many options for Britney Spears tickets it could find, and came up with 37 different prices.

actual recordings in earth-shaking sound delivered by more than 7,000 speakers. ⊠ *Mandalay Bay, 3950 Las Vegas Blvd. S, South Strip* ☎ *855/788–6755* ⊕ *www.cirquedusoleil.com* 🎟 *From $76* ☞ *Dark Tues. and Wed.*

Thunder from Down Under

THEATER | The Australian gents planted their g-strings on the Strip in 2001, as the first male dance revue to counterbalance all the topless burlesque and showgirl revues for men. With table-top dancing and a hands-on approach to their forays into the audience, the Thunder dudes relied on a low-tech, in-your-face appeal, even as *Chippendales* and *Magic Mike Live* brought more theatrical and slickly produced competition. But the *Thunder* struck back in early 2019, with an $8.5-million renovation of the troupe's longtime space at the Excalibur, which now lets them cavort amid immersive technology such as LED screens and pod stages throughout the room. ⊠ *Excalibur Hotel & Casino, 3850 Las Vegas Blvd. S, South Strip* ☎ *702/597–7600* ⊕ *www.thunderfromdownunder.com* 🎟 *From $55* ☞ *Plays nightly.*

Tournament of Kings

THEATER | FAMILY | A rare survivor of Las Vegas's mostly forgotten "family" phase is this Arthurian stunt show, which has lasted more than 25 years in a dirt-floor arena in the basement of the Excalibur. The audience dines on a Cornish hen dinner (warning: no utensils) and cheers on fast horses, jousting, and swordplay. Those familiar with Medieval Times around the country will know the drill. The show remains a great family gathering—especially for preadolescents, who get to make a lot of noise—and the realistic stunts speak to the commitment of the cast. ⊠ *Excalibur, 3850 Las Vegas Blvd. S, South Strip* ☎ *702/597–7600* ⊕ *www.excalibur.com* ⊠ *$75* ☞ *Dark Tues.*

Center Strip

Absinthe

THEATER | Sometimes it's not the elements but how they are combined. *Absinthe* became one of the most popular shows on the Strip by turning Cirque du Soleil's opulent, dreamlike aesthetic on its head. A downscale, shabby-chic vibe unifies circus acrobatics, raunchy comedy, and saucy burlesque numbers inside a cozy tent in front of Caesars Palace. (At least it's a tentlike structure; once it was decided the show would stick around, fire inspectors insisted on a sturdy, semipermanent pavilion.) The audience surrounds the performances on a small, 9-foot stage. The festive, low-tech atmosphere is furthered along by the host, a shifty insult comic known as the Gazillionaire. This is cheap raunch for a discerning audience. And, like Penn & Teller's show, it's a winking salute to the show-business tradition itself. ⊠ *Caesars Palace, 3570 Las Vegas Blvd. S, Center Strip* ☎ *702/534–3419* ⊕ *www.absinthevegas.com* ⊠ *From $99* ☞ *Plays nightly.*

Criss Angel—MINDFREAK

THEATER | Criss Angel lives up to his Goth-rock image with the loudest magic show in town, full of blistering music (some by Korn's Jonathan Davis) from 150 speakers and performed in a Planet Hollywood theater that's been customized with wraparound video walls and surround sound to create a clublike atmosphere. Add dancers to the mix (replacing the comic sidekicks of his previous show), and it gives new meaning to misdirection. What is unchanged from Angel's long run at Luxor is how much this one depends on whether you like the magician. Angel is consistent in his Long Island rock-star image (if you don't count an appearance by his demonic alter-ego Kristos), even as the fast-paced barrage of illusions unfold with a schizophrenic tone that shifts from heavy-metal sinister to rave-up dance party. ⊠ *Planet Hollywood, 3667 Las Vegas Blvd. S, Center Strip* ☎ *702/777–2782, 855/234–7469* ⊕ *crissangel.com* ⊠ *From $69* ☞ *Wed.–Sun. 7 pm.*

★ LOVE

THEATER | Meet the Beatles again—well, sort of—in a certified home run for Cirque du Soleil. Before he died, George Harrison persuaded the surviving Beatles (and Yoko Ono) to license the group's music to Cirque. The remixed music by the late Beatles producer George Martin and his son Giles is revelatory on 7,000 speakers, often like hearing the songs for the first time. In the summer of 2016, Cirque tweaked the show for its 10th anniversary, dialing down the elegiac version of postwar Liverpool, and punching up the dance elements to emphasize the youth culture of Beatlemania. Cirque also added literal depictions of the Fab Four in videos and projection mapping. It's still a great marriage of sensibilities that explodes with joy. ⊠ *Mirage Las Vegas, 3400 Las Vegas Blvd. S, Center Strip* ☎ *702/792–7777, 855/788–6755* ⊕ *www.cirquedusoleil.com* ⊠ *From $87* ☞ *Dark Sun. and Mon.*

Menopause the Musical

THEATER | The campy musical full of song parodies about "the change" has been a female-bonding experience on the Strip since 2006, Of late, Cindy Williams of *Laverne and Shirley* fame has been a billed star amid the usual cast of four women singing song parodies as they cavort through a day at Bloomingdales. ⊠ *Harrah's Las Vegas, 3475 Las Vegas Blvd. S, Center Strip* ☎ *702/369–5000* ⊕ *menopausethemusical. com* ☒ *From $69* ☞ *Dark Sun.*

★ O

THEATER | FAMILY | More than $70 million was spent on Cirque du Soleil's theater at Bellagio back in 1998, and its liquid stage is the centerpiece of a one-of-a-kind show. It was money well spent: *O* remains one of the best-attended shows on the Strip. The title is taken from the French word for water (*eau*), and water is everywhere—1.5 million gallons of it, 12 million pounds of it, contained by a "stage" that, thanks to hydraulic lifts, can change shape and turn into dry land in no time. The intense and nonstop action by the show's acrobats, aerial gymnasts, trapeze artists, synchronized swimmers, divers, and contortionists make for a stylish spectacle that manages to fashion dreamlike imagery from its acrobatics, with a vague theme about the wellspring of theater and imagination. ⊠ *Bellagio Las Vegas, 3600 Las Vegas Blvd. S, Center Strip* ☎ *702/693–8866, 855/788–6755* ⊕ *www.cirquedusoleil.com* ☒ *From $107* ☞ *Dark Mon. and Tues.*

Opium

THEATER | If Cirque du Soleil can multiply with new titles on the Strip, why can't a parody of Cirque? *Absinthe* producer Spiegelworld carries that show's raunchy humor and scantily clad acrobatics over to *Opium* at The Cosmopolitan, where it plays in a very cool venue reminiscent of the supper clubs you see in old movies. This one taps into the swanky retro sci-fi of *Barbarella* and *Forbidden Planet* and leans more into a gay camp aesthetic in its costuming, humor, and overall tone. Your pilots are Captain Ann Tennille and Dusty Moonboots, "the Celine Dion of Uranus," Ponder that while you sip a "Spocktail" such as Kiss My Asteroid, and you have a pretty good idea of what's in store for you on this ride. ⊠ *The Cosmopolitan of Las Vegas, 3708 Las Vegas Blvd. S, Center Strip* ☎ *702/534–3419* ⊕ *spiegelworld.com* ☒ *From $79* ☞ *Dark Tues.*

RuPaul's Drag Race Live

THEATER | Drag shows came close to extinction on the Strip until RuPaul transferred the popularity of his cable TV enterprise into a live spin-off (promoted, of course, with a VH1 dose of cross-promotion, *RuPaul's Drag Race: Vegas Revue*). It's fitting that Derrick Barry, best known for his Britney Spears impersonation, ties back to the bygone days of *An Evening at La Cage* to give this new effort continuity, performing alongside fellow TV stars such as Kameron Michaels, Naomi Smalls, and host Asia O'Hara. (The format allows performers to rotate in and out of the revue, so the lineup isn't consistent, though don't look for the actual RuPaul beyond surprise appearances or special occasions.) The whole enterprise barely got out of the gate before the pandemic shutdown, but seemed poised to come back strong. ⊠ *Flamingo Las Vegas, 3555 Las Vegas Blvd. S, Center Strip* ☎ *702/777–2782, 855/234–7469* ⊕ *caesars.com.*

V—The Ultimate Variety Show

THEATER | FAMILY | This midprice variety show has held its own against the splashier Cirque-type productions for more than 15 years. The lineup varies, but it usually has magic, juggling, and acrobatics such as hand balancing. Perhaps the real secret is the "front of curtain" atmosphere with likable performers making direct contact with the audience in an intimate setting. ⊠ *Miracle Mile Shops at Planet Hollywood, 3667 Las Vegas Blvd. S, Center Strip* ☎ *866/932–1818* ⊕ *vtheater.com* ☒ *From $70.*

Save or Splurge

Save

Carnaval Court. Balmy nights bring a bit of Fremont Street's crazy scene to the heart of the Strip, with this outdoor stage as well as "flair" bartenders, both right off the south door of Harrah's Las Vegas. If the band isn't your favorite, head a few yards in either direction for more free live music in the Harrah's piano bar or O'Sheas section of The LINQ Hotel, or in the Jimmy Buffet–theme Margaritaville minicasino inside the Flamingo.

Fremont Street Experience. Fremont Street's overhead canopy got a $32 million LED upgrade to keep the block-spanning video shows up to date with your HD TV at home. But more of the show is on the ground these days. Glitter Gulch has become a midway, from sidewalk musicians and artists to bar-top go-go dancers and of course, Slotzilla, an overhead zip line. Every weekend live performers play free gigs on two stages on 1st and 3rd Streets. But don't stop walking East (through the noncanopied Fremont East district) until you get to 7th Street, where sunset at Downtown Container Park usually finds a drum circle heralding the first fire-belching blasts from the giant mantis sculpture out front

Mac King. The comedy magic of Mac King is worth every penny of the full $38 ticket price, but various promotions and discounts will get the price down much further, or at least get you upgraded seating.

Splurge

Meet-and-greet tickets. When you have a lot of social media to feed, seeing a show just isn't enough. You gotta have that selfie! Fear not, headliners ranging from Carrot Top to Piff the Magic Dragon offer some form of upgraded ticket with a photo op included. Even the anonymous Blue Men sell you a $175 package that includes a meet-and-greet, choice seats, a free drink, and a piece of merchandise item.

Concert VIP section. Sure you can get a conventional theater seat for a fair price to see Zappos Theater headliners such as Shania Twain and Kelly Clarkson. But if you want to go big, try to score a VIP booth in the crescent-shape row that runs right along the stage extension. You might be paying $225 or more for a ticket, but the booth comes with a bottle of champagne and dedicated cocktail service from Drai's nightclub. And you can't get any closer to the star without being in the show. There was such demand for these in the Planet Hollywood theater that Caesars Palace remodeled its Colosseum, in part to provide a similar VIP set-up with booths and bottle service. At the Virgin Hotels concert hall, the whole second floor is a VIP wraparound; improvements to that area were part of a face-lift when the hotel transitioned from the Hard Rock.

O. Cirque's big water show has been around since 1998, but you won't ever see it go on tour. Pony up the $196 for a prime splash-zone seat, and save on your water bill when you get home.

X Burlesque

THEATER | This is no old-timey burlesque. Instead, an edgy attitude permeates this dance-intensive topless revue with impressive video and lighting effects. A comedian doing a 10-minute set is the only spoken contact with the audience. It's closer to a strip-club vibe than the more theatrical *Fantasy* at Luxor, which should serve as a recommendation to some and a warning to others. But even the more intense gyrations are leavened with a winking humor. ⊠ *Flamingo Las Vegas, 3555 Las Vegas Blvd. S, Center Strip* ☎ *702/777–2782* ⊕ *stabileproductions.com* ✉ *From $56* ☞ *Plays nightly.*

Zombie Burlesque

THEATER | The zombie craze meets retro burlesque and camp humor for a ribald spoof of *Cabaret* that has the undead entertaining us with raunchy songs and a live band in a place called Club Z. *Zombie Burlesque* has found an audience for daring to think small and try something original—and for being more like something you'd find at a fringe festival than on the Strip. (It's recommended for those 16 and up in case parents don't realize "burlesque" gets more weight than "zombie" in the title.) ⊠ *V Theater at Planet Hollywood Resort, 3667 Las Vegas Blvd. S, South Strip* ☎ *866/932–1818* ⊕ *zombieburlesque.com* ✉ *From $79* ☞ *Dark Sun.*

North Strip

Atomic Saloon Show

THEATER | The Strip's third naughty revue from Spiegelworld took its theme from the Western saloon vibe of an inherited venue in The Venetian's retail mall, creating the raucous atmosphere of a theme park revue gone off the rails. The flagship *Absinthe* is a better overall introduction to Spiegelworld's approach. But those who can't get enough of the formula will enjoy this Wild West variation on the campy hijinks, including barely clad acrobats, sexy cowboys and cowgirls, and...a nun. Buy your tickets through axs.com or spiegelworld.com. ⊠ *The Venetian Resort, Grand Canal Shoppes, 3377 Las Vegas Blvd. S, North Strip* ⊹ *Waterfall Atrium, Level 2* ☎ *702/534–3419* ⊕ *Spiegelworld.com* ✉ *$149 (while capacity limited).*

Magic Mike Live

THEATER | Channing Tatum didn't just cash a check to lend the name of his Magic Mike film franchise to a Las Vegas effort. He was an active member of the creative team, working with the movie's two female choreographers for this male revue that debuted in 2017 at the Hard Rock Hotel (now the Virgin Hotels Las Vegas). The pandemic delayed its reopening at the Sahara until the summer of 2021, but there was no reason to believe the approach would change: *Magic Mike Live* pared the g-string antics with a nice-guy vibe and with more wit and modesty—some gals will say too much—than the genre usually allows. It even went so far as to stage a "fake out" opening, spoofing the more typical male revues. ⊠ *Sahara Las Vegas, 2535 Las Vegas Blvd. S, North Strip* ☎ *833/624–4265* ⊕ *MagicMikeLiveLasVegas.com* ✉ *From $89* ☞ *Dark Mon. and Tues.*

Mystère

THEATER | FAMILY | The Strip's first permanent Cirque du Soleil show celebrated its 25th anniversary in late 2018 by completing a gradual overhaul that includes several new acts. It's still the town's most consistent family show, and the Las Vegas Cirque show that most purely preserves the Montreal company's innovative reinvention of the circus. *Mystère* has held up to the increased spectacle of its sister shows by being the funniest of the bunch—and by keeping the spectators close to the action and the human acrobatics in the spotlight. You're intimately involved with this surreal wonderland and the comic characters, who interact with the audience. If you're not careful, you could even end up onstage. ✉ *Treasure Island, 3300 Las Vegas Blvd. S, North Strip* ☎ *800/392–1999* ⊕ *cirque-dusoleil.com* 🎟 *From $75* ☞ *Dark Thurs. and Fri.*

Resident Headliners

The turn-of-the-21st century took Las Vegas back to one of the traditions from its past. The explosion of new room volume on the Strip combined with the hassles of modern air travel opened the doors to a wave of resident headliners, those who live in Las Vegas and perform more or less year-round. Penn & Teller, David Copperfield, and Carrot Top all bet that audiences were ready to embrace the down-front performing tradition (not letting anything get between the performer and the audience) that put Las Vegas on the map.

Now Las Vegas is returning to its 1960s- and 1970s-era concept of stars who don't necessarily live here, but come in several times a year for extended stretches. Celine Dion basically wrote the blueprint for the formula and has returned periodically over the years. There's a full-circle type of symmetry to her fronting the lineup in the new 5,000-seater simply known as The Theatre at Resorts World. Plenty of other stars followed their lead, with Pitbull, John Fogerty, Barry Manilow, and Carlos Santana among those most likely to keep returning. With nonstar production shows having hit a creative wall outside of Cirque and Spiegelworld, count on star-plus-spectacle formulas such as those revolving around Cher, Katy Perry, or Lady Gaga to continue for some time.

South Strip

Carrot Top

THEATER | After years on the college circuit, the prop comic moved his trunks full of tricks into the Luxor, where he became one of the Strip's longest-running year-round names. The Florida native known offstage as Scott Thompson still is most unique when wielding his visual gags, but he sells them with a manic energy, a tourist's street-level view of Vegas, and a running commentary on the act itself, perhaps a sly nod to his eternal lack of respect. ✉ *Luxor Las Vegas, 3900 Las Vegas Blvd. S, South Strip* ☎ *702/262–4400* ⊕ *www.luxor.com/entertainment* 🎟 *From $75* ☞ *Dark Mon.*

David Copperfield

THEATER | FAMILY | The master magician has made Las Vegas a part of his career since the 1980s and now roosts at the MGM Grand for more than 40 weeks per year. At this point, Copperfield is sort of the Rolling Stones of magic; you sense his authority and submit to it from the minute the show opens, and trust him to wow you with illusions such as a recent one involving a T. rex, which take years to perfect. He varies the pace with illusions that can be touching or funny, but most of all they still genuinely fool you. ✉ *MGM Grand Hotel & Casino, 3799 Las Vegas Blvd. S, South Strip* ☎ *800/745–3000, 702/740–7711* ⊕ *www.davidcopperfield.com* 🎟 *From $71* ☞ *Select dates almost year-round.*

Terry Fator

PUPPET SHOWS | Las Vegas has long been a haven for impressionists, only this one lets his puppets do the talking. Fator is the likable second-season winner of *America's Got Talent* who takes ventriloquism into new realms, thanks to his musical range and knack for singing impressions. After 10 years at The

Mirage, Fator has moved to New York–New York in a smaller venue formerly used for private and corporate events. The side views offer new angles on puppet sidekicks such as Walter T. Airedale and Winston the Impersonating Turtle in a show that's always appealed to a wide range of visitors, from older children to baby boomers. ■ **TIP** ➔ **Fator's Christmas show, during the holiday stretch when many titles go on vacation, is even more charming.** ✉ *New York–New York Hotel & Casino, 3970 Las Vegas Blvd. S, Center Strip* ☎ *816/855–4365* ⊕ *terryfator.com* 🎟 *$46* ☞ *Dark Mon.–Wed.*

Center Strip

★ Celine Dion

CONCERTS | Celine Dion transcended her divisive 1990s pop stardom to become a Las Vegas perennial with a loyal, international following. Aging gracefully has worked in her favor, allowing her to blend her own hits into a more universally entertaining showcase that in the past has been far-reaching enough to embrace a James Bond movie medley and tributes to Ella Fitzgerald and Michael Jackson. Details of her new Resorts World show—or even its schedule in a new, 5,000-seat theater—were slow to emerge after its November debut was confirmed during the 2021 Oscars telecast. The star has suggested in interviews that it will be more like her second round at Caesars—more personal and musically focused—than the original production show *A New Day.* ✉ *Resorts World, 3000 Las Vegas Blvd. S, North Strip* ☎ *702/676–7000* ⊕ *www.celineinvegas.com* ☞ *Select dates at 7:30 pm.*

Donny Osmond

CONCERTS | **FAMILY** | No one should question either Donny Osmond's work ethic or his showmanship. What began as a "late career" reunion with sister Marie turned into an 11-year run at the Flamingo. Now, only a worldwide pandemic was able to

slow Donny's plan to reopen next door at Harrah's Las Vegas as a solo act. The show that was set to open in late summer of 2021 shouldn't be hard to imagine. When he shared the stage with his sister, both split off into half-hour solo segments. Donny used his time to show his range: singing piano ballads, reminding audiences of his Broadway credits and serving up bold remakes of old Osmonds hits such as "Yo-Yo" and "Crazy Horses." Whatever the new show offers, you know it will resonate with the stage presence of a perennial who grew up in front of America and wears his variety training with pride. ✉ *Harrah's Las Vegas, 3475 Las Vegas Blvd. S, Center Strip* ☎ *855/234–7469* ⊕ *www.donnyosmond.com* 🎟 *From $65* ☞ *Select dates 8 pm.*

Mat Franco—"Magic Reinvented Nightly"

THEATER | **FAMILY** | A winning smile (and winning *America's Got Talent*) turned out to be a formidable combination for a young magician who settled on the Strip after the TV talent show fast-tracked his fame in 2014. Franco's charm and likable attitude compensated for a streamlined production, which betrayed his days of traveling the college circuit, but his postpandemic show promised more scenic elements and visual appeal. Either way, he makes the classics seem new to a younger audience, and some of the illusions are bound to surprise even the magic-jaded. ✉ *The LINQ, 3535 Las Vegas Blvd. S, Center Strip* ☎ *855/234–7469* ⊕ *matfranco.com* 🎟 *From $44* ☞ *Thurs.–Mon. 7 pm; 9:30 pm Sat.*

Piff the Magic Dragon

THEATER | Billing himself as "The Loser of *America's Got Talent*" fits the droll humor of the British comedy-magician, whose goal of competing on the TV show was to get a berth in Las Vegas. It worked. The magician who stands out for his satin dragon suit, bad attitude and stoic chihuahua sidekick, Mr. Piffles, keeps the jokes coming as fast as the card tricks in a cozy cabaret venue that allows plenty of audience interaction. In perhaps the ultimate sign that he's made it on the Strip, the Flamingo renamed Bugsy's Cabaret as the Piff the Magic Dragon Theater in 2019. ⊠ *Flamingo Las Vegas, 3555 Las Vegas Blvd. S, Center Strip* ☎ *855/234–7469* ⊕ *piffthemagicdragon. com* ⊠ *From $63* ☞ *Dark Tues. and Wed.*

Tape Face

THEATER | FAMILY | Las Vegas and *America's Got Talent* have been great for one another, with Tape Face, the latest variety performer to move in on the Strip—near fellow contestants Mat Franco and Piff the Magic Dragon—after mainstream exposure from the TV competition. Tape Face hearkens back to a simpler era of show business, with his silent mime and prop comedy based on the signature gimmick of gaffer's tape plastered over his mouth. His eyes, gestures and quite a few recruits from the audience, all help propel the charmingly low-fi shenanigans. (A cautionary note: Sam Wills, the creator of Tape Face, generated some controversy when he decided to treat his character more like a Blue Man and less like a Piff. In other words, it's not always Wills doing the show; sometimes it's another performer he trained to do the act.) ⊠ *Harrah's Las Vegas, 3475 Las Vegas Blvd. S* ☎ *855/234–7469* ⊕ *tapeface.tv* ⊠ *From $60* ☞ *7:30 pm daily; dark Mon.*

Downtown

Gordie Brown—Lasting Impressions

COMEDY CLUBS | The Canadian impressionist has been a Las Vegas presence for years, specializing in song parodies delivered with a manic silliness. Women will warm up to a guy good-looking enough to be a retro crooner, and men will recognize the kid from their middle school who memorized *MAD* magazine. ⊠ *Golden Nugget, 129 E. Fremont St., Downtown* ☎ *702/385–7111* ⊕ *www.gordiebrown. com* ⊠ *From $15* ⊗ *No shows Mon. and Fri.* ☞ *Dark Sun.–Thurs.*

West Side

★ Penn & Teller

THEATER | Eccentric comic magicians Penn & Teller are more popular now than when they settled into the Rio in 2002. Ventures such as their durable TV magic contest *Fool Us* expanded the duo into mainstream culture beyond the Strip. Now they turn up almost everywhere it seems. Back in Las Vegas, their off-kilter humor now seems less jarring as they age gracefully at the Rio. Their magic in a gorgeous 1,500-seat theater is topical and genuinely baffling, pushing the form into new creative directions. And their comedy is satiric, provocative, and thoughtful. The duo used some of their pandemic shutdown time to develop new material for the Rio. ⊠ *Rio All-Suite Hotel & Casino, 3700 W. Flamingo Rd., West Side* ☎ *702/777–2782, 855/234–7469* ⊕ *www.pennandteller.com* ⊠ *From $82* ☞ *Dark Thurs. and Fri.*

Venues

In addition to the hotel showrooms and theaters, Las Vegas has four large multipurpose arenas for both concerts and sports, and several smaller performance venues. Check the performance schedules of the following venues to catch a great show.

South Strip

Hollywood Theatre

CONCERTS | Magic maestro David Copperfield has come to dominate the schedule about 40 weeks a year at the MGM Grand. The old-Vegas booths are cool, but at least half the crowd of 700 or so is packed into tight table seating. It's not very comfortable but the sight lines are decent and the sound quality is good in a room that is, oddly, about the only part of the MGM that hasn't been remodeled since the early 1990s. ⊠ *MGM Grand Hotel & Casino, 3799 Las Vegas Blvd. S, South Strip* ☎ *702/891–7777* ⊕ *www.mgmgrand.com.*

House of Blues at Mandalay Bay

CONCERTS | The Las Vegas branch of this chain books one-night concerts which tend to skew toward younger, heavier hard-rock bands and all-ages shows. That said, Carlos Santana emerged from the pandemic before 2021's end to mark his ninth year of resident shows there. Billy Idol and others also explored the potential of classic-rock residencies at the versatile venue. As with other branches, rustic folk art covers the walls. This one is unusual, however, in having a balcony level with reserved theater seating along with the general-admission floor that accommodates about 1,200. ⊠ *Mandalay Bay Resort & Casino, 3950 Las Vegas Blvd. S, South Strip* ☎ *702/632–7600* ⊕ *www.houseofblues.com.*

MGM Grand Garden

CONCERTS | The T-Mobile is now the top dog for concert acts, but home games for the Vegas Golden Knights still require a lot of big concerts to move over to the MGM Grand Garden. The lack of VIP boxes or a second deck of seating means more quality seats for regular folk when the likes of Dave Chappelle or Jimmy Buffett play there. ■TIP➔ **Now that MGM properties charge for parking, remember the Grand Garden is easily accessed by the MGM monorail stop for those on the east side of the Strip.** ⊠ *3799 Las Vegas Blvd. S, South Strip* ☎ *702/531–3826* ⊕ *mgmgrand.mgmresorts.com.*

Michelob Ultra Arena

CONCERTS | This 12,000-seat arena (formerly the Mandalay Bay Events Center) has yielded the big events to the T-Mobile Arena, but after a $10 million upgrade, including new seats, it's become the home court for the WNBA team Las Vegas Aces. Mandalay Bay also has a great outdoor venue, **Mandalay Beach,** set up for general-admission concerts in the hotel's lushly landscaped pool and beach area. Both a monorail and retail mall connect Mandalay Bay to the Luxor and Excalibur, so if you have to drive to a show, parking at either hotel makes for an easier postconcert escape than the Mandalay garage. ⊠ *3950 Las Vegas Blvd. S, South Strip* ☎ *800/745–3000* ⊕ *mandalaybay.mgmresorts.com.*

South Point Showroom

CONCERTS | This small, stylish showroom is a throwback to old Vegas with its coziness and tables-and-booth seating. Visitors are likely to be surrounded by locals for name comedians, tribute acts or veteran musical acts such as Tony Orlando, Frankie Avalon, and Tower of Power. ⊠ *South Point Hotel, Casino & Spa, 9777 Las Vegas Blvd. S, South Strip* ☎ *702/796–7111* ⊕ *www.southpointcasino.com.*

Center Strip

The Chelsea

CONCERTS | The Cosmopolitan's 40,000-square-foot venue is elegantly trimmed, but a versatile bare box in its layout. The floor can offer seating or general-admission standing room, wrapped by a gallery of limited fixed seating, five rows deep, and an in-between area that can be either bleacher seating or more standing room. It usually hosts smaller-capacity concerts for 2,000 or more, with singer John Legend and comedian Bill Burr among those billed for a postpandemic return. ⊠ *The Cosmopolitan of Las Vegas, 3708 Las Vegas Blvd. S, Center Strip* ☎ *702/698–7000.*

The Colosseum at Caesars Palace

CONCERTS | The $95-million theater invented the current model for concert residencies when it was built for Celine Dion in 2003. More recently it's been remodeled to be more versatile and to host younger-skewing acts. A floor area in front of the stage can offer seating as it once did, or retract low enough to become a general admission "pit" without interrupting the sight lines from the seats. A new video system and VIP booth areas were added in time for new bookings such as Sting, while returning favorites include Jerry Seinfeld and Jeff Dunham. The two balconies can seem distant from the ridiculously wide 120-foot stage, but a huge video screen improves the views, and the sound system is impeccable. ✉ *3750 Las Vegas Blvd. S, Center Strip* ☎ *855/234–7469* ⊕ *www.caesars.com.*

The Mirage Theatre

CONCERTS | This comfortable, 1,250-seat theater has long been a multipurpose venue, even if it has been primarily branded with—and had been named for—ventriloquist Terry Fator. But Fator's move to New York–New York opens up the schedule for more stand-up comedy stars such as Gabriel Iglesias, Ray Romano, and George Lopez (collectively branded as the "Aces of Comedy") as well as more days added onto recurring engagements from rotating headliners who have done well in the room, such as magician Shin Lim. ✉ *Mirage Las Vegas, 3400 Las Vegas Blvd. S, Center Strip* ☎ *702/791–7111* ⊕ *mirage.mgmresorts.com.*

Park Theater

CONCERTS | MGM Resorts needed a venue to compete with the Colosseum at Caesars Palace, so the company tore down the Monte Carlo's old showroom to build this flexible arena. The Park can hold up to 6,000 people for concerts, but it also hosts boxing or mixed martial arts. The theater put itself on the map quickly as the exclusive Las Vegas venue for Bruno Mars, Lady Gaga, Cher, and Aerosmith's rocking musical memoir. ✉ *Park MGM, 3770 Las Vegas Blvd. S, Center Strip* ☎ *844/600–7275* ⊕ *parkmgm.mgmresorts.com.*

T-Mobile Arena

CONCERTS | The 20,000-seat, $375-million arena opened in 2016 and instantly became the home of top-tier concerts and events such as the Billboard Music Awards and Academy of Country Music Awards. It's the first Las Vegas arena built with 50 luxury boxes. The arena also is home to the Vegas Golden Knights, the National Hockey League expansion team that went all the way to the Stanley Cup finals in its debut season of 2017–18. ✉ *3780 Las Vegas Blvd. S, Center Strip* ☎ *702/692–1600* ⊕ *www.t-mobilearena.com.*

The Venetian Theatre

CONCERTS | Built for a six-year run of *Phantom of the Opera* and appropriately designed like a European opera house, this 1,800-seat theater has since hosted a variety of short-term and weekend performers. Lately it's under the oversight of concert promoter Live Nation, which has been leaning into classic rock acts such as Styx, Chicago, and ZZ Top. ✉ *The Venetian, 3355 Las Vegas Blvd. S, Center Strip* ☎ *702/414–9000* ⊕ *venetian.com.*

Zappos Theater

CONCERTS | The 7,000-seat concert hall, previously known as the Aladdin Theatre for the Performing Arts, was the only part of the original Aladdin to survive the "implosion" of the resort. It was remodeled in 2013 to host Britney Spears's *Piece of Me* and now has a full rotation of stars ranging from Pitbull to Kelly Clarkson. To create more of a club vibe, a VIP area and two general-admission standing-room areas were added down front, and the balcony isn't used for most shows, bringing capacity down to a cozier 4,500. ✉ *3667 Las Vegas Blvd. S, Center Strip* ☎ *800/745–3000* ⊕ *www.caesars.com.*

Downtown

The Showroom at the Golden Nugget

CONCERTS | The Golden Nugget's upstairs cabaret room is a comfortable movie theater–style layout with 600 roomy seats. Of late it's the home (again) of impressionist Gordie Brown, who is used to sharing the venue with one-night concert acts, which typically play tribal casinos around the country: anyone from the Fabulous Thunderbirds to Jeffrey Osborne. ⊠ *Golden Nugget Hotel & Casino, 129 Fremont St., Downtown* ☎ *702/385–7111* ⊕ *www.goldennugget. com/lasvegas.*

Paradise Road and the East Side

The Theater at Virgin Las Vegas

CONCERTS | Potential naming rights were still up for grabs at the 4,000-seat venue known as The Joint before the old Hard Rock Hotel became the new Virgin Las Vegas. The hotel's closure for a makeover allowed the concert hall to be refurbished with $7 million in upgrades, including new flooring and seating, and redesigned bar and VIP areas. Unchanged is a stage large enough to handle concert tours designed for sports arenas. The property also has a smaller, club-size venue now known as 24 Oxford. In the past, it has hosted stand-up comedy and tribute performers; the latter tradition was preserved with the room's initial booking: *27—A Musical Adventure.* ⊠ *Virgin Las Vegas Hotel & Casino, 4455 Paradise Rd., Paradise Road* ☎ *702/693–5000* ⊕ *virginhotelslv.com.*

Thomas and Mack Center

CONCERTS | This sports arena on the corner of the UNLV campus hosts such sporting events such as the National Finals Rodeo and, of course, Runnin' Rebels basketball. The adjacent **Cox Pavillion** is a smaller venue for women's basketball and the occasional touring children's show. ⊠ *Tropicana Ave. at Swenson St., University District* ☎ *702/739–3267, 866/388–3267* ⊕ *www. thomasandmack.com.*

Westgate Las Vegas Theater

CONCERTS | Once famous as the home base for Elvis Presley, this 1,600-capacity theater (at what was formerly known as the Las Vegas Hilton) has become a bit of an also-ran in recent years, but it regained some of its former profile by luring Barry Manilow out of retirement. Postponed by the pandemic, Manilow had announced a return for at least a few shows in 2021. ⊠ *Westgate Las Vegas, 3000 Paradise Rd., Paradise Road* ☎ *888/796–3564, 702/732–5111* ⊕ *www. westgateresorts.com.*

West Side

Orleans Arena

CONCERTS | The Orleans Arena plays to locals with such family favorites as the Harlem Globetrotters, ice shows, and touring children's productions. The 9,500-seat arena also hosted the debut season of the Henderson Silver Knights, the American Hockey League club of the Vegas Golden Knights while an arena was being built in Henderson. When it comes to concert acts, the Orleans settles for the Strip arenas' hand-me-downs, but has much cheaper beer. ⊠ *4500 W. Tropicana Ave., West Side* ☎ *800/745–3000* ⊕ *www.orleansarena.com.*

Orleans Showroom

CONCERTS | A superwide stage (originally designed to lure TV production) highlights this 800-seat room slightly west of the Strip, which draws a mix of locals and visitors. It hosts the type of headliners who play tribal casinos around the country: Little River Band, Chuck Negron of Three Dog Night, and En Vogue among them. ⊠ *The Orleans Hotel & Casino, 4500 W. Tropicana Ave., West Side* ☎ *702/365–7111* ⊕ *www.orleanscasino.com.*

Did You Know?

Cirque du Soleil plays an outsize role in the Las Vegas entertainment scene, with six shows running simultaneously, including the still-popular aquatic show, *O*.

Summerlin and Red Rock Canyon

Suncoast Showroom

CONCERTS | This local casino, about 15 miles off the beaten path west of the tourist corridor in the Summerlin suburb, has a handsome 450-seat showroom that brings a classic old-Vegas feel to the suburbs. ⌧ *Suncoast Hotel and Casino, 9090 Alta Dr., Summerlin South* ☎ *702/636–7111* ⊕ *www.suncoastcasino. com.*

Performing Arts

Although it's known more for theatrical spectacles than serious theater, Las Vegas does have a lively cultural scene. The arrival of the Smith Center for the Performing Arts Downtown in 2012 was a game-changer, giving new prominence to the city's ballet and philharmonic, which offer full seasons of productions each year. And although some Broadway musicals are still viable on the Strip, The Smith Center also filled the previously missing niche of touring Broadway musicals that drop in for a week or so, and hosts multiweek bookings of extra-commercial musicals such as *Book of Mormon* or *Hamilton.*

Downtown

BALLET

Nevada Ballet Theatre

DANCE | The city's longest-running fine-arts organization (this being Las Vegas, it only dates from 1973) stages five productions each year, anchored by an annual December presentation of *The Nutcracker.* Performing at the Smith Center for the Performing Arts Downtown, the dance company also runs classes from

its studio in Summerlin and builds a bridge from the fine arts scene to the Strip when it partners up with the likes of Cirque du Soleil for its annual Choreographer's Showcase. ⌧ *The Smith Center for the Performing Arts, 361 Symphony Park Ave., Downtown* ☎ *702/243–2623 offices and group sales, 702/749–2000 tickets* ⊕ *www.nevadaballet.org.*

CLASSICAL MUSIC
Las Vegas Philharmonic

MUSIC | Formed in 1998, the Philharmonic performs a nine-show season under the baton of Donato Cabrera, offering monthly concerts during the school year, as well as a four-concert pops series and special events such as playing in sync with a classic film. The orchestra performs at the Smith Center for the Performing Arts Downtown. ⌧ *361 Symphony Park, Downtown* ☎ *702/258–5438 schedule information, 702/749–2000 tickets* ⊕ *www.lvphil.org.*

JAZZ
★ Myron's Cabaret

MUSIC | Tucked alongside the Smith Center's big concert hall is a cozy, 240-seat cabaret (bearing the name of Smith Center president Myron Martin) that creates an upscale vibe and a close communication with performers that's unduplicated in any of the casino venues. Patrons sip wine at tables-for-four while hometown favorites such as Frankie Moreno and Michael Grimm work around visiting headliners that have included trumpet legend Herb Alpert, pianist George Winston, and jazz singer Jane Monheit. Shows are held mostly on weekends but also on occasional weeknights. ⌧ *The Smith Center for the Performing Arts, 361 W. Symphony Park Ave., Downtown* ☎ *702/749–2000* ⊕ *www.thesmithcenter.com* ✉ *From $30.*

THEATER

Away from the Strip, a booming community theater scene caters to the area's many new residents, from retirees to hipsters, who are looking for a low-cost alternative to the pricey shows. Beyond those listed here, most don't have their own performance spaces and instead rent municipal auditoriums or storefront venues for their productions.

Majestic Repertory Theatre

THEATER | Inventive artistic director Troy Heard maximizes a bare-bones storefront space in the heart of a revitalized Main Street to present challenging, consistently interesting titles, often reflecting his interest in immersive theater. Majestic's past triumphs include an aggressive adaptation of *Animal Farm*, and the Las Vegas debuts of *Carrie: The Musical* and *Spring Awakening* ✉ *1217 S. Main St., Downtown* ☎ *702/423–6366* ⊕ *majesticrepertory.com.*

West Side

THEATER

Las Vegas Little Theatre

THEATER | Las Vegas's oldest community theater has branched out beyond the Neil Simon basics. Its main-stage season of six or more titles is augmented by a black-box season of smaller, more adventurous works, and it usually hosts summer festivals of "fringe" comedy or new works. Productions are staged in a sparse but comfortable theater in a strip mall that borders Las Vegas's Chinatown. ✉ *3920 Schiff Dr., West Side* ☎ *702/362–7996* ⊕ *www.lvlt.org.*

Chapter 13

SIDE TRIPS FROM LAS VEGAS

Updated by
Jason Bracelin

👁 Sights	🍴 Restaurants	🛏 Hotels	🛍 Shopping	🍸 Nightlife
★★★★☆	★★☆☆☆	★☆☆☆☆	★☆☆☆☆	★☆☆☆☆

WELCOME TO SIDE TRIPS FROM LAS VEGAS

TOP REASONS TO GO

★ **Alien Encounters:** If you're interested in exploring some government secrets, Area 51 is within a few hours' drive of Las Vegas.

★ **Celebrating Engineering:** It's hard to find a monument to man's ingenuity more impressive than the 1,244-foot concrete span of Hoover Dam.

★ **Enjoying the Outdoors:** With expansive views and acres upon acres of open space, Lake Mead National Recreation Area and Death Valley are great places to reconnect with nature. Death Valley, although prohibitive in summer, is one of the most fascinating national parks in the United States.

★ **Experiencing Geologic History:** The breathtaking 277-mile Grand Canyon was created by the Colorado River over the course of 6 million years, yet it never gets old.

In many ways, the expanse of Nevada to the west, south, and east of Las Vegas is a living museum. The breathtaking Grand Canyon offers a glimpse at 6 million years of erosion, and the Hoover Dam is an incredible exhibit of early-20th-century modern engineering. Beyond these attractions, untrammeled places like Lake Mead National Recreation Area provide a perfect counterpoint to the hubbub of Sin City.

1 Mt. Charleston. Mt. Charleston serves as a lush, "sky island" oasis from the surrounding Mojave Desert, with snow-capped peaks in the winter. It's accessible via a highly scenic drive in under an hour from Las Vegas.

2 Lake Mead National Recreation Area. Lake Mead, the largest reservoir in the United States, and Hoover Dam are about 34 miles from Las Vegas. Nearby, Valley of Fire is a seemingly infinite landscape of sandstone outcroppings, petrified logs, and miles of hiking trails.

3 Area 51. You may not find any aliens, but if it's on your bucket list, the so-called "Area 51" is out in the Nevada desert north of Las Vegas.

4 Grand Canyon National Park. Only about four hours' drive from Las Vegas to the South Rim—less if you head to the West Rim—much of the canyon is a national park. The South Rim is where all the action is, although the North Rim is more for the adventurous. The Skywalk, a relatively new attraction in the West Rim, provides jaw-dropping views straight down.

5 Death Valley National Park. This is a vast, lonely, beautiful place with breathtaking vistas, blasting 120-degree heat in the summer, and mysterious moving rocks. The desert landscape is surrounded by majestic mountains, dry lake beds, spring wildflowers, and Wild West ghost towns.

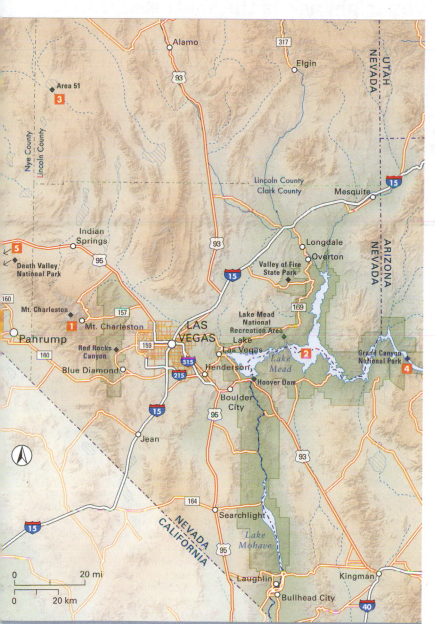

NEVADA
UTAH

Alamo

317

Elgin

93

Area 51
3

Nye County
Lincoln County

Lincoln County
Clark County

Mesquite

15

15

Indian
Springs

Longdale

Overton

5

93

Valley of Fire
State Park

15

Death Valley
National Park

95

169

ARIZONA
NEVADA

160

Mt. Charleston

157

Lake Mead
National
Recreation Area

LAS
VEGAS

1

Mt. Charleston

Pahrump

Lake
Las Vegas

Grand Canyon
National Park

Red Rocks
Canyon

159

2

4

160

Lake
Mead

Blue Diamond

515

Henderson

215

Hoover Dam

Boulder
City

15

95

Jean

93

164

NEVADA
CALIFORNIA

Searchlight

Lake
Mohave

95

15

Kingman

0   20 mi

0   20 km

Laughlin

Bullhead City

40

Nevada takes its name from a Spanish word meaning "snow-covered." So why, you might ask, is the southeastern corner of the state covered in scorching sands and desert landscapes that blend seamlessly with neighboring Arizona? Probably because before Nevada became a state, most of the land in what's now Clark County belonged to Arizona's "lost county of Pah-Ute."

At that time Las Vegas was a tiny settlement situated at the crossroads of the Old Spanish Trail and the Mormon Road. The Mormon town of Callville, later drowned beneath the waters of Lake Mead, was the Pah-Ute county seat. A smattering of agricultural communities sat on the banks of the Colorado River, and steamboats plied the river's waters.

Today the vast majority of the state's population resides in Clark County, and the nearby lakes, state parks, and geological wonders entertain even the most jaded city dwellers. Those pressed for time can take a short drive from Vegas to go hiking in Valley of Fire, rock climbing in Red Rock Canyon, or even skiing on Mt. Charleston in winter. Those with a little more time can explore the wonderland of nearby waterways, stunning rock formations, and laid-back ranching communities. Water enthusiasts head to Lake Mead. Nature lovers find prime wildlife-watching along the Colorado River. And those looking for the grandest spectacle in the region can take the longer drive to the Grand Canyon.

Planning

When to Go

There's no bad time to visit the Grand Canyon, though summer and spring break are the busiest times. Visiting during these peak seasons, as well as holidays, requires patience and a tolerance for crowds. Weather changes on a whim in this exposed high-desert region. The more remote North Rim is off-limits for much of the winter. There are no services, and snow sometimes closes Highway 67 south of Jacob Lake.

Be prepared for hot, exceptionally dry summers in southern Nevada; temperatures can easily hit 105°F. Water destinations such as Lake Mead appeal to sports enthusiasts during the summer and major holiday weekends, while the mild winters are known for attracting retirees. Late fall and early spring are among the most enjoyable times to visit, particularly if you plan on making the trek to destinations such as Death Valley.

As for Death Valley: it's aptly named for the summer months. Believe the hype; summer highs often average 115°F (a record 134°F was set in 1913); winter (primarily February), however, is lovely and the best time for wildflowers, especially if the winter rains are heavy.

Planning Your Time

Plan ahead if you're going to explore Grand Canyon National Park. Reservations for everything fill up during the busy summer months; mule rides and lodging may be reserved up to 13 months in advance. Perhaps the easiest way to visit the West Rim from Vegas is with a tour. **Bighorn Wild West Tours** (☎ *702/385–4676, 888/385–4676* ⊕ *bighornwildwesttours. com*) will pick you up in a Hummer at your Vegas hotel for an all-day trip that includes the shuttle-bus package and lunch for $259. Day-trippers heading to the Lake Mead National Recreation Area can stop at the Alan Bible Visitor Center near Boulder Beach. Death Valley can be reached by car in less than three hours. Leave early in the morning if you go late spring or early fall—midday temperatures can still reach triple digits during this time.

What to Do and Where to Do It

Looking to hook the big one? Head to Lake Mead for excellent year-round fishing. To explore ghost towns and the Old West, check out the eastern reaches of Nevada en route to Death Valley. Nature buffs will find excellent birding and wildlife-watching at nature preserves along the Colorado River, but the grandest natural spectacle's a few hours away at the Grand Canyon. The South and North rims offer outdoor adventure and multiple viewpoints. The privately operated Grand Canyon West, easily accessible from Las

Vegas by a quick flight or a relaxed bus tour, adds a Native American perspective to the world's grandest gorge with three developed viewpoints, horseback and Hummer rides to the rim, and the Skywalk—a glass U-shape bridge 4,000 feet above the Colorado River. Another geological marvel that's a short drive from Las Vegas is the dramatic red sandstone formations and stark views of the Mojave Desert at Valley of Fire State Park.

Drive Times

Approximate drive times from the Center Strip to areas of interest are as follows:

Grand Canyon South Rim: 4½ hours

Grand Canyon North Rim: 6 hours

Mt. Charleston: 45 minutes

Valley of Fire: 1 hour

Hoover Dam: 50 minutes

Area 51: 2½ hours

Death Valley: 2½ hours

Safety Tips

Services can be few and far between in the more remote regions of southern Nevada and northwestern Arizona. Play it safe by packing an emergency car kit with basic automotive repairs, plenty of water, and overnight supplies. To avoid being stranded, let someone know where you're going and which route you plan to take. It's also a good idea to check road conditions (*Nevada* ☎ *877/687–6237*; *Arizona* ☎ *888/411–7623*; *Utah* ☎ *866/511–8824*; *Grand Canyon National Park* ☎ *928/638–7888*) before you set out.

Hotels

Of the nearly 1,000 rooms, cabins, and suites in Grand Canyon National Park, only 203—all at the Grand Canyon Lodge—are at the North Rim. Outside of El Tovar Hotel at the South Rim, frills are hard to find. Rooms are basic but comfortable, and most guests would agree that the best in-room amenity is a view of the canyon. Reservations are a must, especially during the busy summer season.

Lodging options are even more limited on the West Rim. The Hualapai Lodge in Peach Springs and the Hualapai Ranch at Grand Canyon West are run by the Hualapai tribe. The Havasupai Lodge in Supai offers the only rooms in Havasu Canyon. At the South Rim, motel chains make up the most abundant and affordable options in Tusayan, just outside the park entrance (but about 15 minutes from the rim itself) and in Williams, about 50 minutes from the park entrance, and home of the historic railroad line into the park.

Hotel and restaurant reviews have been shortened. For full information, visit Fodors.com.

What It Costs in U.S. Dollars			
$	$$	$$$	$$$$
RESTAURANTS			
under $15	$15–$22	$23–$30	over $30
HOTELS			
under $140	$140–$220	$221–$300	over $300

Restaurants

Dining's generally relaxed and casual in southern Nevada. For the most part you'll find home-cooked American favorites and "South of the Border" specialties.

Dining options in Grand Canyon National Park are limited to the lodge restaurants working under contract with the government. However, you'll find everything from cafeteria food to casual café fare to elegant evening specials. On the Hualapai and Havasupai reservations in Havasu Canyon and at Grand Canyon West, options are limited to tribe-run restaurants.

Mt. Charleston

45 miles northwest of Las Vegas.

In winter Las Vegans drive about an hour to crowd the upper elevations of the Spring Mountains to throw snowballs, sled, cross-country ski, and even hit the slopes at a small ski resort perched atop the eighth-highest peak in the state. In summer they return to wander the high trails, go horseback riding and off-road driving, and escape the valley's 110°F heat (temperatures here can be 20°F–30°F cooler than in the city) in a lush landscape with more than 25 endemic plant and animal species that can only be found in these parts.

Getting Here and Around

Take U.S. 95 from Las Vegas. At the intersection of 95 and Route 157, turn left to Kyle Canyon, home of the township for year-round residents and the two lodge-restaurants. If you're in a hurry to ski, pass this turn and stay on the highway to the next left, Route 156, which takes you to Lee Canyon and the ski resort. But don't stress over the decision. If you take the Kyle road first, there's a scenic 25-minute drive midway up, connecting Kyle to Lee.

■ **TIP→** Speed limits on the drive approaching and climbing Mt. Charleston vary and change quickly; it can be an easy ticket on weekends, when police are out in force. The descending drive especially can lead to

At Mount Charleston winter skiing is only an hour from Las Vegas.

speed violations. It's easy to exceed 55 mph without even realizing it, leading you right into the waiting arms of the law.

Essentials

CAMPGROUND INFORMATION U.S.
Forest Service. ☎ *702/515–5400 Spring Mountains National Recreation Area, 877/444–6777 reservations* ⊕ *www.recreation.gov.*

WEATHER REPORTS Lee Canyon.
☎ *702/593–9500 snow report.*

👁 Sights

⭐ Mt. Charleston
MOUNTAIN—SIGHT | FAMILY | Sin City's refuge for hikers, naturalist, skiers, campers and just about anyone who wants to escape the desert valley for the forest, Mt. Charleston is the highest peak in Clark County and it offers year-round outdoor recreation. Trails include a difficult hike to Mt. Charleston peak, the range's high point. Easier trails lead to seasonal waterfalls or rare, dripping springs where dainty columbine and stunted aspens spill down ravines and hummingbirds zoom. Or they might lead onto high, dry ridges where ancient bristlecone trees have become twisted and burnished with age. ✉ *Kyle Canyon Rd., Outskirts* ✛ *I-15 N to Exit 42A, U.S. 95 N. Turn left onto Kyle Canyon Rd.*

🛏 Hotels

Mount Charleston Lodge and Cabins
$ | HOTEL | At the end of Route 157 at 7,717 feet above sea level you find this lodge—a collection of cabins and a rustic, full-service restaurant, well known among locals—on the perch of Kyle Canyon. **Pros:** seclusion and spectacular views; trails within walking distance; sledding and sleigh rides available during winter. **Cons:** no cable TV (just DVD players); no Wi-Fi; difficult parking on busy weekends, when it's crowded with hikers and diners. ⑤ *Rooms from: $123* ✉ *5355 Kyle Canyon Rd., Outskirts* ☎ *702/872–5408, 800/955–1314* ⊕ *www.*

mtcharlestonlodge.com � *23 rooms* ⦿ *No meals.*

The Retreat on Charleston Peak

$ | HOTEL | This three-story resort is the first stop along Kyle Canyon Road (about 17 miles up). **Pros:** mountain setting; special packages; generally not as crowded as other Mt. Charleston resort. **Cons:** not as high up the mountain as the other lodge; not much to do in immediate vicinity without getting back in a car; bar is small and doesn't seat many. **$** *Rooms from: $129* ✉ *2755 Kyle Canyon Rd., Las Vegas* ☎ *702/872–5500, 888/559–1888* ⦿ *www.retreatoncharlestonpeak.com* ➪ *61 rooms* ⦿ *No meals.*

Activities

HIKING

In summer, hikers escape the heat by traveling 45 minutes up to the Spring Mountains National Recreation Area, known informally as Mt. Charleston, where the U.S. Forest Service maintains more than 50 miles of marked hiking trails for all abilities. Trails vary from the 0.7-mile (one-way) Robber's Roost loop trail to the 6.2-mile Bristlecone Loop trail to the extremely strenuous 10.3-mile (one-way) North Loop Trail, which reaches the Mt. Charleston summit at 11,918 feet; the elevation gain is 4,278 feet. There are also plenty of intermediate trails, along with marathon two-, three-, four-, and five-peak routes only for hikers who are highly advanced (and in peak physical condition). There are trails in the area open for horseback riding, and the Sawmill and Bristlecone trails are open for mountain-bike use. The Mt. Charleston Wilderness is part of the Humboldt–Toiyabe National Forest; for information, contact the **U.S. Forest Service** (☎ *702/515–5400*).

SKIING AND SNOWBOARDING

Hard to believe, but fewer than 50 miles from Downtown Las Vegas there are good skiing and snowboarding trails at the Las Vegas Ski and Snowboard Resort, with a half-pipe, a ski shop, rental equipment, and a day lodge.

★ Lee Canyon

SKIING/SNOWBOARDING | FAMILY | Southern Nevada's skiing headquarters is a mere 47 miles northwest of Downtown Las Vegas. Depending on traffic and weather conditions, it can take less than two hours to go from a 70°F February afternoon on the Strip to the top of a chairlift at an elevation of 9,370 feet. Lee Canyon is equipped with three chairlifts—two quads and a triple—plus a tubing lift (Las Vegas's only one!). The ski resort also offers complimentary coaching for beginners to intermediates, and has a terrain park, a ski shop, rental equipment, and a day lodge with a quick-serve restaurant and full-service bar. Clothing rentals are available. There are 195 acres of slopes: 20% of the trails are for beginners, 60% are intermediate, and 20% are advanced runs. The longest run is 3,000 feet, and there's a vertical drop of nearly 1,000 feet. You know you're at the closest ski resort to Las Vegas when you see the slope names: Blackjack, High Roller, Keno, The Strip, Bimbo 1 and 2, and Slot Alley. In the summer, Lee Canyon is still worth a visit, with scenic chair rides, hiking trails, and an 18-hole disc golf course, which at 9,300 feet, is the highest course in Las Vegas. For skiing, the lifts are open from about late November to early April. Lift tickets are best purchased online and in advance at ⦿ *skilasvegas.com*. Information on transportation and lodging partners in Las Vegas is also found on the website. A telephone call can get you an update on either snow conditions or driving conditions in Nevada. ✉ *6725*

Lee Canyon Rd. ⬧ Take U.S. 95 north to Lee Canyon exit (Hwy. 156), and head up mountain ☎ 702/385–2754, 702/593–9500 Nevada snow conditions, 877/687–6237 Nevada Road Conditions (out of state) ⊕ www.leecanyonlv.com.

Lake Mead Area

Southeast of Las Vegas sits Boulder City, which is quaint, languid, and dotted with a small downtown historic district and neighborhoods, small businesses, and parks—without a single casino. Over the hill from town, enormous Hoover Dam blocks the Colorado River as it enters Black Canyon. Backed up behind the dam is incongruous, deep-blue Lake Mead, the focal point of water-based recreation for southern Nevada and northwestern Arizona, and the major water supplier to seven Southwestern states. The lake is ringed by miles of rugged desert country. The breathtaking wonderland known as Valley of Fire, with its red sandstone outcroppings, petrified logs, petroglyphs, and hiking trails, is along the northern reach of the lake. And all of this is an hour or less from Vegas.

Boulder City

25 miles southeast of Las Vegas.

In the early 1930s Boulder City was built by the federal government to house 5,000 construction workers on the Hoover Dam project. A strict moral code was enforced to ensure timely completion of the dam, and to this day the model city is the only community in Nevada in which gambling is illegal. (Note that the two casinos at either end of Boulder City are just outside the city limits.) After the dam was completed, the town shrank but was kept alive by the management and maintenance crews of the dam and Lake Mead. Today it's a vibrant little Southwestern town.

GETTING HERE AND AROUND
It takes about 30 minutes via U.S. 93/Interstate 515 or Interstate 215/Interstate 515 to get from Las Vegas tourist corridor to Boulder City.

VISITOR INFORMATION
CONTACTS Boulder City Chamber of Commerce. ✉ *465 Nevada Way* ☎ *702/293–2034* ⊕ *www.bouldercitychamber.com.*

👁 Sights

Boulder City/Hoover Dam Museum
MUSEUM | FAMILY | For its size, this small museum inside the Boulder Dam Hotel is well done. It includes hands-on exhibits, oral histories, artifacts from the building of Hoover Dam, and a glimpse at what it was like for Great Depression–era families to pull up roots and settle in the rock and dust of the harsh Mojave Desert. And don't forget to ask museum staff about the city's audio walking tour of 11 historical sites around town. ✉ *1305 Arizona St.* ☎ *702/294–1988* ⊕ *www. bcmha.org* 💲 *Free.*

Boulder Dam Hotel
HISTORIC SITE | Be sure to stop at the Dutch Colonial–style Boulder Dam Hotel, built in 1933. On the National Register of Historic Places, the 20-room bed-and-breakfast once was a favorite getaway for notables, including the man who became Pope Pius XII and actors Will Rogers, Bette Davis, and Shirley Temple. It's still a point of pride for Boulder City and the heart of downtown. The guest rooms have been remodeled to stay competitive but retain a historic feel. There's also a small art gallery featuring the works of local and regional artists, and you can soothe the skin from the dry desert air with a facial at Healing Hands Esthetics by Jeannie. ✉ *1305 Arizona St.* ☎ *702/293–3510* ⊕ *www.boulderdamhotel.com.*

Lake Mead National Recreation Area

Mesquite
TO ST GEORGE, UT →
Riverside
Longdale
Overton
Lost City Museum
Crystal
Valley of Fire State Park
Visitor Center
Nellis Dunes Recreation Lands
LAS VEGAS
SOUTH VIRGIN MOUNTAINS
Jumbo Peak 5,763
ARIZONA
NEVADA
MUDDY MOUNTAINS
Cathedral Peaks
Saddle Peak
BLACK MOUNTAINS
Lake Mead
Lake Las Vegas
Boulder Basin
River
Temple Basin
Gregg Basin
Lake Mead Marina
Boulder Beach
Hoover Dam
Mike O'Callaghan-Pat Tillman Memorial Bridge
Henderson
Boulder City
Alan Bible Visitor Center
Grand Canyon National Park
Lake Mead National Recreation Area
Senator Mountain 5,127
ELDORADO MOUNTAINS
Nelson
Colorado
WHITE HILLS
Dolan Springs
CERBAT MOUNTAINS
Searchlight
TO NEEDLES, CA
Lake Mohave
DETRITAL VALLEY
BLACK MOUNTAINS
Cal-Nev-Ari
NEVADA
CALIFORNIA
Laughlin
Bullhead City
Kingman

0   15 mi
0   15 km

Nevada State Railroad Museum

TRANSPORTATION SITE (AIRPORT/BUS/FERRY/ TRAIN) | FAMILY | The museum pavilion is open daily and features early-20th-century locomotives to check out as well as an elaborate indoor model train exhibit. You can ride the rails aboard the Nevada Southern Railway excursion train, which departs Nevada State Railroad Museum four times a day on weekends for a scenic 35-minute ride through the desert landscape surrounding Boulder City. Some train cars are open-air, allowing you to feel the breeze as you take in the countryside views. For a more participatory experience, book a Rail Explorers rail bike for a 4-mile downhill ride to a rail-side picnic area, then board a train for a ride back to the museum. ✉ *601 Yucca St.* ☎ *702/486–5952* ⊕ *www.boulderrailroadmuseum.org* ✉ *Museum and train rides $10; rail bikes from $85 for 2 riders* ⊘ *No train rides weekdays.*

🍴 Restaurants

The old downtown area of Boulder City has become a fun zone for drinks, dining, and antiques shopping. The center of the action is the 500 block of Nevada Highway (aka Nevada Way).

Boulder Dam Brewing Company

$ | AMERICAN | Across the street from the Boulder Dam Hotel, the Boulder Dam Brewing Company is a lively, family-run brewery decorated with historic Hoover Dam photos and memorabilia. The menu focuses on hearty pub fare and beers with names such as High Scaler Pale Ale and Powder Monkey Pilsner. **Known for:** craft beers; live music; outdoor patio. ⑤ *Average main: $10* ✉ *453 Nevada Hwy.* ☎ *702/243–2739* ⊕ *www.boulderdambrewing.com.*

The Coffee Cup

$ | DINER | The Coffee Cup is a bustling breakfast-and-lunch diner that's been featured on the Food Network's *Diners, Drive-Ins, and Dives*. Tourists line up on weekends for the quintessential small-town diner experience, complete with newspaper-strewn counter seating and the owners' family photos and water-sports memorabilia on the walls. It delivers on the food front, too, with giant portions of favorites such as huevos rancheros, biscuits and gravy, and barbecue sandwiches. **Known for:** hearty breakfasts; large portions; lively atmosphere. ⑤ *Average main: $9* ✉ *512 Nevada Hwy.* ☎ *702/294–0517* ⊕ *www.worldfamouscoffeecup.com* ⊘ *No dinner.*

Milo's Cellar

$ | CAFÉ | Sure, you can sit inside, but what draws locals and tourists alike is the alfresco dining. A well-considered menu offers gourmet sandwiches, soups and salads, platters for wine pairings, and a wide selection of more than 350 vino varieties, 40-plus brands of beer by the glass, and house favorite "Secret Signature Sangria Roja." There are nightly specials that include wine pairings; otherwise, you can sip your cappuccino and watch the tourists stroll by. **Known for:** generous wine selection; alfresco dining; nightly dinner specials. ⑤ *Average main: $12* ✉ *538 Nevada Hwy.* ☎ *702/293–9540* ⊕ *www.milosbouldercity.com.*

Did You Know?

Franklin D. Roosevelt dedicated Hoover Dam on September 30, 1935, and the date is still part of the celestial map found on the dam's terrazzo floor.

Hoover Dam

8 miles northeast from Boulder City.

In 1928 Congress authorized $175 million for construction of a dam on the Colorado River to control destructive floods, provide a steady water supply to seven Colorado River basin states, and generate electricity. Considered one of the seven wonders of the industrial world, the art deco Hoover Dam is 726 feet high (the equivalent of a 70-story building) and at the base it's 660 feet thick (more than the length of two football fields). Construction required 4.4 million cubic yards of concrete—enough to build a two-lane highway from San Francisco to New York.

GETTING HERE AND AROUND

Hoover Dam is about a 45-minute drive from Las Vegas via U.S. 93; it's about 15 minutes from Boulder City.

 ## Sights

★ Hoover Dam

DAM | FAMILY | Originally referred to as Boulder Dam, this colossal structure, widely considered one of the greatest engineering achievements in history, was later officially named Hoover Dam in recognition of President Herbert Hoover's role in the project. Look for artist Oskar Hansen's plaza sculptures, which include the 30-foot-tall *Winged Figures of the Republic* (the statues and terrazzo floor patterns were copied at the Smith Center for the Performing Arts in Downtown Las Vegas).

The tour itself is a tradition that dates back to 1937, and you can still see the old box office on top of the dam. But now the ticketed tours originate in the modern visitor center (or online), with two options. The cheaper, more popular one is the **Powerplant Tour**, which starts every 15 minutes. It's a half-hour, guided tour that includes a short film and then a 537-foot elevator ride to two points of interest: the chance to stand on top of one of the 30-foot pipes where you can hear and feel the water rushing through to the generators, and the more impressive eight-story room housing still-functional power generators. Self-paced exhibits follow the guided portion, with good interactive museum exhibits and a great indoor/outdoor patio view of the dam from the river side. The more extensive **Hoover Dam Tour** includes everything on the Powerplant Tour but limits the group size to 20 and spends more time inside the dam, including a peek through the air vents. Tours run from 9 to 5 all year, with the last Powerplant tour leaving at 3:45 pm daily, and the last Hoover Dam Tour at 3:30. Visitors for both tours submit to security screening comparable to an airport. January and February are the slowest months, and mornings generally are less busy. The top of the dam is open to pedestrians and vehicles, but you have to remain in your vehicle after sundown. Visitors can still drive over the dam for sightseeing, but cannot continue into Arizona; you have to turn around and come back after the road dead-ends at a scenic lookout (with a snack bar and store) on the Arizona side. ■**TIP**➔ **The dam's High Scaler Café offers fare such as cold drinks, ice cream, and hamburgers.** ✉ *U.S. 93, east of Boulder City, Boulder City* ☎ *323/645–2845, 866/730–9097, 888/248–1259 security, road, and Hoover Dam crossing information* ⊕ *www.usbr. gov/lc/hooverdam* 🎫 *Guided Powerplant Tour $15, Guided Dam Tour $30, self-guided visitor center $10; garage parking $10 (free parking on Arizona-side surface lots).*

The Mike O'Callaghan–Pat Tillman Memorial Bridge

BRIDGE/TUNNEL | The Hoover Dam now has sightseer competition from the spectacular bridge that was built to bypass it. The Mike O'Callaghan–Pat Tillman Memorial Bridge (named for the popular Nevada governor and the Arizona football star who was killed in Afghanistan) is the western hemisphere's longest single-span concrete arch bridge. It runs 1,905 feet long, and towers nearly 900 feet above the river and 280 feet above Hoover Dam. You don't see much by driving over it—scarcely anything from a sedan—but walking it is quite a thrill. A pedestrian walkway is well separated from the driving lanes, the access path to the bridge has informational signage, and ramps offer an alternative to the steps. There are restrooms in the parking lot (labeled "Memorial Bridge Plaza"), where it can be hard to find a parking space on weekends. (If you can't get a spot, drive a few yards past the parking lot entrance and turn left into the lot for a trailhead on the other side of the road.) Bring water and sunscreen for the walk, and be prepared for broiling summer temperatures; there is no shade. ■**TIP**→ **Remember to take Exit 2 if you want to go to the dam instead of the bypass bridge, or you will have to drive across it and turn back to visit the dam.** ✉ *U.S. 93, Boulder City.*

🏃 Activities

RAFTING

Black Canyon, just below Hoover Dam, is the place for river running near Las Vegas. Guided raft trips down the Colorado River are available year-round from the Hoover Dam to Willow Beach. It is the Southwest's only natural water trail and includes views of vertical canyon walls, bighorn sheep on the slopes, peregrine falcons, and feeder streams and waterfalls coming off the bluffs. Transportation to and from Las Vegas is available.

Black Canyon/Willow Beach River Adventures

WHITE-WATER RAFTING | FAMILY | If you're interested in seeing the canyon and Hoover Dam on large motor-assisted rafts, Black Canyon/Willow Beach River Adventures has group excursions launching from the base of the dam for both 3-hour and 90-minute tours. The half-day excursion includes lunch; the shorter "postcard" tour lasts about 90 minutes but includes only 30 minutes on the raft. Round-trip Las Vegas transportation is available. All tours depart from Lake Mead RV Village. ✉ *Lake Mead RV Village, 286 Lakeshore Rd., Boulder City* ☎ *800/455–3490* ⊕ *hooverdamtouradventures.com* 🛏 *From $69.*

Desert Adventures

WHITE-WATER RAFTING | For a more hands-on approach, try a guided kayak trip through Black Canyon with Desert Adventures. The daylong excursion, including a soak in hot springs, slot-canyon hike, and lunch, requires an additional $27 permit fee, which are limited and best purchased in advance. They'll pick you up at the Hoover Dam Lodge or from your hotel on the Strip. ✉ *Hoover Dam Lodge, 18000 U.S. Hwy. 93, Boulder City* ☎ *702/293–5026* ⊕ *www.kayaklasvegas.com* 🛏 *From $195.*

Lake Mead

About 4 miles from Hoover Dam.

Lake Mead is actually the Colorado River backed up behind Hoover Dam, making it the nation's largest man-made reservoir: it covers 225 square miles, is 110 miles long, and has an irregular shoreline that extends for 550 miles.

GETTING HERE AND AROUND

From Hoover Dam, travel west on U.S. 93 to the intersection with Lakeshore Drive to reach Alan Bible Visitor Center, which reopened in 2013 with a new welcome film and exhibits after two years and nearly $3 million in renova-tions. It's open every day, 9 to 4:30. Call ☎ 702/293–8990 for more information.

VISITOR INFORMATION
Alan Bible Visitor Center

The main information center for Lake Mead National Recreation Area is complete with a high-def film about the park, and open seven days a week. Also here are a bookstore, nature exhibits, and a cactus garden. It's at the Lake Mead turnoff from U.S. 93, before you get to the pay booth for park entry. A second, smaller visitor center at the park head-quarters is in downtown Boulder City at 601 Nevada Way. ⊠ *10 Lakeshore Dr., Boulder City* ☎ *702/293–8990* ⊕ *www.nps.gov/lake.*

● Sights

Lake Mead

BODY OF WATER | People come to Lake Mead primarily for boating and fishing. Adjacent marinas offer watercraft rentals, restaurants, and paddle-wheeler cruises; the turn-off for them is just past the entry gate. A few cultivated areas allow for swimming but they are not desig-nated swim beaches, so no lifeguards are on duty. In fact, the National Park Service highly recommends wearing life jackets, as high winds come up fast on the lake making for potentially dangerous swimming conditions. The rocky Boulder Beach swimming area is about 2 miles past the visitor center. ⚠ **A fishing license is required within the states of Nevada and Arizona, so if you plan on fishing Lake Mead, get one.** ⊠ *Alan Bible Visitor Center, 10 Lakeshore Dr., Boulder City* ☎ *702/293–8990* ⊕ *www.nps.gov/lake* 🎫 *$25 per vehicle, good for 7 days; lake-use fee $16 for 1st vessel, good for 7 days. Annual pass is $45 per vehicle or $50 per vessel. Regular camping is $20 per site, per night; group camping (12–30 people) is $80 per site, per night.*

⛹ Activities

BOATING
Las Vegas Boat Harbor and Lake Mead Marina

BOATING | These side-by-side marinas are accessed via Lakeshore Road from a branch road; look for a right turn soon after you pass through the Boulder City admission gate near the Alan Bible Vis-itor Center. They are jointly operated, with combined slips of nearly 1,500. In addition to boater amenities, both have marina stores and casual restaurants. A variety of watercraft and boats can be rented by the day or hour, and the marinas provide the closest services to nearby Boulder Beach, a popular public swimming beach. ⊠ *490 Horsepower Cove Rd., Boulder City* ☎ *702/293–1191* ⊕ *www.boatinglakemead.com.*

LAKE CRUISES
Lake Mead Cruises

BOATING | At Lake Mead Cruises you can board the 275-passenger *Desert Princess,* an authentic Mississippi-style paddle wheeler that plies a portion of the lake, offering impressive views of Hoover Dam, the bypass bridge, and ancient rock formations such as an extinct volcano called Fortification Hill. Brunch and dinner cruises are available seasonally, while 90-minute sightseeing cruises are offered year-round. Advance tickets are offered online. ⊠ *490 Horsepower Cove Rd., Boulder City* ⊹ *Just north of Alan Bible Visitor Center, look for signs to Hemenway Harbor* ☎ *866/292–9191* ⊕ *www.lakemeadcruis-es.com* 🎫 *From $35.*

Valley of Fire

50 miles northeast of Las Vegas.

The 56,000-acre Valley of Fire State Park was dedicated in 1935 as Nevada's first state park. Valley of Fire takes its name from distinctive coloration of its rocky landscape, which ranges from lavender to tangerine to bright red, giving the vistas along the park road an otherworldly appearance.

GETTING HERE AND AROUND

From Las Vegas, take Interstate 15 north about 35 miles to Exit 75–Route 169 and continue 15 miles. If you're coming from the northern Overton Arm of Lake Mead, look for the sign announcing the Valley of Fire and head west onto Valley of Fire Highway for a few miles to the park's visitor center. ■ **TIP→ It may also be possible to see some of the remnants of St. Thomas, a settlement within the park that was washed away by the Colorado River after completion of the Hoover Dam, as drought conditions have lowered lake levels dramatically. It's located off unpaved St. Thomas Road north of Overton Beach.**

👁 Sights

Lost City Museum

MUSEUM | FAMILY | The Moapa Valley has one of the finest collections of ancestral Puebloan artifacts in the American Southwest. Lost City, officially known as Pueblo Grande de Nevada, was a major outpost of the ancient culture. The museum's artifacts include baskets, weapons, a restored Basketmaker pit house, reconstructed pueblo houses, and black-and-white photographs of the excavation of Lost City in the 1920s and '30s. To get to the Lost City Museum from Valley of Fire, pass the park's east entrance and head north onto Northshore Drive, which becomes state route 169, toward Overton. ✉ *721 S. Moapa Valley Blvd., Overton* ☎ *702/397–2193* ⊕ *lostcitymuseum.org* 💲*$5* 🕐 *Closed Mon. and Tues.*

★ Valley of Fire State Park

NATIVE SITE | FAMILY | Valley of Fire's jumbled rock formations are remnants of hardened sand dunes more than 150 million years old. You find petrified trees and one of the park's most photographed features—Elephant Rock—just steps off the main road. Mysterious petroglyphs (carvings etched into the rocks) are believed to be the work of the Basketmaker and early Puebloan people, with their occupation in the area estimated from 300 BC to AD 1150. The easy, essential trail is Mouse's Tank, named for an outlaw who hid out here and managed to find water; so will you in cooler months (but not for drinking). It's a short walk with views of petroglyphs and shaded by steep canyon walls. Sci-fi fans also might recognize Fire Canyon as the alien planet in *Starship Troopers* and several other movies.

The **Valley of Fire Visitor Center** was remodeled in 2011 and has displays on the park's history, ecology, archaeology, and recreation, as well as slide shows and films, and information about the two campgrounds (72 campsites, 20 of them with power and water for RVs) within the park. Campsites at Atlatl Rock and Arch Rock Campgrounds are available on a first-come, first-served basis. The park is open year-round; the best times to visit, especially during the heat of summer, are sunrise and sunset, when the light is truly spectacular. ✉ *29450 Valley of Fire Rd., Overton* ✛ *I–15 N to Exit 75. Merge onto Valley of Fire Hwy. Entrance to park is about 14 miles* ☎ *775/684-2770* ⊕ *parks.nv.gov/parks/valley-of-fire* 💲*$10 per vehicle; $15 for non-Nevada vehicles; camping is $20 per vehicle, per night; $25 for non-Nevada vehicles.*

Area 51

148 miles north of Las Vegas.

It's a long way to drive just to buy a T-shirt and take some quirky photos, but for those with Area 51 on their bucket list it can be worth it. It wasn't until 2013 that the CIA, following a Freedom of Information Act request, acknowledged the existence of the restricted Air Force installation, but conspiracy theories have been swirling around the desert facility for years. It's been rumored to contain everything from scientists replicating crashed alien spacecraft to those creating time travel. What we actually do know is the Air Force does, in fact, test top-secret aircraft and related technology here, resulting in many of the strange sights and sounds that have been reported for years. But it's all the mystery and secrecy, wrapped up in a desolate enigma in a locale that looks like the set of a 1950s sci-fi flick. And it's kept folks from around the world driving to the edge of the landmark (also known as Groom Lake and Dreamland) and its closest neighbor, the tiny hamlet of Rachel, Nevada, population about 100.

Keep in mind, it's illegal to get too close to the installation, launch drones in the area, or take photographs in the nearby vicinity. Fines are high, and military police have the authority to use deadly force if necessary. Locals can fill you in on the particulars, or simply heed the posted signs.

Getting Here and Around

To get to Rachel, head north from Las Vegas on Interstate 15, then take U.S. 93 north for about 85 miles; you'll pass Alamo and Ash Springs, then go left onto Highway 318 and stay on it for less than a mile before veering left onto Highway 375, Nevada's officially designated "Extraterrestrial Highway." Drive about 40 miles to reach Rachel and the famous Little A'Le'Inn. Little more than a simple roadside diner, it's the main destination for most visitors since places to stop and eat are few and far between. Keep in mind gas stations are also limited in this area, so fuel up before the trip or in Alamo, and look out for cows grazing in the area as they tend to cross the E.T. Highway. The drive from Las Vegas can take 2½ hours.

Tours

Adventure Tours
DRIVING TOURS | This tour company provides daylong Area 51 photo tours in luxury SUVs, stopping in Rachel and taking in the Air Force installation's guarded perimeter as well as highlights along the way, including ancient petroglyphs and dry lakes associated with UFO lore. The tour includes lunch, unlimited snacks, and pickup at your Las Vegas hotel. It operates regularly on Monday, Wednesday, and Saturday (or other days if you have a group of four or more). ☎ 702/889–8687 ⊕ www.vegassightseeing.com ⊠ From $199.

⊙ Sights

Pahranagat National Wildlife Refuge
NATURE PRESERVE | If you're looking for a bookend to your trip to Area 51 that, well, is just more down-to-earth, drop by these spring-fed wetlands, which serve as a stopover for thousands of birds migrating along the Pacific Flyway. The 5,380-acre Pahranagat National Wildlife Refuge is a chain of lakes, marshes, and meadows that provides a convenient stop on the Pacific Flyway for ducks, herons, egrets, eagles, and other species. The Upper Lake is the most accessible, with campsites, picnic tables, and observation points. For a bird list, stop at the refuge headquarters located 4 miles south of Alamo, at milepost 32 off U.S. 93, which also features interactive exhibits, a

15-minute movie and short nature trails. The best times to see more than 230 species of birds are early morning and late evening during the spring and fall migrations. ☎ 775/725–3417 ⊕ www. fws.gov/refuge/pahranagat ⊠ Free.

🍴 Restaurants

Little A'Le'Inn

$ | **AMERICAN** | Even if you aren't hungry for a tasty "alien burger," a pilgrimage to this restaurant/bar is practically a requirement to earn those Area 51 bragging rights. While the food is typical diner fare such as chili and sandwiches, it's very reasonably priced, and the owners put some tender loving care into keeping their oddly famous outpost in top shape. **Known for:** reasonably priced diner fare with pretty good burgers; colorful owners; alien-inspired gifts. ⑤ Average main: $7 ⊠ 9631 Old Mill St., Alamo ⊹ Hwy. 375, about 45 miles northwest of Ash Springs ☎ 775/729–2515 ⊕ www. littlealeinn.com.

Grand Canyon

If you take only one side trip from Las Vegas, make it to the Grand Canyon. The Colorado River has carved through colorful and often contorted layers of rock, in some places more than 1 mile down, to expose a geologic profile spanning a time between 1.7 billion and 2.5 billion years ago—one-third of the planet's life. There's nothing like standing on the rim and looking down and across at layers of distance, color, and shifting light. Add the music of a canyon wren's merry, descending call echoing off the cliffs and spring water tinkling from the rocks along a trail, and you may sink into a reverie as deep and beautiful as the canyon.

Getting Here and Around

There are two main access points to the canyon: the **South Rim** and the **North Rim,** both within the national park and both about the same distance from Las Vegas by road. The canyon is doable on a very long day-trip, but because of the amount of driving and traffic you might encounter, an overnight is more desirable if you are going on your own. The hordes of visitors converge mostly on the South Rim in summer, for good reason. Grand Canyon Village and the gateway community of Tusayan are here, with most of the lodging and camping, restaurants and stores, and museums in the park, along with the airport and the most popular rim roads, scenic overlooks, and trailheads into the canyon. The South Rim can be accessed either from the main entrance near Tusayan or by the East entrance near the Desert View Watchtower.

Directions to the South Rim: The South Rim is 278 miles southeast of Las Vegas (about a four-hour drive from Hoover Dam). Take Highway 93 south to Interstate 40 heading east. At Highway 64 drive 60 miles north to the park's southern entrance. ■**TIP**➔ **In summer, roads are congested, so park your car and take the free shuttle to visit popular sights along the South Rim. Traffic's lighter and parking is easier October through April.**

The North Rim, by contrast, stands 1,000 feet higher than the South Rim and has a more alpine climate, with twice as much annual precipitation. Here, in the deep forests of the Kaibab Plateau, the crowds are thinner (only 10% of the park's total visitors), the facilities fewer, and the views, arguably, even more spectacular.

Directions to the North Rim. The North Rim is 275 miles northeast of Vegas. Drive 128 miles north on Interstate 15 to Route 9 and then travel east 10 miles to Route 59/Route 389. Continue east 65 miles to U.S. 89A and head 30 miles east to

Route 67 which dead-ends at the North Rim entrance.

If you don't have time for the 4½- to 6-hour drive to the North or South Rim, the **West Rim**—about 2½ hours from Las Vegas—is a more manageable excursion, especially now that the once-pitted road up to the entrance is entirely paved. As an alternative to driving, you can look into a helicopter, Hummer, or coach tour. Many tours will transport you to and from your Vegas hotel; park fees and lunch are usually part of the package. At the West Rim, which isn't part of the Grand Canyon National Park and is run by the Hualapai tribe, you can view the canyon from the horseshoe-shape Skywalk.

Directions to the West Rim: Grand Canyon West is 121 miles southeast of Las Vegas. Travel 72 miles south on Highway 93 to Pierce Ferry Road (about 30 minutes from Hoover Dam) and travel north 28 miles to Diamond Bar Road. Drive 21 miles on Diamond Bar Road to the entrance at Grand Canyon West Airport, where a shuttle takes visitors to the West Rim.

Safety and Precautions

To report a security problem, contact the Park Police stationed at all visitor centers. There are no pharmacies at the North or South Rim. Prescriptions can be delivered daily to the South Rim Clinic from Flagstaff. A health center is staffed by physicians from 8 am to 6 pm, seven days a week (reduced hours in winter). Emergency medical services are available 24 hours a day.

CONTACTS Emergency services. ☎ *911, 9–911 in park lodgings.* **North Country HealthCare Grand Canyon Clinic.** ☎ *928/638–2551.* **Park Police.** ☎ *928/638–7805.*

Admission Fees and Permits

A fee of $35 per vehicle or $20 per person for pedestrians and cyclists is good for one week's access at both rims.

The $70 Grand Canyon Pass gives unlimited access to the park for 12 months. The annual $80 America the Beautiful **National Parks and Recreational Land Pass** (☎ *888/275–8747* ⊕ *store.usgs.gov/pass*) provides unlimited access to all national parks and federal recreation areas for 12 months.

No permits are needed for day hikers, but **backcountry permits** (☎ *928/638–7875* ⊕ *www.nps.gov/grca* ✉ *$10, plus $8 per person per night*) are necessary for overnight hikers. Permits are limited, so make your reservation as far in advance as possible—they're taken up to four months ahead of arrival. **Camping** in the park is restricted to designated campgrounds (☎ *877/444–6777* ⊕ *www.recreation.gov*).

Tours

You can take organized bus and air tours from Las Vegas to the Grand Canyon. Once you are in the park, transportation-services desks are maintained at El Tovar, Bright Angel, Maswik Lodge, and Yavapai Lodge (closed in winter) in Grand Canyon Village. The desks provide information and can handle bookings for sightseeing tours, taxi and shuttle services, and mule and horseback rides. On the North Rim, Grand Canyon Lodge has general information about local services.

AIR AND BUS TOURS
Ground tours to the Grand Canyon can be had from the Grand Canyon Tour Company, but if you're short on time (and can check your fear of heights at the bell desk), consider winging your way there in a small plane or helicopter.

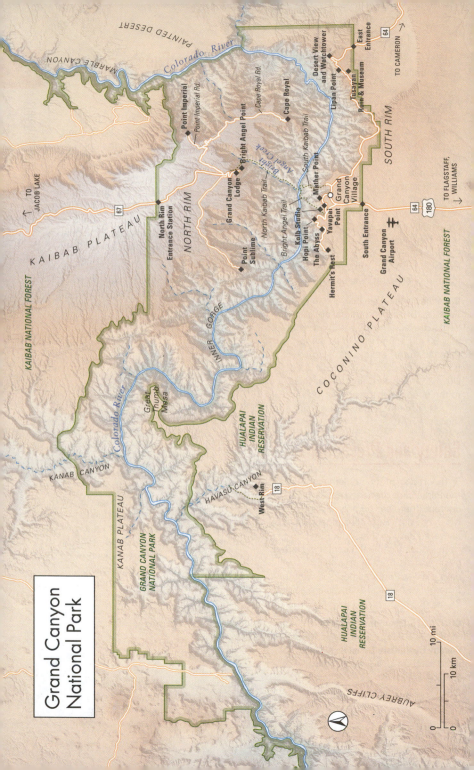

Grand Canyon National Park

PAINTED DESERT

MARBLE CANYON

Colorado River

TO CAMERON

East Entrance

TO JACOB LAKE

KAIBAB PLATEAU

North Rim Entrance Station

NORTH RIM

Point Imperial

Point Imperial Rd.

Cape Royal Rd.

Bright Angel Point

Cape Royal

Grand Canyon Lodge

North Kaibab Trail

Bright Angel Creek

South Kaibab Trail

Desert View and Watchtower

Lipan Point

Tusayan Ruin & Museum

SOUTH RIM

TO FLAGSTAFF, WILLIAMS

Mather Point

Point Sublime

Bright Angel Trail

Kolb Studio

Hopi Point

Yavapai Point

Grand Canyon Village

The Abyss

South Entrance

Grand Canyon Airport

Hermit's Rest

KAIBAB NATIONAL FOREST

INNER GORGE

Colorado River

COCONINO PLATEAU

Great Thumb Mesa

HUALAPAI INDIAN RESERVATION

KANAB CANYON

KAIBAB NATIONAL FOREST

KANAB PLATEAU

HAVASU CANYON

West Rim

GRAND CANYON NATIONAL PARK

HUALAPAI INDIAN RESERVATION

AUBREY CLIFFS

10 mi

10 km

A host of air-tour companies will give you a bird's-eye view of the Strip, Hoover Dam, and Lake Mead on the way to the Grand Canyon rim and even down to the Colorado River bed itself on tours as brief as two hours and as inexpensive as $200 per person. Helicopter tours are usually more expensive than those in a small fixed-wing plane. All possible permutations of flight plans and amenities are available, from lunch to river rafting to overnight accommodations. Most tours include pickup and drop-off service from your hotel (sorry, Hotshot, you get picked up in a van or limo, not by a chopper). Weekday tours actually fill up faster than weekends; it can't hurt to book a few days in advance. The scenery is spectacular, but the ride can be bumpy and cold, even in summertime.

Grand Canyon Helicopters

AIR EXCURSIONS | If you are looking for an aerial day tour to the Grand Canyon, this company can provide you with a trip to either the South, North, or West Rim, by helicopter. You can also book overnight lodging through the company to extend your trip. Air tours leave from the company's terminal at McCarran Airport. ⊠ *McCarran International Airport, 275 E. Tropicana Ave., Las Vegas* ☎ *702/835–8477, 855/326–9617* ⊕ *www.grandcanyonhelicopter.com* ✉ *Tours from $249.*

Grand Canyon Tour Company

AIR EXCURSIONS | The largest company in Las Vegas offering day-trip bus tours to the Grand Canyon, this company offers several different alternatives, many of which are day-trips. But you can also book lodging at the Grand Canyon if you want to do an overnight. The company picks up at most major Las Vegas hotels. ☎ *702/655–6060, 800/222–6966* ⊕ *www.grandcanyontourcompany.com* ✉ *Tours from $79.99.*

Maverick Helicopter Tours

AIR EXCURSIONS | Travelers with more money than time will want to arrange an air tour with Maverick. The cheapest options take you over the canyon and back to Las Vegas. If you pay more, you'll get to land and do a tour in the canyon itself, either at the West or South Rim. ⊠ *Henderson Executive Airport, 1620 Jet Stream Dr., Henderson* ☎ *702/261–0007, 888/261–4414* ⊕ *www.maverickhelicopter.com* ✉ *Tours from $199.*

Papillon

AIR EXCURSIONS | Offering a bird's-eye view of either the West or North Rim, these aerial tours travel by either plane or helicopter. Helicopter tours leave from Las Vegas while airplane tours leave from Boulder City. The company offers pickup at all major hotels in Las Vegas. Papillon also offers bus tours of the canyon to the West Rim. ☎ *702/736–7243, 888/635–7272* ⊕ *www.papillon.com* ✉ *Tours from $104.*

Scenic Airlines

AIR EXCURSIONS | Flying out of Boulder City, Scenic offers either flyover tours of the canyon by airplane or tours that include a land component. Or you can simply take a bus tour to the South or West Rim. The company offers pickup and drop-off service from all major Las Vegas hotels. ☎ *702/638–3300, 800/634–6801* ⊕ *www.scenic.com* ✉ *Bus tours from $79; air tours from $104.*

Sundance Helicopters

AIR EXCURSIONS | Take a luxury tour of the Grand Canyon by helicopter or bus. More expensive options drop you off at the bottom of the West Rim for a champagne picnic. Hotel pickups and drop-offs are made in a stretch limousine. ☎ *702/736–0606, 800/653–1881* ⊕ *www.sundancehelicopters.com.*

Visitor Centers

SOUTH RIM

Desert View Information Center

INFO CENTER | Near the watchtower, at Desert View Point, this nonprofit Grand Canyon Association store and information center has a nice selection of books, park pamphlets, gifts, and educational materials. It's also a handy place to pick up maps and info if you enter the park at the Eastern entrance. All sales from the association stores go to support the park programs. ⊠ *Eastern entrance, Grand Canyon National Park* ☎ *800/858–2808, 928/638–7888.*

Grand Canyon Verkamp's Visitor Center

INFO CENTER | This small visitor center is named for the Verkamp family, who operated a curios shop on the South Rim for more than a hundred years. The building serves as an official visitor center, ranger station (get your Junior Ranger badges here), bookstore, and museum, with compelling exhibits on the Verkamps and other pioneers in this region. ⊠ *Desert View Dr., Grand Canyon Village* ⊕ *Across from El Tovar Hotel* ☎ *928/638–7146.*

Grand Canyon Visitor Center

INFO CENTER | The park's main orientation center provides pamphlets and resources to help plan your visit. It also holds engaging interpretive exhibits on the park. Rangers are on hand to answer questions and aid in planning canyon excursions. A daily schedule of ranger-led hikes and evening lectures is available, and a 20-minute film about the history, geology, and wildlife of the canyon plays every 30 minutes in the theater. The bicycle rental office, a small café, and a huge gift store are also in this complex. It's a 5-minute walk from here to Mather Point, or a short ride on the shuttle bus, which can take you into Grand Canyon Village. The visitor center is also accessible from the village via a leisurely 2-mile walk on the Greenway Trail, a paved pathway that meanders through the forest. ⊠ *East side of Grand Canyon Village, 450 Hwy. 64* ☎ *928/638–7888.*

Yavapai Geology Museum

INFO CENTER | Learn about the geology of the canyon at this Grand Canyon Association museum and bookstore that doubles as a visitor center. You can also catch the park shuttle bus or pick up information for the Rim Trail here. The views of the canyon and Phantom Ranch from inside this historic building are stupendous. ⊠ *1 mile east of Market Plaza, Grand Canyon Village* ☎ *928/638–7890.*

NORTH RIM

North Rim Visitor Center

View exhibits, peruse the bookstore, and pick up useful maps and brochures at this visitor center. Interpretive programs are often scheduled in summer. If you're craving refreshments, it's a short walk from here to the Roughrider Saloon at the Grand Canyon Lodge. ⊠ *Near Grand Canyon Lodge at North Rim, Grand Canyon National Park* ☎ *928/638–7864* ⊕ *www.nps.gov/grca.*

Visitor Information

PARK CONTACT INFORMATION

Grand Canyon National Park

Before you go, you can view and print the complimentary *Pocket Map and Service Guide,* updated regularly, from the Grand Canyon National Park website. You can also pick up a copy at the entrance stations and the visitor centers. ☎ *928/638–7888* ⊕ *www.nps.gov/grca.*

South Rim

278 miles east of Las Vegas.

Visitors to the canyon converge mostly on the South Rim, and mostly during the summer. Believe it or not, the average stay in the park is a mere four hours, so those doing the canyon as a day-trip from Las Vegas aren't really being short-changed by the short stay. The 25-mile rim road (Desert View Drive) allows easy access to several highlights, including canyon viewpoints, the Tusayan Ruin, and the Yavapai Geology Museum with its incredible glassed-in views from the observation room. Day trekkers can also take a short hike down into the canyon to experience it close-up.

GETTING HERE AND AROUND

By car, travel south on U.S. 93 to Kingman, Arizona; Interstate 40 east from Kingman to Williams; then Route 64 and U.S. 180 to the edge of the abyss. The South Rim is open to car traffic year-round, though access to some of the overlooks west of Grand Canyon Village is limited to shuttle buses from March through November. Roads leading to the South Rim near Grand Canyon Village and the parking areas along the rim are congested in summer as well. If you visit from October through February, you can usually experience only light to moderate traffic and have no problem with parking.

When driving off major highways in low-lying areas, watch for rain clouds. Flash floods from sudden summer rains can be deadly.

There are also free shuttle routes. Hermits Rest Route operates from March through November between Grand Canyon Village and Hermits Rest; it runs every 15 to 30 minutes from as early as 5 am to 30 minutes after sunset, depending on the season. The Village Route operates year-round in the village area from one hour before sunrise until as late as 9 pm depending on the time of year; it's the easiest access to the Grand Canyon Visitor Center. The Kaibab Rim Route travels from Grand Canyon Visitor Center to viewpoints such as Yaki Point and the Yavapai Geology Museum.

TOURS

Narrated motor-coach tours on the South Rim cover Hermits Rest Road and Desert View Drive. Other options include sunrise and sunset tours. Prices range from around $22 to $65 per person.

👁 Sights

SCENIC DRIVES
Desert View Drive

SCENIC DRIVE | This heavily traveled 25-mile stretch of road follows the rim from the east entrance to Grand Canyon Village. Starting from the less congested entry near Desert View, road warriors can get their first glimpse of the canyon from the 70-foot-tall watchtower, the top of which provides the highest viewpoint on the South Rim. Six developed canyon viewpoints in addition to unmarked pullouts, the remains of an Ancestral Puebloan dwelling at the Tusayan Ruin and Museum, and the secluded and lovely Buggeln picnic area make for great stops along the South Rim. The Kaibab Rim Route shuttle bus travels a short section of Desert View Drive and takes 50 minutes to ride round-trip without getting off at any of the stops: Grand Canyon Visitor Center, South Kaibab Trailhead, Yaki Point, Pipe Creek Vista, Mather Point, and Yavapai Geology Museum. ✉ *Grand Canyon National Park.*

Hermit Road

SCENIC DRIVE | The Santa Fe Company built Hermit Road, formerly known as West Rim Drive, in 1912 as a scenic tour route. Nine overlooks dot this 7-mile stretch, each worth a visit. The road is filled with hairpin turns, so make sure you adhere to posted speed limits. A 1½-mile Greenway trail offers easy access to cyclists looking to enjoy the original 1912 Hermit Rim Road. From March through November, Hermit Road is closed to private auto traffic because of congestion; during this period, a free shuttle bus carries visitors to all the overlooks. Riding the bus round-trip without getting off at any of the viewpoints takes 80 minutes; the return trip stops only at Hermits Rest, Pima, Mohave, and Powell points. ✉ *Grand Canyon National Park.*

Continued on page 310

EXPLORING THE
COLORADO RIVER

High in Colorado's Rocky Mountains, the Colorado River begins
as a catch-all for the snowmelt off the mountains west of the
Continental Divide. By the time it reaches the Grand Canyon,
the Colorado has been joined by multiple tributaries to become
a raging river, red with silt as it sculpts spectacular landscapes.
A network of dams can only partially tame this mighty river.

Snaking its way through five states, the Colorado River is an essential water source to the arid Southwest. Its natural course runs 1,450 miles from its origin in Colorado's La Poudre Pass Lake in Rocky Mountain National Park to its final destination in the Gulf of California, also called the Sea of Cortez. In northern Arizona, the Colorado River has been a powerful force in shaping the Grand Canyon, where it flows 4,000 to 6,000 feet below the rim. Beyond the canyon, the red river takes a lazy turn at the Arizona–Nevada border, where Hoover Dam creates the reservoir at Lake Mead. The Colorado continues at a relaxed pace along the Arizona–California border, providing energy and irrigation in Arizona, California, and Nevada before draining into northwestern Mexico.

A RIVER RUNS THROUGH IT

Stretching along 277 miles of the Colorado River is one of the seven natural wonders of the world: the Grand Canyon ranges in width from 4 to 18 miles, while the walls around it soar up to a mile high. Nearly 2 billion years of geologic history and majesty are revealed in exposed tiers of rock cut deep in the Colorado Plateau. What caused this incredible marvel of nature? Erosion by water coupled with driving wind are most likely the major culprits: under the sculpting power of wind and water, the shale layers eroded into slopes and the harder sandstone and limestone layers created terraced cliffs. Other forces that may have helped shape the canyon include ice, volcanic activity, continental drift, and earthquakes.

WHO LIVES HERE

Native tribes have lived in the canyon for thousands of years and continue to do so. The plateau-dwelling Hualapai ("people of the tall pines") live on a million acres along 108 miles of the Colorado River in the West Rim. The Havasupai ("people of the blue green water") live deep within the walls of the 12-mile-long Havasu Canyon—a major side canyon connected to the Grand Canyon.

ENVIRONMENTAL CONCERNS

When the Grand Canyon achieved national park status in 1919, only 44,173 people made the grueling overland trip to see it—quite a contrast from today's nearly 5 million annual visitors. The tremendous increase in visitation has greatly impacted the fragile ecosystems, as has Lake Powell's Glen Canyon Dam, which was constructed in the 1950s and '60s. The dam has changed the composition of the Colorado River, replacing warm water rich in sediments (nature's way of nourishing the riverbed and banks) with mostly cool, much clearer water. This has introduced nonnative plants and animals that threaten the extinction of several native species. Air pollution has also affected visibility and the constant buzz of aerial tours has disturbed the natural solitude.

Above and right, views of Colorado River in the Grand Canyon from Toroweap.

Did You Know?

The North Rim's isolated Toroweap overlook (also called Tuweep) is perched 3,000 feet above the canyon floor: a height equal to stacking the Sears Tower and Empire State Building on top of each other.

RIVER RAFTING THROUGH THE GRAND CANYON

Viewing the Colorado River from a canyon overlook is one thing, but looking up at the canyon from the middle of the river is quite another experience. If you're ready to tackle the churning white water of the Colorado River as it rumbles and hisses its way through the Grand Canyon, take a look at this map of what you might encounter along the way.

You'll hear the roar of **Lava Falls** before you see it—this large rapid is the fastest navigable white-water stretch in North America.

South Cove, on Lake Mead, is the final destination for many river trips.

Many outfitters end their trips at **Diamond Creek**, where the river begins to slow down. One-day trips are operated by the Hualapai Tribe.

NEVADA / ARIZONA

KANAB PLATEAU

GRAND CANYON

Tuweep

Mile 179 · Lava Falls

Hava Falls

Lake Mead
Mile 296

South Cove

GRAND CANYON NATIONAL PARK

Kolb Rapid

Whitmore Wash

Colorado River

GRAND WASH CLIFFS

Mile 225

Diamond Creek

Dirt

1

HUALAPAI INDIAN RES.

Dirt

Peach Springs

COLORADO RIVER TRIPS

Time and Length	Entry and Exit points
1 day Float trip	Glen Canyon Dam to Lees Ferry (no rapids)
1 day Combo trip	Diamond Creek, then helicopter to West Rim
3–4 days	Lees Ferry to Phantom Ranch
6 days, 89 miles	Phantom Ranch to Diamond Creek
9–10 days, 136 miles	Lees Ferry to Diamond Creek
14–16 days, 225 miles	Lees Ferry to South Cove

*Trips either begin or end at Phantom Ranch/Bright Angel Beach at the bottom of the Grand Canyon, at river mile 87

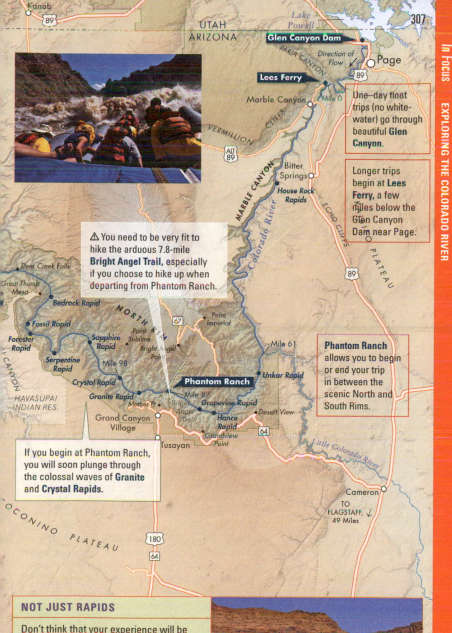

UTAH
ARIZONA

Lake Powell

Glen Canyon Dam

Direction of Flow

Page

Lees Ferry

Mile 0

Marble Canyon

VERMILLION CLIFFS

PARIA CANYON

ALT 89

Bitter Springs

ECHO CLIFFS

House Rock Rapids

MARBLE CANYON

Colorado River

89

One–day float trips (no white-water) go through beautiful **Glen Canyon**.

Longer trips begin at **Lees Ferry**, a few miles below the Glen Canyon Dam near Page.

Deer Creek Falls

Great Thumb Mesa

NORTH RIM

Point Imperial

67

Bedrock Rapid

Fossil Rapid

Forester Rapid

Sapphire Rapid

Point Sublime

Bright Angel Point

Mile 61

⚠ You need to be very fit to hike the arduous 7.8-mile **Bright Angel Trail**, especially if you choose to hike up when departing from Phantom Ranch.

Serpentine Rapid

Mile 98

Crystal Rapid

Unkar Rapid

HAVASUPAI INDIAN RES.

Granite Rapid

Mather Pt

Phantom Ranch

Mile 87

Bright Angel Trail

Gropevine Rapid

Grand Canyon Village

Hance Rapid

Desert View

64

Tusayan

Grandview Point

Little Colorado River

Phantom Ranch allows you to begin or end your trip in between the scenic North and South Rims.

If you begin at Phantom Ranch, you will soon plunge through the colossal waves of **Granite** and **Crystal Rapids**.

Cameron

TO FLAGSTAFF, ↓ 49 Miles

COCONINO PLATEAU

180

64

NOT JUST RAPIDS

Don't think that your experience will be nonstop white-water adrenaline. Most of the Colorado River features long, relaxing stretches of water, where you drift amid grandiose rock formations. You might even spot a mountain goat or two. Multi-day trips include camping on the shore.

Kanab

89

PLANNING YOUR RIVER RAFTING TRIP

OAR, MOTOR, OR HYBRID?

Base the type of trip you choose on the amount of effort you want to put in. Motor rafts, which are the roomiest of the choices, cover the most miles in less time and are the most comfortable. Guides do the rowing on oar boats and these smaller rafts offer a wilder ride. All-paddle trips are the most active and require the most involvement from guests. Hybrid trips are popular because they offer both the opportunity to paddle and to relax.

THE GEAR

Life jackets, beverages, tents, sheets, tarps, sleeping bags, dry bags, first aid, and food are provided—but you'll still need to plan ahead by packing clothing, hats, sunscreen, toiletries, and other sundries. Commercial outfitters allow each river runner two waterproof bags to store items during the day—just keep in mind that one of these will be filled up with the provided sleeping bag and tarp. ■TIP➔ **Bring a rain suit: summer thunderstorms are frequent and chilly.**

WHEN TO GO

Lots of people book trips for summer's peak period: June through August. If you're flexible, take advantage of the Arizona weather and go from May to early June or in September. ■TIP➔ **Seats fill up quickly; make reservations for multiday trips a year or two in advance.**

TRIP LENGTH

Rafting options on the Colorado River range from one-day trips at either the east or west end of the Grand Canyon to leisurely, two-week paddle trips through the full length of Grand Canyon National Park. If you're short on time, take a one-day trip near Grand Canyon West, where you'll run several rapids and fly back to the West Rim by helicopter. Another action-packed choice is to raft the river for 3 or 4 days, disembark at Phantom Ranch, then hike up to the Grand Canyon South Rim. "Full Canyon" rafting trips can take 9 to 16 days.

Above, Getting wet—and loving it—on an oar boat.

Did You Know?

As you're hanging on for dear life, consider this: Civil War veteran John Wesley Powell chartered these treacherous rapids in 1869—not only were conditions more dangerous then, but he had only one arm.

HISTORIC SITES

Kolb Studio

HISTORIC SITE | The Kolb brothers began building their photographic workshop and residence in 1904, a time when no pipeline meant Emery Kolb descended 3,000 feet each day to get water to develop his prints; he operated the studio until he died in 1976 at age 95. Today the building provides a view of Indian Garden and houses a gallery with paintings, photography, and crafts exhibitions. There's also a small Grand Canyon Association store here. In winter a ranger-led tour of the studio illustrates the Kolb brothers' role in the development of the Grand Canyon. Call ahead to sign up for the tour. ⊠ *Grand Canyon Village, Grand Canyon National Park* ⊹ *Near Bright Angel Lodge* ☎ *928/638–2771* ⊕ *www.nps.gov/grca* ⊠ *Free.*

Tusayan Ruin and Museum

ARCHAEOLOGICAL SITE | This museum offers a quick orientation to the prehistoric and modern indigenous populations of the Grand Canyon and the Colorado Plateau, including an excavation of an 800-year-old Pueblo site. Of special interest are split-twig figurines dating back 2,000 to 4,000 years and other artifacts left behind by ancient cultures. A ranger leads daily interpretive tours of the Ancestral Pueblo village. ⊠ *Grand Canyon National Park* ⊹ *About 20 miles east of Grand Canyon Village on E. Rim Dr.* ☎ *928/638–7888* ⊠ *Free.*

SCENIC STOPS

The Abyss

VIEWPOINT | At an elevation of 6,720 feet, the Abyss is one of the most awesome stops on Hermit Road, revealing a sheer drop of 3,000 feet to the Tonto Platform, a wide terrace of Tapeats sandstone about two-thirds of the way down the canyon. From the Abyss you'll also see several isolated sandstone columns, the largest of which is called the Monument. ⊠ *Grand Canyon National Park* ⊹ *About 5 miles west of Hermit Rd. Junction on Hermit Rd.*

Desert View and Watchtower

VIEWPOINT | From the top of the 70-foot stone-and-mortar watchtower with its 360-degree views, even the muted hues of the distant Painted Desert to the east and the Vermilion Cliffs rising from a high plateau near the Utah border are visible. In the chasm below, angling to the north toward Marble Canyon, an imposing stretch of the Colorado River reveals itself. Up several flights of stairs, the watchtower houses a glass-enclosed observatory with telescopes. ⊠ *Grand Canyon National Park* ⊹ *Just north of East Entrance Station on Desert View Dr.* ☎ *928/638–7888* ⊕ *www.nps.gov/grca* ⊠ *Free.*

Hermits Rest

VIEWPOINT | This westernmost viewpoint and Hermit Trail, which descends from it, were named for "hermit" Louis Boucher, a 19th-century French-Canadian prospector who had a number of mining claims and a roughly built home down in the canyon. The trail served as the original mule ride down to Hermit Camp beginning in 1914. Views from here include Hermit Rapids and the towering cliffs of the Supai and Redwall formations. You can buy curios and snacks in the stone building at Hermits Rest. ⊠ *Grand Canyon National Park* ⊹ *About 8 miles west of Hermit Rd. Junction on Hermit Rd.*

★ Hopi Point

VIEWPOINT | From this elevation of 7,071 feet, you can see a large section of the Colorado River; although it appears as a thin line, the river is nearly 350 feet wide. The overlook extends farther into the canyon than any other point on Hermit Road. The incredible unobstructed views make this a popular place to watch the sunset.

Across the canyon to the north is Shiva Temple. In 1937 Harold Anthony of the American Museum of Natural History led an expedition to the rock formation in the belief that it supported life that had been cut off from the rest of the canyon. Imagine the expedition members' surprise when they found an empty Kodak film box on top of the temple—it had been left behind by Emery Kolb, who felt slighted for not having been invited to join Anthony's tour.

Directly below Hopi Point lies Dana Butte, named for a prominent 19th-century geologist. In 1919 an entrepreneur proposed connecting Hopi Point, Dana Butte, and the Tower of Set across the river with an aerial tramway, a technically feasible plan that fortunately has not been realized. ⊠ *Grand Canyon National Park* ✥ *About 4 miles west of Hermit Rd. Junction on Hermit Rd.*

★ Mather Point

VIEWPOINT | You'll likely get your first glimpse of the canyon from this viewpoint, one of the most impressive and accessible (next to the main visitor center plaza) on the South Rim. Named for the National Park Service's first director, Stephen Mather, this spot yields extraordinary views of the Grand Canyon, including deep into the inner gorge and numerous buttes: Wotans Throne, Brahma Temple, and Zoroaster Temple, among others. The Grand Canyon Lodge, on the North Rim, is almost directly north from Mather Point and only 10 miles away—yet you have to drive 215 miles to get from one spot to the other. ⊠ *Near Grand Canyon Visitor Center, Grand Canyon National Park* ☎ *928/638–7888* ⊕ *www.nps.gov/grca.*

★ Yavapai Point

MUSEUM | Dominated by the Yavapai Geology Museum and Observation Station, this point displays panoramic views of the mighty gorge through a wall of windows. Exhibits at the museum include videos of the canyon floor and the Colorado River, a scaled diorama of the canyon with national park boundaries, fossils, and rock fragments used to re-create the complex layers of the canyon walls, and a display on the natural forces used to carve the chasm. Dig even deeper into Grand Canyon geology with free daily ranger programs. This point is also a good location to watch the sunset. ⊠ *Grand Canyon Village* ✥ *1 mile east of Market Plaza.*

🍴 Restaurants

Arizona Steakhouse

$$$ | **STEAKHOUSE** | The canyon views from this casual Southwestern-style steak house are the best of any restaurant at the South Rim. The dinner menu leans toward steak-house dishes, while lunch is primarily salads and sandwiches with a Southwestern twist. **Known for:** views of the Grand Canyon; Southwestern fare; local craft beers and wines. ⑤ *Average main: $28* ⊠ *Bright Angel Lodge, 9 N. Village Loop Dr., Grand Canyon Village* ☎ *928/638–2631* ⊕ *www.grandcanyonlodges.com.*

Fred Harvey Burger

$$ | **SOUTHWESTERN** | **FAMILY** | Open for lunch and dinner, this casual café at Bright Angel Lodge serves basics like salads, sandwiches, and burgers. Harvey House favorites like strip steak and spaghetti round out the menu. **Known for:** reasonably priced American fare; family-friendly menu and setting; some limited vegetarian and gluten-free options. ⑤ *Average main: $14* ⊠ *Bright Angel Lodge, Desert View Dr., Grand Canyon Village* ☎ *928/638–2631* ⊕ *www.grandcanyonlodges.com.*

★ El Tovar Dining Room

$$$ | SOUTHWESTERN | Even at the edge of the Grand Canyon it's possible to find gourmet dining. This cozy room of dark wood beams and stone, nestled in the historic El Tovar Lodge, dates to 1905. **Known for:** historic setting with canyon views; local and organic ingredients; fine dining that's worth the splurge. ⓢ *Average main: $28* ✉ *El Tovar Hotel, 1 El Tovar Rd., Grand Canyon Village* ☎ *928/638–2631* ⊕ *www.grandcanyonlodges.com.*

Maswik Food Court

$ | AMERICAN | FAMILY | You can get a burger, hot sandwich, pasta, or Mexican fare at this food court, as well as pizza by the slice and wine and beer in the adjacent Maswik Pizza Pub. This casual eatery is in Maswik Lodge, ¼ mile from the rim, and the Pizza Pub stays open until 8 pm (you can also order pizza to take out). **Known for:** good selection (something for everyone); cafeteria-style dining; pizza to go. ⓢ *Average main: $10* ✉ *Maswik Lodge, South Village Loop Dr., Grand Canyon Village* ⊕ *www.grandcanyonlodges.com.*

Yavapai Lodge Restaurant and Tavern

$$ | AMERICAN | FAMILY | If you don't have time for full-service, the restaurant in Yavapai Lodge offers cafeteria-style dining for breakfast, lunch, and dinner, including hot and cold sandwiches, pizza, barbecue ribs, and rotisserie chicken. Wine and beer, including craft brews from nearby Flagstaff, are also on the menu; or enjoy drinks on the patio at the adjacent Yavapai Tavern. **Known for:** quick bites or hearty meals; convenient dining in Market Plaza; patio with firepit at Yavapai Tavern. ⓢ *Average main: $12* ✉ *Yavapai Lodge, Yavapai Lodge Rd., Grand Canyon Village* ☎ *928/638–4001* ⊕ *www.visitgrandcanyon.com.*

🏃 Activities

HIKING

Remember that the canyon has significant elevation changes and, in summer, extreme temperature ranges, which can pose problems for people who aren't in good shape or who have heart or respiratory problems. ■TIP➔ **Carry plenty of water and energy foods.** The majority of each year's 400 search-and-rescue incidents result from hikers underestimating the size of the canyon, hiking beyond their abilities, or not packing sufficient food and water.

⚠ **It's not advised to attempt a day hike from the rim to the river and back.** Canyon rangers will try to talk you out of the idea. It's legal, but only very fit, athletic people with proven hiking skills should attempt it. Remember that when it's 80°F on the South Rim, the temperature may be 105°F on the canyon floor.

★ Rim Trail

TRAIL | The South Rim's most popular walking path is the 12.8-mile (one-way) Rim Trail, which runs along the edge of the canyon from Pipe Creek Vista (the first overlook on Desert View Drive) to Hermits Rest. This walk, which is paved to Maricopa Point and for the last 1½ miles to Hermits Rest, visits several of the South Rim's historic landmarks. Allow anywhere from 15 minutes to a full day, depending on how much of the trail you want to cover; the Rim Trail is an ideal day hike, as it varies only a few hundred feet in elevation from Mather Point (7,120 feet) to the trailhead at Hermits Rest (6,650 feet). The trail can also be accessed from several spots in Grand Canyon Village and from the major viewpoints along Hermit Road, which are serviced by shuttle buses during the busy summer months. On the Rim Trail, water is available only in the Grand Canyon Village area and at Hermits Rest. *Easy.* ✉ *Grand Canyon National Park.*

White-water rafting is just one of the many activities you can experience in the Grand Canyon.

★ Bright Angel Trail

TRAIL | This well-maintained trail is one of the most scenic (and busiest) hiking paths from the South Rim to the bottom of the canyon (9.6 miles each way). Rest houses are equipped with water at the 1½- and 3-mile points from May through September and at Indian Garden (4 miles) year-round. Water is also available at Bright Angel Campground, 9¼ miles below the trailhead. Plateau Point, on a spur trail about 1½ miles below Indian Garden, is as far as you should attempt to go on a day hike; the round-trip will take six to nine hours.

Bright Angel Trail is the easiest of all the footpaths into the canyon, but because the climb out from the bottom is an ascent of 5,510 feet, the trip should be attempted only by those in good physical condition and should be avoided in mid-summer due to extreme heat. The top of the trail can be icy in winter. Originally a bighorn sheep path and later used by the Havasupai, the trail was widened late in the 19th century for prospectors and is now used for both mule and foot traffic. Also note that mule trains have the right-of-way—and sometimes leave unpleasant surprises in your path. *Moderate.* ✉ *Grand Canyon National Park* ✛ *Trailhead: Kolb Studio, Hermit Rd.*

South Kaibab Trail

TRAIL | This trail starts near Yaki Point, 4 miles east of Grand Canyon Village, and is accessible via the free shuttle bus.

Because the route is so steep (and sometimes icy in winter)—descending from the trailhead at 7,260 feet down to 2,480 feet at the Colorado River—many hikers take this trail down, then ascend via the less demanding Bright Angel Trail. Allow four to six hours to reach the Colorado River on this 6.4-mile trek. At the river, the trail crosses a suspension bridge and runs on to Phantom Ranch. Along the trail there is no water and shade. There are no campgrounds, though there are portable toilets at Cedar Ridge (6,320 feet), 1½ miles from the trailhead. An emergency phone is available at the Tipoff, 4.6 miles down the trail (3 miles past Cedar Ridge). The trail corkscrews down through some spectacular geology. Look for (but don't remove) fossils in the limestone when taking water breaks. *Difficult.* ⊠ *Grand Canyon National Park* ⚓ *Trailhead: Yaki Point Rd., off Desert View Dr.*

MULE RIDES

Mule rides provide an intimate glimpse into the canyon for those who have the time, but not the stamina, to see the canyon on foot. ■TIP➜ **Reservations are essential and are accepted up to 13 months in advance.**

These trips have been conducted since the early 1900s. A comforting fact as you ride the narrow trail: no one's ever been killed while riding a mule that fell off a cliff. (Nevertheless, the treks aren't for the faint of heart or people in questionable health.)

★ **Xanterra Parks & Resorts Mule Rides**
TOUR—SPORTS | These trips delve either into the canyon from the South Rim to Phantom Ranch, or east along the canyon's rim. Riders must be at least nine years old and 57 inches tall, weigh less than 200 pounds for the Phantom Ranch ride or less than 225 pounds for the rim ride, and understand English. Children under 18 must be accompanied by an adult. Riders must be in fairly good physical condition, and pregnant women are advised not to take these trips.

The two-hour ride along the rim costs $155. An overnight mule ride with a stay in a cabin at Phantom Ranch at the bottom of the canyon, with meals included, is $705 ($1,226 for two riders). Package prices vary since a cabin at Phantom Ranch can accommodate up to four people. From November through March, you can stay for up to two nights at Phantom Ranch. Reservations are a must, but you can check at the Bright Angel Transportation Desk to see if there's last-minute availability. ☎ 888/297–2757, 303/297–2757 ⊕ *www.grandcanyonlodges.com* ⚓ *Reservations essential.*

North Rim

276 miles northeast of Las Vegas.

The North Rim stands 1,000 feet higher than the South Rim and has a more alpine climate, with twice as much annual precipitation. Here, in the deep forests of the Kaibab Plateau, the crowds are thinner, the facilities fewer, and the views even more spectacular. Because of snow, the North Rim is off-limits in winter. The park buildings are closed mid-October through mid-May. The road closes when the snow makes it impassable—usually by the end of November. Driving to the South Rim makes more sense if you are just going to the Grand Canyon for the day. Despite the fact that the mileage is similar to both North and South Rims from Las Vegas, the travel time to the North Rim is significantly more. If you head to the more remote North Rim it will take at least five hours one-way, and bus tours are lengthy. There is also more to see in a limited amount of time at the South Rim. If it's possible—and if your heart is set on the more secluded North Rim—look into an overnight stay, but remember a room at Grand Canyon Lodge means booking months in advance.

Lodgings are available but limited; the North Rim offers only one historic lodge and restaurant, and a single campground. The canyon's highest, most dramatic rim views can be enjoyed on two wheels (via primitive dirt access roads) and on four legs (courtesy of a trusty mule).

Top Picnic Spots

Bring your picnic basket and enjoy dining alfresco surrounded by some of the most beautiful backdrops in the country. Be sure to bring water, as it's unavailable at many of these spots, as are restrooms.

Buggeln, 15 miles east of Grand Canyon Village on Desert View Drive, has some secluded, shady spots. **Cape Royal**, 23 miles south of the North Rim Visitor Center, is the most popular designated picnic area on the North Rim because of its panoramic views. **Grandview Point** has, as the name implies, grand views; it is 12 miles east of the Village on Desert View Drive. **Point Imperial**, 11 miles northeast of the North Rim Visitor Center, has shade and some privacy.

GETTING HERE AND AROUND

To get to the North Rim by car, take Interstate 15 east to Hurricane, Utah; Routes 59 and 389 to Fredonia; and U.S. 89 and Route 67 to the North Rim. Since it's so high in elevation (at 8,000 feet), the remote North Rim is closed to automobiles after the first heavy snowfall of the season (usually in late October or early November) through mid-May. All North Rim facilities close between October 15 and May 15. AZ 67 south of Jacob Lake is closed by the first heavy snowfall in November or December and remains closed until early to mid-May.

When driving off major highways in low-lying areas, watch for rain clouds. Flash floods from sudden summer rains can be deadly.

◉ Sights

HISTORIC SITES
Grand Canyon Lodge

HISTORIC SITE | Built in 1937 by the Union Pacific Railroad (replacing the original 1928 building, which burned in a fire), this massive stone structure is listed on the National Register of Historic Places. Its huge sunroom has hardwood floors, high-beamed ceilings, and a marvelous view of the canyon through plate-glass windows. On warm days, visitors sit in the sun and drink in the surrounding beauty on an outdoor viewing deck, where National Park Service employees deliver free lectures on geology and history. The dining room serves breakfast, lunch, and dinner; the Roughrider Saloon is a bar by night and a coffee shop in the morning. ✉ *Grand Canyon National Park* ✛ *Off Hwy. 67 near Bright Angel Point* ☎ *928/638–2611 May.–Oct., 877/386–4383 reservations* ⊕ *www.grandcanyonforever.com* ☾ *Closed mid-Oct.–mid-May.*

SCENIC DRIVE
★ **Highway 67**

SCENIC DRIVE | Open mid-May to roughly mid-October (or the first big snowfall), this two-lane paved road climbs 1,400 feet in elevation as it passes through the Kaibab National Forest. Also called the North Rim Parkway, this scenic route crosses the limestone-capped Kaibab Plateau—passing broad meadows, sun-dappled forests, and small lakes and springs—before abruptly falling away at the abyss of the Grand Canyon. Wildlife abounds in the thick ponderosa pine forests and lush mountain meadows. It's common to see deer, turkeys, and coyotes as you drive through such a remote region. Point Imperial and Cape Royal branch off this scenic drive, which runs from Jacob Lake to Bright Angel Point. ☒ Hwy. 67, Grand Canyon National Park.

SCENIC STOPS
★ Bright Angel Point

TRAIL | Bright Angel Point is one of the most awe-inspiring overlooks on either rim. To get to it, follow the trail that starts on the grounds of the Grand Canyon Lodge and runs along the crest of a point of rocks that juts into the canyon for several hundred yards. The walk is only ½ mile round-trip, but it's an exciting trek accented by sheer drops on each side of the trail. In a few spots where the route is extremely narrow, metal railings ensure visitors' safety. The temptation to clamber out on precarious perches to have your picture taken should be resisted at all costs. ☒ North Rim Dr., Grand Canyon National Park ✛ Near Grand Canyon Lodge.

Cape Royal

TRAIL | A popular sunset destination, Cape Royal showcases the canyon's jagged landscape; you'll also get a glimpse of the Colorado River, framed by a natural stone arch called Angels Window. In autumn, the aspens turn a beautiful gold, adding even more color to an already magnificent scene of the forested surroundings. The easy and rewarding 1-mile round-trip hike along **Cliff Springs Trail** starts here; it takes you through a forested ravine and terminates at Cliff Springs, where the forest opens to another impressive view of the canyon walls. ☒ Cape Royal Scenic Dr., Grand Canyon National Park ✛ 23 miles southeast of Grand Canyon Lodge.

Point Imperial

VIEWPOINT | At 8,803 feet, Point Imperial has the highest vista point at either rim; it offers magnificent views of both the canyon and the distant country: the Vermilion Cliffs to the north, the 10,000-foot Navajo

Need a Break?

If you've been driving too long and want some exercise, along with great views of the canyon, it's an easy 1.25-mile-long hike from the Information Plaza to El Tovar Hotel. The Greenway path runs through a quiet wooded area for about half a mile, and then along the rim for another three-quarters of a mile.

Mountain to the northeast in Utah, the Painted Desert to the east, and the Little Colorado River canyon to the southeast. Other prominent points of interest include views of Mt. Hayden, Saddle Mountain, and Marble Canyon. ☒ Point Imperial Rd., Grand Canyon National Park ✛ 11 miles northeast of Grand Canyon Lodge.

★ Point Sublime

VIEWPOINT | You can camp within feet of the canyon's edge at this awe-inspiring site. Sunrises and sunsets are spectacular. The winding road, through gorgeous high country, is only 17 miles, but it will take you at least two hours one-way. The road is intended only for vehicles with high road clearance (pickups and four-wheel-drive vehicles). It is also necessary to be properly equipped for wilderness road travel. Check with a park ranger or at the information desk at Grand Canyon Lodge before taking this journey. You may camp here only with a permit from the Backcountry Information Center. ☒ North Rim Dr., Grand Canyon National Park ✛ About 20 miles west of North Rim Visitor Center.

HIKING
EASY
Transept Trail

TRAIL | FAMILY | This 3-mile round-trip, 1½-hour trail begins near the Grand Canyon Lodge at 8,255 feet. Well maintained and well marked, it has little elevation change, sticking near the rim before reaching a dramatic view of a large stream through Bright Angel Canyon. The trail leads to Transept Canyon, which geologist Clarence Dutton named in 1882, declaring it "far grander than Yosemite." Check the posted schedule to find a ranger talk along this trail; it's also a great place to view fall foliage. Flash floods can occur any time of the year, especially June through September when thunderstorms develop rapidly. *Easy.* ⊠ *Grand Canyon National Park* ⊹ *Trailhead: near Grand Canyon Lodge east patio.*

🍴 Restaurants

Deli in the Pines

$ | AMERICAN | Dining choices are limited on the North Rim, but this deli next to the lodge is your best bet for a meal on a budget or grabbing a premade sandwich on the go. Selections also include pizza (gluten-free or standard crust), salads, custom-made sandwiches, and soft-serve ice cream. **Known for:** convenient quick bite; sandwiches to take on the trail; outdoor seating. 💲 *Average main: $9* ⊠ *Grand Canyon Lodge, Bright Angel Point, North Rim* ☎ *928/638–2611* ⊕ *www.grandcanyonforever.com* ⊗ *Closed mid-Oct.–mid-May.*

★ Grand Canyon Lodge Dining Room

$$$ | SOUTHWESTERN | The high wood-beamed ceilings, stone walls, and spectacular views in this spacious, historic room are perhaps the biggest draw for the lodge's main restaurant. Dinner includes southwestern steakhouse fare that would make any cowboy feel at home, including selections such as bison and venison. **Known for:** incredible views; charming, historic room; steaks, fish, game, and vegetarian selections.

💲 *Average main: $25* ⊠ *Grand Canyon Lodge, Bright Angel Point, North Rim* ☎ *928/638–8562* ⊕ *www.grandcanyonforever.com* ⊗ *Closed mid-Oct.–mid-May.*

🛏 Hotels

★ Grand Canyon Lodge

$$$ | HOTEL | This historic property, constructed mainly in the 1920s and '30s, is the only lodging on the North Rim. The main building has locally quarried limestone walls and timbered ceilings. **Pros:** steps away from gorgeous North Rim views; close to several easy hiking trails; historic lodge building a national landmark. **Cons:** fills up fast; limited amenities; most cabins far from main lodge building. 💲 *Rooms from: $200* ⊠ *Hwy. 67, North Rim* ☎ *877/386–4383 reservations, 928/638–2611 May–Oct.* ⊕ *www.grandcanyonforever.com* ⊗ *Closed mid-Oct.–mid-May* ⇄ *218 rooms* 🍽 *No meals.*

🏃 Activities

MULE RIDES

Canyon Trail Rides

TOUR—SPORTS | FAMILY | This company leads mule rides along the easier trails of the North Rim. Options include one- and three-hour rides along the rim or a three-hour ride down into the canyon (minimum age seven for one-hour rides, 10 for three-hour rides). The one-hour ride is $50, and the three-hour rides are $100. Weight limits are 200 pounds for canyon rides and 220 pounds for the rim rides. Available daily from May 15 to October 15, these excursions are popular, so make reservations in advance. ☎ *435/679–8665* ⊕ *www.canyonrides.com* ⇆ *From $50.*

Death Valley

The desert is no Disneyland. With its scorching summer heat and vast, sparsely populated tracts of land, it's not often at the top of the list when most people plan their California vacations. But the natural riches of Death Valley—the largest national park outside Alaska—are overwhelming: rolling waves of sand dunes, black cinder cones thrusting up hundreds of feet from a blistered desert floor, riotous sheets of wildflowers, bizarrely shaped Joshua trees basking in the orange glow of a sunset, tiny pupfish that enthrall youngsters, and a silence that's both dramatic and startling.

When to Go

Most of the park's 1 million annual visitors come between late fall and early spring, taking advantage of moderate temperatures and the lack of rainfall. If you visit in summer, believe everything you've ever heard about desert heat—it can be brutal, with temperatures often topping 120°F (a record 134°F was set in 1913). The dry air wicks moisture from the body without causing a sweat, so drink plenty of water. Bring sunglasses, a hat, and sufficient clothing to block the sun's rays and the wind. Flash floods are fairly common; sections of roadway can be flooded or washed away, as they were after a major flood in 2015. The wettest month is February, when the park receives an average of 0.3 inches of rain.

Getting Here and Around

It can take more than three hours to cross from one side of the park to another, so it's important to choose an entrance point that makes sense for what you want to see. From Las Vegas, enter from the north at Beatty, Nevada, or via the central entrance at Death Valley Junction.

Distances can be deceiving within the park: what seems close can be very far away. Much of the park can be viewed on regularly scheduled bus tours, but these often don't allow time for hikes to sites not seen from the road, such as Salt Creek, Golden Canyon, and Natural Bridge. The best option is to drive to a number of the sites, get out of the car, and walk.

When driving in Death Valley, reliable maps are important, as signage is often limited or, in a few places, nonexistent. Bring a phone but don't rely on cell coverage exclusively in every remote area, and pack plenty of food and water (3 gallons per person per day is recommended). Cars, especially in summer, should be prepared for the hot, dry weather, too. Some of the park's most spectacular canyons are only accessible via four-wheel-drive vehicles but if this is the way you want to travel, make sure the trip is well planned and use a backcountry map. Be aware of possible winter closures or driving restrictions because of snow. The National Park Service's website (⊕ *nps.gov/deva*) stays up-to-date on road closures during the wet (and popular) months. ⚠ **One of the park's signature landmarks, Scotty's Castle, and the 8-mile road connecting it to the park border will be closed until at least 2022 due to damage from a 2015 flood.**

Death Valley in One Day

If you begin the day in Furnace Creek, you can see several sights without doing much driving. Bring plenty of water with you, and some food, too. Get up early and drive the 20 miles on Badwater Road to **Badwater,** which looks out on the lowest point in the Western Hemisphere and is a dramatic place to watch the sunrise. Returning north, stop at **Natural Bridge,** a medium-size conglomerate rock formation that has been hollowed at its base to form a span across the canyon, and then at the **Devil's Golf Course,** so named because of the large pinnacles of salt present here. Detour to the right onto **Artists Drive,** a 9-mile one-way, northbound route that passes **Artists Palette.** The reds, yellows, oranges, and greens come from minerals in the rocks and the earth. Four miles north of Artist's Drive you'll come to the **Golden Canyon Interpretive Trail,** a 2-mile round-trip that winds through a canyon with colorful rock walls. Just before Furnace Creek, take Highway 190 3 miles east to **Zabriskie Point,** overlooking dramatic, furrowed red-brown hills and the **Twenty Mule Team Canyon.** Return to Furnace Creek, where you can grab a meal and visit the museum at the Furnace Creek Visitor Center. Heading north from Furnace Creek, pull off the highway and take a look at the **Harmony Borax Works.**

DRIVING INFORMATION California Highway Patrol. ☎ *800/427–7623 recorded info from CalTrans, 760/872–5900 live dispatcher at Bishop Communications Center* ⊕ *www.chp.ca.gov.*

Visitor Information

PARK CONTACT INFORMATION
Death Valley National Park. ☎ *760/786–3200* ⊕ *www.nps.gov/deva.*

PARK FEES AND PERMITS
The entrance fee is $30 per vehicle and $15 for those entering on foot or bike. The payment, valid for seven consecutive days, is collected at the park's ranger stations, self-serve fee stations, and the visitor center at Furnace Creek. Annual park passes, valid only at Death Valley, are $55.

PARK HOURS
Furnace Creek Visitor Center, open daily 8–5.

VISITOR CENTERS
The popular visitor center at Scotty's Castle is closed until at least 2022 as a result of a major flash flood in 2015 that damaged the structure and destroyed the access road.

Furnace Creek Visitor Center and Museum
INFO CENTER | The exhibits and artifacts here provide a broad overview of how Death Valley formed; you can pick up maps at the bookstore run by the Death Valley Natural History Association. This is also the place to find out about ranger programs (available November through April) or check out a live presentation about the valley's cultural and natural history. The helpful center offers regular showings of a 20-minute film about the park, and this is the place for children to get their free Junior Ranger booklet, packed with games and information about the park and its critters. ✉ *Hwy. 190, Death Valley* ✛ *30 miles northwest of Death Valley Junction* ☎ *760/786–3200* ⊕ *www.nps.gov/deva.*

Only 710 feet above sea level, Zabriskie Point nevertheless offers amazing views in a very accessible location, just 5 miles south of popular Furnace Creek.

Tours

Furnace Creek Visitor Center programs

GUIDED TOURS | This center has many programs, including ranger-led hikes that explore natural wonders such as Golden Canyon, nighttime stargazing parties with telescopes, and evening ranger talks. ⊠ *Furnace Creek Visitor Center, Rte. 190, 30 miles northwest of Death Valley Junction, Death Valley* ☎ *760/786–2331* ⊕ *www.nps.gov/deva/planyourvisit/tours. htm* 🎫 *Free.*

Pink Jeep Tours Las Vegas

GUIDED TOURS | A 10-passenger luxury vehicle with oversized viewing windows will pick you up at most Strip hotels for visits to park landmarks. The tours run from about 7 am to 4 pm from September through May, are professionally narrated, and include lunch and bottled water. ⊠ *3629 W. Hacienda Ave., Las Vegas* ☎ *800/873–3662* ⊕ *pinkadventure-tours.com* 🎫 *From $275.*

👁 Sights

Scotty's Castle, one of the most iconic sights in Death Valley is closed until further notice after a major flash flood in 2015 caused damage to both the sight and its access road.

SCENIC DRIVE
Artists Drive

SCENIC DRIVE | This 9-mile, one-way route skirts the foothills of the Black Mountains and provides intimate views of the changing landscape. Once inside the palette, the valley's expanses are replaced by the small-scale natural beauty of pigments created by volcanic deposits or sedimentary layers. It's a quiet, lonely drive, and shouldn't be rushed. Reach Artists Palette by heading south on Badwater Road from its intersection with Route 190. ⊠ *Death Valley National Park.*

SCENIC STOPS
Artists Palette

NATURE SITE | So called for the contrasting colors of its volcanic deposits and sedimentary layers, this is one of the signature sights of Death Valley. Artists Drive, the approach to the area, is one-way heading north off Badwater Road, so if you're visiting Badwater from Furnace Creek, come here on the way back. The drive winds through foothills of sedimentary and volcanic rocks. About 4 miles along, a short side road veers right to a parking lot that's a few hundred feet before the "palette," whose natural colors include shades of green, gold, and pink. ⊠ *Off Badwater Rd., Death Valley* ✛ *11 miles south of Furnace Creek.*

Badwater Basin

NATURE SITE | At 282 feet below sea level, Badwater is the lowest spot of land in North America—and also one of the hottest. Stairs and wheelchair ramps descend from the parking lot to a wooden platform that overlooks a sodium chloride pool, a small but remarkably persistent reminder that the valley floor used to contain a lake. You can continue past the platform on a broad, white path that peters out after a ½ mile or so. Badwater is one of the most popular and easily accessible sites within the park. From this lowest point, be sure to look across to Telescope Peak, which towers more than 2 miles above the valley floor. ⊠ *Badwater Rd., Death Valley* ✛ *19 miles south of Furnace Creek.*

★ Dante's View

VIEWPOINT | This lookout is 5,450 feet above sea level in the Black Mountains. In the dry desert air you can see across most of 160-mile-long Death Valley. The view is astounding. Take a 10-minute, mildly strenuous walk from the parking lot toward a series of rocky overlooks, where, with binoculars, you can spot some signature sites. A few interpretive signs point out the highlights below in the valley and across in the Sierra. Getting here from Furnace Creek takes about an hour—time well invested. ⊠ *Dante's View Rd., Death Valley* ✛ *Off Hwy. 190, 35 miles from Badwater, 20 miles south of Twenty Mule Team Canyon.*

Devil's Golf Course

NATURE SITE | Thousands of miniature salt pinnacles carved into surreal shapes by the desert wind dot this wildly varied landscape. The salt was pushed up to the surface by pressure created as underground salt- and water-bearing gravel crystallized. Get out of your vehicle and take a closer look; you may see perfectly round holes descending into the ground. ⊠ *Badwater Rd., Death Valley* ✛ *13 miles south of Furnace Creek. Turn right onto dirt road and drive 1 mile.*

Mesquite Flat Sand Dunes

NATURE SITE | These dunes, made up of minute pieces of quartz and other rock, are ever-changing products of the wind-rippled hills, with curving crests and a sun-bleached hue. The dunes are the most photographed destination in the park, and you can see them at their best at sunrise and sunset. Keep your eyes open for animal tracks—you may even spot a coyote or fox. Bring plenty of water, and note where you parked your car: it's easy to become disoriented in this ocean of sand. If you lose your bearings, climb to the top of a dune, and scan the horizon for the parking lot. ⊠ *Death Valley* ✛ *19 miles north of Hwy. 190, northeast of Stovepipe Wells Village.*

Titus Canyon

SCENIC DRIVE | This popular, one-way, 27-mile drive starts at Nevada Highway 374 (Daylight Pass Road), 2 miles from the park's boundary. Highlights include the Leadville Ghost Town and the spectacular limestone and dolomite narrows. Toward the end, a two-way section of gravel road leads you into the mouth of the canyon from Scotty's Castle Road (closed until at least 2022). This drive is steep, bumpy, and narrow. High-clearance vehicles are strongly recommended. ⊠ *Death Valley National Park* ✛ *Access road off Nevada Hwy. 374, 6 miles west of Beatty, NV.*

Zabriskie Point

VIEWPOINT | Although only about 710 feet in elevation, this is one of the park's most scenic spots, overlooking a striking panorama of wrinkled, multicolor hills. It's a great place to watch the sunrise, but it can be bustling any time of day. Pair it with a drive out to magnificent Dante's View. ⊠ *Hwy. 190, Death Valley* ✛ *5 miles south of Furnace Creek.*

🍴 Restaurants

★ Inn at the Oasis at Death Valley Dining Room

$$$$ | **AMERICAN** | Fireplaces, beamed ceilings, and spectacular views provide a visual feast to match this fine-dining restaurant's ambitious menu. Dinner entrées include salmon, free-range chicken, and filet mignon, and there's a seasonal menu of vegetarian dishes. **Known for:** views of surrounding desert; old-school charm; can be pricey. ⑤ *Average main: $42* ⊠ *Inn at the Oasis at Death Valley, Hwy. 190, Furnace Creek* ☎ *760/786–3385* ⊕ *www.oasisatdeathvalley.com.*

Index

Photo Credits

Front Cover: icona / Alamy Stock Photo [Description: The Venetian hotel and casino in the evening in Las Vegas, Nevada, USA]. **Back cover, from left to right:** Sean Pavone/Shutterstock, DNY59/iStockphoto, somchaij / Shutterstock. **Spine:** Galushko Sergey/Shutterstock. **Interior, from left to right:** MBPROJEKT_Maciej_Bledowski/istockphoto (1). PGPHOTO.INFO/ Courtesy of Caesar's (2). LOOK Die Bildagentur der Fotografen GmbH / Alamy (5). **Chapter 1: Experience Las Vegas:** BENEDETTA BARBANTI (6-7). MGM Resorts International (8). The High Roller Observation Wheel (9). Kevin Mazur (9). Eataly Las Vegas (10). MGM Resorts International (10). Tomek Pleskaczynski (10). Kobby Dagan/Shutterstock (10). MGM Resorts International (11). Black Raven Films/Fremont Street Experience (11). NHLI (12). MediaPunch Inc / Alamy Stock Photo (12). The Venetian Resort Las Vegas (12). The Venetian Resort Las Vegas (12). Las Vegas News Bureau (13). Emily Wilson (13). Kobby Dagan/Shutterstock (13). Courtesy of The Vox Agency (13). Fremont Street Experience (14). Courtesy of The Neon Museum (14). Brian Jones/Las Vegas News Bureau (14). Erik Kabik Photography/ erikkabik.com (15). Waldorf Astoria Hotels & Resorts (16). Matt Beard Photography/Cirque du Soleil (16). The STRAT Hotel, Casino & SkyPod (16). Anthony Mair/The Cosmopolitan of Las Vegas (16). Springs Preserve (17). Esther Lin/SHOWTIME (17). Bureau of Reclamation (17). BLM Nevada (17). Courtesy of The Mob Museum/Chris Wessling (20). Deidra Wilson Photography (21). Geri Kodey (22). Courtesy of The Cosmopolitan (23). MGM Resorts International (24). Terrence Mahanna (24). Downtown Grand Las Vegas (24). Thomas Hart Shelby/Goat Rodeo Productions (25). Robert Miller (25). Jeff green photography/Jaleo Las Vegas (26). GOURMET TV PRODUCTIONS (26). Erik Kabik Photography/ erikkabik.com (26). GIADA at The Cromwell (26). Gordon Ramsay Steak at Paris Las Vegas (27). MGM Resorts International (27). MGM Resorts International (27). MGM Resorts International (27). © Pictorial Press Ltd / Alamy (31). Library of Congress Prints and Photographs Division Washington, D.C. (32). Author Unknown [Public Domain]/Wikimedia Commons (32). Library of Congress Prints & Photographs Division (32). Harrah's Entertainment (33). Pictorial Press Ltd / Alamy (33). Everett Collection Historical / Alamy Stock Photo (33). Content Mine International / Alamy (34). Pictorial Press Ltd / Alamy (34). Public Domain (34, center top). Library of Congress [Public Domain]/Wikimedia Commons (34). Allstar Picture Library / Alamy (35). Carol M. Highsmith [Public domain]/Wikimedia Commons (35). LOOK Die Bildagentur der Fotografen GmbH / Alamy (35). **Chapter 3: South Strip:** Yaacov Dagan / Alamy Stock Photo (61). Amy Cicconi / Alamy Stock Photo (80). Eataly Las Vegas (83). **Chapter 4: Center Strip:** Courtesy of MGM Resorts International (87). Las Vegas News Bureau, Las Vegas Convention and Visitors Authority (93). Denise Truscello (94). Courtesy of MGM Resorts International (97). Kobby Dagan/Shutterstock (104). Kobby Dagan/Shutterstock (111). **Chapter 5: North Strip:** Benson Truong/Shutterstock (119). f11photo/Shutterstock (127). Megan Blair/Resorts World Las Vegas (133). **Chapter 6: Downtown:** Fremont Street Experience (139). fukez84/Shutterstock (147). Hakat/Shutterstock (151). **Chapter 7: Paradise Road and the East Side:** Kitleong | Dreamstime.com (157). Virgin Hotels Las Vegas (167). **Chapter 8: Henderson and Lake Las Vegas:** Lisaturay | Dreamstime.com (171). CelineMichelle/istockphoto (176). Green Valley Ranch (179). **Chapter 9: West Side:** MediaPunch Inc / Alamy Stock Photo (181). Kate Russell/Meow Wolf Las Vegas Exhibit (187). Mark Waugh / Alamy Stock Photo (193). **Chapter 10: Summerlin and Red Rock Canyon:** dmodlin01/shutterstock (195). Chee-Onn Leong/Shutterstock (198). Nagel Photography/shutterstock (203). **Chapter 11: Gambling and Casinos:** Homolo lavani/istockphoto (207). shotsstudio/istockphoto (229). Lee Foster / Alamy (240). Kit Leong/Shutterstock (245). Thomas Hart Shelby (250). Kobby Dagan/Shutterstock (253). **Chapter 12: Shows:** Pamelaberry86 | Dreamstime.com (257). David Hawe/BMP (263). Véronique Vial/Cirque du Soleil (276). **Chapter 13: Side Trips from Las Vegas:** Tara McCrillis (279). jpellgen [CC BY-NC-ND 2.0]/Flickr (285). Photoquest | Dreamstime.com (291). Christophe Testi/Shutterstock (302-303). Kerrick James (304). Geir Olav Lyngfjell/Shutterstock (305). Kerrick James (306). Kerrick James (306). Kerrick James (307). Grand Canyon NPS [CC BY 2.0]/Flickr (307). Pacific Northwest Photo/Shutterstock (308). Kerrick James (309). MARK LELLOUCH, NPS (313). Rodney Ee, Fodors.com member (320). **About Our Writers:** All photos are courtesy of the writers.

*Every effort has been made to trace the copyright holders, and we apologize in advance for any accidental errors. We would be happy to apply the corrections in the following edition of this publication.

Notes

Notes

Notes

Notes

Notes

Fodor's LAS VEGAS

Publisher: Stephen Horowitz, *General Manager*

Editorial: Douglas Stallings, *Editorial Director*; Jill Fergus, Amanda Sadlowski, Caroline Trefler, *Senior Editors*; Kayla Becker, Alexis Kelly, *Editors*

Design: Tina Malaney, *Director of Design and Production*; Jessica Gonzalez, *Graphic Designer*; Mariana Tabares, *Design and Production Intern*

Production: Jennifer DePrima, *Editorial Production Manager*; Elyse Rozelle, *Senior Production Editor*; Monica White, *Production Editor*

Maps: Rebecca Baer, *Senior Map Editor*; Mark Stroud (Moon Street Cartography), *Cartographer*

Photography: Viviane Teles, *Senior Photo Editor*; Namrata Aggarwal, Ashok Kumar, *Photo Editors*; Rebecca Rimmer, *Photo Intern*

Business and Operations: Chuck Hoover, *Chief Marketing Officer*; Robert Ames, *Group General Manager*; Devin Duckworth, *Director of Print Publishing*; Amber Zhou, *Business Analyst*

Public Relations and Marketing: Joe Ewaskiw, *Senior Director of Communications and Public Relations*

Fodors.com: Jeremy Tarr, *Editorial Director*; Rachael Levitt, *Managing Editor*

Technology: Jon Atkinson, *Director of Technology*; Rudresh Teotia, *Lead Developer*; Jacob Ashpis, *Content Operations Manager*

Writers: Steven Bornfeld, Jason Bracelin, Matt Villano, Mike Weatherford

Editor: Douglas Stallings

Production Editor: Monica White

31st Edition

ISBN 978-1-64097-410-4

ISSN 1542–345X

All details in this book are based on information supplied to us at press time. Always confirm information when it matters, especially if you're making a detour to visit a specific place. Fodor's expressly disclaims any liability, loss, or risk, personal or otherwise, that is incurred as a consequence of the use of any of the contents of this book.

SPECIAL SALES
This book is available at special discounts for bulk purchases for sales promotions or premiums. For more information, e-mail SpecialMarkets@fodors.com.

PRINTED IN CANADA

10 9 8 7 6 5 4 3 2 1

MIX
Paper from responsible sources
FSC® C016245
www.fsc.org

About Our Writers

 Steve Bornfeld has been an award-winning journalist since 1983. He has been based in Las Vegas since 1997, where he has been covering its global entertainment activities and Strip scene for daily newspapers, city magazines, and alternative weeklies, including *The Las Vegas Review-Journal, Las Vegas Sun, Las Vegas Weekly, Las Vegas Life, Desert Companion,* the *New York Post, Boston Herald,* Gannett News Service, and Hearst Wire Services. His other endeavors include being a published playwright, essayist, and poet, as well as an AM radio talk show host. He updated Downtown and all the Strip chapters for this edition.

 Jason Bracelin is a veteran journalist and music critic who currently serves as a features writer for the *Las Vegas Review-Journal,* where he began working in 2006. Upon graduating from the University of Illinois in 1998, Bracelin served as a music writer and editor for Cleveland-based alt-weeklies *Free Times* and *Scene* while contributing to numerous publications such as *Spin, Complex, Alternative Press, Revolver,* and more. He's also a boxing writer for Premier Boxing Champions. He updated Henderson & Lake Las Vegas, Summerlin & Red Rock Canyon, and Side-Trips from Las Vegas.

 Matt Villano is a writer and editor based in Healdsburg, California, but spends much of his time in Las Vegas. He contributes to CNN, *The Wall Street Journal, The New York Times,* the *San Francisco Chronicle,* AFAR, and *Entrepreneur,* to name a few. When he's not researching stories or working on Fodor's Las Vegas book, he's running, hiking, or playing with his three daughters. He updated Experience, Travel Smart, and Casinos & Gambling for this edition.

 Mike Weatherford came to us well prepared for the task of revising the Shows chapter of this book (not to mention Paradise Road & the East Side and Westside chapters). He's lived in Las Vegas since 1987 and is the author of *Cult Vegas—The Weirdest! The Wildest! The Swingin'est Town on Earth.* He was a longtime entertainment reporter and columnist for the *Las Vegas Review-Journal,* and he still sees a lot of shows as a freelancer. He updated Paradise Road & the East Side, Westside, and Shows for this edition.